Read *Roswell Rising – a Novel of Disclosure*, precursor to *Roswell Revealed – a World after Disclosure* and *Roswell Redeemed – Humanity After Disclosure*.

Available now from The Aldyth Press!

Review of *Roswell Rising*:

"This month's incredible book! ...I quickly became fascinated, wanting to know the very next outcome... Explore the Roswell Incident from an alternative angle... This book would make an excellent movie and is most certainly a must-read for any UFO enthusiast!..."

★★★★★ Five stars.

Steve Mera – Phenomena Magazine

Roswell Redeemed – Humanity After Disclosure

Roswell Redeemed - Humanity After Disclosure
by Ben Emlyn-Jones

The Aldyth Press

Published by
The Aldyth Press

© Copyright 2018
Ben Emlyn-Jones

Ben Emlyn-Jones asserts the moral right to be identified
as the author of this work in accordance with the
Copyright, Designs and Patents Act of 1988

All Rights Reserved
No part of the publication may be reproduced, stored or transmitted
in any form by any means without prior permission of the publisher.

This book is sold subject to the condition that it shall not, by way of
trade or otherwise, be resold, lent, hired out or otherwise circulated
without the publisher's prior consent in any form of binding or cover
other than that which it is published and without a similar condition,
including this condition, being imposed on the subsequent purchaser.

This is a work of fiction. Not all the characters are imaginary
and some relate to real people, few of whom are alive at the
publication date, however the setting and actions in which
they are portrayed do not relate to any real occurrence.

First published in 2018

ISBN: 978-0-9542229-9-4

"The pain of an injury is over in seconds. Everything that comes after is the pain of getting well... I'd forgotten that you see. Coming back to life. It hurts."
Tessa Dare

Chapter 1

Brendan Quilley opened his eyes. It was morning and light glinted off the walls and ceiling of his bedroom. There was a brightness and texture to the sheen that was different to the usual. He hardly dared hope as he got out of bed, but when he looked out of his bedroom window his hopes were confirmed and his heart soared. The world outside was blanketed with snow. Almost before he knew what he was doing he had dashed out of his bedroom and was thundering down the stairs. His father was already waiting for him, stood at the bottom of the stairs holding Brendan's winter jacket and woolly hat. "You'll need these, son." he said with a wry smile on his face.

"Thanks, dad." He bundled into his warm clothes as quickly as he could.

His mother called from the kitchen. "Brendan, what about your breakfast?"

"Can I have it later, mom?"

She chuckled. "Okay."

Brendan pushed the front door open; immediately he was met with resistance. He pushed harder at the drift blocking the door. The sound of the snow being displaced by the door was like a smoother version of the rustling of leaves. He stepped outside and his feet were enveloped in the chilled caress of fresh powdery fall. The sky above was almost as white as the ground and the overcast was featureless. He took a few steps, relishing the obstruction the snow caused. He could feel the popping, crackling sensation of the snow compacting under the soles of his feet, through the thick material of his boots. The chilled air on his face made his cheeks glow. Condensation formed on his eyelashes. His father had already retrieved his son's sledge from the garage. It was a wooden one that the two of them had built the previous spring and this was the first time he had used it. Brendan dragged the sledge behind him by a loop of blue nylon cord as he clumped down the garden path and out into the street. There were only a few rows of footprints at this early hour on this small residential road. They were neat foot-shaped depressions in the fall that resembled cookie-cutter holes in the pure, smooth icing whiteness. The beds of the spoors were compressed down without melting.

He reached out and pulled a clump off the top of a garden wall. It felt soft and fluffy through his insulated mittens. He chided himself for spoiling the immaculate perfection of the fallen snow, that magical substance. He looked behind him and saw his own footprints filing between the lines made by the runners of his sledge. He reached the main road and there were a few more footprints. There were places on the pavement where they merged to create irregular patches of trodden snow where it was easier to walk. The wheeled snow-mountains of cars trundled past, their engine sound muted by the acoustics of the snow. The low rumble of petrol engines, the roar of diesels and the high-pitched warble of Digby Carrousels sounded more alike today. A snowplough was working its way down the carriageway. It was a large yellow council vehicle with a rotating scoop at the front. It excreted a prism of broken snow behind it in the gutter. There was a bleeping sound from Brendan's roamphone. He took of his mittens and pulled the device out of his pocket. There was a cascade of social media posts from his friends; they were all heading for the golf course. He seethed with excitement. It was just perfect for him that the snow had fallen today. It was a Saturday; that meant no school and no church. He was completely free to have fun all day.

The Red Gate Golf Course enjoyed a mystical status in the culture of Brendan and his friends. It was private property and access was strictly forbidden, which was one of the factors that most drew them towards it. There was a high fence around the course but it was full of rusty holes so that it was not hard to squeeze through. Once inside there was no end to the supply of amusements; climbing trees, rolling down the fairways, games of soccer and baseball, hide-and-seek; and, their favourite, dodging the groundsmen. Today, however, there would be nobody there and it was safe to enter through the main gate. The view of the open spaces drenched in pure white took his breath away. Snow turned familiar surroundings into another world. He began trudging over the clean unbroken cover as if he were an arctic explorer. He knew where everybody would be; the seventh hole. The fairway was a steep concave drop from the line of trees in the rough to a row of bunkers at the bottom of the hill.

A perfect place for sledging. As the location came into view he saw that a number of boys were already there. Many of them had shop-bought sledges injection-moulded from brightly coloured plastic. As he approached, one of the bigger boys straightened up and stared at him. "Hey, Quilley! What are you doing here?"

Brendan pulled up dead in his tracks. Because of their winter clothing he had not recognized any of the boys ahead of him. The one who had challenged him was Walt Nomatski, a sixth-grader at the new junior high school Brendan had started attending at the start of the last term. There had been an instant mutual dislike between them; indeed Walt seemed to enjoy that hostility. He felt it for many fifth-graders, especially those who were considerably smaller and less aggressive than he was. If Brendan had known Nomatski was there he would have given the place a wide berth.

Nomatski sneered. "Quilley, this hill is for cool kids with cool sleds only, not dumb kids with stupid sleds made of sticks their dads built for them. So scram!" A few of Nomatski's big ugly friends were standing at his shoulder, glaring at Brendan from under their woolly hats. Their mouths were hard thin horizontal lines above their scarves.

Brendan turned around and walked away; there was nothing else he could do. He felt no anger or humiliation at his dismissal by Nomatski's gang; this was just normal life for him. He pulled his sledge over the rise through some more rough, and the fairway beyond was empty. He knew from his roam that some more likeable companions were congregating on a neighbouring hole, but he was quite happy to have some time to himself first. He watched the fragments of snow being kicked up by his boots as he plodded along. He stopped. He kicked a big clod across the surface of the fall and it rolled into a small ball. He suddenly had the desire to build a snowman, but then a noise in front of him made him stop. The noise was coming from the tree-line ahead on the next rough at the side of the fairway; it was the beehive buzzing of a flyer engine. For a moment he was worried that it might be his father, come to take him away from this ice crystal idyll; but when he saw the vehicle he relaxed. It was a far bigger craft than his father's. The flyer rose above the treetops, interlaced for a moment with the skeleton of winter branches. It was a blank grey coin-like disc against the steely miasma of the sky. In moments it had vanished into the drooping cloud base. A new text message appeared on his roam: *"Bren, I'm by the fourth green. Dave."* Brendan smiled to himself and changed course; his trail of footprints banked to the left. His heart soared; Dave was his best friend. All adversity would be forgotten when he managed to reach Dave's side. He was heading right towards where the flyer had taken off.

Dave looked very small. He was hunched over, hugging his knees, on the slope at the edge of the green. In the snow of the flat surface of the green was a circular depression where the flyer had landed. "Who was that?" asked Brendan.

"Who was who?" Dave was wrapped tightly in tartan-coloured winter clothes. His dark face was framed by the lace edges of his hood.

"Who was in that flyer?"

Dave stared hard at him. His chestnut eyes seemed more intense surrounded by the snowy landscape. He gave a very long pause. "Friends."

"Dave, are you okay?" Brendan sensed that something was on his friend's mind."

"Just thinking how much I love the snow."

Brendan sat beside him, the fall on the berm through his insulated trousers making a most comfortable seat. "Me too... Do you want to do some sledding?"

He hesitated again, failing to meet Brendan's gaze, making his friend feel more awkward. "I'll miss the snow. I won't be seeing it again most likely."

"What do you mean?"

After Dave explained, they felt uncomfortable with each other. They made a pretence of play for a while, taking it in turns to drive Brendan's sledge down the slopes, but it was a relief when Brendan managed to think of an excuse and say goodbye to his friend. As he walked back across the golf course, following his own approaching footsteps from earlier, tears budded in Brendan's eyes. He looked around himself, hoping that the old Indian was there, but there was no sign of him; and Brendan dared not contemplate the other friend he had recently lost because if he did he would simply break down and cry all day in the snow. He headed straight home as quickly as he could, hoping he could get there before the dam broke. Tears were rolling down his face as he ran up the garden path as fast as the snowfall allowed. He left his sledge by the door. "What the matter, honey?" His mother ran forward as soon as she saw him come in.

"It's Dave... He's moving away! I'm never going to see him again."

"Oh, baby!" His mother put her comforting arms around him and gathered him up onto her lap in the armchair.

"He's my best friend." Brendan sobbed.

"Where's he moving too?"

"Africa."

His father came into the room. "I'm sorry, son. I had heard rumours about this, but didn't want to say anything till I knew for sure."

Brendan looked up at him. His vision was warped by tears. "Why, dad?... Why's he moving to Africa?"

"David's dad's a physician. The word's got round that he'd signed up for the Return to Africa programme."

Brendan had heard that term before on TV, but didn't know what it meant. "What's 'Return to Africa'?"

"A few countries in Africa have asked for Americans, especially those with skills and education, to go and live and work there."

"But why Dave's dad?"

His father paused. "Because he's a black man."

Brendan frowned in confusion. "What does that matter?"

"Black people in America all come from African families."

"Dave doesn't! His family come from Baltimore."

"Back to his granddad or great-granddad's time maybe, but what about before that?"

"Who cares who was before that? It's too long ago."

"Some people do care about that, Bren... I'm sorry." His father reached down and patted his head.

Brendan started weeping again. "He was my best friend."

"You can stay in touch." said his mother. "Talk to each other on the Mesh. We can even take you to visit him now we've got flyers."

"Dr King is black; why is he not moving to Africa?"

"Dr King is the president-elect." said his father.

Brendan went to his bedroom and lay down on his bed. Snow was falling outside his window again, but all the wonder it had filled him with that morning was gone. He felt a stab of anger for his parents. The heartbreak he was feeling was one he had had to deal with many times because his family were always uprooting themselves and moving. Each time he expected it to become easier but it never did. He had been born in Ireland and had moved to New York City when he was four. He had started kindergarten there and had experienced the newfound joy of extra-familial relationships with the other children. These relationships were instantly and totally cut off when the Quilleys packed up and moved to Las Vegas where he went through elementary school making new friends; Harry, John, Marcus, Pete, Charlie and many others. He enjoyed a certain status among the other boys there because his adult sister Siobhan was on television; she presented the news on CBS. He was growing bigger, stronger and happier every day, but then everything went wrong and his life fell apart. His father had a stroke and almost died; and then a sinister old lady entered the household and arranged medical treatment for him... Brendan stomped on the brakes of his train of thought. There were some things he could not allow himself to think about.

....

The following morning the family got into the ground car and, like they did every Sunday morning, drove to church. Sometimes when the weather was warm they walked together along the streets of Rockville, Maryland USA, their hometown; but usually they drove or flew. Mass began at ten AM sharp, although sometimes they would attend the later short masses without music or the other frills. The church was a strange dome-shaped structure with a thin central spire and high narrow-arched gables for the windows and main door. Neighbouring it was an older chapel of a more traditional architecture that was only used for special occasions. There was a life-size white marble statue of Jesus Christ in the driveway. They walked into the narthex with the other parishioners, saying hello to familiar faces. Brendan kept a lookout for his own acquaintances among the younger members of the congregation. He dipped his finger in the holy water and crossed himself, feeling revolted as he always did. The water in the pot might be holy, but it looked very dirty and usually had slime floating in it. After all the fingers that were stuck in it there were probably all kinds of bacteria and viruses in suspension. The family tended to sit in the same pew, as all the regular congregation did, even though there was no official seat allocation. It was just mutually-agreed habit. They sat quietly while they waited for the mass to start. The organ played soothing ambient music. A few people were kneeling and praying. Brendan's parents sometimes sat quietly, muttering the rosary. Then the organ music would change to a grander tone and a server would ring a bell. Everybody stood up and sang the opening hymn as the priest walked in from the sacristy. The parishioners' attitude to the local clergy was very paradoxical. They regarded them with reverence, as vicars of Christ ordained by the holy sacraments from God. At the same time they often made affectionate fun of their quirks and mannerisms. Several of them had humourous nicknames. When a priest appeared that they had recently been lampooning Brendan's father would often nudge his son and look down with a smile. Brendan would return his gaze and giggle.

Today it was Father Costello, a tall and extremely thin Jesuit with a highly set nose and sunken cheeks. His vestments hung off his ancient frame as if he were a coat hanger. Behind his back he was sometimes called "Dr Relic". His physical opposite, the chubby young deacon, carried the liturgical texts behind him. As the music stopped, Father Costello took his place at the front of the nave. "In the name of the Father, the Son, and the Holy Spirit." He said in his high-pitched nasal Southern accent.

"Amen." everybody replied in unison. Then there followed the rites of penitence and then the Gloria. After that the children would leave the nave for a small room adjoining the sacristy where they would receive the children's liturgy; bible stories told by a teacher from the local elementary school in a manner intended for children to understand and enjoy them. Here finally Brendan was able to interact with his friends.

At the end of the children's liturgy they all returned to the nave for the Eucharist, the principal part of the mass; then the priest would end the service with a blessing and they headed for the church hall for tea and biscuits.

There was a burst of excitement from his parents and several other people there when Siobhan arrived. There was the humming sound from outside and people rushed to the windows to see a dark blue flyer descending into the carpark and his parents bubbled over with delight as Siobhan decamped from it. Brendan's sister was seventeen years his elder. She was an adult; and this felt strange from the point of view of his friends whose siblings were all just a handful of years' difference in age. They often talked about their brother or sister in the grade below or above them. Brendan found it normal to have a sister who was out of school and in the same alien world of adulthood as his parents. He remembered lying in her arms as much as he remembered doing so with his mother. Often she used to pick him up and cuddle him when he cried. She looked very like his mother, with a similar face and hair; she always had. He had not seen her for a month and he was surprised how much she had changed. Her hair was cut shorter and she had put on a lot of weight. Her abdomen was swollen like a beach-ball. Accompanying her as always was her best friend Jenny, a bright-eyed older woman with unkempt greying hair and a lively intelligent face. The whole family walked home from church together and gathered in the lounge to talk. Jenny drove Siobhan's flyer over and was waiting for them in the driveway. Brendan was given the job of fetching tea and biscuits for everybody. When he came back into the room they all turned and stared at him with quizzical smiles on their faces. "Brendan." said his father. "We have something to tell you... You're going to be an uncle."

"Eh?" Brendan shook his head in confusion.

"Siobhan is having a baby, honey." added his mother.

Brendan stared at Siobhan. "Really?"

Siobhan nodded her head almost imperceptibly.

"But... how?"

They all laughed.

"What's so funny?"

"It's nothing to worry about, Bren." said his mother.

"It's just Siobhan's time to have a baby, just like it was my time to have you when you were born."

Brendan sat down, his mind churning. "I'm a... an uncle?"

"Yes."

"But I can't be! I'm a kid. Uncles are all grown up."

They chuckled again. "Not necessarily, baby." said his mother. "To be an uncle all you need to do is have a brother or sister who has a child. I've heard of uncles and aunts who are younger than their nieces and nephews."

He nodded his head after processing this information.

"And I'm going to be a grandpa." said his father with a rueful half-smile.

"When will the baby come out?" asked Brendan.

"The end of February." said Siobhan. "Also it's not just one baby; it's two."

His parents' and Jenny's heads swung away from Brendan and focused on Siobhan like a trio of high-speed lighthouses. "What!?" exclaimed his mother.

"It's twins, mom."

"Are you sure? Have you been tested?"

Siobhan shrugged. "Kind of."

His father whistled in surprise. "Wow!"

....

Brendan felt perturbed as he trudged through the ageing snow to school the following morning. He met up with his friends and put on a good act of being his normal self; but inside, his mind was in turmoil. The bell rang in the playground. He dropped the snowball he had been about to throw and headed inside to his locker to collect the books he needed. He sat at his desk in his classroom in silence, staring at the Stars and Stripes hanging above the waxboard. The girls on the row of desks to his left were turning to face each other and talking. They giggled inanely at some joke that was both inaudible and incomprehensible. Girls, Brendan mused, were surely the most repulsive creatures in all of God's creation. Their obsessive vanity, their banal chatter about irrelevant subjects, their fixation on their clothes, their hair and cosmetics; their propensity to play with dolls, meaningless objects that were good for nothing except targets on a catapult range... However they were essential for human reproduction.

For some reason, known only to Himself, God had made humanity with the inherent burden of a degenerate lower half. Brendan had known about the facts of life for quite a while. It was the previous year that a seventh-grader he knew had let him borrow a biology textbook he had just taken out of the senior library all about "the birds and the bees". It was entitled *Sex and Childbirth- an Introduction.* Brendan had pored through its pages with a mixture of fascination and horror. It had taken several weeks, but he had managed to put this upsetting reality into the slow oven of his mind for long-term integration. However the announcement of his sister's pregnancy brought the whole sordid quandary crashing down on his head again. The process involved unthinkable acts, such as inserting parts of a male body into parts of a female body, the emission of substances and objects that he couldn't even have imagined existing. The engendering of evil-looking piscine mutants with ropes of flesh sprouting from their navels that unbelievably took on human form and eventually squeezed their way out into the world and became a baby. He still could not accept that he, like everybody else, had begun his own life as one of those deformed homunculi... He shivered and a wave of nausea passed over him. He knew that he could never become a father. How on earth was any baby ever created when adults were forced to perform such disgusting actions? Is that the best method God could come up with? It amazed Brendan to think that his own parents had had sexual intercourse, not just once, but *twice*; in order to create both himself and Siobhan. How did they achieve this feat while keeping their mental health intact?

Brendan's first class of the day was art, one of his favourites. The main reason he liked it was that he got to sit next to Dave, however when they sat down together his friend was strangely distant. He greeted Brendan far more formally than usual and declined to enter into their usual conversation. To begin with Brendan felt hurt by his reticence, but when he looked at Dave's face, and realized how sad his friend was, he understood. Dave was as dejected at the prospect of being parted from Brendan as Brendan was from him. Their mutual company had now become painful with the knowledge that it was finite and leading up to an appointed permanent end.

Dave just wanted to get it over with now.

"Now then." said Miss Spreale, the art teacher. "Today I'd like you all to produce a picture of a friend you have not seen for a long time and really wish you could. Somebody you really miss badly."

The class nodded their collective head. The teacher placed a sheet of paper and a jar of coloured pencils and crayons in front of them and they got to work. Brendan looked at the jar closest to him. His hand reached out and picked up the blue and green crayons. He had a strange feeling while he did so, as if he knew something terrible was about to happen, he was the one doing it and he still couldn't stop himself. He drew a line of green across the paper and then drew a line of blue on top of it. He stopped and stared. The two superimposed crayon marks mixed like paint. The resulting purple colour made his breath catch in his throat and tears fill his eyes. He felt as if he had split into two separate entities locked in combat. One half of him yelled at him not to risk it; these were forbidden fortresses within his memory. The other urged him on. He carried on drawing, his hand moving automatically. It took him twenty minutes to complete the image. Miss Spreale walked over to his desk. "Oh Brendan." she shook her head sadly. "Why do you always have to be difficult?"

He didn't dare look up at her. He hoped his voice would not betray his emotions. "Miss?"

"The assignment I set you, like I set this whole class, was to draw a picture of a friend, one you haven't seen for a long time and one you miss. All you have done is drawn some kind of cartoon character."

Suppressed sniggers broke out from around him; the entire class were eager spectators to his reprimand.

Brendan felt his cheeks blazing like radiators. He wished badly that he had been able to stop himself drawing that picture. He shrugged evasively.

"I'm waiting for an explanation, Brendan." growled the teacher in a threatening tone.

"He is a friend, miss. His name's Boggin."

His classmates burst into raucous merriment.

"Quiet!" snapped Miss Spreale at them. "Brendan." she began is a gentler tone. "Was this your imaginary friend?"

"He wasn't imaginary. He was real." He sniffed loudly.

There was a long pause. "Alright, Brendan. Carry on." The teacher moved to the next desk. Brendan looked up at her departing back.

....

"How does it feel to be ten years old?"

"Cool, mom." A couple of years earlier Brendan's mother would have scooped him onto her lap, but today she merely embraced him as he stood in front of her. He felt nostalgic regret about that. It struck him very much at that moment how much he had grown. He really was significantly bigger than he had been on his previous birthday. His eyes were on a level with his mother's shoulder and she looked diminished in size. In a world where every adult previously appeared like a giant, he began to perceive scale among them. It actually felt very odd to be ten years old. For the first time ever there were two digits associated with his age. He recalled being six or seven and thinking how ancient ten years old appeared; but now he was there it was unearthly. Time seemed to be passing so quickly.

"Happy birthday, son." His smiling father clapped him hard on the shoulder. "Ten years; it's quite a milestone."

"I guess so." Brendan replied.

"Have you given any thought to your outing?"

"Not really, dad."

"We should make it a special one this year." Every year on his birthday, Brendan's parents took him and a handful of his school friends, as many who could fit in the car, out for a day trip to somewhere of his choosing. Sometimes his father would help him by suggesting a place. On his previous birthday his father had been recovering from a stroke and so they had had a trip in the spring and Brendan got the feeling his father felt that was insufficient. Sometimes his friends asked Brendan if he minded his birthday being so close to Christmas. Brendan had never given it much thought seeing as it was when his birthday happened to be, and he knew of no other. He got the feeling his friends who had birthdays at other times imagined that the significance of Brendan's birthday was diminished because Christmas was only two weeks later, but he didn't feel that way. In fact he regarded his birthday as a happy prelude to Christmas; both festivals enhanced the other. He regarded New Year the same way. "Look at this." His father was sitting at the kitchen table with his matchbook computer open in front of him. "A place has just opened in London called 'the London Planetarium'. Shall we go there?"

A thrill rose within him and he jumped in the air. "Yeah!" He had no idea what a planetarium was, but the thought of going all the way to London was delicious regardless of the purpose of the adventure.

"London?" his mother frowned. "London, England?"

"That's the only London I know of." His father grinned at his wife sardonically.

"But, Clane; it's not safe."

"It's perfectly safe."

"It's a war zone!"

"No it's not, Gina." he scoffed. "Not any more. It's under full LoW control these days. I've seen travel brochures urging people to go to England."

"Of course; they want people's hard American money... Clane, I don't feel comfortable with Brendan going to England. There are plenty of other planetariums he can go to. There's a very neat one in Chicago."

Brendan stared at his father in fear, silently begging him. His two parents had a debate for about three minutes. When he was younger they used to get angry and shout at each other, but they had mellowed in the last couple of years; probably because they had both suffered serious illness. In the end Brendan could bear it no longer. "But please!" he interjected. "Mom, dad; I really want to go to England!"

They both turned their heads in unison and looked at him blankly.

....

The evening before the outing Brendan's father went to pick up the flyer. Brendan stood in the driveway, the slush soaking into his slippers, waiting for his father to come back. The vehicle was a large sleek black object with tinted windows. It descended over the treetops in the garden opposite and settled gently on the tarmac, buzzing smoothly. Like most flyers it resembled a large family car without wheels. "Wow, dad!"

exclaimed Brendan.

"Pretty hot, huh?" His father got out and ran his hand along the shiny roof.

"Can we keep it?"

He guffawed. "Oh, I wish!... No, we have to take it back to Jenny's factory when we come home. We're only borrowing it."

"It's way cooler than our flyer, dad."

"Damn right; she's got a lot more power. Four disc, sixty-seven lateral G's. Very sexy! We could have done the trip in our own, but it's only got five seats. You couldn't bring as many friends. Also this baby has a life-raft which we should have really." His father opened the luggage hatch at the rear and showed his son a bright yellow box attached to the sidewall.

"Why do we need that?"

"In case we have a breakdown transatlantic."

Brendan found it difficult to sleep that night. He lay in bed seething with anticipation. He got up before everybody else and ran downstairs to make breakfast. His parents rose from slumber in more leisurely manner. They snapped at their son a few times as he tried to cajole them along. Eventually, after enough cups of coffee, they both stopped yawning and the bags under their eyes retracted into their faces. They returned to their bedroom to put on their clothes and finally they were ready to leave. The interior of the flyer was immaculate and smelled of rubber like a new car in a showroom. It had a similar layout to a car, with a driving seat and front passenger seat at the front; then a row of three seats in the middle and two seats at the back. "Don't make a mess back there!" warned his father. "I promised Jenny we would bring this thing back in the same condition we took it. She has to sell it to somebody next week." He started the engine and the vehicle drifted upwards. He moved uncertainly to begin with, getting used to the unfamiliar controls. "Jeez, the pitch lever on this bird is heavy." he muttered. After a few minutes of circling over their street at about two hundred feet he set a course for Henry's house. Brendan relished Henry's gaping face as he looked up at their flyer in awe as it descended elegantly into his back garden. After that they went and picked up Chris, Pete and

Albert. Brendan was enthused by the presence of his friends and they all eagerly stared out of the windows as his father drove the flyer higher and faster. Soon they were breaking through the clouds and the sky above was vanilla blue.

The flight to London took an hour and a half. They traversed the eastern seaboard. New York and the snowy backdrops of Nova Scotia and Newfoundland passed below them. Once over the Atlantic Ocean his father brought them down to four thousand feet so they could watch the sea scrolling beneath them like an old movie. They passed a few ships; coloured blobs that whipped below their undercarriage before they had a chance to have a good look at them. A haze appeared ahead of them that solidified into a green landscape free of snow. His father eased back on the throttle and the vehicle slowed so that they could see more of the fields, rivers, roads and towns that they flew over. "Welcome to England." he said.

"Have you been here before, Mr Quilley?" asked Pete.

His father's face became grim. "A long time ago, before Saucer Day."

The countryside below them grew more built up and soon they were flying over a huge city. A wide meandering river flowed through the metropolis. Some boats floated along it, looking like twigs from this altitude. Brendan recognized many of the buildings because they were famous historical landmarks and tourist attractions, Big Ben, Tower Bridge and St Paul's Cathedral. He and his friends had their noses pressed to the windows. "Wow!" "Look at that!" and other exclamations were their only words.

"Where can we land?" asked his father.

"Not sure." replied his mother. She was studying the navigation display in front of her seat. "I can't see any official flyer pads listed."

"Damn it! I'm going to put down where I can and hope the LoW don't give me a ticket." He dived towards a triangular patch of green, a verdant wedge among the grey rooftops. He levelled up and slowed until he was hovering above a small park in the middle of a busy urban district. He landed the flyer on the grass and they all eagerly decamped. The air was warmer than at home. The sky was blue with small clean clouds. A road lay beside the park with a wide pavement on the far side. Multiple vehicles drove past including a very tall red bus with two floors like a moving house. "Stay close to me, everybody." commanded Brendan's mother. "Clane, where do we go from here?"

"To the nearest subway station; they call it the 'Underground'... There." He pointed to a sign which showed a thick red circle with a blue equatorial line overlaying it. "Now be careful, all of you! Especially when crossing the streets. They drive on the wrong side of the road over here. We need to get a move on; it's already mid-afternoon in England." They walked along the wide pavement, looking at the shop fronts that skirted the tall grey-brick buildings. When they got closer they saw that the Underground station was called Shepherd's Bush. "Shepherd's Bush?" They all laughed. "Do shepherds have bushes?... What a crazy name." The adults bought tickets for them all and they descended via an escalator to the subterranean platforms. It was very similar to the New York Subway only more compact. The trains were cylindrical in shape and the carriage roofs curved in overhead giving the interior a suffocating atmosphere. A few times on the journey the train was so full of people that they had to stand; their shoulders, chests and backs pressed against other passengers. They had to change trains at one point and walked along passageways and escalators to another platform. It was quite a relief to climb back up onto another bustling city street. "Ladies and gentlemen." announced his father grandly. "We are now on Baker Street. This is where Sherlock Holmes lived."

"Hey!" "Neat!" "Wow!" they all called out in unison. "Is he still there, dad?" asked Brendan. "Can we go visit him?"

His parents laughed loudly.

There was some commotion at the junction as they walked towards their destination. Traffic was at a standstill because of it and some of the drivers were sounding their horns. A squad of riot police with light blue helmets were holding back a crowd of angry people who were blocking the road. Brendan recognized the uniforms as the League of the World Peace Corps. The crowd was a political demonstration; the people held aloft placards that read: "*ELECTIONS NOW!*", "*LoW OUT!*" and "*FREE BRITAIN!*" "They want their own government." explained his father. "They've been under LoW occupation for a long time now. A bit like our own Provisional Government, except so far there are no plans to change that situation in Europe..." He cut off and gasped. "Look!" He pointed at a banner sporting a strange emblem, a red oblong centred by a blue circle inside a white circle. A white jagged line, like a bolt of lightening, cut the blue one in two.

"What's that, dad?"

"Mosleyites!"

"What are they?"

"Fascists!"

His father led him swiftly away from the protesters. "God, I thought all that was over." he muttered uneasily. A few hundred yards down the road they came to a steep dome-shaped structure neatly embedded into a street corner like an eyeball in its socket. It had a signboard above its entrance that said *LONDON PLANETARIUM*. "A show is about to start." said his mother. "Come on in, kids." They bought tickets and entered the softly-lit auditorium. The place resembled a cinema except the seats were arranged in a circle around the centre. The space in the middle of the dome, right under its apex, was taken up by a strange machine that looked like a robot or a spacecraft mounted on a stand. When he sat in a seat Brendan was surprised at how far back it was reclined. It was more like a dentist's chair than a cinema seat. The room darkened and the done above their heads lit up. The device in the centre was a projector and it beamed a realistic image onto the curved ceiling. "*Welcome to the London Planetarium...*" said a deep masculine voice through a loudspeaker. The voice gave a running commentary as the concave screen displayed very vivid images of the night's sky. Planets came into close view, stars wheeled around the zenith; constellations were highlighted and described. To Brendan the display looked as if the roof had been lifted off and they had moved forward six hours in time. It was as if he were looking at the real night's sky. A yellow globe appeared and the commentator announced that they were looking at a diagram of the sun. "*The sun is a star, a luminous globe of gas producing heat and light by nuclear fusion. It was born from a nebula and consists mostly of hydrogen and helium gas. The brightest stars have masses one hundred times that of the sun and emit as much light as a million suns. They live for less than a million years. The faintest stars are the red dwarfs, less than one thousandth the brightness of the sun. They can live for hundreds of billions of years. Towards the end of its life, a star like the sun swells up to become a red giant. Eventually it explodes with enormous force. This is called a* stella nova. *It loses its outer layers and these become a planetary nebula. Finally it will shrink to a fraction of its former size to become a white dwarf. During this process, the earth and most of the planets will be completely destroyed, but don't worry. The scenario I have just described will not begin for at least six billion years...*" The show ended soon afterwards and the lights came on. The audience got up out of their couches to leave, including his parents and friends. "Hey, what's the matter with Brendan." Henry said. Brendan couldn't move. He was totally paralyzed. He lay in his couch staring at the white dome above his head. His heart was pounding; his mouth was dry. He heard his mother's voice: "Brendan?... Brendan!... BRENDAN!... Brendan, what's wrong!?" Brendan couldn't reply. All he could see was the blazing fiery sphere of the swollen sun engulfing the planet earth. Everything around him was bursting into flames; the trees were igniting like matchsticks, the mountains were melting, the oceans were boiling.

....

He couldn't remember how he left the London Planetarium. He had some vague recollection of his father coaxing him to stand up onto his feet. He was being half-carried down the London street they had walked along earlier. It was now dark and the shop windows were glowing with electric light. He was trying to walk, but could not support is own weight; his legs felt like noodles. Henry and his father had a hand each under his armpits to support him. "We need to call a goddamn ambulance!" he heard his mother yell.

"No!" his father retorted. "We need to get him home!"

"I told you we shouldn't have brought him here!"

"How the hell was I to know this would happen!? Are you saying in Chicago it wouldn't have!?" They travelled on the Underground back to Shepherds Bush and returned to the flyer. Brendan lay on the back seat, his eyes out of focus, as they flew back across the Atlantic as fast as they could. Slowly the sky lightened as if at dawn. When they arrived home they were back in the US Eastern Time zone and it was still early afternoon. After dropping off Brendan's friends, his parents took him to the doctor. The family's GP was an old man with wispy grey hair and a long pointed nose. He looked very much like a creature from a science fiction film Brendan had seen a few years ago. He examined Brendan as the boy lay on his examination table. He took his temperature, blood pressure and listened to his heartbeat. While he was doing this Brendan's parents told him what had happened. The doctor looked down Brendan's throat, in his ears and shone a light into his eyes. "Well, Mr and Mrs Quilley, I can't find anything wrong with him. His observations appear normal; although his heart-rate is up a bit."

"But there *is* something wrong with him!" insisted his mother. "He can hardly walk! He hasn't said a word for hours. He's in some kind of trance."

"I think he has suffered some kind of emotional trauma. I'd like to treat him for shock. I'll also make you an appointment with the child psychiatrist."

His parents gasped. "Emotional shock!?" shrilled his father. "Why!?... How!?..."

"Dr Flynn, we were having a day out in London for Christ's sake!" said his mother. "Nothing, absolutely nothing happened that could cause Brendan emotional trauma. We were having a lovely day..."

"Mrs Quilley, I can only address this case based on the symptoms I observe." The doctor shrugged. After the appointment was arranged they went home. By now Brendan could walk properly, but he still had not spoken. When they got home he collapsed onto the settee. His father went to the kitchen and came back with a tub of chocolate ice cream. He held it in front of Brendan's face. "Look at this, son. Can I interest you in a scoop or two?"

"No thanks, dad. There's no point." Brendan's voice cracked slightly as he spoke. He coughed.

His father leapt back and yelled: "Gina! He said something! He spoke!" There was the clatter of feet on the floor and in moments both his parents were crouching in front of him.

"Brendan!" His father stared hard into his eyes. "Can you say something else? You said there was no point eating ice cream. What did you mean, son? Why is there no point eating ice cream?"

"Because we're all going to die. The whole world is going to die."

"What do you mean?"

"What do you mean, honey?" chimed in his mother.

"The sun is going to blow up and destroy the earth. It said so in that planetarium place."

They both gasped; then they almost laughed. "Son!" said his father. "Is that it? Is that what has been bothering you all day?"

"Baby!" his mother leaned forward and caressed his shoulders. "You don't have to be concerned about that. It's not going to happen for millions and billions of years!"

"That's true, son." said his father. "I had no idea you were so upset by this. I'm so sorry. I should never have taken you there... But you must know, we could never have guessed such a minor thing would distress you so much."

....

Brendan felt a bit better the next day. It was Sunday so they all went to mass at church as always. Then they spent the afternoon visiting a few family friends. They got home when dusk was falling and Brendan went out for a walk. He strolled along the streets to Rock Creek Park where the dregs of the snow were most abundant. It lay in crusty, granular patches, vitrified by a week of partially melting and freezing every day and night. He walked along the pathway through the trees until he came to an open patch of grass with a number of logs one could sit on. The overcast was breaking up and the sun peeked through a gap between two thick clouds. It glowed red like the eye of Satan. Brendan glared at it hatefully. The same sun which gave life to the earth would eventually take it, destroying everything it had sustained throughout the history of the solar system in a bath of fire. He then noticed that there was a man sitting on one of the logs on the far side of the glade; Brendan had seen him when he'd sat down. The figure was the size of a small adult man and was clad in a parka and Wellington boots. There was something wonderfully familiar about his posture. Brendan stood up and walked over towards him, hardly daring to hope. The man lifted his head and smiled from beneath his hood. Brendan's heart leaped for joy. "Indian!"

"Hello, Brendan." said the old Indian.

Brendan threw his arms around his friend as far as they would go and squeezed his insulated body. "Indian!... Indian!"

"It's good to see you too, Brendan. I'm sorry you did not have a happy birthday this year."

Brendan looked at him hard. "Is it true, Indian? What they said at that place, the London Planetarium?" The brief pause that followed before the old Indian spoke was like an adrenalin-soaked temporal singularity. Brendan felt like the defendant in the dock waiting for the foreman of the jury to say *guilty* or *not guilty*. At that moment he would have given everything he had, or would ever have, to hear the Indian say *no*.

"Yes."

A second eternal moment passed as Brendan dug his nails into his sanity to stop it falling away. "So it's true? The sun will one day swell up and burn up the earth?"

"Yes it is, Brendan. I'm sorry... But it will not happen for eight and a half billion years. Astronomers have underestimated the sun's life cycle by two-point-five billion years... Do you know how long a time that is? How long do you think a billion years are?"

"I don't know. Will it happen after I've died as an old man?"

The Indian chuckled. "Oh yes... A billion years is a thousand times one million years; and a million years is a thousand times one thousand years. And that has to happen more than eight times. You will not live more than just over one hundred years, if you're lucky; and that is just one tenth of one thousand years. An event that far in the future? For practical purposes it might as well be never. The earth is only about five billion years old; it's barely middle aged. You know how old the dinosaurs are? Well they never even appeared until about a quarter of a billion years ago. So you have no cause to be concerned, Brendan."

Brendan had buried his face in the Indian's jacketed lap. "Why, Indian?"

"Brendan, look up at the sky."

Brendan raised his head. The sun was now just a smudge on the horizon, filtered by the leafless undergrowth, and some of the stars were visible in the lavender zenith.

"Do you know how many stars there are up there, Brendan? More than anybody could ever count. More than anybody could even imagine... But one day, all of them will be dead; in the same way one day, far sooner, all the people alive in the world today will be dead. But when that time comes, there will still be stars in the universe; in the same way when all people today are dead there will still be people on earth... Everything dies, but everything also carries on. When stars explode they release a huge quantity of material that eventually transforms into new stars and new planets. This is the same as people having children who grow up and outlive their parents, and eventually have their own children who outlive them in an everlasting cycle."

"Why did God make the universe this way? Make it so that everything has to die. Why couldn't He just make it so that everything lasts forever?"

He felt the Indian shrug inside his winter jacket. "I don't know."

Brendan gasped. "Why not? I thought you knew everything!"

"I don't. I am not God... No more than you are anyway."

"I thought you knew all the things God knows."

"I do not... The only reason I know more than you is because I have a better view. I'm like a man standing on a high mountain. I can see far more than a man standing in a valley, but it doesn't make me any smarter than the man in the valley."

Brendan sat next to him silently, mulling over this concept. He felt the weight of misery that had been crushing his shoulders for the last twenty-four hours lift slightly.

"Do you feel better now?" asked the old Indian.

"I guess. A bit."

"Good. You will continue to recover your spirit, young Brendan. It will take a long time, but it will happen; slowly but steadily."

"Thanks, Indian." Brendan leaned forward with his face on his knees and his eyes squeezed shut. "How's Boggin?"

The Indian began stroking his head as if he were a cat. "Very well. He sends his love as always. He watches you regularly."

"Does he have a new friend now?"

"Yes."

"Who?"

The Indian paused. "A young girl."

"Who is she?"

"I can't tell you. She lives a very long way from here."

"Where?"

"She doesn't live on this earth."

Waves of curiosity and envy flowed though him. "How many earths are there, Indian?"

"More than there are years before the end of the world... Be patient, young Brendan; one day I will tell you all about it." He stopped stroking Brendan's head.

"Why not tell me now?" He waited for the old Indian to reply and when he didn't Brendan raised his gaze and saw that the Indian had gone. Brendan was sitting alone on the log. He shrugged to himself. The Indian always vanished into thin air like that, but usually less suddenly; usually he said goodbye first. It was almost dark now and thousands more stars shone from between the clouds. He stood up and went home, feeling happier.

Chapter 2

The house was full of people; some were neighbours, some were his father's friends and colleagues from Washington DC. Siobhan and Jenny had also turned up. There was loud friendly chatter from downstairs in the kitchen and lounge. Brendan sat on his bed reading a comic book under his bedside lamp. Outside his window the night was as black as oil. He knew it was almost time for bed and, as always, the soothing canon of adult voices downstairs would lull him off to sleep. The New Year party would still be going strong long after he had dropped off. He heard his mother's footsteps coming up the stairs and put the comic down, preparing himself to wish his mother goodnight. There was the standard evening knock on the door and his mother poked her head round. Normally she just walked in and kissed his cheek. "Brendan?... Brendan, honey?"

"Mom?"

"Would you like to come downstairs?"

"What?"

"You're ten years old now; old enough to see in the New Year... Put on some nice clothes and join us in the den."

Brendan felt excited as he slipped on his black terylene trousers and a white shirt. He descended the familiar stairs of his home into the alien world of adulthood. All the strangers in the lounge greeted him. The men were in suits and women were in low-cut gowns; glittering jewellery shone from their wrists and earlobes. His father was rosy-cheeked and smiling. He thrust a glass into Brendan's hand. "There you are, son. Get that down your neck!"

"What is it, dad?"

"Blue Nun."

Brendan sipped. The drink's taste reminded him slightly of the shampoo the school nurse had once given him to treat his head lice, but it was much more pleasant. He circulated, moving from the lounge to the kitchen, but he was disappointed to find there were no other children there. The forest of adults towered over him and their arcane conversations bored him. The television was on in the corner of the lounge and he found a fairly good view of the screen; only once every few minutes did somebody walk in front of it. It was showing the standard New Year variety broadcast with locations shot in Times Square. A rock and roll band played; a journalist gave a political commentary of the year about to end. A giant clock on the wall of the square counted down the minutes and seconds to midnight. His glass was almost empty. The drink was making him feel strange. His head was dizzy and sounds were muted, but he felt abnormally relaxed and content.

"Have some more, son."

Brendan jerked slightly with shock as his father poured some more drink into his glass. "Thanks, dad."

"It's almost twelve." The adults gathered around him to watch the TV. Their trouser legs and skirt hems brushed against Brendan's shoulders. The TV announcer chanted excitedly and the adults copied him: "Ten... nine... eight... seven... six... five... four... three... two... one... ZERO! Happy New Year!" Fireworks cracked and flashed on the screen. The illuminated numbers "1963" lit up above the streets in far off New York City. Outside the window Brendan heard more fireworks from elsewhere in his own neighbourhood, booming like distant thunder. The adults all linked arms and sang *Auld Lang Syne* above Brendan's head. Their voices were raucous and amplified with alcohol so he plugged up his ears. The quiet then allowed him to ponder. So this was now a whole new year, 1963. He wondered what came next, presumably 1964. What happened when they got to 1969; would the year after that then be nineteen-sixty-ten?

"Come on, Bren."

He started again as his mother laid a hand on his shoulder.

"You've seen in the New Year now, honey; time for bed."

....

Brendan woke up feeling ill. He had a pounding headache and an unpleasant taste in his mouth. He could tell by the quality of the light in his bedroom that he had slept in late. "Mom?" He got out of bed and went downstairs. A twinge of nausea passed through him as he walked. His surroundings orbited around him as if he were on a merry-go-round. His mother was in the kitchen mopping the floor. "Mom, I don't feel too good." he said.

"What's wrong, Bren?" She sat down at the table and pulled forward a stool for him to sit on.

When he described his symptoms he was astonished and annoyed to see his mother laugh. "Why is that funny, mom?"

"Brendan, you've got a hangover."

"A what?"

"I'm sorry to laugh, honey. It's your dad's fault. He shouldn't have given you a second glass of wine... Whenever somebody drinks too much liquor they get a hangover; but don't worry, it won't last long." She got up and poured him a large glass of water. "Here, honey. Drink this. You'll feel better in a couple of hours."

Sure enough, Brendan's hangover had eased by midday. He read some comic books and looked at a few Meshboards on his matchbook for a while; and then he began to feel his familiar craving for a sugar rush. He went downstairs and approached his mother again. "Mom, can I have some money for candy?"

She scowled at him. "After all the candy you got over Christmas? You must have eaten your weight in chocolate. God help your teeth!"

"Please, mom."

"No. You can have some more candy when school starts again." She went back to her chopping board.

Brendan knew from her gestures and tone of voice that her decision was non-negotiable. He returned to his bedroom growling to himself in disappointment. He lay down prostrate on the carpet to pull out some old comics from the archive under his bed. A cloud of dust was kicked up as he removed the ream, making him cough slightly. Along with the old comics came a few fragments of loose crumpled paper. One of them made Brendan stop and look more closely. Its texture and dark greenish-white colour was familiar, and it filled him with a wild hope. He unravelled it and saw that, sure enough, it was a one dollar bill. His heart leaped. He looked over his shoulder at the open door to his bedroom, making sure nobody was watching him, and then he slipped the banknote into his pocket. He put on his outdoor clothes and walked down the stairs as calmly as he could so as not to arouse suspicion. "Mom, I'm just going out for a while." he called.

"Okay." his mother responded from the kitchen.

It was a cold and dry day with no snow, so Brendan got out

his bicycle for the journey to the market square. He locked it up at a rack by a shopping centre. There had been a lot of development in Rockville during the last few years including a network of pedestrian malls in the town centre. Brendan had explored them all thoroughly and had a very accurate mental map in his head of all the best places to buy sweets. There were a number of supermarkets with confectionary aisles, Giant Eagle, Walmart and K-mart; but Brendan's favourite was *Melissa's Candy*, a small independently-run shop on a corner Gibbs Street. "Hi, Brendan. Happy New Year." The rotund but pretty young woman behind the counter greeted him as he walked into the shop.

"Happy New Year, Mel." he smiled back at her.

"I've got some Mini-Bristols in, 'specially for you." she grinned. "Your favourite."

"Cool! Thanks!"

"How's your ma and pa?"

Brendan conversed with Mel as he stocked up from the shelves, his mouth watering. He took his goods over to the counter and produced the repossessed dollar bill from his pocket. Mel froze and gasped as she took it from his hand. "Sweet Jesus!"

"Is there something wrong with it, Mel?"

"Brendan, where did you get this?"

"It's mine."

She handed it back to him. "I can't accept this, Brendan. I don't know where you got it from, but you shouldn't have it."

"What are you talking about?"

"Get it out of my shop!" she yelled at him. Her rosy cheeks were now glowing crimson with rage.

He paused and then opened his mouth to speak; unsure of what to say.

"GET IT OUT!" Mel shouted.

Brendan backed towards to the door and fled. He felt tearful as he dashed into a nearby public garden and crouched behind a shrubbery. He had never seen Mel so angry. After taking a few minutes to recover, he walked back to where he'd parked his bicycle, his brain churning with upset and confusion. He sat on his saddle and took another look at the dollar bill. It looked completely normal; it had the usual portrait of George Washington on one side and the Reverse Great Seal on the other. What was the problem? He rode his bicycle northwards through Rockville along the main road. It had a wide cycle track which made the journey safer and easier than usual. After several miles he came to Johns Hopkins University where he knew there would be the traditional New Year American football game; something he hoped would take his mind off his troubles. As soon as he arrived he saw that something strange was going on. The stadium was in the grounds of the new campus and on a bowl game day it would normally be bustling with students, fans, cheerleaders and family members cheering on the players as they walked out onto the gridiron. Astonishingly it was almost empty. Only a few gloomy-looking groundsmen wandered around. Brendan went and double-checked and there was still a banner above the gate that clearly said: "*Johns Hopkins Montgomery New Year 1963 Bowl. January 1st, 3 PM*". There was no mention of a cancellation. He left the campus and rode back into central Rockville. In doing so he realized something that he had noticed subconsciously on his journey out, but it had not registered at the time. There was very little traffic on the roads, even for a public holiday. He passed an occasional car, but far fewer than normal; and there were no buses or lorries. When he arrived back in town he saw a group of people standing on a street corner. They were clustered close together outside the door of a solicitors' office. Brendan thought there was something wrong about their posture. He slowed down to listen to their voices. They were all weeping. Their heads were bowed, they were covering their face with their hands and they wailed pitifully together. Brendan pedalled harder and sped away from them, feeling afraid for some reason. He turned his bicycle onto Park Road and followed it under the railway bridge into a residential district. He then spotted four people sitting in a front garden outside a house; three men and five women. They were crouched on the grass crying. Brendan was so surprised that he pulled up by the kerb and stared. The people didn't notice him; they never looked up. They stayed where they were, half-sitting on the grass with tears dropping from their noses. Brendan rode on. Less than a minute later he passed an old man walking down a lane crying openly. Then he saw a married couple whom he knew by sight, but whose names he couldn't remember. They were also weeping profusely. Brendan was unnerved so he headed home as quickly as he could. On the way he encountered a number of other people all in tears. It was as if the entire town had turned into one big funeral. When he got home he left his bicycle in the garage and entered his home. "Mom, dad, are you there?" He walked into the lounge and saw his mother and father hunched forward on the settee watching television. "Mom, dad, why is everybody crying...?" His words caught in his throat as he saw tears in his parents' eyes. They were clutching each other's hands as if seeking support from each other. His eyes moved to the TV screen where a narrator was speaking in a sombre voice: "...*the true magnitude of what has been done for more years than we currently know...*" His mother leaped for the TV remote control in a panic and almost threw herself on top of it. The screen went blank. She got to her feet and faced her son, her face trembling. "Brendan, go to your room now."

"Why? What's going on?" Brendan asked as a very half-hearted interrogation. He knew he had no choice but to obey. As he reached the top of the stairs he heard her bark behind him: "Wait!" She ran up the stairs and pushed past him into his bedroom and came out carrying his matchbook.

He reached out for it. "Oh no, mom!"

"Go to bed!" she responded in a tremulous voice and pointed at the door.

"It's only four o'clock!"

She slammed the door of his bedroom behind him as soon as he was inside.

He passed an anxious evening reading his books, cut off from the outside world because of the loss of his matchbook. He stared out of the window as the sky darkened. He went to the bathroom a few times and tried to overhear the conversation or TV dialogue from downstairs but was unable. He changed into his pyjamas and got into to bed early; he struggled to fall asleep.

....
The following morning Brendan awoke while it was still dark outside. He poked his head out of his bedroom and heard somebody moving about downstairs. He descended to the kitchen and saw his father sitting at the table eating a bowl of cereal. A coffee mug sat at his elbow. He was dressed in a well ironed white shirt and tie. His suit jacket hung on the back of the neighbouring chair. His work identity photo badge glinted in the piercing glare of the neon lights on the ceiling. The window blinds were raised and the darkness outside reflected the interior of the room on its panes like a heavily tinted mirror. "Morning, dad." said Brendan.

His father looked up sharply, a trickle of milk running down his chin. He wiped it away with a serviette as he stared at his son, appearing not to recognize him. It reminded Brendan of the heartrending days when his father had been incapacitated by a stroke. "Hello, son." he said breathlessly. "It's only six-thirty. What are you doing up this early?"

He shrugged. "Because I went to bed early I guess."

His father chuckled sadly. "We can't keep you in bed forever can we?"

"What's going on, dad?"

He sighed tremulously. "Sit down, Bren."

Brendan poured himself a glass of orange juice from the fridge and took his place on a stool opposite his father.

"We didn't want to expose you to what's happened. It's too horrible. The reason I'm up so early is I'm heading into DC to deal with it. I've got a meeting with Jack scheduled for eight AM."

Brendan felt adrenalin surge through his body. His father looked genuinely perturbed, more so than he had ever done before. "What's going on, dad? Why was everybody crying yesterday?"

"Jack told the country something awful yesterday afternoon, some really bad news. He's been holding it back for a long time; keeping it secret, just like in the old days... He never even told me. I was pissed off at first, but now I understand why. I know why Jack made sure nobody could know; and anyway he's told the nation now."

"Told the nation what?"

His father bowed his head and raised his hands to his brow, as if experiencing a headache. "It's... it's all to do with children."

"What about children, dad?"

"Before R-Day... in fact even before Saucer Day, the government kept children prisoner. Some were children taken away from their moms and dads; some were children who never had a mom or dad. Some were only part human; they were hybrids."

"What's that?"

"Kids with one parent who is human and another who is ET; like Kerry, Siobhan's friend... There were millions of these children, mostly living in the underground bases. And..." he shuddered. "And the government did some really cruel things to them."

"Like what?"

"I can't tell you; you're too young to know." he tittered ironically. "I think we're *all* too young to know."

Brendan gazed at him curiously.

His father looked up with a different expression and said in a stronger voice: "Right, I've got to go to work and you should go back to bed till your mom wakes up. She's still asleep but she'll be up soon."

"Dad, can I come with you to work?" Brendan blurted out the question before he knew why he was asking it.

His father made the facial expression he did just before he said the word "*no*"; then he paused. "You really want to come with me into DC?"

"Yeah."

"You'll get bored."

"Can't I go off and explore while you work?"

"I guess so. And your mom's going to be out all day so you'll be stuck on your own otherwise." He looked sad again. "And... I could well do with your company."

Brendan smiled. "So I can come?"

"Yeah, why not; but I'm leaving in a minute so go get your clothes on now."

Dressing took Brendan about thirty seconds; he simply tore on the clothes he had been wearing the day before which he'd left lying on the floor. He reached the bottom of the stairs as his father was buttoning up his jacket and picking up his briefcase. "Right, let's go." said his father. "Your mom needs the flyer today so we'll have to take the ground car."

The air outdoors was cold, damp and fresh, and the sky was as dark as night. The streetlamps bathed the silent pre-dawn street with a carotene glow. His father drove the ground car out of the garage and Brendan got in. To his excitement he was allowed to sit in the front passenger seat. The Digby driven car accelerated slowly along the lane, lacking the power of the petrol engine saloon the family used to drive before they sold it. There was more traffic when they reached the highway into Washington DC. His father sat hunched forward in agitation, cursing other drivers for minor mistakes. "First thing I've got to do is go through some of the arrest warrants with Jack." he muttered. "He's ordered the FBI to start rounding up some of these folks."

"The ones who hurt the children?"

His father nodded. "We don't know where they all are; there were too many to monitor. Some of them might work out what's going to happen and split."

"Jack's the president. He'll find them."

"He's not the president." His father's voice was deadpan. "He's head of the US Provisional Government; that's not the same thing. The United States doesn't have a Federal executive at the moment. It won't get one till Dr King is inaugurated in a couple of weeks... This is the last thing Jack needs right now. He's up to his ass in the transitional process with MLK." he chuckled. "Funny how practicalities still rear their ugly heads, even during incidents like these."

Brendan nodded, not understanding.

The traffic became thicker and the buildings grew taller as the car approached the US Capitol. The line of cars and other vehicles grew slower and slower until it eventually ground to a halt. "Shit!" His father thumped the steering wheel with the palm of his hand.

Brendan felt his cheeks redden at his father's exclamation. "Dad! Mom says it's bad to cuss." he reproached.

His father laughed. "You're a good boy, Brendan... Sorry, it's just annoying. It's seven-thirty and we've got a gridlock."

Brendan looked out of the window. A man on a motor

scooter pulled up beside the car. He looked down and his eyes met with Brendan's. He smiled. He appeared to be sucking something in his mouth, a toffee or gobstopper. Brendan looked away. He recalled the incident the previous day in Mel's sweet shop and related the story to his father as they waited stationary in the traffic jam.

"Have you got the dollar on you now?"

He reached into his pocket and found it there. He pulled it out and handed it to his father.

"Ah! No wonder. This is a pre-Disclosure bill. It's no longer legal tender today."

"You mean it's not proper money anymore?"

"Unfortunately not. You can't buy anything with this."

"But I didn't know that... And why was Mel so angry with me?"

"A lot of people feel really uncomfortable about the old single; look at this." He flipped the note over and pointed to the motif on the right hand side of the reverse. "Do you know what that is?"

"Looks like a pyramid, one of those big stone things they have in Egypt. I've seen it on TV a few times."

"It's the reverse of the original Great Seal of the United States. The people were told the eye in the capstone of the pyramid was supposed to be the eye of God watching over the nation. What it really means is the Illuminati own the nation."

"I thought the Illuminati was supposed to be secret. That's what they told us in school. Why would they leave clues like that on our dollar bill if they didn't want us to know?"

His father pondered for a moment. "I'm not quite sure. Perhaps they just liked to laugh at us for being too dumb to see what they were showing us. Maybe they felt that if they showed us they were the real boss and we did nothing to stop them, then it was kind of our own fault."

Brendan nodded; this time he understood perfectly. He recalled that a few months ago some of the sixth-grade bullies at school had assaulted him in the toilets and told him that it was his own fault for not being able to stop them. It was a moral equation that everybody at school was very familiar with and accepted.

"So these days when some people see that symbol it upsets them a lot. Mel must be one of them. It's like in Germany after the war; people burst into tears if they saw the Nazi Swastika. Here." His father leaned over to pull his wallet out of his pocket and extracted a banknote from it. He handed it to Brendan.

"What's this?"

"The new dollar bill. If you feel like some candy today go buy some."

"Thanks, dad." The new dollar was very different to the old one. It was not made of paper, but instead felt more like plastic. It was also slightly larger and was a different colour and shape.

"It's made of polymer instead of paper; that means it won't turn to mush if you forget to take it out of your pocket when you put your pants in the laundry."

The obverse looked fairly unchanged, with the portrait of George Washington in the middle, but on the back there was no reverse of the US Great Seal. Instead there was simply the obverse Great Seal on the left and on the right was a circle of glinting shiny yellow material. Brendan pointed to it. "What's that?"

"Gold." his father grinned. "One dollar's worth of gold leaf, straight from the reserves at Fort Knox. Jack is changing the monetary system back to the gold standard. What better way than to put the gold itself inside the bills. Of course when you get up to the Benjamins you have a problem. Jack is currently getting the Treasury to design a bill with a hundred dollar's worth of gold in it. It'll probably end up being some kind of hard plastic thing, like a credit card... Oops, we're moving!" The queue of cars ahead started trundling forward in a caterpillar-like undulation. By the time the crest of the wave reached their car, his father had the Digby rolling and the vehicle in gear. They drove the rest of the way to the Capitol in ten minutes. The glowing dome appeared ahead in the distance as they turned a corner onto a long straight boulevard and it grew bigger and bigger as they approached it. They parked the car in his father's reserved space and walked across the lawn towards the grand building. The sky was beginning to brighten and the overcast was now lit dark grey by the invisible sunrise. The Capitol was illuminated by hundreds of lights. In daylight it was ivory white. To Brendan it resembled an enchanted castle from a fairytale. They climbed a long wide stairway up to the entrance. A single Stars and Stripes hung from a pole in front of the doors. Brendan looked behind him and saw the National Mall stretching all the way to the obelisk of the Washington Monument; looking as if some giant pharaoh had lived in Washington long ago and that was the remains of his palace. At the entrance, a uniformed policeman greeted them. "Morning, Mr Quilley."

"Hi, Eddie. Long night?"

"Almost time for bed now, sir." The officer examined his father's ID badge and then smiled down at Brendan. "And who's this young man?"

"This is my son, Brendan. I thought I'd show him round."

"By all means, sir; so long as you let the security chief know... Hi there, Brendan."

"Hello." Brendan returned the man's greeting blandly.

They were then allowed under a classical portico and through a pair of black wooden doors. They walked down an echoing marble corridor with a spotless shining floor that emerged into a huge circular open space stretching upwards like a cathedral. Brendan craned his neck to see the space above him, which he guessed correctly from its shape and size must be the interior of the dome. "Wow!" he exclaimed.

"Pretty neat, huh?" His father grinned at him proudly. "Welcome to the Rotunda."

A stiff-looking man in a suit approached them. "Mr Quilley, sir. Chief Executive Kennedy is in the House Speaker's office and will receive you now."

"Very well." His father led him along an opposite corridor and turned a few corners before coming to an archway where he had to be vetted by another security guard. Beyond that was a surprisingly small and cosy room with several settees and a low table. Jack sat in an adjacent armchair. "Clane, how's it going?" he waved as they entered.

"Hi, Jack. You're going downmarket a bit aren't you, meeting here?"

"Ooh!" Jack hissed in mock-reproach. "Don't let Lennie hear you say that!" He moved his gaze downwards and slightly to the right. "Hey, Brendan. I heard you were joining us."

"Hi, Jack." Brendan smiled at his father's friend. Jack was a lively and kind adult who often brought Brendan presents and told him jokes whenever they met. He had two children of his own whom Brendan had encountered a few times. One was a rather aloof girl called Caroline, a few years younger than him; and the other was a toddler called John Jr. Neither were much fun to play with. Jack's wife Jacqueline was a calm and maternal lady. To Brendan, the Kennedys were rather like a popular uncle and aunt.

There were half a dozen other people on the settees, only one of which Brendan knew; Martin Luther King who sat at the end beside Jack's chair, his elbow propped on the velvet arm. Next to him was a thin and loose-limbed white man wearing a college blazer and brogues. His hair was smooth, light brown and neatly parted. It seemed strangely unattached to his head as if it were a toupee. His facial expression was constantly changing and he responded to everything everybody else said with a sly half-smile, a half-wink with his electric blue eyes and an impudent flicker of his eyebrows as if teasing the person he was addressing. He spoke in a transatlantic upper class accent and radiated arrogance. When he was introduced to Brendan he merely responded: "Greetings, little boy!" before turning away and ignoring him. His name was William F Buckley and he was described as the "vice president-elect". Brendan assumed that this would make Martin Luther King his boss. Seeing them sitting together on the sofa, Brendan got the distinct impression that Dr King and Buckley did not like each other very much. He felt sorry for Dr King having to work with such an unpleasant man.

The adult's conversation was very hard to follow and, as his father predicted, he soon became bored. He whispered in his father's ear that he was going off to explore the city and his father nodded. Brendan left the office and headed out of the Capitol building. Before they'd arrived, his father had given him instructions to report back to the security guard at the entrance when he returned and his father would be informed to come and pick him up. Brendan wandered along an extensive road leading away through the Capitol with a leafy park on both sides with lawns as smooth and thin as baize. He crossed over at a set of pedestrian lights and beyond were the tall, oblong buildings of various Federal government departments and agencies; and then, further along, private banks, corporations, public buildings and grand hotels. There were few people around. Nobody was crying today, but the handful of passers by he encountered had gloomy and frightened faces. He arrived at a concrete corner block with the chrome-framed letters *National Press Building* above the door. He remembered his father talking about this place and so went in. He saw from a direction signboard that there was a "national Disclosure museum" on the sixth floor. He took the lift up and followed the arrows on the wall until he came to the museum. More plaques on the wall explained that this used to be the Charles Ross Television Suite, but had been converted into the museum. The TV studio had been preserved and Brendan was amused to see that there was a waxwork model of his father sitting in front of a TV camera facing another dummy of a man in a suit wearing glasses. The effigies were very lifelike and his father was easily recognizable, although he was clearly many years younger. All this happened before his son was born. Brendan left the National Press Building and continued walking along the street. He was lost, but quite enjoyed the thrill of that. He stopped at a supermarket to buy some sweets with the money his father had given him. An open space appeared ahead and the River Potomac stretched out before him. The far bank was thickly wooded, promising a rich opportunity for frolics. The shore was a spider's web of pale winter branches. He felt the urge to reach it and started looking for a bridge. Sure enough, there was one a short distance downstream to his left. It was a wide road-bridge, but there was very little traffic that day and there was a narrow pavement behind a row of crash barriers. At the crest of the bridge he got a much better view and could see that the forested far bank was actually an island and there was another reach of the river beyond it. Even better! He had to climb over the parapet and slide down a tree bough to reach the land; there was no official access from the bridge. He was disappointed to find that the woods were not as impenetrable as they had first appeared from a distance and there were many well-tended pathways and patches of mowed grass. It was more like a park than a jungle. He decided what was the most overgrown part of the island he could find and then crawled into the gap between three bushes where he settled down on a patch of leaves to eat his sweets. He could peek out from between the branches to spy on one of the green spaces and he saw an old man sitting on a bench nearby eating a sandwich and reading a newspaper. Brendan reclined back onto a patch of leaves to eat his sweets when he felt a jagged lump under his back. He sat up and turned round to remove what he suspected were stones concealed by the ground litter, but he saw they were bones instead. They were clean, dry white bones. He wondered what animal they had come from; they were quite large. He poked around, picking them out one at a time, until he came across the skull. He had been worried for a while that he might have found human bones, based on the size of them, but when he saw the skull he was relieved to find that this beast had been something very different. The skull was elongated and tapering. It had huge orbits and a nasal cavity at the very front. Its jaw was straight, its mouth very wide and it had fifty to sixty teeth all of which were the same type, long and jagged like a shark's.

Brendan dropped the skull, his hands were shaking. He knew instantly what it was. He remembered R-Day as much as anybody else did; it was still less than a year ago. There were some facts of life his parents could not shelter him from and millions of people suddenly shape-shifting into reptilian humanoids was one of them; not least because his own family played a crucial role in making it happen. He found that out when the reptilians all suddenly dropped dead after his sister and her friends broke down the method by which the creatures disguised themselves and then destroyed the particle collider in Canada. Afterwards, Jack had ordered that all the rotting corpses of the reptilians be cleared up as quickly as possible, but naturally they would end up missing a few. This one must have died right here in Washington DC, just a short walk from the White House. Laying under a bush on this river island it went unnoticed and decomposed quietly while the world passed it by. Brendan climbed out from under the bush. The man who had been sitting on the bench had got up. He was standing by the bench examining his folded newspaper one last time; then he threw it down on the bench and walked away, perhaps because he had finished reading it and was leaving it for the next person who sat there. Brendan waited until he had gone then he went up to the bench and sat down. He picked up the newspaper. It was that day's edition of *The Washington Post* and the headline read: *UNDERGROUND CHILDREN- MORE DETAILS EMERGE* and underneath in slightly smaller lettering: *PROV-GOV PUBLISHES NEW L.N.E. FILES*. Brendan read the front page article and the inside features. The story carried on through half the pages of the newspaper, all the way to the centrefold. The paper was, of course, aimed at adults, so Brendan did not understand every word of it; but he managed to grasp the general gist. His father had told him the truth, but had omitted the devastating details. The underground bases that had been discovered after Disclosure, such as Area 51, were far larger and more extensive than had previously been thought. They existed in a massive network that covered the entire earth, like a secret rabbit warren of evil beneath their feet. The explorers who were sent in to survey the network after R-Day had come across many locations where crimes were committed against children on a horrifying scale and severity. These crimes included kidnapping, non-consensual medical experimentation, satanic ritual abuse, sexual abuse, torture, mutilation, murder and many other atrocities that Brendan couldn't comprehend. Bodies had been found in their millions. Some were children who had lived their whole lives down in that artificial hell and others had been taken from human families in the surface world. They were some of the thousands of children who were reported missing every year. The Provisional Government had decided not to release this revelation immediately to the general public; partly because it was so appalling, but also because there was a criminal investigation involved. The FBI believed that there were a great number of people still at large; in other words they were not reptilians, but they had colluded with the reptilians and the Illuminati, to a greater or lesser degree, to aid and abet these offences. The FBI had begun arresting the suspects and so Jack had decided to publish the truth after the New

Year. Brendan now understood why so many people had been weeping in the streets yesterday. He understood why a black cloud of gloom still hung over everything around him.

He jumped to his feet and threw the newspaper onto the ground. He felt a sudden desperation to be with his father. He ran along the path looking for a way off the island. Eventually he had to use a footbridge on the far side of the island that deposited him on the right bank of the Potomac at Arlington, Virginia. From there he made his way along the riverbank to the bridge he had come over on so that he could cross back into the District of Columbia. He could see the Washington Monument poking above the treeline and so found it easy to navigate his way back to the Capitol. He walked along the Mall from the Lincoln Memorial but had to take a diversion to avoid a gang of rough-looking adults who had gathered outside the Smithsonian. They had the mien of protesters. Brendan had seen several street demonstrations during the turbulent years of his young life and subconsciously knew all the signs. He checked in at the security office and his father came to fetch him. Brendan embraced him wordlessly and hard. "Hey, Brendan!" His father hugged him tight back laughing. "Are you alright?"

He nodded.

"Cool beans. I'm nearly done here. One more hour and we can go home, okay?"

It was still overcast as Brendan and his father headed back to the carpark. The January afternoon was dimming slightly as the clock's hand drooped below three PM. His father was talking on his roamphone as they walked to the car. When he'd hung up he explained to Brendan. "That was the Secret Service. There's some trouble in Georgetown and they've recommended we take a detour."

"What trouble, dad?"

"Some people blocking the roads, yelling and throwing things around. Apparently they're targeting cars with Federal government plates."

"Has our car got Federal government plates?"

His father nodded grimly. "The police are dealing with it, but we should go home a different way just to be on the safe side."

Brendan and his father drove slowly and steadily through the evening traffic, heading out of Washington. There were more police around than usual, and several helicopters and flyers hovered above the rooftops. His father kept pressing buttons on his sat-director to recompute a different route home. After a quarter of an hour they turned off onto a smaller road through a residential district of terraced houses and shops. It was much darker now and streetlights had come on. They pulled up at a red light...

BOOM!... Both Brendan and his father yelped in shock. A large heavy object had just struck the windscreen. The glass was starred and warped. "What the fuck...!?" his father swore. A group of men had surrounded the front end of the car. They hammered on the bonnet and rocked the vehicle on its suspension. Their faces were contorted with hate. One of them was carrying a crudely-painted placard. In his state of adrenalin-washed terror Brendan's senses were enhanced and he noticed every detail. The words had been applied with a thick paintbrush, but they were still legible: *STOP THE ARRESTS! KENNEDY OUT!* His father shifted the car into reverse and backed jerkily; he swung round to look over his shoulder and swerved to avoid hitting the car behind him which was also backing. "Motherfuckers!" he yelled. The Digby Carrousel under the bonnet strained with the effort. His father shifted the gears again and the car leaped forward around the gang of troublemakers. It accelerated into the opposite lane until they had cleared the junction and were safe. Brendan stared at the damaged windscreen. "Dad! Why did they do that!?"

"I don't know, son."

By the way he avoided his gaze, Brendan could tell his father was holding something back.

....

Brendan woke up crying. He sat up in bed, shocked by the nightmare he'd just had. Along with the shock was the relief that it had not been real. He switched on his bedside lamp and looked around himself at all the reassuringly normal things in sight. He jumped out of bed and was about to head for his parents' bedroom so he could be comforted by them, especially by his mother, like he always did whenever he had a bad dream; but when he remembered content of the dream he stopped and returned to his bed to lie there alone.

Like with most of his dreams, he found it difficult to recall individual details; however he was left with a very powerful sense of presence and ambiance. He had been back in his old home in Las Vegas during the terrible few months when his father had been in hospital recovering from his stroke. During this period his mother had brought home a very old and bad-tempered Scottish woman called Millicent. Millicent was a chain-smoker who filled their home with her noxious fumes, giving Brendan a continuous cough. Her mother had been obsessively devoted to Millicent calling her "the best friend I've ever had!" and wanting to spend every moment of every day with her. In doing so, his mother's personality had radically changed. She had once been such an affectionate parent, yet now she paid little or no attention to her son at the best of times. During the worst of times she was openly hostile and cruel, especially when Millicent was in the house, as if his mother were showing off for her friend. It was as if Millicent were brainwashing his mother into hating her own children. It pained Brendan to recall even a moment of that period in his life, but now he had no choice. In the dream his mother and Millicent were both scolding him violently for some misdemeanour he had allegedly committed; but he wasn't sure what it was. He either couldn't understand or failed to remember. He just stood trembling in front of the baleful glare of his mother and Millicent; two pairs of flaming eyes, two screeching voices and two wide open, sneering mouths. His mind churned helplessly in Kafkaesque bewilderment. The two women paused, panting with exertion and waited for him to reply. "But... but you haven't heard my side of the story yet." he protested.

"I don't *need* to hear your side of the story!" Millicent shouted at him in her discordant Scottish growl. Then she turned to his mother. She produced a long silver butcher's knife from her pocket and handed it to his mother. "Gina, take your only begotten son, Brendan, whom you do NOT love... and offer him up as a sacrifice to ME!"

Brendan's mother obeyed without hesitation or question. She took the knife from Millicent's hand and seized Brendan by the scruff of his neck. It was a very vivid dream; he could feel her knuckles against his nape and his T-shirt collar tighten around his throat. She dragged her son over to the kitchen table. Brendan screamed and kicked in terror but his mother's hand was too strong. She hoisted him up onto the tabletop and pushed him flat onto his back. Her face was robotic, deadpan, totally devoid of all emotion and thought; a face with no humanity. She raised the knife above her head ready to plunge it into her son's heart... At that point Brendan woke up.

He knew what part of this dream related to. When he was in first grade he had been mortified when he was told the bible story from the Book of Genesis- Chapter 22 where God tells Abraham to sacrifice his son Isaac. Abraham is about to comply, but at the last moment an angel steps in to stay Abraham's hand. God then reveals that His commandment was just a test of Abraham's faith and obedience to God. For days afterwards Brendan pestered his parents with the question: "Would you kill *me* if God told you to?" And he didn't stop asking until his parents had reassured him in the negative at least a dozen times.

Brendan tried to return to sleep but couldn't. Luckily it was almost daybreak and soon the sky became lighter outside. He heard his parents moving about in their room followed by the sound of them descending the stairs. He got out of bed and followed them. The family drank coffee and ate breakfast together. His father straightened his tie. "I've got to go back to Washington today. Lots of mess to sort out following yesterday's debacle."

Brendan's heart skipped a beat as he remembered their journey home the previous evening. "Will you be safe, dad?"

"Sure. The police have regained their control of the streets."

"But what if those men come back; the ones who tried to break the car's windshield?"

His father grinned affectionately at him. "Are you really worried about me?"

Brendan nodded.

"What if I take the flyer?" He looked at his mother. "Do you need it today, Gina?"

His mother shook her head.

Brendan felt a wash of relief. "Thanks, dad." In the flyer, his father could soar over the ineffectual raised arms of the bloodthirsty mob, totally safe from harm. He went out into the front garden to see his father leave for work. His father waved and smiled as he closed the door of the flyer. The antigravity drive inside the vehicle activated and began buzzing with that familiar bees' nest sound. The craft rose slowly into the air and moved forward, accelerating in both speed and altitude until it was a black oblong against the early morning sky. It vanished behind the roofs of the houses opposite and Brendan returned into the warm interior of his home.

He finished his breakfast, had a bath and then was about to go out on his bicycle, determined to enjoy the last few days of freedom before his return to school the following week. "Brendan!" his mother shouted. At the moment he heard her voice he also heard the sound of a flyer outside. He ran into the kitchen; his mother was looking out of the window, her head pressed to the glass to see upwards. "It's not your father. It's the police I think. It's coming down in the backyard... Oh my God!" She opened the backdoor and ran out onto the patio. The flyer was a large black vehicle with the words *UNITED STATES SECRET SERVICE* on the flank. It settled down in the middle of the lawn and its humming dropped in volume. The door opened and a woman in uniform decamped. "Mrs Quilley?"

"Yes." said his mother.

"We need you to come with us."

"Why?"

"We need to take you to a secure location."

"Why?"

"Come now! We'll explain on the way."

They gave Brendan no time even to collect a comic book from his room; his mother just had time to lock the back door and then they were soaring into the air. The two USSS agents in the front seats told them what was happening. "The rioting has returned this morning, Mrs Quilley. The gangs are deliberately targeting senior Provisional Government officials and their families. Your husband is the senior assistant executive to Chief Executive Kennedy; therefore we have reason to believe that you're not safe at home.

We're therefore evacuating you to Andrews AAF Base as a temporary security measure."

"What about my house? Will it be damaged?"

"We will ask the Maryland state police to keep a lookout for it."

His mother paused. "What about my husband?"

"He is ensconced at the Capitol and we believe he is safe, ma'am."

She sighed.

The flyer landed outside a huge metallic building with a wide open door. Vast rivers of flat concrete stretched away in all directions and Brendan could see several aircraft parked at varying distances. He stopped to study them, but the Secret Service personnel urgently ushered him on until they were all inside the building. There were several dozen people inside the large empty room; one that he realized was an aircraft hangar. Almost all of them were women and children and they were clustered on a few circles of plastic seats, like the ones he sat on at school. He recognized some of them as family of his father's colleagues. Two women with a large steel urn on a trolley served the refugees coffee. They also had a luscious pile of comics that the youngsters quickly burrowed into, Brendan included. An hour later, a uniformed airman wheeled in a large television set and a shelf full of videodisks. After a brief dispute they all agreed to watch a new Disney animation. Within a few hours Brendan had made several friends and it was almost disappointing when the USSS crew came in to tell them that it was now safe to return home. To his mother's relief, the house had not been touched since they'd left. One of the Secret Service officers stayed with them.

Twilight fell and before long a burring sound outside announced the return of his father. Clane came into the lounge and ripped off his tie. His face was creased and overwrought. "I'm afraid the Secret Service folks will be staying with us, for the foreseeable future at least... *All* of us."

His mother sighed. "So they'll have to walk round the mart with me?"

"Yes... And Brendan, one will have to accompany you to school."

"What?" Brendan thought for a moment how that would

feel. An armed man in a suit would be standing by the wall in all his classes. Was that a good or bad thing? It would give him a certain mystique among the other boys, but... maybe that could have a downside. "But dad, what if the other kids think I'm weird?"

"I'm sorry, Brendan. It has to be this way for safety reasons... Hopefully it won't be for too long." He collapsed wearily into an armchair. His mother went and made them all coffee. He sipped it slowly like a sick man lying in a hospital bed.

"Are you alright, Clane?" asked his mother.

He gazed at her. "Oh, Gina... will this ever be over?"

"What was it like in Washington today?"

"Like the Siege of Yorktown."

"Oh my God!... Why? We have Disclosure, goddammit! We've freed ourselves from the Illuminati! We've exposed the reptilians! In a few weeks a new president is going to be sworn in!... Isn't *that* enough? Why are people still not happy?"

Brendan's father sighed and his eyes looked upwards as he reminisced. "I remember during the war. We'd taken the boat out of Pearl on an exercise. There was a westerly blowing, force seven. Just right for an underway line-handling drill. Anyway this guy called Hank fell overboard; a young guy straight out of New London, junior boatswain's mate. We put her about and started looking for him. He had his Mae West on so we knew he'd stay afloat. This was warm water too; central Pacific is like a Turkish bath that time of year. We were well away from shark waters too so we weren't too bothered for his safety. It took us three hours, then we saw him bobbing in the swells and waving his hands. We dragged him onto the casing and he was okay; swallowed a bit of seawater, sure, but nothing serious... But, I tell you; he was never the same again. He was alright at first; totally normal, but then he totally lost his shit the following week and had to be sent to Bethesda. You see... those three hours floating in the sea destroyed him. He didn't know whether he'd live or die, he couldn't see anything but water and sky. No sounds but splashing waves, nothing solid under his feet... He was saved, he was rescued uninjured; yet he couldn't get over the shock. Trauma is a very strange thing. It often hits you much later than when you experience what caused it. Delayed reaction."

"Why do you bring that up now, Clane?"

He chuckled with bitter knowingness. "We're like Hank, all of us, as a people, as the whole of mankind."

"You mean we've got trauma?"

He nodded. "Did you really think it would be so easy? We got Disclosure, kicked out the reps, kicked out the Loomies... and then what, Gina? Everything in the garden will just be lovely forever and ever? We suddenly become like priests of High Atlantis or something?... No! The real problem is in here!" He pointed at his heart. "We're like... like a guy who's hooked on liquor or opium. It's killing him, it's breaking apart his very body and mind; but he can't stop. And if you take his habit away from him he loses his wits... You see, in the same way as a guy hooked on drink and drugs, mankind was hooked on the Illuminati. There are no rehab clinics for us to check into, no helplines we can call. We're going to have to do cold turkey."

Brendan got up and wandered through into the kitchen. He found his parent's conversation extremely alarming. He looked out of the window. Flyers and helicopters were once again filling the sky. He felt an inexplicable sense of foreboding.

Chapter 3

The collar was choking him. Brendan tugged at it to stretch it every few minutes. He was sitting on the back seat of the family flyer, tucked in between Siobhan and his Aunt Mary. "There's a no-fly zone over Capitol Hill." said his father from the driver's seat. "We're going to land at Anacostia Park." The journey only took about five minutes, then flyer came to rest and they all decamped. Siobhan found this difficult because of her pregnancy bulge and somebody had to tug on her arm to get her to her feet. "Brendan." Brendan looked up to see the severe brow of his father frowning down at him. "Listen carefully, son. You must be on your best behaviour today. Remember the TV cameras will be on us; millions of people across the world might be seeing us. So, no funny faces, no picking your nose, no scratching your ass and no other things like that; okay?"

"Yes, dad."

He grinned. "Well done, son. Now, this is a wonderful moment for America and the world. A rebirth of civilization, so enjoy yourself."

Anacostia Park was a patch of grass and woodland that had been converted into a huge flyer-pad. Everybody was standing around in a crowd dressed in their best clothes. All his parents' friends were there as well as most of their family. Jenny, Siobhan's best friend, came over and gave him a hug. They moved to a row of black vans for the short remainder of the journey. Ushers wearing suits escorted them from the ground vehicles into a side entrance of the United States Capitol. The white walls of the building had been washed and were shinier than ever. The whole edifice was draped with huge Stars and Striped flags. The interior corridors were thronging with people. Brendan's view was cut off by walls of adult bodies covered in mohair and satin. The next time he got a reasonable view of his surroundings he was passing through a doorway outside again. He felt a moment's precariousness as he realized that he was at the top of a steep slope leading down to the west front of the Capitol. Ahead of him in the distance he could see the National Mall and the Washington Monument. The slope consisted of an aisle of spotless blue carpet and rows of folding seats. His father and mother pushed his shoulders gently to guide him into his place. The sun was peeking through thin cloud. It was a mild and dry day with a fresh but tepid breeze. People were walking up and down continuously; some were in military dress uniform. A group of people wearing black robes marched down the aisle together in a row, like a conclave of priests. "Dad." Brendan plucked his father's elbow and pointed. "Who are they?"

"The Supreme Court." said his father. "Look, that's Chief Justice Marshall at the front. He'll be administering the oath."

A brass orchestra played various patriotic tunes from an invisible place below their feet. A choir crooned gently in harmony. Crowds slowly gathered in the Mall until it looked as if a tide of people was washing in from a sea of multicoloured dots, like decorative beads. Brendan's eyes drifted across the scene in a leisurely way. He leaned his head back and looked up at the translucent clouds. Something caught his eye; it was a black oval, plainly visible against the creamy overcast. It looked like a chocolate egg hanging in the sky; its apparent size was about that of a coin held at arms length. He couldn't tell how high up it was; it was impossible to get a range on it, but it was below the clouds; almost at the zenith. "Dad, what's that?" he pointed.

His father's hand shot out like a whip and dragged his hand down. "Brendan, don't point!" he hissed.

"Why? What is it?"

"Nothing."

"What? It's not nothing, dad; it's right up there."

His father blushed and ignored him.

"Is it a flyer?" Brendan muttered. The object resembled the flyer he had seen taking off from where he's met his friend David in the snow last December.

"No." replied his father after a pause.

Brendan remembered his father telling them that there was a no-fly zone above Capitol Hill. "What is it, dad?" he repeated in a furtive tone.

His father sighed and rolled his eyes. "It's not one of ours."

"Then whose..." Brendan began, but then he suddenly understood. He gasped. "You mean it's a flying saucer!?"

"Shh!" his father leaned at him with his extended finger pushed desperately against his lips. "Keep your voice down. Brendan!... Jesus!"

"You mean it is?"

"Yes."

A blend of excitement and dread filled him. "Then... shouldn't we tell these people?"

"No need; I'm sure they can see it too."

Sure enough, every few seconds Brendan saw one or two of the other VIP's glance upwards at the mysterious ovoid. "Dad, shouldn't we stop the inauguration if there's a flying saucer overhead?"

"Not a chance! This is way too important. It's business as usual until we have our president... Now just act like it's not there. That's what everybody else is doing."

Everything around seemed the same. Nobody flinched at the uninvited guest above their heads. The band didn't drop a note; the US Marine Corps honour guards remained standing like statues by the sides of the door. Despite his father's command, Brendan continued to flick his eyes upwards to observe the MFO, Mysterious Flying Object, every so often. "They must be watching us." he murmured, but nobody heard him.

"Ten-hut!" yelled one of the guards and the military contingent came to attention. Everybody in the seating area rose to their feet. His father nudged him edgily while Brendan was already getting up. "I know, dad!" he snapped. An announcer on a loudspeaker introduced a number of the senior dignitaries as they paraded through the door in formation and took their seats. Brendan recognized Martin Luther King's three children who were a few years his junior. Dr King's wife had not arrived yet. She had looked pregnant in the same way Siobhan did when Brendan had last seen her. He wondered how she would cope with the ceremony, or whether she had had her baby yet. The family of the Provisional Chief Executive followed them. Jacqueline Kennedy was a quiet and slightly nervous woman, similar to her daughter Caroline who walked down the steps behind her. John Jr held his mother's hand tightly as he traversed the stairs one at a time. Coretta Scott King, the future first lady, was indeed walking with difficulty as she descended to her seat accompanied by a number of House and Senate officials. Her belly protruded like the dome of the Capitol itself from between the folds of her pink velvet jacket.

"Ladies and gentlemen." said the master-of-ceremonies in a climactic voice. "Please welcome the Chief Executive of the Provisional Government of the United States of America... Mr John Fitzgerald Kennedy!" There was a momentous cheer when Jack appeared. He waved to the crowd as he almost jogged down the steps to take his place at the front by the podium. There were handshakes all round. The band then stopped playing for the first time since Brendan had arrived. There was a long pause and then the band played a fanfare and drum roll. "And now... ladies and gentlemen, the vice-president-elect of the United States, Mr William Francis Buckley... and now the president-elect of the United States, Dr Martin Luther King Junior!" Brendan was almost deafened by the roar from the crowd. A hundred thousand admiring voices called out in unison. Dr Martin Luther King Jr was dressed in a heavy greatcoat that fell to his knees. A long blue tie fell loosely in front of his chest and he paused at the top of the stairs to smile and wave to the adoring masses. He looked tired and slightly nervous; there was no sign of self-satisfaction in his manner. If anything he appeared excessively modest, Brendan thought. The band played a triumphal match to serenade him to his place of office. When he took his seat the guests sat down and the honour guard stood at ease.

A congressman went to the podium and made a speech to open the ceremony. He gave a history of inaugurations; about how the United States had carried out one every four years, without fail, once every four years since 1789. The American Civil War didn't stop it, the Great Depression didn't stop it and the world wars of the current century didn't stop it. The quadrennial cycle was broken by Disclosure and R-Day. It gave him pride that even in such an unparalleled and extremely unpredictable crisis, the United States of America had slipped out of its dedicated rhythm for just three years. The Provisional Government had only been necessary for ten months. Today's inauguration was the most important in American history. "...We continue, as we are and always were..." He paused and sniffed loudly. Brendan could only see the back of his head, but he got the distinct impression that the man was crying. It shook him slightly; a grown man weeping was an uncomfortable sight. "As we inaugurate our new president we declare to the forces of evil that they have failed. The darkness is banished." Brendan looked up at the sky. The MFO was still hovering there like a bird of prey, although it had moved westwards slightly and so was at a lower elevation. It also looked slightly bigger indicating that it had dropped in altitude. When the congressman had sat down a trio of clergymen came to the podium to lead a prayer. They were followed by a Jewish rabbi who gave a brief sermon followed by a blessing in Hebrew. Then the congressman who had made the previous speech came forward and called for Vice-President-Elect Buckley to step up and take his oath of office. The choir sung a short song and then Chief Justice Marshall came forward and called for the president-elect. Dr King and his wife stepped uneasily up to the podium, like a schoolboy called into the headmaster's office. Mrs King held up the inaugural bible and Dr King laid his left hand on top of it.

"Mr President-Elect, please raise your right hand and repeat after me." said Marshall. "I, Martin Luther King, do solemnly swear."

"I, Martin Luther King, do solemnly swear." replied Dr King.

"That I will faithfully execute."

"That I will faithfully execute."

"The office of President of the United States."

"The office of President of the United States."

"And will, to the best of my ability."

"And will, to the best of my ability."

"Preserve, protect and defend."

"Preserve, protect and defend"

"The constitution of the United States."

"The constitution of the United States."

"So help me God."

"So help me God."

"Congratulations, Mr President." President King and the Chief Justice shook hands. The orchestra struck up the presidential anthem *Hail to the Chief*, a tune that had been strictly prohibited in official function for ten months. The applause of the crowd almost drowned out the twenty-one gun salute from an artillery battery set up on the National Mall. The president and Jack Kennedy embraced warmly. The former Chief Executive of the US Provisional Government clearly had tears in his eyes. He was probably sad because his government had just ceased to exist, Brendan concluded. A new sound rose above that of human voices and cannon fire, a steady thundering roar. A squadron of jet fighters flew low overhead trailed smoke behind them coloured red, white and blue. They passed underneath the MFO, so giving the unusual object a minimum range.

The congressman then announced: "Ladies and gentlemen, it gives me great pleasure to introduce the thirty-ninth president of the United States, Martin Luther King!"

As President King gave his inaugural address all the thousands of people in sight were completely silent. Brendan could easily imagine that the entire city, or even the entire world, were silent; their ears and mind focused in rapt attention. There were a large group of protesters at the far end of the Mall, held in check by a phalanx of policemen. There seemed to be protesters at every event those days, Brendan thought; but at this moment even they were stilled and attentive. The silence lasted for a few moments after King had stepped back from the microphone. The show of approval that followed was more subdued than Brendan expected. Many people around him couldn't clap their hands because they were wiping their eyes and noses. He looked at the ground in disgust. He never in his life expected to see thousands of adults all crying. After people had recovered their emotions there were more benedictions from the men of the cloth; then a large old lady came forward and everybody stood while she led the singing of *The Star-Spangled Banner* in an operatic voice. Everybody had been given a sheet of paper with the lyrics and Brendan looked up to see his father reading from it carefully as he sung. Brendan was surprised that his father didn't know them off by heart. Everybody remained on their feet as the new president and first family departed the podium, the honour guard saluted him as their commander-in-chief for the first time. Slowly everybody else shuffled after him. Brendan held on to his mother's hand so he wouldn't get lost. They retired to a hall full of statues where dozens of tables were set up for them to have a luncheon. He sat in a red velvet chair and admired the sparkling gold cutlery and fine china plates. The menu was printed in cursive writing that Brendan had trouble reading. His parents were in good spirits as white-coated waiters served them some very nice food. The president and his family sat on a dais by the wall raised above the rest of the impromptu restaurant on a long straight table facing the room. After the luncheon there were more speeches; Brendan had begun to find them rather tedious. Colonels, secretaries and senators came forward to present the new executive with various ornaments and mementoes. After that they were ushered out of the dining hall to a seating area at the east front of the Capitol where a parade of military marchers, emergency service workers and even farm tractors rolled by for an hour and a half. President King's arm must have been aching, Brendan thought, as he saluted one after another of the parade groups. The MFO had gone.

It was getting dark when the festivities finally broke up. Dr King and his family left by limousine for their first night in their new home, the White House. Brendan was feeling sleepy as his mother and Siobhan escorted him back to where the vans had dropped them off that morning. Jackie Kennedy and her children went with them. Brendan's father had walked off by himself a few minutes earlier and he caught up with them in the courtyard. He had Jack Kennedy with him. The former Provisional Government leader was is very high spirits. The sadness he has displayed when the president took his oath had inexplicably metamorphosed into exuberance. He was almost jumping for joy as he walked along beside Brendan's father. "I'm free!... I'm free!" he kept repeating. "The strife of the goddamn country is now Martin's problem. I'm free and I can finally relax!"

"May Jack and I invite you all home to dinner?" Jackie Kennedy smiled at the Quilley family. "I think we deserve a little private celebration."

Jack smiled back in a self-conscious way. "Jackie... Clane and Gina are always welcome and I'm sure we can host them another time, but... well..."

Jack's wife frowned subtly. "'Well' what, Jack?"

"Erm..."

Brendan's father interrupted. "Jackie, we appreciate the offer, but Jack and I have made other arrangements for this evening."

"What kind of arrangements?" asked Jackie in an apprehensive tone."

Clane laughed. "We're off down the feckin' pub!"

....

Brendan sat in the back of Jackie Kennedy's spacious flyer next to Caroline. John jr was asleep in the baby-seat on his other side. The landscape below was scattered with electric lights and the sky was dark. Jackie piloted the aircraft while Gina Quilley sat in the front passenger seat. Both women were grim and silent for a long time; then Jackie sighed. "Dear God, I hope nothing goes wrong."

Brendan's mother chucked sarcastically. "Two middle-aged Irishmen spending the evening downtown; what could possible go wrong?"

They landed by the front door of the Kennedys' grandiose mansion in rural Massachusetts and a butler came out to escort them into the house. They were then served a light dinner at a well-polished rosewood table; and Brendan felt very sleepy afterwards so Jackie took him to one of the guest bedrooms. Brendan fell asleep on a bed the size of a trampoline.

He was woken up in the middle of the night by a noise coming from outside. He sat up and switched on the bedside lamp. It was the buzzing of a flyer's engines very close, as if the vehicle were hovering just above the roof of the house. He jumped out of bed and ran down the curved staircase in his pyjamas. He wrestled with bolt for about thirty seconds and then managed to open the front door. He ran out into the driveway and looked up. A flyer was indeed moving through the air just above the gable. Its headlights shone down at the tiles. It was wheeling back and forth as if out of control; the buzzing sound kept rising and falling as if the pilot were continuously adjusting the throttle. Brendan leapt back instinctively as the aircraft collided with a chimney. There was creaking crackling noise as its body panel was torn by the brickwork. The flyer reversed and flew over the drive. It descended sharply and Brendan ran onto the lawn to avoid it. It landed directly onto its chassis; the pilot did not lower the landing gear. The engine fell silent and the doors opened. Raucous laughter burst from the flyer's interior and two men rolled out onto the ground. They used the sidewalls of their shattered vehicle to steady themselves as they clambered to their feet. Brendan recognized them as Jack and his father. They both immediately broke into a slurred and cacophonous duet: *"Oh, Eire! Must we leave you, driven by the tyrant's hand? Must we ask a mother's welcome from a strange but happy land? Where the cruel cross of England shall never more be seen and in that land we'll no more hang for the wearing of the green. The wearing of the green! The wearing of the green!..."*

Jackie and Gina came running out of the front door. They both exclaimed in outrage at the sight that met their eyes. "John Fitzgerald Kennedy! What the hell have you done!?" yelled Jackie.

"Clane! Jesus Christ! You could have broken your necks!"

The two men stopped singing and staggered towards their wives; their hands round each other's shoulders for support. "Gina!... Love o' my life!" giggled Clane.

"I'm sorry, honey." said Jack in a similar tone. "We wanted to come home and protect you from the protesters..."

"God bless America and God bless President King!" bellowed Clane at the top of his voice.

A flashing red light appeared between the trees of the grounds and a police car turned into the driveway. Its siren sounded briefly as it braked beside the crashed flyer. Two state troopers stepped out and strode forward aggressively. The women then noticed Brendan standing to one side. "Brendan, get upstairs to bed now!" commanded his mother. Brendan obeyed but his room was right above the entrance hall and he left his door open a crack. He couldn't make out much of the conversation, but the tones were very comprehensive. The women continued to rebuke their husbands while the men continued to laugh drunkenly. The calm and professional voices of the policemen interjected occasionally. Eventually his mother and the officers approached the front door where

Brendan could hear them better. "I'm afraid there is no doubt that your husband was driving, Mrs Quilley." said the trooper.

"Will he lose his license?" asked Gina urgently.

"No, Ma'am. If he had been driving a ground car we would have arrested and charged him. The law has not yet caught up with the new tech yet."

"That's good." she sighed.

"I would advise him to take more care in future though, Ma'am. There is a bill running through the state house right now which will extend the driving-under-the-influence legislation to personal aerial vehicles."

"I will. Thank you, officer."

"Goodnight, Ma'am."

Chapter 4

Brendan jumped and woke up with a start. His mother was leaning over his bed shaking his shoulder. The window was filled with the pre-dawn gloom. "Mom?"

"It's okay, honey. It's just time for Siobhan to have her baby. We have to head for the hospital now."

He nodded and got out of bed without another word. His mother and father were both subdued as they gathered in the hallway. They didn't even pause for breakfast. The sun rose as they headed northeast in the family flyer. They glided down over the New Jersey hospital just as Jenny's ground car pulled into the carpark below them. Clane brought the antigravity aircraft down into the neighbouring space. Jenny got out of the driving seat and ran round to the far side of her car. "She's getting contractions every ten minutes." she said urgently. Gina and Jenny both helped Siobhan out of the front passenger seat. Brendan looked at her sister as she struggled to get out of the car and stand up. Her huge belly hung in front of her like a beach ball. She caught her brother's eye and smiled confidently. A porter with a wheelchair came up to the car and he pushed Siobhan in through the sliding doors of the hospital entrance. She was booked in at reception and taken straight through a set of double doors. Her mother went with her, leaving Brendan alone with his father. The entrance hall was a long, clean space with a low ceiling, whitewashed walls and a parquet floor. There was an open-plan cafeteria at the far end so Clane took his son for their belated morning cup of coffee. They sat in silence for a while, sipping from their cardboard cups. His father stared down at the table, deep in thought. "Jackie's pregnant." he eventually muttered.

"Pardon, dad?"

"Jackie Kennedy is expecting another baby." Clane repeated in a louder voice. "Don't tell anybody that. Jack asked me to keep it a secret. They've only just found out."

Uncomfortable thoughts ran through Brendan's mind involving Jack, Jackie and the biology book he had read the previous year. "I guess it happens all the time."

"Always feels weird when it's you though, Bren. One day it *will* be you."

Brendan shuddered. "I don't think I could be a daddy."

His father chuckled affectionately. "You say that now, kid; but... you're young."

They remained silent again for a few minutes. "Dad?"

"Yes?"

"Who's the daddy of Siobhan's babies?"

He sighed. "Julian."

Brendan rustled up the memories of his sister's former lover. He had been a tall and calm man with thick, dark hair and an English accent. He had been very kind to Brendan and Brendan had liked him. "But Siobhan and him aren't boyfriend and girlfriend any more."

"I know, but they met up again last year for a short time. I'm not sure exactly how. Siobhan doesn't like to talk about it."

"But... if he's the daddy of her babies, he needs to be here with her while they're being born."

His father nodded. "You're right of course. Sadly life doesn't always work out like that."

"Does he know about the babies?"

Clane shrugged. "I don't know if she told him about them. I don't think she knows where he is. He's a strange kid, very single minded. Very political... He was a communist; maybe he still is."

Brendan nodded. He didn't know what a communist was, except that the word referred to people adults generally considered disreputable.

"It's strange how time passes." his father was now speaking half to himself. "I can still remember Siobhan's birth perfectly. I can still feel her tiny little body resting in my arms, her bright blue eyes blinking up at me, her mouth opening and closing... And now *she* is a parent herself. In a short time another little face...no, *two* little faces... will be gazing up at *her*... As for me? It'll be my turn to be grandpa Quilley." He chuckled. "You never met my grandfather, Brendan. He died when Siobhan was six years old. He had huge thick white hair, missing teeth, a face wrinkled and sunburnt. I used to think he looked like a walnut." he laughed and then turned to his son. "Brendan, do I look like a walnut?"

"No, dad." Brendan studied his father's face; his watery blue eyes, prominent nose, his greying ginger hair spread down over both sides of his head like a thatched roof. It was as if it were a short exposure photograph of water flowing away from the small bald patch at his crown.

"I'm *not* old!" Clane asserted. "I don't *feel* any different being a grandfather. I still *feel* like a young man!... Bren, you're so lucky not having to worry about things like this. One day though, you'll understand... You'll perhaps be a grandpa yourself."

They continued drinking coffee for twenty minutes or so. Then Clane looked up urgently and gawped. He put down his cup suddenly, spilling some of its contents. Brendan swung round. His mother had come out of the double doors she had entered a while before. She was staggering towards the cafeteria with a dazed look on her face. "Gina!" Clane exclaimed.

"It's a boy and a girl." Gina gasped. "Siobhan's fine... They're all fine!" Both Brendan's parents embraced and wept profusely.

A uniformed midwife escorted them to a room with a large bed. It was full daylight now and the windows let in white sunbeams. Brendan stopped himself in the doorway with shock. He felt himself blush. His sister Siobhan was lying in the bed with white cotton sheets up to her waist. She had a gown on made of the same material that was open at the front and both her breasts were exposed. There was a pair of oblong fabric bundles resting on each of her forearms and two miniature faces poked out from them. Both of their mouths were puckered up around each of her nipples, sucking furiously. Siobhan smiled at him with an expression he had never seen on her face before. "Brendan, this is your niece Colleen..." She glanced down to the baby on the left then moved her eyes to the one on the right. "And this is your nephew William."

Brendan recovered himself and looked.

"It's okay; come closer." The babies had their eyes clamped shut. Their skin was covered with traces of a white greasy substance. He looked up at his parents. Their faces were glowing like angels.

....
Brendan jogged across the long dry grass of Rock Creek Park. He'd just left his friends playing hide-and-seek down in the valley and was heading for the main road, the first stage of his half-hour walk home. The sun beat down painfully on his brow; it dazzled his eyes and squeezed sweat out of every pore. This was the last week of the school holidays; in five days time, the following Monday, he would have to return to school. The thought appalled him. This summer break had been the happiest he'd ever experienced. He'd made new friends, lost touch with ones he didn't like and, even better, Siobhan had come home to live with them. He had not felt any conscious positive love for his adult sister since he was a small child, but when she arrived in April he almost cried when he gave her a hug. William and Colleen were growing bigger every day and had transformed since he had first seen them suckling straight after they were born. They could sit up and use their hands. They would flash him the most wonderful smiles whenever they saw him. Sometimes they laughed at almost nothing. They also cried a lot. Often they woke him up in the middle of the night and he would hear Siobhan's voice coming from her room, soothing them until they stopped. Occasionally they would argue with each other. Usually this was caused by William or Colleen picking up a teddy bear or rattle or some other implement of play that the other wanted to pick up at the same time. Then they would burst into tears and glare at each other before looking up at their mother to adjudicate over the conflict. It was a humid August afternoon and even with the increasing use of transport powered by Digby Carrousels and antigravity drives there were still enough internal combustion engine vehicles on the highway to make a film of fumes that lingered in the oppressive heat. As usual the sun was periodically filtered by the chemtrails that crossed the summer sky most days. The vapour dumped in long lines through the atmosphere took away a little of its light and heat. He arrived home and saw his mother and father sitting in the lounge on the settee. William and Colleen were both asleep in one of their favourite places, sitting on each of their grandfather's thighs with their heads reclined on his stomach. "Hi, mom; dad. Where's Siobhan?"

"In her room having a nap, honey." said his mother. "The babies kept her up last night."

Clane laughed. "Well they're making up for it now." He patted the heads of his grandchildren lovingly.

Brendan went into the kitchen and poured himself a glass of Coca Cola from the fridge. Then he went and sat between his parents and looked at the television. A sports channel was on and it showed a baseball game about halfway through. Colleen's chest rose and fell steadily as she slept. Her grandfather's hand gently supported her right arm. She trembled slightly as Gina's roamphone started ringing, but did not wake up. The device was lying on the coffee table. Gina leaned forward and stretched out her arm. She couldn't quite reach it from a sitting position so she groaned at the annoyance and stood up. As soon as she had it in her hand she collapsed back onto the settee with a sigh and said: "Hello?... Oh hi, Jackie..." After a few seconds of silence she sat bolt upright and said: "What?... But you're not due for six weeks!... Right... Does Jack know?... Okay, let us know how you get on."

"What is it?" asked Clane, alarmed by her manner.

"That was Jackie Kennedy. She's gone into labour." Gina's facial expression matched his concern.

"When was she due?"

"September twenty-third."

"Can the doctors make her wait?"

"You mean stop the labour? I'm not sure... If the baby comes now it's only six weeks early. These days they just put it in an incubator until it's big enough."

Clane went out to the kitchen and called Jack Kennedy on his own roam. After a brief conversation that Brendan couldn't interpret his father came back to the lounge and said deadpan. "I'm heading up to Boston to help take care of things." He went straight to the garage and within a minute his flyer was buzzing up into the sky outside the window. The rest of the family sat subdued, watching the TV. Just after one PM Gina's roam bleeped. She looked at it. Brendan leaned over to read the instant message too. It was from his father and it said: "*Jackie has had it. It's a boy.*" Gina frowned. There was something subtextual to that short factual message that lacked the usual happiness a birth should bring. It gave him a chill and clearly his mother picked it up too.

A dour atmosphere hung over the house. At five PM Gina made dinner for the family. Siobhan changed William and Colleen's nappies and then sat down next to Brendan at the table. A humming sound came from outside and his father's flyer settled gently in the driveway. A sad and tired-looking Clane walked slowly into the room. His head was hung low and his face was flushed. Everybody jumped to their feet.

"Well?" asked his wife.

He sighed. "Perhaps we should speak outside." he said hoarsely.

"No, Clane. Tell us all now... Something's gone wrong, hasn't it?"

He paused and then nodded. "The baby... he's got a problem with his lungs. The doc told me what it's called, but I can't remember it. It means he can't breathe properly. It's because he's premature."

"Can they fix it?"

"They're not sure. They're doing all they can. They told me he's got a fifty-fifty chance. We'll know soon enough. It all depends on the first forty-eight hours."

Siobhan gasped and put a hand to her face. "Oh God!"

Clane collapsed into a chair and leaned his arms on the table. "Jackie had to have a C-section. She's recovering in the maternity ward. The baby's been transferred to the children's hospital... Jack is shuttling back and forth between the two of them."

"What's happened to the baby?" blurted out Brendan. A deep horror was rising within him.

Gina looked at him; her eyes were damp with tears. "Brendan honey... The baby is very sick. He might die."

"But he's a newborn baby. He *can't* die!"

....

It was the morning after next that Brendan's mother called the entire family into the lounge and told them all, in a painfully controlled and formal voice, that the baby had died. "Jack brought in the hospital padre and he baptized Jack and Jackie's little boy. His name was Patrick Bouvier Kennedy. Patrick passed away peacefully at four o'clock this morning with his father by his side. The angels are carrying him up to Heaven right now, where he will go straight away, as a pure spirit."

The family went to mass as usual on Sunday. It was the second day after the baby had died. There was widespread public grief all over the country and it was distilled inside the small Maryland church. A few reporters stood outside the driveway, but they kept a respectful distance. The congregation sat in the pews with their heads bowed quietly through the whole service. All the usual lively banter was hushed. There was no children's liturgy. At the homily, Father Peterson, the parish priest, spoke fervently about the tragedy: "John F Kennedy helped bring America back from the brink of destruction at her darkest hour. As head of the Provisional Government, he led us all, like Moses in the wilderness, when we were lost and uncertain about everything we used to believe in... He believed! He walked firm and fast as we recreated our own promised land from nothing!... For such a man, this loss of his newborn son is a loss for us all. Let us pray. May the Lord guide and comfort our beloved John Kennedy at this, his own darkest hour; and also console the grieving mother, his wife Jacqueline. May the Lord bless the soul of little Patrick, gone from his mother and father. Gone from the world. Now living eternally in Heaven at the side of our Lord Jesus Christ, with all the other children..."

After the mass, the congregation gathered in the hall for a cup of tea and biscuits, although there were fewer who stayed behind afterwards this Sunday. Clane told them all about the baby's funeral. It had taken place the previous day and been a quiet affair at the private chapel of Cardinal Richard Cushing in Boston. President King had attended as well as Clane, with other close family members and friends. Patrick had then been buried in Holyhood Cemetery. The family went home accompanied by two friends from the church. Siobhan had skipped mass that Sunday to take care of her babies. As they all walked into the house Colleen was asleep in her mother's arms, but William was awake and alert, oblivious to all the misery around him. He looked up at Brendan as he walked into the room and gave him his usual infantile toothless grin. William lifted his hand and pointed it towards his young uncle with the palm spread wide. He then made a noise that sounded like "Buh-buh." Siobhan laughed. "I think he's trying to say your name, Bren." she said. "What a clever boy you are, Will."

Brendan felt dizzy. His vision clouded over. "Why is God such a motherfucker?" The words were out of his mouth before he even realized he was saying them. He didn't remember where he had learned the expletive he had just used. He had never uttered it or thought of it before.

There was a stunned stillness in the room. Everybody turned slowly and looked at him.

"How can He let a little baby die? Why does He decide to kill a kid who has not even lived? Two days; that was all he got! He never had time to do anything. Never learned to talk, never learned to walk, never saw anything of the world! God is not good! He can't be! He must be evil! He must be a bully! He must like seeing people sad! He must hate us!... He must *really* hate Jack and Jackie!" He was crying now. The thoughts and feelings he had crammed up for the last two days were gushing out of him like a dam that was bursting. "Why, dad? Why, mom? It doesn't make sense! It's not fair! It's wrong, I tell you! WRONG!"

His parents took him to his bedroom where he wept continuously for several hours. Eventually he ran out of tears and could only lie on his bed staring at the ceiling, his thoughts offlined, his sense of time absent. His mother knocked on his door later and came in with a bowl of ice cream and some water. She rubbed his shoulders affectionately as he ate and rank. He was ravenously hungry and thirsty. "It's natural to feel angry, honey." his mother said. "You'd have to be brainless and heartless not to be. A lot of things in the world don't make sense. I wish I knew why God does the things He does; I wish that all the time. But God *is* good. God moves in mysterious ways, but His ways can only result in good. I think He will tell us the answers to our questions, but not on this side of the grave. Until then our challenge is to accept what happens as His will and carry on with life. Be thankful for what He has given us. Jack and Jackie are very thankful for John Jr and Caroline. Your father and I are thankful for you and Siobhan, and for William and Colleen.

God has been good to us, He really has."
....

School started the next day, but Brendan couldn't face it. He was grateful when his parents immediately agreed that he should be allowed to stay at home until the following day. At seven PM John F Kennedy turned up at their front door. His face was as grey as a corpse and his eyelids looked like tortoiseshells. He staggered into the entrance hall with a dazed expression, as if he'd been drugged. Clane stood up and the two men embraced; Kennedy's nape heaving as he wept silently against his friend's shoulder. Gina gave Brendan a hard and meaningful look. "Brendan, I think you should go to bed early. I'm going to take a walk down the road and see Leticia." Siobhan also took the hint and carried the twins upstairs to her room. Within a minute Clane and Jack were alone. Brendan climbed into bed and lay still for a minute. Then he gingerly stood up and opened his door. There were loud voices coming from downstairs. Jack was crying and spoke in an animated voice through his tears. Brendan tiptoed out onto the landing and descended the stairs. He sat on the fifth step from the bottom opposite the open door to the lounge. "I'm a bastard!" Jack lamented. "I'm a goddamn fucking bastard!"

"No, you're not." His father's voice was calmer. Brendan heard the cracking noise of a bottle of spirits being opened and the gurgle of glasses being filled.

"I am, Clane!... All this! It's all my fault! I think it's punishment from God. He took Patrick from me and I deserved it."

"Don't talk crap, Jack."

"I wasn't even there when he was born. I'm never there when she needs me. I never even went home when Arabella happened. I stayed on in Capri. I just told Bobby to deal with it... If she'd fucked him the way Marilyn did I wouldn't have blamed either of them; it would have still been *my* fault. The only thing that changed my mind was when George called me and told me I'd jeopardize my US Senate seat if I didn't haul my ass back home. What kind of man is driven more by ambition than the love of his wife?... I've shit on her, Clane! I've shit on the woman I love. I don't deserve her. She doesn't deserve me!" His voice dissolved slightly at the end of the sentence as he took a gulp of drink. "Why can't I just say 'no'? Why can't I just turn these bitches away? Why is that so difficult?... You can do it. Remember that whore you told me about, the one you met in London? You said 'no' to her, didn't you?"

"Yes I did. That was way back in fifty-five." He chuckled. "But I don't get asked as often as you, Jack."

"But you do get asked?"

Clane paused. "Occasionally."

"And you've always said 'no'?"

"Every time."

There was a long silence. "I prayed, Clane. On Wednesday night. I knelt on the floor of my hotel room and prayed for an hour. Dave Powers stayed with me on a spare cot. I just couldn't bear to be alone. I... I told God that I would exchange Patrick's life for my own. I asked Him to spare my son and take me instead... And I meant it! I truly meant it... But God took my son and left me here, trapped in life!... He was such a beautiful baby. He fought so hard. I saw another baby in the burns ward, covered in bandages. I was so moved; I wrote the mother a little note. Right now I so want *that* child to live... When Patrick was gone I told Jackie and... you know what she said?" He began crying again. "She said: 'The only thing I couldn't stand would be losing you.'... She couldn't stand losing a man as worthless as me!"

"You're far from worthless, Jack." said Clane. "You're not a saint, but then again who is?"

Kennedy burst into sudden raucous laughter. He sounded drunk. "You!... You are, Clane."

His father laughed too. "I'm not, Jack."

There was another long pause. "What am I going to tell Caroline and Junior? How can I possibly explain it to them?"

"Do they know about Arabella?"

There was a pause and Brendan got the impression that Jack had just nodded.

"You'll just have to tell them it's happened again."

Brendan heard the clicking of a key in the front door lock; his mother was coming home. He jumped to his feet and vaulted back up the stairs on the tips of his toes before she saw him. He closed his bedroom door silently and slipped back into bed. He heard her voices mixed with the other two, muffled by the floorboards. After a while she came upstairs to kiss him goodnight as usual and he pretended to be asleep.

The following morning Brendan's father drove him to school in the ground car. Brendan felt huge trepidation at starting again after the long summer break. "Dad." he said as they waited by some traffic lights.

"Yeah?"

"Who's Arabella?"

His father had been watching the road ahead, but now he suddenly swung his head round and stared at his son. "What? Where did you hear that name?"

Brendan panicked. He realized that he might have just confessed to his eavesdropping, but his father didn't pick up on it.

"Oh, you heard me and Jack last night from your room did you? I suppose our voices were a bit loud."

"Who is she?"

He sighed sadly. "We don't like to talk about it much, but Arabella is Jack and Jackie's first baby. She was born and died back in fifty-six, three years after they got married. They named her after the famous Winthrop ship, the one that carried the founding fathers of Massachusetts from England."

"So she died as a little baby too, like Patrick?"

"Not quite. Arabella was stillborn."

"What does that mean?"

"She died before her birth."

Brendan wondered if he had misheard his father. "What do you mean 'died before her birth'? How can a baby die before being born?"

"Well..." The traffic lights changed and Clane paused for a moment to steer the car through the junction. "Babies grow inside their mom for nine months before being born. During those nine months sometimes they die. It's very sad, but it happens." Clane's face suddenly took on a mournful mien. "I think it always will. It's funny, but people reckon Disclosure will create a paradise on earth, but it won't. Even if the new tech delivers everything it promises, it won't stop tragedies like Arabella from happening. This is something that will continue to hurt moms and dads for as long as there *are* moms and dads. It's just the way the world is."

His father dropped Brendan outside the school gates. Brendan strolled mindlessly into the building. He heard his friends speaking to him, teachers greeting him after their long absence, but these experiences held no substance for him. Everything around him, of every kind, even his very thoughts, felt stripped of all meaning. He had entered a plastic world, a non-physical facsimile of reality. When the bell rang for his first class he walked across the yard feeling like nothing more than a shadow. It took him a while to notice when he had changed direction and was not walking to his class. He was exiting the school via a back alleyway. Nobody stopped him; it was as if he were invisible. He was soon on the sports fields, empty at this time in the morning. For the first time in months he started thinking about Boggin, his ethereal friend who used to be his companion when he was younger, but whom he had stopped seeing after a stay in a hospital. "Indian?" he asked aloud. Then he shouted; he cried out for help: "INDIAN!... INDIAN!... INDIAN!... Please come to me!" Nothing happened. The old Indian would not come. It was as if he had never existed; that he was as devoid of substance as everything else now was.

....

This feeling of emptiness and nihilism followed Brendan around all week like a dark cloud. He remained functional. It was not an acute incapacitating blow like his trip to the planetarium had been. It was more a slow, drawn out scratch across his cheek; or a repetitive tapping of his forehead. He finally gained some solace on Saturday when he saw a film at the cinema about a group of young children who die and go to Heaven. He recalled what his mother and Father Peterson had said about how the baby Patrick was now in Heaven with Jesus. Obviously Arabella was there too, also being a little baby. On Sunday there was a special event in church. A nun from a convent in New York City was paying them a visit. Sister Margarita van de Kerk was a legend throughout the Roman Catholic community of the north-eastern United States for her charity work and dedicated service as a volunteer schoolteacher and nurse in some of the poorest neighbourhoods in the country. She walked into the church hall in Rockville with a broad smile on her face and her hands raised in blessing. She was a short and plump old woman with a long wimple on her head. If she had hair then it was completely covered by the garment. Her face was cracked and lined with age. Her true antiquity was a closely guarded secret, but she was rumoured to be over eighty. Despite this, she was filled with seemingly boundless energy. She worked almost every waking moment when she wasn't praying or taking mass. Brendan and the other children cheered as she greeted them. She was renowned for her love of the youths and her ability to emulate their sense of play. Despite being an old lady, Brendan did sense something girlish about her. He could imagine her leaping over a skipping rope like somebody seventy years her junior. She spoke in an exotic foreign accent that Brendan didn't recognize as she preached to her young audience. He zoned out somewhat as she recited lines from the Gospels, but he snapped into an alert state when the subject came up of the recent celebrity bereavement. Sister Margarita recited Matthew, Nineteen-Fourteen: "...But our lord said 'Suffer the little children. Do not forbid them to come to me, for theirs is the Kingdom of Heaven.'... The young Kennedy child is sitting in the arms of our Lord. His is the Kingdom of Heaven and God rejoices in the return of His youngest son."

Brendan thrust his hand into the air.

Sister Margarita spotted him and pointed. "Yes, my dear."

"There's Arabella too, Sister. Jack and Jackie first baby. She was stillborn before all their other kids were born."

The old nun sighed and the creases of her face bunched up as she frowned sadly. "I remember that well; it was in all the papers when it happened. I felt deeply for Senator Kennedy and his lovely wife. I prayed for them daily... As for the child, alas! As an unbaptized infant she will have died in a state without sin, but also without grace. Therefore she cannot enter the Kingdom of Heaven."

The cloud that had been hovering above Brendan's head all week suddenly descended and enveloped him in black horror.

"The child was born into original sin, for there is no salvation except through the Lord Jesus Christ. As a mere baby she is without personal sin and so would never be punished in hellfire, but she died without salvation via baptism into the Kingdom of God and so is blighted with the fall of Adam. Therefore her soul can never come to God. She will have entered the realm of Limbo, the outer edge of Hell. Limbo is a place without the tortures of Hell but also without the joys of Heaven. It is a land of darkness, silence and stillness. There she will endure for all eternity." Sister Margarita looked distressed at the expression of Brendan's face. "I'm so sorry, my dear. I wish it could be otherwise, but it is not."

Brendan's father managed to find out what was wrong with his son after a persistent discussion that afternoon when they went for a walk in Rock Creek Park. "Come on, Bren; you've been on a downer all week. It can't just be the baby. What's wrong?"

Brendan told him everything. It gave him a relief that he had never expected; he had up till then being suppressing the unthinkable thoughts, keeping them away from his consciousness.

Clane's eyes bulged and his cheeks turned crimson with rage as he listened. "What the *feck* do they think they're doing!? Bringing in that dried up old prune to spout that evil obscurantist bullshit to young kids like you! This parish sucks to hell! I had this upsetting drivel fed to me when I was a boy; I can't believe it's still going on in this day and age!... Listen, son; there's no such feckin' place as Limbo! It's a dirty lie made up by obsolete, evil-minded, vinegar-cunt virgins like that Margarita!" He gasped. "Every single sensible theological thinker knows that baptism-by-desire is the reality. As if God in His mercy would actually condemn unborn babies to eternal oblivion!? It's an abomination to even suggest it!"

They sat down to rest on a bench. Brendan leaned close to his father's firm, warm body, resting his head on his chest. His ear was against his shirt, listening to the pleasant buzz of his voice through his skin as he spoke.

Siobhan took a third position when Brendan raised the matter with her that evening. "Take no notice of that old witch, Bren." She was bathing the babies as they talked. Brendan was standing by the bathroom door. William and Colleen were screeching with fun, slapping the water with their hands. "The church is a mountainous pile of lies."

"So is Arabella in Heaven right now with Patrick?"

Brendan's question was a rhetorical one so he was astonished and confused when Siobhan shrugged. "Maybe; I don't know."

"What do you mean?"

She paused. "What if *none* of it is true? Neither the bad stuff nor the good stuff. If there's no Hell or Limbo then maybe there's no Heaven either."

"How can that be?"

She looked up at him. "Maybe God doesn't exist."

Brendan was silent for a moment as his brain churned over that completely novel concept. "But that's not possible. Of course God exists; how else could the world exist, you and me exist, if He hadn't made it?"

"Things can make themselves." She jerked her thumb over her shoulder in the direction of the frosted bathroom window. "If I drop something out of the window it will fall to the ground. God doesn't make that happen; it's the force of gravity that makes it happen."

Brendan had to cogitate intensely again before he could generate an answer. "But God made the force of gravity."

"Did He? Gravity might be just a part of the universal functioning. Scientists have worked it all out. It's like you and me. We're human beings, sure; but human beings are a kind of ape. We're related to chimps and gorillas and we all came from an ancestor who gave birth to all of us. All the animals and plants are like that. They grow and change over millions of years. This sort of thing just happens naturally. No God is needed to draw it all up beforehand; it just happens as part of the way the world works."

"But, Siobhan; you go to mass every Sunday! You pray with us. You say grace with us before meals..."

"Yes I do, I know." she interrupted. "And I wonder more and more about why I still do it. It's kind of a routine that comes from being in this family, and it is a way of belonging to the group of people that makes up our friends and families...

That's all it is to me now. I sometimes question whether some of the others have the same doubts as I do, but they just don't tell anybody."

"So if there's no Heaven or Hell; where do people go when they die?"

She hesitated, looking down at her two children playing in the bathwater. "Nowhere. They simply die."

"Are you sure, Siobhan?"

"No." she answered immediately. "I could be wrong. Maybe God is real... I'm just not sure about anything anymore. I'm confused by the whole subject to be honest; I have been for a long time."

Neither of them said anything for several minutes. Siobhan lifted the twins out of the bath and dried them with a towel on a foam mat. "What about the Indian? He talks about God sometimes."

She looked over her shoulder at him with a nostalgic smile. "Flying Buffalo? Are you still seeing him?"

"Yeah, he turns up every now and again... If he is real then surely God is real."

She shook her head. "Not necessarily. When did you last see him?"

"Round about Christmastime."

"That's a long time ago. Have you not seen him since then?"

He shook his head.

"Have you ever thought that maybe you made him up?"

"No! He was there! I swear I'm not lying..."

"No, no, no! I didn't mean that you *pretended* he's real when he's not. I meant that maybe you *imagined* he was real when he's not."

"That's not possible. I saw him! I talked to him!"

"People can sometimes see things that aren't there. Your brain plays tricks on you."

Brendan paused. "But you saw him too. So did Dad."

Siobhan fastened Colleen's nappy and then looked up at him with a desolate expression. "Maybe we all imagined him, Bren. Maybe we all saw him because we went through some rough times and deep down we all needed somebody like that in our lives. It's as simple as that."

Brendan stared at her blankly.

"I'm sorry." she said.

Brendan left the bathroom and went downstairs. He took his bicycle from the garage and pedalled along the narrow twisting streets of the area until he came to Rock Creek Park. He found the clearing where he had seen the old Indian the previous winter and looked around at the trees, now covered with lush green leaves. The sun was setting and it shone in glinting fragments, muffled by the woodland again. He sat on the same log where he had seen the Indian nine months earlier. He recalled their conversation about stars exploding and people dying. He also remembered the previous Tuesday morning on the school playing field when he called desperately for the Indian. "Indian?" he asked aloud again. "Where are you?"

A light breeze whistled through the trees and the leaves rustled delicately.

"Indian, have you gone? Have you left me?... *Why* have you left me?"

In the distance he could hear the voices of children playing, the familiar music of the park. A woodpecker drummed away against a tree nearby.

"Indian... do you exist? Are you real?"

Brendan sat in silence for a few more minutes, then he stood up and walked away down the path, pushing his bicycle. Just before the log went out of sight behind the bushes, he stopped and looked over his shoulder at it, half-expecting to see a human figure sitting there. He waited a few moments to see if anything would change. It didn't. He rode home and went to bed.

Chapter 5

The ambient buzzing of the gravitators reduced as the school flyer descended. The aerial vehicle, the size of a bus, bumped against the ground and came to rest. Mr Briengard stood up at the front beside the driver. "Alright, boys and girls." he began. "Pay attention!... Step down from the flyer one at a time and assemble on the sidewalk to the right." He pointed. Brendan and Charlie stood up and pushed into the aisle between the other excited pupils. They emerged into blazing sunlight and Brendan shielded his eyes as his irises adjusted. He was standing in a concrete carpark and around him slopes of dry broken rock rose steeply in all directions. The sky was framed by orange mountains above a deep gorge that glinted in the piercing sunshine; they were lumpy and granular like waste cement. All over the mountain range were the signs of human intervention. The peaks were wrapped in an interconnecting spider's web of electric cables supported by stick-like pylons. In the bottom of the gorge were vast concrete structures simply-shaped; squares, cylinders and blocks, like a giant child's play-set. "You been here before, Bren?" asked Charlie.

Brendan nodded. "I used to live just a few miles away." The place did indeed resurrect memories years in the past, earlier and sadder times from his childhood.

Mr Briengard had been studying his slate; he then raised his voice. "Right, class. We've just had a last-minute word from the weather forecasters. The wind is blowing from the northeast so we will have to move to the spectators' platform on the far side. Let's start walking now; stay close together. No misbehaving or you can go back and sit on the bus!" The children started walking in file down the sloping roadway towards the concrete shapes with their teacher in the lead. Ground vehicles had been restricted on this last leg of the journey so they could stroll down the middle of the carriageway. Several hundred other people, mostly adults, were walking with them in the same direction; some of them alone, but a few in small groups. A pane of blue water emerged on the right side of the highway and on the left the ground dropped away into a chasm so deep that the bottom was invisible from Brendan's viewpoint. He felt a wave of dizzy precariousness, as if he were walking along a huge tightrope. The road took one more bend and then opened out onto a smooth curve with art deco parapets on either side. To their right the lake gleamed in the sunlight. Four gigantic fluted columns emerged out of the water, connected to the road by small footbridges. The rocky hillsides leading down into the water changed colour to white a few yards above the waterline, as if the gorge was a draining bath of white paint. To their left the parapet descended into an artificial precipice, sloping down just a few degrees from vertical. The base of the canyon was now visible and it was a dry gulch housing a double row of low grey structures and yawning tunnel portals. Close to them, on higher ground, a column of tunnel-filling machines were waiting like inanimate vultures; the teeth of their diamond drill-heads glittered like glass shards. Flyers filled the air. Some buzzed continuously back and forth like wheeling seagulls and others sat still in the sky. Two large ones were hovering low above the apex of the curve. They held a banner stretched out between them displaying the words: "*SAVE HOOVER DAM*". A man was leaning out of one of the flyers' windows brandishing a megaphone. His voice rose in apparent volume as they approached, tinny from the amplifier; but eventually his words became comprehensible: "...a hundred and twelve men were killed making this dam! Men destitute and desperate! Right in the depths of the Depression! We bored the tunnels and choked on carbon monoxide! It was a hundred and forty-five degrees in there! High-scalers hung from single ropes on the cliffs, falling to their deaths or being knocked dead by falling rocks! For the sake of the memory of those men, we oppose the demolition of this dam!..." A group of supporters stood on the walkway cheering the speaker. They were all middle-aged or elderly men wearing builders' hardhats.

"Mr Briengard." asked one of Brendan's schoolmates. "What are those men saying?"

"They're protesting, Johnny." said the teacher. "They're some of the men who constructed the dam thirty years ago. They don't want to see it destroyed. They think it should be turned into a national monument."

"Maybe it should, sir." said Johnny.

Mr Briengard shook his head. "It's not possible. Lake Mead needs to go; its environmental impact is too severe. Hoover Dam created the reservoir so it has to go first. Then the Colorado River can return to its natural flow..."

The teacher's voice was loud enough for one of the old builders to overhear him. The man turned round and called out: "Hey, Mack! That ain't true. The river can flow totally normally through the penstock tunnels now the gennies have been removed. The lake will still drain..."

Mr Briengard ignored him. "Come along, children." he commanded.

The troupe of schoolchildren reached the far side of the dam and entered the state of Nevada, Brendan's old homeland. The road led directly along the side of the canyon with the dam over their left shoulders. Eventually they came to a long flight of steps that led upwards to a wide ledge that gave a spectacular view over the vista. A terrace of seats had been constructed and around two hundred people were settling down into them. Brendan followed his peers along the walkway between the seats and took his place. He was shocked to find that he was sitting next to Heather McManus; this was completely unintentional. He looked at her out of the corner of his eye and felt himself blush. Heather ignored him as usual. She was scribbling something in her rough book and fiddling with her coloured bracelet. Brendan looked quickly at her again, this time to admire her intense beauty. She had flowing blonde hair, smooth skin and elegant freckles. He could only allow himself tiny sips of sight; if he lost self-control he would end up staring at her obtrusively. He recalled an incident that took place at Christmas two years earlier, just after his eleventh birthday. He had been invited to a sleepover at a friend's house and Heather had been there with about a dozen other children. After they had all eventually fallen asleep on put-you-ups and inflatable mattresses on the floors, Brendan had woken up when somebody prodded his shoulder. He rolled over and saw Heather crouched beside him. "Brendan." she whispered. "I've got something to show you."

He sat up. "What?"

She smiled and stood up. Then to his utter astonishment she removed her pyjamas and stood in front of him completely naked. "Do you think I'm sexy, Brendan?" She giggled.

Brendan lay back down and rolled over to turn his back on her. He wondered if he were still asleep and having a nightmare. She lifted the covers and climbed into the bed beside him. She threw her arms around his body and began caressing him. Her breath was hot against the back of his neck. He panicked. He jumped out of his bed and ran. He spent the rest of the night in a broom cupboard using a mop-head as a pillow. Now, two and a half years later, as he looked at Heather sitting beside him with the Hoover Dam beyond her neat profile, he understood what she had done. He wished he could go back in time and stay in the bed with her. Over the last few months he had been seeing the world very differently to how he used to. Always a person to be troubled by his own thoughts and feelings, he experienced a redoubling of this problem. It was partly his changing attitude towards girls, but also many other things. His own mind and body were transforming radically. He had grown in size enormously and his mother had had to buy him an entire new wardrobe. He lost his craving for sweets, but at the same time developed a passionate taste for other foods. He always felt hungry and ate more than ever. His voice became very hoarse for about a month, as if he had a bad cold. Every time he spoke a husky rasp would come out. Now it had returned, but it had a very different tone, much lower in pitch. He didn't like it. Hair started sprouting from parts of his body where it had never grown before. A small thin beard appeared on his chin and his father showed him how to remove it with a razor (For some reason this made his father cry). Brendan also developed painful and ugly pustules on his face, his testicles ached every day, his skin felt greasy and clammy, his armpits developed an unpleasant smell. He knew what it was; puberty. He had learned about the process in biology the previous year. However he never really grasped the obvious reality that it would happen to him too. He was only thirteen years old after all. The biology lesson taught him that puberty occurred at the approximate ages of eleven to thirteen with girls and thirteen to fifteen with boys. Why did he have to catch it at the earliest time in that period? Most of his male friends had not been hit with it yet and he envied them. Couldn't it have waited a while longer with him?

To take his mind off his worries he took his slate out of his satchel and switched it on. He put *Hoover Dam* into the search engine and came up with thousands of Meshpages. He looked up and saw a group of people still moving around in the distance on top of the dam. There seemed to be some kind of commotion going on and he could make out the hardhats of the builders among the throng. He looked back at his slate and clicked wmn.SaveHooverDam.pv.us. On the Meshboard's newspage it stated that the dam builders had made plans in advance. They were attempting to thwart the destruction of their masterpiece by occupying the structure itself. As he read, Brendan felt a twinge of sadness. Hoover Dam clearly was an engineering wonder. Wasn't it possible to keep it intact just for that reason alone? He shrugged and turned to the board showing the details of the demolition. It was to be a semi-important media event, being covered live on television. The operation was being managed personally by Dr Jenny Bulstrode. Because no explosives were being used, the demolition of the dam would be far safer than any conventional one. Indeed, people were permitted to walk on the dam just a short time before it would happen. Dr Bulstrode was in the control room a few miles away. Her transmitters were visible on two of the mountain peaks; others were out of sight from the observation platform. A squadron of five police flyers swooped down from the west towards the dam to remove the insubordinate builders. They landed in a row on the doomed megastructure and there was some activity for about twenty minutes that was too distant to follow. Then the police vehicles took the air again and the dam top was deserted.

A wailing siren echoed across the valley; the onlookers around Brendan lowered their chatter in anticipation. Wisps of smoke began rising from the concrete semicircular bulk of the Hoover Dam. It looked like a wet object steaming in the sun. Brendan smiled to himself as he remembered the spontaneous lectures Jenny gave people who used the wrong terminology: "No! This is something entirely new that requires comprehensive new terminology! It's not smoke; that is a result of combustion and this is not combustion. It's not steam either; that is a product of water evaporation.

It's also not dust; that is a product of mechanical abrasion..." Whatever the proper name was for the substance, more and more of it was rising from the dam. Suddenly there was a massive eruption of brown fume that expanded outwards like a puffball. The audience gasped. The only noise from the location was a penetrating two-tone hiss. The top of the fume cloud rose above the highest mountain peaks. It blotted out the sun and made the world around them turn dark. A few audience-members muttered nervously, fearful that it would engulf their unprotected observation post, but after a minute or so the wind began to eat into the discharge and mould the cloud away from the terrace. It rolled and billowed as it blew away to the east over the Arizona side of the gorge. The gap in the canyon where the Hoover Dam used to be slowly emerged from the murk. Nothing was left of the construction except a pair of regular scrapes in the wall of the canyon where the rock had been extracted to build the dam's foundations. One half of the two-tone hiss remained and Brendan could now see that it was caused by a huge torrent of white foaming water bursting through the space where the dam used to be, like a giant's mill race. The noise of it rose from a rumble to a roar as more of the released water hurtled towards the unexpected new exit. The level of Lake Mead had been lowered as far as possible in preparation for the demolition, but it could not be drained altogether while the dam was still there. It would do so now within a few hours; then the River Colorado would return to its natural flow, in the same way it had flowed for thousands of years before its brief thirty-year hiatus behind the dam. The Hoover Dam had been made of six and a half million tons of solid concrete. It had taken five years to build and cost seventy million US dollars. It had cost lives, limbs, sweat and blood; yet it had been dissolved into a cloud of fine dust within two minutes. The audience were struck dumb. Long ago, nineteen years ago, the world had changed forever when a billion people stood still and gaped as the tallest building in New York City had been destroyed in the same way. Brendan imagined other buildings mutating into clouds of dust, entire cities, entire nations, entire continents... the whole earth? By the pale faces and slack jaws on either side of him, he could guess that similar thoughts were going through the heads of the other spectators too.

....

The school outing continued. The aerial coach picked the class up from another carpark on the Nevada side of the open gorge where the Hoover Dam used to be. The subdued mien of the children wore off as they flew westwards and soon they were chatting normally. Half and hour later the coastline approached and the vehicle descended, and they came to rest in Pismo Beach. The class giggled when Mr Briengard mispronounced the name when he declared where they were. The seaside town was a holiday resort. As the class walked down the promenade they saw bars, restaurants, souvenir shops, amusement arcades and a theme park. A flat wooden pier stretched out over the beach into the sea. Lots of people were walking around in light clothes and bathing costumes and there were rows of deckchairs on the beach where people sunned themselves. A few hundred yards further along the road the seaside frolics immediately gave way to an enormous block-like windowless building, painted light blue and with a darker blue steel roof. Five huge shiny metal pipelines emerged from its eastern wall and led away up the steep inland hills. Strangely the pipelines were not straight but ran in regular sharp meanders like huge novelty drinking straws. Another similar set of pipes, this time conventionally straight ones, sprouted from the opposite wall and ran several hundred yards out to sea on a pier. Mr Briengard gestured proudly at the facility. "This is why the Hoover Dam was demolished!" he exclaimed. "This is the Pismo Beach Desalination Plant. It is the largest forward osmosis desal waterworks in the United States. It's one of eighteen that run right along the Pacific coast from San Diego to Seattle. Together they supply the entire western United States with water for drinking, agriculture... that means farming... industry, hygiene and leisure. The plant draws in seawater there," He pointed at the pipes on the pier. "and removes the salt from it. Then it pumps the water through those pipes on the other side to wherever it is needed, Los Angeles, Denver, San Francisco, anywhere. The technology to desalinate seawater has been known for hundreds of years, but it was never practical before Disclosure because of mankind's access only to limited energy; five kilowatt-hours for every thousand litres made it economically impossible on a large scale. There were just a few local desalination plants that served coastal communities. Now we have free energy we are liberated from that restriction... The need to corral and siphon fresh water on land, or to wait hopefully for rain, is no longer a problem. This is why large inland reservoirs are no longer necessary; hence the removal of Hoover Dam and the draining of Lake Mead. Natural fresh water can now go completely back to its old job of serving nature."

The class were taken on a tour of the inside of the desalination plant by an eager young engineer with Chinese features. He was wearing a white coat and a hardhat, one ironically similar to those toted by the protesting builders at the now departed Hoover Dam. He showed the children the brightly-coloured machines and pipes, explaining how they worked. Brendan didn't understand much and waited patiently for the man to finish so he could raise his hand and ask a question. "Why are the pipes taking the fresh water out of the plant curved?"

The man grinned, clearly relishing the chance to explain. "The pumping system we use is based on the Schauberger flume. It was invented in Austria over thirty years ago by an amazing man called Viktor Schauberger, but it was classified along with the rest of the new tech. The shape of the pipes employs energy within the water itself to drive it along them. No additional mechanics are necessary and it requires no fuel at all. The water will even flow through the pipes uphill, as you can see outside."

On the flight home Brendan sat quietly, not talking much to Charlie. Instead he browsed through some of the takeaway pamphlets he'd been given at the desalination plant's visitors' centre. It described the processes of the outfit in simple language, obviously aimed at younger readers. Brendan contemplated the flowing of water, eddies and vortices, with a brand new thrill. "I'm going to be an engineer when I grow up." he said, half to himself.

"Come again?" Charlie was startled by the statement after his friend's long silence.

"Yeah, that's what I'm going to be; an engineer. I want to be somebody who runs waterworks like that one."

....
Brendan awoke to the sound of his parents arguing downstairs. It was daylight outside, but the daylight had the quality that told his subconscious mind that it was about half an hour from when he would normally wake up. He padded out onto the landing and listened. He heard Siobhan's voice occasionally interject at an equally high volume. He moved a few steps down the staircase so he could hear their words. "What the hell were you thinking of, woman!?" roared his father. "You knew! You *knew* we would need the flyer to get there!"

"Why!?" retorted his mother. "Why should I know that when you never tell me!? You never tell me any damn thing! You planned it all behind my back and you blame my ass when it all screws up! What am I? A goddamn mind-reader!?"

"You never ask him!" yelled Siobhan.

Brendan retreated to the upper floor. He found William standing in the corridor looking frightened. He had a teddy bear clutched to his chest. Colleen peeked out from the door to their room behind him, sucking her thumb plaintively. "Uncle Brendan, why are grandma and grandpa shouting?" asked William.

"I don't know, Will." Brendan told his three-year-old nephew. "Go back to bed."

It was over an hour later, and during a somewhat tense breakfast of smouldering exchanges, that Brendan got the basic gist of his parents' contretemps. His mother's friend, a woman Brendan hardly knew called Laurel, had needed emergency transport because of a sick relative in Oregon and Gina had generously allowed her to borrow the family flyer. However this was also the day that Brendan's father had arranged with his parents to take the entire family to visit their relatives in New York. This resulted in a situation whereby the family would have to use alternative transportation. Clane munched toast while he spoke stressfully on the telephone to his parents: "I know, dad. We said we'd be there this morning, but now we've got to go in the ground car and that will take all day... About four or five PM; I'm sorry... Well, could you apologize to Stephen for us and tell him we'll have to see him later in the year?..." After breakfast the family packed their luggage into the boot of their Buick Eternal and hit the road. Clane grasped the steering wheel with white knuckles as he turned off his usual route to Washington and headed for the interstate. "It's years since I drove long distance on the ground." he muttered.

"Well if you've forgotten how to do it you could let me drive." said Gina in an acidic tone.

"I remember perfectly." Clane retorted after a furious pause. Brendan saw a red patch appear on the skin below his father's hairline. Brendan was sitting in the backseat of the sedan with William squashed in to his right and the door handle jammed against his left hip. Siobhan sat on the right side with Colleen on her lap. They drove down the dual carriageway towards the eastern junction with the I-Ninety-Five, early morning commuter traffic honking madly in the wheeled dance of the rush-hour. Clane took the turning before he noticed the red signboards a hundred yards from the junction. He braked sharply. "What the hell!?" The slip-road was blocked by barriers bearing the words "*ROAD CLOSED.*" Beyond it through the windscreen a pair of yellow-painted combine road-breaking machines were at work, crawling along, slow as slugs, eating the tarmac lanes of the interstate as they went. "Shit." cursed Clane, quietly and calmly, although the red patch on his nape flared up. He put the car into reverse. "I should have checked beforehand."

"Yes, you should!" spat his wife.

Clane ignored her. "The big highways are used a lot less these days now most people have flyers. So a lot of them are being shut down and torn up... Never mind, we'll go cross-country."

The mood in the car lightened slightly, at least on the back seat, as the car headed away down a small rural highway. Green fields and leafy forests passed on both sides. "Reminds me of Ireland." Clane mused wistfully at one point. They passed through small towns and isolated farms. The sky was blue and the sun shone brighter and brighter as the morning aged. They opened to windows to enjoy the fresh summer air. There was little traffic on the road and they mostly passed tractors or lorries full of livestock and hay bales. William and Colleen were laughing amiably at a juvenile joke of their own when a screeching wail broke out from the front of the car.

Brendan's hands covered his ears as a reflex. Everybody in the car exclaimed. The twins screamed in alarm. Clane jerked the car to a crawl and the noise eased. He coasted up onto the verge and the vehicle stopped. The noise disappeared, but Brendan's ears were ringing. "What the hell have you done, Clane!?" shouted Gina.

"What have *I* done!?" he yelled back. He got out of the car and opened the bonnet.

Brendan leaped out and joined him. "What's happened, dad?"

He leaned over, looking down into the depths of the car. "The engine's fucked."

Brendan looked at the machinery in the dark engine cavity and began studying the contents carefully.

His mother was out of the passenger seat and striding towards her husband. "Oh my God, what is this!? Jesus, Clane! Can't you even get inside a goddamn car without wrecking it!?"

"What the *feck* are you talking about!? How is this *my* fault!? It's a Digby Carrousel! The mill cycle has clashed! It happens all the time!"

"You should have had it checked over at the garage before we left!"

"I would have if I'd known some dumb broad was going to lend out our *feckin'* flyer to all-comers the very day we've got to travel!...." After a few more exchanges the argument broke down into a practical discussion. Clane was a member of the American Automobile Association; he took out his roamphone and tried to call them but couldn't get a signal. "Alright, I'm going to take a walk and see if the reception improves. If it doesn't then when I get to a town I'll call on a payphone."

"Don't leave us, for Christ's sake!" shouted Gina. "There are bandits in this area!"

"Bullshit! That's a tabloid myth."

"I don't suppose you've brought any of the guns have you?" she asked sarcastically and rhetorically.

He glared at her and then strutted off. "I shall return as soon as I can with help. If I'm not back in two hours then it means the bandits got me."

The car had broken down in a very pleasant location. The road was a gentle bend to the right. On the inside of the bend were thick bushes and trees; on their left a curtain of shrubs and then a slope of pasture where sheep grazed. The paddock led down to a river beyond which was more farmland and forest, making a lush valley that glowed in the July sunshine. Birds cooed in the woodland and squirrels bolted across the road. Gina, Siobhan, Brendan and the two children waited patiently; sitting on the edge of the car seats with their legs dangling out. Sometimes they would take a stroll a few hundred yards up and down the road. Unfortunately they had planned to stop for meals at the interstate travel services and so had brought no packed lunches. William and Colleen chased each other along the grassy verges. An hour after Clane left, a tractor drove past and the driver paid them no attention. To pass the time, and also because he was genuinely curious about anything to do with machines, Brendan continued to examine the car's shattered engine. He had learnt about the Digby Carrousel from books and from surfing the Mesh. It was a declining technology since R-Day and the burgeoning transformation to flyers. There was an attempt to revive it since somebody had found a way to synthesize mantalite, one of the vital ingredients that had previously only been a very rare natural mineral and had threatened to make the entire system obsolete; but it was clear the technology would only ever be needed for short-range, low-power ground cars; hence the destruction of the country's major roads. Its unreliability was still its foremost problem that no engineer had yet found a good way to solve. The counter-rotating mills that provided the power sometimes suffered from "hunting", a damaging oscillation that also affected railway wheels. It caused the delicate balance of motion within the engine to break down and jam it. This had just happened to the Quilley's ground car. All automobile manufacturers were now producing lines of ground cars powered by electric motors. These were simpler and more reliable than the Digby and had batteries that could simply be charged up from the free energy mains supply. The tractor that had passed them earlier was clearly electric. Many of the firms were predicting the end of their Digby-powered products. A flyer passed by at about midday. It descended to about two hundred feet and slowed as if to watch them. Brendan stared at it through the tree branches. He couldn't be sure, but he thought it contained a group of men. He was momentarily nervous, remembering what his mother had said about bandits. The craft cruised past and he saw the faces of the occupants looking down at them, but then it accelerated and ascended seconds later and was soon just a speck in the sky. A chemtrail, or "lifetrail" as they were sometimes called at that time, operation began soon afterwards and the blue sky was quickly covered by a lattice of translucent white lines. This lowered the temperature slightly. The fact that the chemtrail programme was now public and would be done openly for the next few decades did not make it any less uncomfortable to experience.

At one PM there was the noise of more than one ground vehicle approaching from ahead. A vehicle recovery truck rounded the corner followed by a large beige saloon with the name of a car hire firm stencilled on the side. The latter sounded its horn and the driver wound down the window. Clane Quilley leaned out and grinned. "Greetings all! This is our new car... temporarily of course."

His wife frowned at him. "What took you so long, Clane?"

"I had to walk to the nearest town; that's about five miles away. Then I had to get hold of the Triple-A and arrange a pick-up and a replacement car." The family piled into the hire car while the recovery truck driver loaded their own vehicle and took it away to the garage for repairs. The journey finally resumed after a two-hour break. The replacement ground car was an old pre-Disclosure Pontiac. It was very dated, but looked in good condition. Brendan's parents' irritation with each other continued and this time Siobhan was more vocal, perhaps because William and Colleen had both fallen asleep. She chimed in almost completely in alliance with her father against Gina. Brendan sat quietly on the worn leather backseat and watched the two-ings and fro-ings in dismay. A sudden realization came to him, one that he felt he had known a long time but not really integrated until now: Siobhan did not love their mother; in fact she didn't even like her. What's more their mother did not love her either.

"Dad, what's that red light on the dash?" asked Siobhan.

Clane looked down. "Goodness me, it means we're running out of... gas." His voice took on a subtle note of surprise as he uttered the word *gas*.

"Gas?" Gina looked alarmed. "You mean this car is an IC?"

"Yes, of course it is; one this old." He tapped the petrol gauge. "We'd better find a filling station."

"There aren't many of those around nowadays." said Brendan. He knew that IC's, internal combustion engines, were quickly becoming obsolete in the post-Disclosure world."

"Nonsense!" riposted his father. "We'll find one soon."

Gina rolled her eyes and tutted. "Didn't you check that the garage had filled up the tank?"

"No." her husband replied deadpan. His knuckles once again whitened on the wheel and the red patch on his nape returned. The family was quiet as they drove on; everybody was watching the needle on the antiquated petrol gauge as it clicked closer and closer to the *EMPTY* symbol. They entered a small town and Clane gasped with relief and pointed. "A gas station; thank you, God!" Around a corner above some bushes was a tall post sporting a brightly-coloured signboard: *S.V. MOBIL*. They pulled in towards it and ground to a halt. The petrol pumps had all been removed, the shop was boarded up and the forecourt was cracked with grass growing on it. "Closed." muttered, Siobhan. "They're hardly going to keep open a gas station almost nobody ever uses."

"Alright." said Clane in a tight, commanding voice. "Has anybody got a roam signal?"

"I have." Gina studied her roamphone.

"Search 'IC fuels' on the maps page."

There was a pause. "There's a garage in Sparks Glencoe that sells IC fuels."

"How far is Sparks Glencoe?"

"About eight miles."

Siobhan whistled.

"Can we make it?" asked Gina.

"We'll soon find out." Clane accelerated gently, as if softer driving would preserve the scant remains of their petrol load. They were cruising along a straight well-surfaced road between two cornfields when the engine began misfiring. "Come on!" hissed Clane. He kicked the accelerator in a temper as the Pontiac coasted to a standstill. "Shit!"

There was a minute's silence, as if they were attending a funeral for the car; then Gina looked up from her roam and spoke: "Sparks Glencoe is just another mile and a half away."

Clane nodded and stepped out of the car. Without another word he strode away swiftly in the direction of the village. Gina, Siobhan and Brendan pushed the car closer to the verge to keep the road clear and then sat down for a second time that day and waited. It was four PM when a hunched human figure appeared in the distance. When it got closer they all identified it as Clane Quilley carrying two metal cans. He smiled with relief as they greeted him; sweat was dripping off his sunburnt brow. He removed the petrol cap and poured the contents of both cans into the car's parched tank. "Right!" he said triumphantly. "Nothing can stop us now. Get in everybody; we have a journey to complete."

He started the engine and the car pulled away from the verge. Immediately the engine began making a strange chugging sound. "What's happening *now*?" demanded Gina.

"I don't know." Clane growled, shaking his head. The car stalled again and Clane jumped out. "What's wrong *this* time!?" He lifted up the bonnet in frustration, running a hand through his greying hair.

"Clane, what did you do with the empty cans?" asked Gina, a tone of fear in her voice that made Brendan sit up.

"I put them in the trunk... The motor looks okay; I don't get it."

Gina opened the boot of the car and Brendan heard her sigh. "Clane."

"What?"

She held up one of the empty cans. "This is diesel..."

....

Brendan woke up the next morning in a hotel. The bedroom window was open a crack and the sounds and smells of lower Manhattan wafted into the room. He met the rest of his family for breakfast where they sat and ate in silence. Their reticence was not from tension, but simply from exhaustion. They had no more energy left for arguing. When Gina asked Clane to pass her the bottle of tomato ketchup he did so immediately, neutrally and willingly. William and Colleen were back to their usual cheerful and playful selves as Siobhan helped them eat their soldiers with scrambled egg. The previous day they had both cried non-stop all afternoon. Nobody wanted to recall that time; they occasionally looked around themselves in wonder at how they had even arrived at where they were. The expedition had involved hitchhiking, being picked up by a friendly old farmer in a rusty cattle truck who Brendan was afraid might be a bandit, lying for half and hour in the back of the truck on reeking floorboards covered with dry cowpats, waiting for two hours at an isolated bus stop and, finally, running to catch a train. They had staggered into the hotel at around ten PM barely able to stand. Siobhan and Clane carried a sleeping William and Colleen; and Gina's eyes were bloodshot from continuous weeping and her voice hoarse from shouting. After breakfast Clane made an apologetic phone call to the AAA and told them where to pick up the hire car he had damaged. The family then paid their bill and walked along Wall Street to the nearest Subway station. The concrete canyons of New York City towered above them; police car sirens echoed shrilly off the lofty ceramic facades. There was a commotion outside the neoclassical portico of the New York Stock Exchange; a cluster of men in smart suits were pouring out of the doors and running around like disturbed ants. They were waving sheets of paper above their heads and exclaiming inaudibly. The Quilleys crossed the street to bypass the throng. Outside the Subway station was a temporary kiosk where a young boy was handing out newspapers from huge piles that were being unloaded from a van. "Extra! Extra! Read all about it" he yelled. "Big trouble at the Big Board!... Read all about it!" Clane handed the youth a coin and took a paper.

"What is it?" asked Gina.

"A special edition of *The Wall Street Journal*. There's been a stock market crash!"

"Not another one. What caused it this time?"

Clane scanned the pages as they queued to buy Subway

tickets. "A commodities crash. 'Black Friday' it says. They're talking about a 'new Great Depression'!... Mind you they've been saying that every year since Disclosure."

"Commodities?"

"Energy commodities to be precise."

She paused. "The oil companies?"

He nodded and pointed at the newspaper. "This columnist is calling it 'market readjustment', but basically it's the end for them because of the new tech."

She put her hands on her hips. "They could always try selling diesel oil to gasoline IC owners."

He glanced at her briefly, but did not react to her sarcasm. It was the closest Gina had come to relighting yesterday's animosity.

They rode the Subway to Pennsylvania Station and caught a train on the Long Island Rail Road. An hour later they finally reached their destination; Syosset, New York. The town was flat and broadly-spaced. The family trudged across the sprawling carpark and then used Clane's roam to navigate to their destination in a leafy residential park beside a golf course. Luckily the weather remained calm and warm. The clear sky was tainted in one sector by chemtrails. The roads of the district were long and straight and the houses all detached; either low suburban mini-mansions with large windows and heavy roofs, or boxy clapperboard 1920's prefabs with small dormers. Every home had a pretty garden and well-pruned hedges lined the road for most of their journey. "Here it is." said Clane, pointing to a house that combined both architectural styles. They walked up the driveway and he knocked on the door. Brendan's grandfather opened it with a frown. "So, you finally made it."

"Hi, dad." Clane replied flatly.

Brendan's paternal grandparents greeted him lovingly, as they did Siobhan, William and Colleen. As soon as they had sat down and had a cup of tea, Colleen and William jumped up onto their great-grandfather's lap and kissed his cheeks, much to his delight. His wife embraced them all, remarking that Siobhan was now thirty-one years old, much to Siobhan's obviously suppressed annoyance. The old couple's home was simply but elegantly furnished. The carpets were clean and thin. The ornaments and wall decorations consisted mostly of mementoes and family photographs. On the hearth mantelpiece were a row of free-standing gilt frames featuring photographs of Clane and Gina's weddings... both of them, Siobhan, himself and the twins. There was also a black-and-white print of his father during the war; he looked young and was wearing a US Navy uniform. Next to that were pictures of Clane's brother Mark and sister Daisy. There was a wooden shield in pride of place embossed with the silver relief of a dead mouse lying on its back; a retirement present from the pest control company Brendan's grandfather worked for. There was a long conversation of light-hearted recriminations and apologies for the "journey from hell!" as they had all dubbed it. The family had been due to arrive Thursday morning and it was now over twenty-four hours later. After just one more night they would have to return home. Arthur and Marianne Quilley had finally retired, despite their working class background and the lingering economic recession. The house had been bought partly out of a gift from Clane's family. Clane Quilley had enjoyed several well-paid jobs during the immediate post-Disclosure years. He had been the first US Secretary for Interplanetary War. The fact that said war was a false-flag fabrication, a last-ditch attempt to suppress the truth about flying saucers, grated on Arthur even more. Clane had then worked in Ireland on the US embassy staff. After that he had taken a job with a defence contractor, again as part of a fraudulent operation. Brendan gathered that this caused some tension between father and son. Behind their back, Brendan's mother and father had often told him about the family's own past. When Clane was a child, his parents had tried to raise the family's social status using various different methods. This project failed and left the family almost bankrupt from all the loans they had taken out. They lost the big house they had bought and had to move to the small apartment in Prospect Park where they spent the next thirty-five years. It irked Arthur that his son had been far more materially successful than he had. He saw this as a fluke; a piece of undeserved serendipity emerging from Disclosure rather than any natural talent or hard work. Arthur loved his new house, but his enjoyment of it was tainted from the fact that he had not paid for it all himself.

The whole family went out for the afternoon. Arthur and Marianne were aged in their late seventies and had limited energy, but they were determined to show the family the Montauk Museum. Brendan sensed also that Arthur was running out of conversational topics and feared long hours of small-talk with his son. He brought his Digby ground car out of the garage and the family squeezed in. The drive to Montauk took two hours. Their destination lay on the very tip of the longer southern peninsula of Long Island's forked Atlantic seaboard. The drive was a pleasant one; the sun continued shining through the chemtrails and they opened all the windows to bask in the fresh breeze. The sea shone like a sapphire to their right for much of the journey. As they approached Montauk a sombre mood descended over the family, the traffic and, it felt, even the very land. The town itself was a small and bustling seaside resort, reminding Brendan of Pismo Beach. They followed a sign for the museum into some thick forest and the road led to a carpark outside a place that had the atmosphere more of a crematorium than a museum. A finely-cultivated garden of turf and roses led up to an ancient square structure made of grey concrete topped by a huge radar antenna. There was a much newer marble edifice next to it on which were carved rows and rows of people's names; thousands of them. "They're the people who were kidnapped and brought here to die." explained Clane in a sad voice. "Runaway kids, tramps, anybody they could get their hands on." There were stone benches beside the memorial where a number of people sat staring at it. Some were in tears. The family descended down flight of stairs into a huge basement area beneath the radar tower. The place consisted of long dirty corridors with rooms leading off; signboards on the walls told the visitors what the spaces were used for. "Genetic engineering laboratory..." Clane read aloud while reading them. "Radiation exposure test chamber... Psychotropic drugs laboratory..." They went down another bare stone staircase to a huge cavern filled with a gigantic doughnut-shaped object. "They were experimenting with the fabric of the universe down here." said Gina, flicking through a guidebook she had bought from the gift shop. "Like a miniature version of that

SQEC place in Canada... Where you went, Siobhan."

Siobhan nodded in reply; she looked very uncomfortable. "I'm going to take the twins back up." she said abruptly and left with her children. The rest of the family was not far behind her, even though there was far more to visit in the museum. Brendan felt relieved to return to the sunlit outdoors, a sight the prisoners taken to the secret government laboratory of the Montauk base perished without ever seeing again. They met up on a nineteenth century gun turret, made out of concrete like everything at the Montauk base. Next to it was another memorial, this time a granite one with a plaque that read: "*For the innocents who died here whose names are not known.*" Above the plaque was a carving in black stone of a pair of children's shoes. The Quilleys gazed out to sea, feeling weighed down by the knowledge of the inhuman atrocities that had been committed beneath their feet for almost twenty years before Disclosure. "It's like a small Area 51." put in Clane grimly.

It was dusk when they arrived back at Arthur and Marianne's house. Marianne cooked a light dinner and then they sat in a circle around a table and looked though the family photographs, a tradition during Quilley family get-togethers. Arthur and Marianne possessed a dozen doorstep-sized albums full of photographs, some funny, some sad, some moving. Brendan saw his father as a baby, a faded daguerreotype of his great-grandparents, his great uncle's body lying in a coffin and a panorama of the Irish countryside. Marianne turned over a page and a new set of photographs appeared, and suddenly Arthur gasped and leaned forward. He pointed at a pair of prints at the bottom of the verso page. Brendan followed his finger. The first print was of a man in his thirties with a cheery half-smile. He was sitting on a settee in a room with a French window behind him. He had wide staring eyes and a thick pompadour of wiry hair. Despite the fact that the photograph was sepia, Brendan sensed that the man's eyes were blue and his hair brown. In the next image the man was standing behind a woman sitting in a chair. The woman was thin and wore thick spectacles. He was looking down at the top of her head. His hands were resting on her shoulders, partly affectionately; but his palms were turned inwards as if he was contemplating the notion of strangling her. Beside him stood Arthur Quilley when he was younger, just a few years older than the man. Both were wearing identical hand-knitted pullovers which Brendan recognized as the style of his grandmother's needlework. His grandfather was grinning happily at the side of the man's head. The man appeared not to notice. The entire family's gaze lingered over these two photographs more intensely than any of the others in the whole album. Brendan looked up and was astonished to see the most peculiar expression on the faces of his grandparents. Their eyes were beaming and wide; thin grins stretched across their features. The strangest thing was not just the alien nature of their expressions, but that both of them were identical. His grandmother and grandfather had very different personalities and mannerisms, but suddenly they looked as identical as William and Colleen. Arthur's voice was breathy and trembled with passion as he spoke. "That... is Karl Dennison."

"We haven't seen him for five years." added Marianne. "He came here just before Christmas in sixty-one. He came all this way to visit us. It was wonderful to see him again..."

Brendan had been at church a few weeks ago and an old lady had told him how she had once seen the Virgin Mary; her demeanour was exactly the same as his grandparents' was now. It was not completely exotic to him though. His mother used to gaze at Dr Millicent Arbroath-Laird with a similar look of hypnotic adoration. He checked the rest of the family to see how they reacted. His mother and sister appeared unmoved, yet his father had also developed a strange look on his face; but it was strange in a very different way. His cheeks were flushed purple with outrage, his eyes were bulging and tears welled up in the corners. His mouth was ripped into an agonized rictus. His lips were pure white. He looked as if he desperately wanted to scream manically, but the very maximum effort of self-control barely reined him in.

....

The family went home the following afternoon. The AAA generously provided a courtesy-flyer for the trip. The final morning at Arthur and Marianne Quilley's house had been surreal. Everybody was acting completely normally apart from Clane. He was taciturn and very sullen. He hardly spoke at all and when he did it was with a prickly snap; however his grandparents didn't notice, or pretended not to. This worried Brendan and after breakfast he waited outside the upstairs bathroom door while Clane was using it. Everybody else was downstairs so they could talk in private. When Clane came out Brendan blurted: "Dad, what's wrong?"

His father paused. "I'll tell you later, son."

He did not, however. The family were home within an hour and the rest of the weekend passed fairly normally. They went to mass as usual on Sunday morning and spent the rest of the day visiting people. Brendan went out and played with his friends. He had no school because it was the summer break so he went to watch a baseball game in Silver Spring. He was surprised to find his father standing in the entrance to the park after the game. His friend Harry gave Brendan a furtive look and ran ahead after greeting his father with a mumbled "Hi, Mr Quilley."

Brendan frowned. "Dad, what are you doing here?"

Clane paused. "I knew you were here so I wanted to meet up with you afterwards."

"Why?"

He paused. His face was mournful, almost guilty. Was he about to confess to some kind of criminal action? "I'm about to... go somewhere. Would you like to come with me?"

"Go where?"

"Come with me to the flyer." His father had parked the flyer a hundred yards away. When they got in he took off and headed west over Bethesda, ascending rapidly. "If you change your mind and want to go home at any time; just let me know and I'll take you straight away."

Brendan nodded from the front passenger seat. "What's all this about, dad?"

"We're going to pay somebody a visit."

"Who?"

"Karl Dennison."

"The man in the photo?"

Clane nodded. "I think you're old enough to witness this; in fact I want you to witness this. When I was a kid, younger than you even, I remember clearly thinking to myself that when I grew up, if I ever had a child of my own, I promised; I would never... *never*... allow what happened to me to happen to them!"

"What do you mean?"

Clane seethed bitterly. "My dad... he doesn't know how to pull up the drawbridge. He can stand up to me, to mom, to Mark and Daisy, to Siobhan; because we're good people who treat him kindly... but when it comes to scumbags, he just falls to his knees and spreads his ass-cheeks. He cannot say 'no' to some people... and it's only the people who abuse him and his family."

Brendan found it odd to hear Clane say *my dad* and *mom* when talking to him about his own parents. He normally always used the phrases *your granddad* and *your grandma*.

"What did this Karl Dennison guy do?"

Clane bowed his head and gritted his teeth. To Brendan's shock, his own father suddenly now looked like a frightened young boy, no older than himself. "I had no idea the motherfucker was even still alive. Certainly I assumed mom and dad had not been in contact with him... and then I find out they're still in touch; and that he visited them at Christmas a few years ago... My dad actually opened the door, said 'come in, Karl', and welcomed him into his house to treat him as a guest, the same house we've been staying at!... Did you see the way dad looked at that photo? Starry eyed! It was pathetic! That man still has a hold over his heart and mind, after all these years, after everything he did. I've tried to talk to him about this, but he will not listen to me! I can't stop him fawning over Dennison in public like some lovesick groupie! He can fall to his trembling knees and lick that shit's asshole till it's as clean as his eyeballs as far as I'm concerned... but the thought that they are still inviting him to stay... after everything he did!... Why!? Jesus Christ, *why*!?"

There was a long silence. "What are you going to do when we get there?" asked Brendan.

"I'm going to kick the crap out of him... I'm going to kick the sweet dry living crap out of him!" Clane punched the dashboard like a boxer, making Brendan jump.

"Won't you get in trouble with the cops if you do that?"

"Maybe; I could care less... Actually the asshole lives in

some kind of nature commune miles from anywhere so I doubt if anybody will find out."

Within twenty minutes they were speeding over the forested mountains of West Virginia. Clane pitched the aircraft downwards and it descended. He was flying much too fast, eager to sate his lust for revenge. Brendan spotted a collection of large brown buildings nestling between the trees and a farmer's field. Clane brought the flyer down onto a narrow country lane where he switched to "ground-hugging" mode. The flyer then behaved like a car, skimming the road about a foot above the tarmac as if it could not fly and had invisible wheels. A limestone wall appeared to their left and they followed it to a wide gate that led to a drive lined by an avenue of fine trees. At the end was a small carpark beside a long two-storey house that looked like a very old European stately home. Clane lowered the landing pads and brought the flyer to a standstill. He got out and strode like a trooper towards a flight of stone steps leading to an old wooden door. Brendan followed, his heart thumping. He didn't know what the right thing to do was; he was a helpless observer. The door was one of five built into the wall of the mansion; the place had clearly been converted into a terrace of private flats. Clane knocked hard on the door. After a few seconds he knocked again. Brendan heard the bolt being drawn on the other side and it creaked open. Clane stepped back, poised and ready for action. A thin-faced elderly woman appeared; her eyes were covered by think spectacles. She was clearly the woman in the photograph whose shoulders Karl Dennison had had his hands on, albeit around forty years older. "Clane?" She smiled. "Is that you?" She gasped with delight. "My goodness you've grown!"

"Hello, Susannah." Clane replied, clearly taken aback at the amicable greeting.

"Come in! Come in!" She opened the door wide. Then she stared at Brendan in delight. "Is this your son?"

"Yes, this is Brendan."

The old lady patted Brendan's shoulder. "I've heard all about you; it's really good to meet you finally." She escorted them through the door into a small and antiquated but very charming farmhouse kitchen. She placed an ancient copper kettle on a cast iron range to brew some tea. The heavenly scent of burning wood rose from beneath the hob. The cracked wooden mantel held many portraits and photographs of people. Horse brasses hung from the walls and a sprig of dried wildflowers decorated the window. "How are the rest of the family?" asked Susannah as the water boiled.

"Very well, thank you." answered Clane politely. "How are yours?"

"Doing alright. Harriet is working in Los Angeles; Bobby has just finished college; got a degree in climatology."

"I'm happy to hear that." Clane opened his mouth and hesitated. "Susannah... is Karl home?"

She stopped what she was doing and sighed, then she turned to look at him with a blank expression. "No."

"Does he... not live here any more?"

She gave a sad half-smile. "Kind of." She walked towards an inside door. "Let me show you something." She left the room and came back two minutes later with a cardboard box about a foot and a half along each side. She opened it and brought out an object that made Brendan yell in alarm and jump to his feet. He knew what it was; indeed he had seen one himself three years ago. He had found it under a bush while playing on an island in the River Potomac. It was a reptilian skull. "I don't know why I keep it." continued Susannah. "We didn't bury him; we couldn't. We were all too scared. At the same time I couldn't bear to let the clean-up squads just dump him on a pile in the back of a truck with all the others."

Clane gaped at the object in Susannah's hands. "So *that* is Karl... Karl was one of *them*!"

"Nobody knew. I don't think he knew himself. He changed on the same day as all of them. I was out in the garden pulling up weeds. He called to me from the kitchen, asking me if I wanted to attend the community concert that evening. I called back 'yeah sure!'; then it was just a few minutes later I stood up and took off my gloves..." Her eyes misted over with tears. "I went into the kitchen and there was this... *thing* just standing there. I screamed for Karl, warning him to get out of the house. When I couldn't find him I assumed he had got out to safety. It was only hours later I found out the truth... He wandered through the house, growling and hissing, looking for an exit. When he got lost and ended up in into the basement I slammed the door on him and locked it. He tore around the place, roaring, ripping everything apart, but he couldn't get out. There was not much more we could do here except look after each other. We got together, gathered weapons, stocked up on food. The police were too busy in the cities to care about what happened to us. I wasn't the only one in the area who had lost a family member to... had one turn into..." She squeezed her eyes shut with the painful memory. "A few of them changed in Elkwater just down the road. Those ones just wandered off into the woods. Of course, two weeks later when they all dropped dead... I had to check. I unlocked the door and peeked into the basement; and, sure enough, Karl... that thing that used to be Karl... was lying on the floor completely still." She plucked a tissue out of a box and blew her nose.

There was a long silence. Clane was trembling. His hands were spread on the old wooden table and they shook. His gaze was levelled at them in horror. "Susannah... I'm so sorry... I... I don't know what to say."

She smiled at him sympathetically. "It's okay, Clane. I guess nobody told you. Well, I didn't tell anybody. I should have written to your mom and dad, but..."

He nodded. Soon afterwards he and Brendan bade Susannah a fond farewell and then flew home. They never spoke a single word for the entire journey.

Chapter 6

Brendan walked home from school. It was Tuesday, the day after Labour Day, and he had been surprisingly happy to return to school as a ninth-grader. He always longed for the holidays when he was in the middle of a semester, but the length of the summer break was becoming more tedious at each annual return. This was his final year at the junior high school and he had some new teachers who appeared quite nice at primary classroom encounter. He hoped all his friends would be accompanying him to the same senior high the following year. It was a warm and fresh day in late summer and he watched the shadows of tree branches play across the pavement as he strolled in a leisurely manner. He came to a junction where an orange brick wall ran along one side of the road. Occasionally graffiti appeared on it; always the usual crude erotic frescoes, taboo obscenities or incoherent threats. He knew who most of the artists were because they went to his school. There was a new graffito on the wall that he'd not seen before and Brendan could tell it was different from the standard even from a distance. It was simple text in black spray paint and it said: *"IT'S NOT TOO LATE."* Brendan took a photograph of it with his roam and went home. He remembered seeing the same words somewhere else, but it had escaped his attention at the time. He felt an itch on his left shoulder and he reached under his shirt to rub it. Siobhan was in the kitchen when he arrived. She had just served William and Colleen a meal and was washing up the oven tray. She had a strange look on her face. "Bren..." She looked over her shoulder at the twins, who were munching contentedly on their low table, and then motioned him into the conservatory where they were out of earshot. "How would you feel if we came to live here; Will, Colleen and me?"

He shrugged. "You pretty much do already."

"I mean all the time, permanently. I'm thinking of selling the apartment. It's miserable there with just the three of us alone; that's why we spend most of our time here."

"What about mom?"

Siobhan frowned. "What about her?"

Brendan cursed himself and wished he'd not spoken. "Well... you and her... you fight a lot."

Siobhan looked at him for a moment and sighed. "That's true... Well, maybe this can be a chance for us to learn to fight less."

"There's also..." Brendan hesitated. "Will and Colleen's daddy. Will he mind?"

Siobhan blinked a few times and flushed. Then she guffawed dismissively. "He wouldn't care either way. It's not his business anyhow." He pursed her lips. "They've started asking me about him. They were bound to eventually. They're getting too old not to think about it, not to be curious. All the other kids have daddies; why don't they?"

"What have you told them?"

"Nothing... yet. I just can't."

Brendan nodded and scratched his shoulder again.

"What's the matter, Bren?"

"Just got an itchy shoulder."

"Maybe a bug bit you. Can I look?"

Brendan undid his shirt buttons and pulled his collar wide over his upper arm. Siobhan studied his skin. "Can't see any marks, except from your fingernails... Stop scratching it or that will make it worse. It'll probably go away soon."

Brendan went to his room and fired up his personal computer. He was delighted to see he had an E-gram from Dave. It was only the second time he had heard from his friend since Dave had moved away three years earlier. The letter was long and detailed and included photographs of Dave's new home in Africa. At the end he said: "*My dad has written to your dad to invite you all over to stay. Hope you can come visit.*" Brendan seethed with excitement. He ran downstairs and sat by the front door for half an hour, waiting for his father to come home from work. As soon as Clane had crossed the threshold his son ran up to him. "Dad! Have you had an E-gram from Dr Pearson?"

"Yes, yes, Brendan. Let me get indoors for Christ's sake!"

"Can we go? Can we?"

"Hold your horses! Can I get changed and have a coffee first?"

Eventually, when he was finally settled in the lounge with the family, Clane answered in the affirmative. Brendan cheered and hugged him. A few minutes later he remembered something. "Hey dad, what does 'it's not too late' mean?"

"Why do you ask?"

Brendan explained.

"It's kind of a slogan. It came up at the Dubai summit a few years ago. Since then people have been saying it everywhere, like it's symbolic. The League of the World Earth Healing Organization has even adopted it as its motto. That's not the first time somebody has scrawled it on a wall... What's up with you, Bren?"

Brendan's shoulder was still itching and he had his hand under his shirt again.

"Brendan, I told you not to scratch it!" scolded Siobhan.

"I can't help it, Siobhan, I..."

"Hey look!" Gina pointed at the television. A news programme was on. It showed a city street full of cheering people. A row of cars and trucks were driving along in a convoy. They were all overloaded with passengers; some were sitting on the roofs and bonnets, waving their arms in the air with huge grins on their faces. Brendan started listening to the narrator's voice: "*...formal resignation of the provisional government. The triumphant parade in Canberra by the CPA-Labour alliance has been going on all afternoon. Prime Minister Sharkey has just been sworn into office...*"

"What's going on, mom?" asked Brendan.

"The communists have taken power in Australia."

"Holy shit!" cursed Clane. "There's been talk of this for a while, but I never thought it was serious. I didn't think it could happen in Australia of all places. Just the other day on *This Week in Politics* I heard..."

"Shh!" Gina raised her hand. The news story had changed to a recording of a thin elderly man making a speech: "*The revolution is finally here.*" the man said. "*The working class of this nation have called for a state of their own and they have one.*" The crowd cheered. "*As the prime minister...*"

"Who's that dude standing behind him?" asked Clane, pointing at the TV screen.

"Which one?" asked Gina.

"Him on the left, right beside the guy making the speech."

The person Clane indicated was a much younger man than the new prime minister. He was wearing a baseball cap and sunglasses, but Brendan sensed that he looked vaguely familiar. His mouth scowled from behind a rough beard and his body was covered by a dirty and torn T-shirt. "I think I've seen him before." said Brendan.

"Isn't that Julian?" asked Gina, her voice was raised in surprise.

"Nah! Surely not." answered Clane. "Looks a bit like him, but it's not the same guy."

However the next shot was an interview with that man. He yelled manically at the camera, ignoring the reporter, and pointed at the audience: "*Let the capitalist pigs of the ruling class watching me speak hear this. I say to you: tremble in your beds in terror! We have taken one of the biggest jewels from your crown! The nation and continent of Australia has just been liberated through class struggle! We will not stop until...*" His familiar youthful English accent removed any doubt, even before the caption appeared on the screen saying: "*JULIAN SPENCER- C.P.A. MILITIA LEADER.*"

"My God!" hissed Gina.

Siobhan had been silent since the news programme began. She stood up and walked slowly towards the television, her eyes fixed on the screen. The long silence was broken by Colleen. "Who's that man, mommy?" Her face and voice were absent of any suspicion or concern; it was just one of the casual childlike questions that she always asked.

Everybody turned to look at her, struck dumb with indecision. Siobhan walked back to her seat and lifted Colleen up onto her lap. Then she did the same for her son. It was clearly more of an effort than it had been in the past because the twins were now three-and-a-half years old and growing rapidly. "Colleen, Will; that... is your daddy."

....

"What's this place called again?" asked Gina from the front passenger seat.

"Bawku." replied Clane. "Or however you pronounce it."

"Weird name."

Brendan had his matchbook open on his lap on the backseat and was studying the map. The Volta Union was a mushroom-shaped country, sprouting out of the coast of West Africa and their destination was at the top of the geographical stalk, where it met the cap. They were transatlantic in the family flyer. Brendan sat alone in the backseat; Siobhan and the twins were not coming with them. They had been in the air for half an hour when his father suddenly changed course. "Sorry folks, we're going to take a swift detour. I want to see how Britain's doing."

Gina groaned. "Is that wise, Clane; there's a civil war in progress?"

"Not exactly. But it looks like the New Republic is not going to last. If violence breaks out, the LoW will move in and take over again."

"Okay, but don't fly too low." He didn't. They cruised over London with the dotted clouds flowing below the chassis. From that altitude everything looked normal. Plenty of cars were moving along the roads, looking like mites along a blade of grass. Brendan recalled his own visit there in 1962. Gina sighed tremulously. "At least Siobhan doesn't want to go here." Clane nodded. The fortnight since they had seen Julian on television had been a tough one. Siobhan had become fixated on the idea of going immediately to Australia and taking her children with her. Her parents had to calm her down during her various bouts of obsession. They almost had to block the door to the garage and physically prevent her jumping in her flyer. She had no idea what she would do if she went straight there. She didn't know if Julian was willing to see her or their children. She didn't even know how to contact him. Revolutionary Australia was also a very dangerous place. Three nations, New Zealand, Japan and Thailand, had all declared war on the new socialist regime; there had already been a number of air-strikes and threats of invasion. Refugees were pouring out of the continent by any means they could. Internal dissidents had attempted a counter-coup. Eventually, through dedicated persuasion, Siobhan and her parents had reached an agreement. Siobhan would stay at home and try to communicate with Julian from there. In return, they would assist her in any way they could when they came home from Africa.

From Britain they turned due south along the Greenwich Meridian. They crossed France, Spain and the Mediterranean Sea; then they caught their first sight of Africa. It consisted of the vast yellow dry plain of the Sahara Desert interspersed by desolate mountain ranges. After another twenty minutes flying across this lonely place like a swallow, a tinge of green mixed with the yellow. The green grew in power until it overcame the yellow. Clane dipped their aircraft into descent and more details of the ground emerged. There were patches of bright verdant forest mixed with grey savannah and patches of red and yellow barren earth. Slate-blue rivers meandered across the landscape. Clane followed the satellite-navigator lower and lower until signs of human habitation emerged; rows of large low houses beside straight, square streets. Bright and neat gardens surrounded them, along with smooth parks. "Here it is." said Clane. Like many post-Disclosure buildings, the Pearson's house had a flat space on its roof for parking flyers. The family were standing beside their own vehicle smiling and waving as Clane pulled up carefully into the slot next to it. They greeted the Quilleys warmly as they stepped out of their flyer into the sun. The heat was stifling and Brendan broke out in a sweat immediately. "Welcome to Africa!" said Dr Pearson with a broad smile. Dave ran up and embraced him joyfully.

Dave's family quickly led the Quilleys down a flight of stairs into the house where it was beautifully cooled by the caress of air conditioning. The Pearson home was large and spacious with big windows. Everything was clean and the furniture was all covered in leather. It was clearly a brand new building. "Built especially for us." said Dr Pearson proudly. Pearson was a cheerful fit-looking man, tall and muscular with a deep voice. He and Brendan's father had been semi-acquainted back in the United States. His wife was an athletics coach and an ex-FBI agent; and she had the lean figure of a runner, accentuated by her natural negress curves. She had long frizzy hair cut in a round bob; a style that was currently fashionable among black women in America. Their clothing was also American, as was that of Dave and his older brother Michael. "I think almost everybody in this area is American." said Dr Pearson, gesturing out of the lounge window at the neighbouring houses. "Well, there are a few Brits, a couple of Cubans, some Brazilians." After a light meal the adults retired to the lounge to talk and the children went out. It was five PM and the air had cooled. The sun was low in the sky and dusk was falling. This felt incongruous to Brendan who lived in a latitude where hot weather was always associated with long summer evenings. Here, close to the equator, night always fell early the whole year round. The neighbourhood had a surprisingly unexceptional atmosphere for a corner of the Dark Continent. It was very much like a typical east coast suburban new town in the USA, except for the hot weather and different biology. The trees were of an unfamiliar species and the evening birdsong had a different tone. The public spaces were pretty and flowers poked at them out of pots, smelling wonderful. There was a park half a mile from the Pearson's home with several basketball courts. Dave, Michael and Brendan shot a few hoops with some other local boys, all American expatriates, and then went to a nearby leisure centre where there was a cinema, amusement arcade, indoor sports hall and diner. It was pitch dark when they left to go home. Crickets sang loudly from the verges and frogs croaked from garden ponds. Insects wheeled around the streetlamps. "The whole of Africa is not like this place, surely?" asked Brendan rhetorically. He had been slightly disappointed by the lack of exotic ambiance. He had met plenty of different people, but none were native Africans, even though every one of them was black. Everybody had been friendly to him, but he himself felt he stood out by being the only Caucasian.

"Hell, no." said Dave. "In the morning we'll show you the rest of town."

Brendan slept well in a comfortable spare bedroom. The air conditioning protected him from the heat; and he didn't get bitten by mosquitoes because the house also had a neat repellent system using a device on the wall of the house that fired tiny laser beams at flying insects. He was woken up at two AM by a violent thunderstorm. Lightning strobed repeatedly, illuminating his room like a disco; thunder made the ground shudder and torrential rain thrashed the roof and drowned the gutters. In the morning at breakfast Dr Pearson explained that they were in the "rainy season". By the time Dave and Michael took Brendan out, the morning sun was shining and the pavements steamed as the rays dried them. Dave and his brother took him in the opposite direction to where they had gone the previous evening and soon they came to a road with smaller houses of a different architecture. These were bungalows with lightly sloping roofs. They had no gardens and were surrounded by the bare red earth, a signifier of the area, dotted with scrub. Small areas by their facades were concreted over and covered by sunshades where flyers and ground cars were parked. There were a lot of motorcycles, usually small scooters, leaning against most of the houses. Many homes were surrounded by waist-high white brick walls. There were people walking in both directions along the cement roadway. There was no pavement and they simply strolled along at the edge to avoid the cars and motorcycles. As with the expatriates' colony, everybody was a Negro, but they were dressed very differently. The men wore bland knee-length short trousers with loose pastel shirts and the women had on brightly-coloured dresses with beautiful complex patterns. Some also had bright scarves and turbans on their heads. Others, particularly the young girls, braided their hair and added beads or flowers. "These are the natives." said Michael. The local people were not hostile; Dave and Michael appeared at ease with them, but there was no interaction or greetings. Brendan felt as if he and his two friends were invisible. "They have their own languages that make no sense to me." said Dave. "Although a lot of them speak English. A few speak French. I've learned some French at school."

"We're right on the border of the old British and French empires." explained Michael.

The road was long and completely straight. Soon it emerged into a bustling open-air market. There were rows of stalls selling every product imaginable; piles of fruit and vegetables of which some were recognizable and others not; meat, fish, canned or wrapped products. There were clothes, shoes, hardware, books, videodisks, old vinyl records, crockery and cutlery. The smells were intoxicating. Loud voices were everywhere. Sellers pushed past them carrying sacks of wares on their backs, music played from loudspeakers, officials in uniform patrolled the aisles between the stalls. Flyers circuited overhead like hawks, their drivers leaning out to find places to land and unload their stock. At the other side of the market were a number of cafes and restaurants in low structures resembling beach huts. Then they came to a handsome church and another ornate white stucco building next to it with a dome on top and a Middle Eastern feel. Dave pointed at the latter. "That's a mosque. A lot of people here are Muslim... Look!" He pointed to a group of about six people in the forecourt of the mosque who were carrying out a strange dance involving high leaps into the air and rotating their bodies very quickly. They chanted rhythmically as they jumped. Many people in the church garden were leaning over the wall and watching with interest. "The Sufis are performing. I love that spinning, but they must get so dizzy." A hundred yards down the road another much larger group of people were engaged in a synchronized dance of a kind Brendan had never seen before to a quartet of drummers banging bongos. The troupe laughed and cheered as they rocked from side to side and waved their hands. They looked like generally happy people, Brendan thought. He had not seen a single face that morning which was not either cheerful or at least content.

"Would you like to see some elephants?" asked Dave.

"Yeah." said Brendan. "Why, have you got a zoo here?"

The two boys laughed and shook their heads. "Come with us." Dave and Michael led Brendan up a smaller side street. Eventually the cement road gave way to the dry red dusty soil and it narrowed into a footpath through a forest. The heat and humidity were stifling. Brendan dripped with sweat. The alien birdsong was mixed with the rustle of millions of insects. The sounds and colours of nature were totally different to the countryside of his home. The tree leaves were greener, the bark of their trunks darker, the grass was taller and the smells were more intense. There was no doubt, Brendan mused, that he was now in a foreign land. Michael led the way; seeming to know instinctively the right route even though the path had narrowed to a rut between the patches of grass. The tips of the grass stems tickled their ankles. Brendan felt nervous. "Hey, Dave. Are there any snakes or anything round here?"

"No."

"That's good news." he sighed.

"The snakes all got eaten by the giant spiders." Dave laughed and added: "Only kidding." when he saw Brendan's expression. "Yeah, there are some snakes, but they usually avoid people. So long as we stay on the path we'll be safe. If you hear about somebody who's been bitten by a snake then it's almost always some schmuck who was trying to catch it or kill it."

"Look!" Michael stopped dead and the two other boys instinctively copied him. Michael pointed. "Over there." He was whispering. Brendan parted some rushes with his hand and in front of him, about two hundred yards away, were the gigantic barrel-shaped grey bodies of a herd of elephants. There were six of seven of them. He was astonished. He'd seen elephants several times in zoos, but here he was in the wild with them, with no bars or glass separating him from them. The elephants flapped their huge ears and swished their tails. Their snow-white tusks gleamed in the sunlight. They reached up with their trunks to grasp leaves from the canopy to eat. "We can't risk getting any closer than this." hissed Michael. "They've got kids with them; look." Sure enough a gaggle of miniature elephants without tusks, about the size of small cows, trotted around by the feet of the adults. "They can get real nasty when they've got kids. Protective I guess."

Another worrying thought occurred to Brendan. "Are there lions round here?"

"No." This time there was no jocularity on Dave's face. "They live further south. Same with leopards and other big cats. Like the snakes they don't generally attack humans, not as much as in the movies anyhow. Thing is, since Disclosure, the farms have shrunk and so the jungle has been growing; and the big animals have wandered beyond the old game reserves. This means in this part of the country people have to take more precautions. It's not really that much more dangerous though."

"Our dad wants to show you some crocodiles this afternoon." added Michael with a playful grin.

The crocodiles were actually tame ones that lived in a reserve in the town of Paga which was a ten minute flyer flight to the west. The reserve consisted of a large meadow and wetland surrounding large muddy ponds. After the huge reptiles had been fed with raw chickens, that the visitors had to buy, they simply lay contentedly on the grass while everybody clustered round them taking photographs. Brendan even sat on the sedate horny back of one of the beasts. It unnerved him to begin with, but the creature didn't move; its eyelids only flickered once in a while. Clane crouched down and lifted the tail of one of the crocodiles, following instructions from the sanctuary staff. The family all snapped pictures of him and uploaded them to social media. Clane's face was pale as he looked at what was in his hands. "Sweet Mary! This thing could bite me in half if it wanted."

"It won't." replied Pearson. "There's a local legend that the people of Paga reincarnate as one of these crocs when they die, and that's why they never hurt humans. Local children even swim in these lakes in complete safety."

"I see." said Clane dubiously.

Pearson grinned ghoulishly. "It's probably got more to do with the fact that they are constantly kept well-fed. If they ever got hungry then this place would become a death-trap."

Brendan stood up and dismounted the crocodile he had been sitting on. He reached under his shirt and rubbed his skin. The itch on his shoulder had started again.

....

Brendan awoke slowly from a half-sleep. His room was full of light; almost as if the sun was shining in through the windows or that there was a dazzling floodlight outside. It was like the lightning the previous night, but was steady. Then the light vanished as if somebody had flicked a switch. He was wide awake now and sat up; wondering if the light had been part of a dream. He often had strange visions in the transitional zone between waking and sleep, usually while waking. He would find himself unable to move any part of his body except his eyes. He would sometimes call out for help, but his voice made no sound at all. In this state he would be able to perceive his surroundings, but with the addition of strange phenomena, such as dark figures in his peripheral vision. However he had never before had a vision of a huge bright light. He got out of bed and walked towards the window. He looked out at the Pearsons' back garden, dimmed by the night. He glanced at the illuminated clock on his bedside table: two-fifty-two AM. The bushes in the garden were rocking in a breeze and a light rain was falling; he could just make out water dribbling down the window pane in the wash from cloud-filtered moonlight. He heard an almost imperceptible sound behind him, but in his silent reverie it made him start. He tiptoed over to the door and opened it. There was a low-powered nightlight at floor level which allowed him to see across the landing to the other bedrooms. The door to Dave's room was ajar. Brendan left the doorway and walked slowly, one step at a time, over to his friend's bedroom; the thick carpet felt pleasant on the soles of his feet. He peeped around the jamb apprehensively, as if unsure of what he would find, although Dave had shown Brendan round his room the previous evening. Everything looked fairly normal, the posters on the wall, books on the shelves, a soccer ball on the floor, a baseball bat leaning against a chest of drawers, an inert PC on the desk; although everything was colourless and hazy in the gloom. Dave was not in his bed; the covers were pulled back in a chaotic pile as if he had leapt out in a hurry. Brendan looked over his shoulder. The bathroom was down a corridor to the left of the landing, but the door was open and no light showed from it. Brendan went over to check just in case, but it was empty. He padded back to the landing and looked down the stairs. There was no light coming from the ground floor. Brendan saw a brief flicker of movement, but immediately recognized it as one of the Pearson's two cats running around. He shrugged his shoulders and went back to bed.

When Brendan woke up it was eight-thirty AM. He went downstairs and saw everybody sitting round the kitchen table in their dressing gowns eating breakfast. The big patio doors were wide open and a fresh breeze filled the house; it was less humid today than it had been previously. The sound of church bells rang in the distance and he realized that today was Sunday. "Good morning, Brendan." Mrs Pearson smiled at him. "Take a seat; would you like grapefruit again?" The two families talked cheerfully as they ate while drinking coffee. Dr Pearson told them all about his job at a local hospital. He was part of a regional emergency surgical team. His wife nodded approvingly and interspersed descriptions of her own work, coaching the athletics team for the same region. This was done without animus or rivalry between them. Clane and Gina told them about life in America, Clane's work for the government, their extended family. "Were you okay last night, Dave?" asked Brendan when there was a gap in the conversation.

The response from Dave, Michael and his parents was a tense silence. They all exchanged glances.

Brendan felt uneasy and continued, feeling he should explain. "You were gone from your bed and weren't in the bathroom."

"I saw the owl again last night." said Dave abruptly, looking at his parents.

"That's right." added Mrs Pearson, smiling calmly at Brendan. "An owl got into Dave's bedroom last night and it scared him a bit so he came and slept in bed with Terry and me."

Brendan shrugged. "Okay." The atmosphere around the table changed. The carefree banter was gone. The Pearsons all looked perturbed, as if somebody had just blurted out a carefully guarded family secret. The Quilleys picked up on this and looked embarrassed. Brendan felt confused. What had he said wrong?

After breakfast Brendan went to his bedroom and examined the window. It was made of heavy plate glass. Like many post-Disclosure houses in regions of the world with a hot climate, the Pearson's home was built with air conditioning as part of its integral design. The window could not be opened except by breaking an emergency fire-seal. He went to Dave's bedroom to talk to him, making up an excuse that he wanted to borrow one of his friend's videodisks. What he really wanted to do was look at Dave's window. It was exactly the same as the one in his own room. He went back to his room turning the videodisk aimlessly over and over in his hands and he wondered. "How did the owl get in?" he asked aloud to himself.

....

"Hey, Brendan; what's up with your shoulder?" Dr Pearson asked. "You keep scratching. Have you got some skin irritation there?"

"Yeah, a bit." answered Brendan.

"Can I take a look?" He carbon-copied his permission with a glance at Clane and Gina. They both nodded.

"Take your shirt off and let me see."

Brendan blushed slightly as he undid his buttons.

Dave's father chuckled affectionately. "Trust me, I'm a doctor." He examined Brendan's shoulder in a very medical way, pushing and prodding the skin. "Hmm... Yes, you have some inflammation there; a patch just at the top of your left shoulder blade... I'm not sure what that is. It doesn't look like a burn. How long have you had it?"

"About two weeks."

"Did you hit it or have any other kind of injury there?"

"No."

"Could be an allergic reaction of some kind; a bug bite wouldn't last that long. How often does it itch?"

"Every couple of days."

"Okay. I've got some cream I can rub in that might ease the irritation; can I put it on you?"

Brendan nodded. The cream felt cooling on his skin as the doctor applied it and the itching mercifully eased afterwards.

After breakfast the two families gathered in the lounge and Dr Pearson stood up with an element and theatre and said grandly: "Right! I have an announcement to make. The arrival of Clane Quilley and his family in the Volta Union has not gone unnoticed by the nation and I'm pleased to tell you that you have all been invited for an audience with the President in the nation's capital this very afternoon."

"Wow!" replied Clane.

"Thank you very much!" said Gina.

They took the flyer to the nearby town of Bolgatanga where there was a railway station. A train was already waiting at the platform and the staff showed them to a private VIP coach. Brendan's parents were somewhat overwhelmed by this. The train was a modern one that Clane said reminded him of the one he'd ridden on in Britain in 1955. It was called the "Trans-VU Express, Ouagadougou to Accra." The Pearsons and Quilleys were served with drinks and snacks by polite waiters as they lay back in their extra-large seats. Clane chuckled and joked with the staff. The train began moving and its motion was so smooth Brendan didn't notice until he looked out of the window. The landscape shot past so fast that it was hard to see; one of the crew informed Brendan that the top line speed was over two hundred miles-per-hour. There was a flat plain of short dry grass stretching away to the horizon, punctuated by single trees every few hundred yards. They crossed several rivers on concrete bridges. After an hour, the vista became greener and hillier. Cocoa farms appeared, consisting of small trees planted in neat rows stretching as far as the eye could see. The railway passed over more bridges and through several tunnels. Buildings scrolled into view and these became denser and denser until the train was running through a low-roofed, but very tightly-constructed city. Multiple communications masts bristled above the narrow streets and above the flat, oblong houses. The train slowed and entered a steel and glass-covered railway terminal. "We've arrived." said Dr Pearson in a lively tone. As soon as it stopped, they stepped off the train onto a shiny marble platform and to their amazement a dance troupe of about twenty were carrying out a performance right in front of the train. A choir next to them chanted in the traditional African style in one of the outlandish local languages. A man in a suit came forward and held out his hand. "Mr Quilley, Mrs Quilley. Welcome to Accra, capital of the Volta Union. President Nkrumah will see you now." The suited man led them out of the station into a busy urban street and straight into a ground limousine. The city beyond was darkened by the tinted glass as the doors shut and the chauffeur pulled out into the traffic. A pair of policemen on motorcycles rode in front and behind, their sirens blaring. "What am I, the Queen of Sheba?" asked Gina with a half-smile. All the pomp and ceremony had begun to make her feel uncomfortable.

"It was the president's birthday last week." said Mrs Pearson. "He traditionally holds parties at this time. There won't be too much publicity; it's just standard. Clane, you are a foreign dignitary; there's no way that your presence here would pass unnoticed. The VU is a young nation, less than ten years old. They're conscious of their position on the world stage." The centre of Accra was an impressive sight with numerous tall, elegant buildings. The VIP motorcade drove down a long boulevard and curled right into a long driveway through a lovely grand garden. At the end of the driveway was a white-walled palace with a slightly pyramidal feel. Its style was typical of a British colonial mansion, but on the flagpoles flew not the Union Jack, but the flag of the VU. It consisted of three horizontal stripes; green at the top, gold in the middle and red at the bottom. On the gold stripe were two stars; one black, one red. The car decelerated slowly in front of the grand entrance. A reception committee was lined up consisting of people wearing suits, military uniforms and local fashions. The chauffeur opened the door and the families climbed out. "Good afternoon." A man stepped forward to greet them. He was dressed in a gown flowing over his right shoulder like a Roman toga. It consisted of several differently coloured strips. His feet moved underneath it, clad in dark plimsolls. "I am Kwame Nkrumah, president of the Volta Union. He shook all their hands. He had a heavy gold watch on his left wrist. He grinned at Brendan as he shook his hand; "Hello, young Master Brendan." he said sincerely and Brendan felt sudden emotional warmth flowing from him. The man had kindly features, a long high forehead with swept-back hair that stuck out at the sides almost like cinnamon buns. "Mr Quilley, it is an honour to welcome a great American to this nation. I spent many years in the United States. How is President King? He and I are good friends and we communicate when we can, but I haven't seen him for many years."

"He's well, Mr President." Clane was returning Nkrumah's infectious grin.

"I'm sorry, I have not yet looked up your own role in Dr King's administration."

"I'm the Secretary for Disclosure Affairs. I've been working alongside Dr King for years, in the US Provisional Government and now in his executive, so we've known each other a long time. He's a fine man."

"So are you, sir. So are you! I have read a lot about your exploits. We in the VU have you to thank for so much."

"Why me?"

"You brought the world Disclosure and Disclosure has revolutionized my country, more so even than yours I think... Please, come inside where it is cooler." President Nkrumah and his posse escorted the guests up the flight of steps through some glass screen doors that were clearly much newer than the house, and into the entrance hall that was lined with polished wood panelling. "The new tech has turned my nation from a colony of poverty and enslavement into a land flowing with milk and honey. We have the highest standard of living in Africa." He gave a look that made it clear that this was not a competition. "But the rest of the continent is catching up."

The president and his visitors had drinks in a sumptuous lounge. "Nice place you've got here." said Gina.

"Indeed, Mrs Quilley. This used to be the home of the British colonial governor when this country was a chattel state. I enjoy it as poetic justice with a clear conscience. I spent a year in a prison that was just a short distance from here; I was incarcerated on the orders of the former resident of this palace."

"So you've embraced the new tech here?" Clane asked rhetorically.

"Very enthusiastically." answered Nkrumah. "Do you know, before Disclosure I had all kinds of wild plans; I had a vision of building a dam across the Volta and turning the river into a hydroelectric plant. Disclosure has made that all unnecessary."

Nkrumah and his officials took the Quilleys and Pearsons out to a restaurant at a beach resort. Like everything in Accra, it was clean and grand, mixing modern architectural styles with local traditional themes. They sat in a reserved section of the patio. A fresh breeze blew in from the sea and seagulls wheeled above them. Nkrumah was very engaging as he had been at his home, but he kept his slate and roam close by, and at one point broke off to take an urgent call. Afterwards his mood was slightly subdued. "Everything alright, Mr President?" asked Clane. He had had a few glasses of wine and it had made his manner more informal.

Nkrumah nodded. "Yes, it's just there's been another attack by communists in the north. Nothing major; nobody killed." He shook his head pensively. "I can't believe I once supported those people..."

Half an hour later when the meal had ended, Clane tapped Brendan's shoulder in a way that Brendan recognized as his father's usual indicator that he wanted a private conversation. The two of them got up and walked off the patio onto the beach. The sand was white and clean. It felt warm and soft on the feet. A few hundred yards away the bright blue Atlantic Ocean burst onto the land as white surf. "Do you like it here, son?" asked Clane.

"Yeah, dad. It's a neat place." replied Brendan.

"I think it's beautiful. I've really fallen in love with it... I mean, I do feel a bit like a lump of chalk that's just been dropped into a sack of coal."

"What do you mean, dad?"

Clane chuckled and laid his finger on his forearm, indicating his white skin.

"Yeah, I guess we do stand out a bit."

"I've never felt threatened though. Everybody's been nothing but friendly to me."

"Yeah, same here."

Clane paused cryptically. "I'm glad to hear you say that."

"Why?"

"I've been talking to your mom about the future, have been for some time now. If Dr King doesn't get re-elected next year, I'm thinking of taking retirement. I'm a bit young, but I can afford it. I think I've done my duty, getting the country back on its feet. I've guided the new administration through a whole presidential term. What more can I do? The country can stand on its own two feet; it doesn't really need my help anymore... When I do retire, I think I'd like to retire here. I talked to your mom and she thinks it's a good idea. What about you?"

Brendan looked up at his intense but gentle gaze. "I... I don't know, dad."

"It's alright, son; no need to decide now. Your mom and I haven't for sure."

They strolled back up the beach. Brendan's shoulder was itching again. He asked Dr Pearson to put some more cream on it and he did. His friend's father and he went into the spotless and scented washroom to apply the medication. Pearson paused as Brendan pulled his shirt down. "Goodness, Brendan. The inflammation has really worsened. I'll put on some more of this cream, but you really need to get this looked at when you get home."

"What's wrong with me, Terry?"

"I'm afraid I'm not sure. My best bet is an allergy or

autoimmune reaction of some kind, but I'm not a specialist in that field. Your GP will refer you to a dermatologist, that's a doc who knows everything about skin complaints."

The cream initially cut into the irritation, but its effect was far shorter and weaker than the last time he used it. They said goodbye to President Nkrumah and were taken back to the railway station in the ground car. The sun was setting as the train pulled out of the Accra terminal and it was pitch dark when it pulled into Bolgatanga. The bad patch on Brendan's shoulder was now worse than it had ever been. Along with the prickling itch was mixed in a burning crawling pain, like pins and needles. It felt as if some creature with sharp claws was under his skin trying to break out. His mother noticed the distress in his face. "Brendan, honey; what's wrong? Is it your shoulder again?"

He nodded. "It's really bad now, mom. Feels like there's bugs in my skin scratching at me."

She caressed his head. "We'll be home soon. I'll have a look at it then."

When they arrived back at the Pearsons' house Brendan removed his shirt. The material stuck to his skin where his bad shoulder was. The family closed round and stared at his back in concern. "Oh my!" Dr Pearson looked much more concerned this time. "You've got a lesion now."

"A what?" Brendan asked fearfully.

"What's happening to him?" asked his mother, also sounding alarmed.

"I'm sorry, Gina; I don't know... His skin is broken. I'll need to apply an antiseptic, put on a dressing... I have no idea what's causing this."

Brendan wondered how he was going to sleep with such terrible pain and irritation on his mysterious shoulder wound, before Dave's father put some different cream on the sore spot that made the entire area go numb. He also put on some antiseptic cream and stuck a large plaster over it; so Brendan settled down in his bed in relative comfort, feeling grateful to Dr Pearson. In the morning the numbness had worn off, but the original discomfort had lessened. Dr Pearson removed the dressing and was about to put on some more cream when he stopped. Brendan sensed his confusion. "What is it, Terry?"

"Erm... One moment, I'd like to just..." He got up and went to his study. Clane and Gina looked concerned. He came back with a pair of tweezers wrapped in a sealed sterile packet. "Brendan, there appears to be some foreign objects in your lesion; I'd like to remove them and examine them. Is that okay?"

"Sure."

Brendan felt some probing with the cold metal of the tweezers; then Dr Pearson lifted the tweezers and wiped the contents onto a wad of gauze. He frowned as he studied what he had retrieved. "What the hell...?"

Brendan turned to look at the wad and saw a collection of short thin hairs, like the down on his forearms. "Did they come from me?"

Pearson nodded. "Yes, from inside your lesion. They're fibres of some kind. At first I thought they were just bits of cotton from the dressing that had got trapped in the scab, but no; these are not cotton. Look at the colours. That one's pink; there's one that's blue, and... My God! Are they moving? Am I imagining that?"

Gina bent over and examined the wad. "No, they are moving. They look like little worms or something." She sounded worried. The tiny filaments from Brendan's wound were arching and writhing like something alive.

"What's wrong with me?"

Dr Pearson paused and shook his head. "I'm afraid I don't know... Can I take another look at the lesion, Brendan?" After a few more minutes with the tweezers, Pearson had recovered a dozen more of the mysterious strands. He also found what looked like a miniscule fragment of green glass and a stubby piece of copper wire.

"Bren, we'd better take you to Dr Flynn this afternoon." said Clane. "I'll make an appointment for straight after school."

"I don't think Brendan should travel today." interjected Dr Pearson immediately.

"But he has to go to school." This was a Monday morning and the Quilley family planned to leave Africa around eleven AM. Because of the time difference they would arrive home exactly when Brendan would normally be heading for school.

"I know, but..." Pearson sighed. "Under the circumstances, considering we don't know what his condition is, it's best that he doesn't move around too much... I mean, for all I know this could be contagious."

Gina gasped. "Terry, are you saying you intend to put my son into quarantine?"

"Not formally, but it is my strong recommendation that Brendan stays put for now... It is my duty as a physician to prevent anything that has the potential to infect from doing so, especially across international borders."

Everybody in the room fell into shocked silence. Brendan felt his heart thumping in his chest. "Am I going to be alright?"

Pearson chuckled. "Yes, you'll be fine, Brendan. I promise I'll take very good care of you... First thing I need to do is call the hospital. You guys all go get breakfast; I'll be in my study for a while."

Mrs Pearson brewed coffee and served everybody cereal and fruit. There was a subdued atmosphere at the kitchen table, although Dave was cheered by the prospect of his beloved friend not leaving when he was due to. An hour later Dr Pearson joined them. He had his slate with him and he read from it as he spoke. "I've been doing some reviews of the literature and I can't find anything in recent journals that matches Brendan's symptoms. However, I remember reading a strange story long ago, way back in medical school, and I've managed to track it down again. It's a very old report, three hundred years old in fact, and it's by an English doctor called Sir Thomas Browne. He describes a terrible dermatitis suffered by infants around two years old in southern France. He called it *Morgellons*. These days it's thought to have probably been just simple scabies, but it included fibres a bit like those in Brendan's lesion."

"You mean our son has caught a three hundred year old French skin disease?" asked Clane.

Pearson shrugged. "It may not be the same pathology, but the symptoms are similar."

That afternoon Dr Pearson drove Brendan to Bawku Regional Hospital in his ground car. His parents accompanied him. Clane spent the journey talking on his roam to Siobhan, explaining what had happened. Seeing as he was a senior doctor there, Pearson quickly arranged a series of tests for Brendan. Brendan was X-rayed, made to run a treadmill, had blood taken, was made to urinate into a plastic pot, was made to spit into another and had lights shone in his eyes and ears. The doctors and nurses who did the tests were all local people; they were kind and accommodating. His parents stayed with him for every stage of the examination. Then they all went and sat in a waiting room while the doctors processed the results. An elderly lady served them with tea and coffee. An hour passed, then two. Luckily there were plenty of books to read and Brendan had a long talk with his parents. Outside the waiting room hospital staff walked to-and-fro; nobody paid them any attention. "How long are they going to be?" moaned Clane. A few minutes after he spoke some commotion began in the clinic outside the waiting room. They heard urgent raised voices and then the sound of footsteps as people all hastily exited. The door to the waiting room flew open and five men entered. They were all clad in white plastic overalls like a police forensic team. They wore goggles over their eyes, Wellingtons on their feet, and masks over their noses and mouths like painters' masks. Despite this, Brendan recognized one of the men as Dr Pearson. "Brendan." Pearson said sharply. "I'll need you to come with me right away."

Brendan instinctively got to his feet at the doctor's urgent tone. His parents copied him.

"No!" the doctor held up his hand. "Sorry, Clane, Gina. Not you."

"What!?" shrilled Gina.

"What the fuck's going on, Terry!?" demanded Clane.

"I'll explain everything soon. " said Pearson. "But you must stay here now; please!... Come on, Brendan; let's go."

....

Brendan awoke instantly; dawn was just breaking outside the window. He was alert very quickly, as was normal for him, and climbed out of his cot with ease. The other children in the dormitory were all still fast asleep; their snores washed around the room from their bunk beds, barely audible above the dry, cold blast of the air vents. The canned and processed air flowed through the room, cooling his body. He walked over to the window and laid his hand on the pane. The hard transparent plastic felt much warmer to the touch than glass. The window was thick, hermetically sealed and very strong. The view was simple and restricted; he could see the rooftops of neighbouring buildings in Fort Detrick. Winter was here and the morning was a chilly one; frost glinted on the drainpipes and skylights in the breaking sun. He suddenly longed to feel cold air on his cheeks, to blink snowflakes from his eyes. That moment, as that thought passed through his mind, he felt the presence. It had happened a few times since he had been at Fort Detrick. "Indian?" he breathed. He didn't dare turn round; he knew he would see nothing and feared renewed disappointment. However, he could feel the Indian's presence. He couldn't see him, hear his voice or feel his hands, but he simply sensed him. It was a new kind of perception that he had not had before his incarceration. Rather than swinging round and staring, this time Brendan simply whispered: "Thank you, Indian. Thank you for being with me."

The other children were aroused soon after and they all trooped casually into the dining room for breakfast. Food was good at Fort Detrick and Brendan had also made a few friends. School time began soon afterwards and this took place in a room full of desks where the children all sat in front of consoles and slates. Brendan was connected to his classroom thirty miles away in Rockville, Maryland by a camera and microphone on the Mesh via the Mootster app. The other children, who came from all over North America, were similarly linked to theirs. Brendan had become used to this kind of remote interaction and so had his teachers and classmates. However, he could see the backs of Henry's and Charlie's heads, sitting behind their desks; and he wished he could sit beside his friends and talk to them face-to-face. After school they had to see the doctors. The doctors, as always, examined him behind windows with holes in. The holes were covered by long rubber gloves which the doctors put their hands through so that they could treat their patients safely. This originally frightened Brendan, but now he was used to it; like he had become used to so much else that he originally found weird. He now had four extra Morgellons lesions along with the original one on his shoulder; two on his legs, one on his forehead and one on his bottom. Brendan's favourite part of the day was around six PM when he received a visit from his family. This happened every evening. They had not missed a single day since Brendan had been admitted two months earlier. Luckily Fort Detrick was close to home, but his mother had once told him tearfully that she would have regularly visited him if he'd been at the North Pole. Brendan sat in the visitors' booth in front of the window, another hard plastic airtight window like all the others that separated him from the outside world. On the other side was a similar booth with a number of chairs. His mother and father were there every day; and every three or four days Siobhan would appear with William and Colleen. He had also had visits from his grandparents, uncles, aunts and other relatives. Today it was just his parents. They walked in with big smiles on their faces. Gina pressed her pursed lips to the window and Brendan did the same on the other side at the same place; an inch of armoured synthetics lay between their kiss. "Hi, son. How are you today?" asked Clane; his voice came through the speakers on the wall.

Brendan put his mouth close to the microphone to prevent feedback. "I'm okay, dad. How are you guys?"

"Will asked after you. He cried because he couldn't come and see you today."

"When can he come?"

"Siobhan promised to bring them both over tomorrow."

"Cool."

There was a moment's silence; then Clane said: "I don't know how much TV they let you watch in this place, but you're pretty famous out here."

"Like you are, dad." Brendan laughed.

"Like I was." Clane was happy to see his son cheerful. "You are officially Patient Zero."

"What does that mean?"

"You're the first person in the world to catch Morgellons disease."

"So that old name has stuck?"

"Terry is really pissed off it wasn't named 'Pearson's disease' after him... God, aren't docs a mother lode of ego?"

Brendan paused. "When can I get out of here?"

Gina looked pained at her son's distress. "Soon, honey. Very soon."

"Before Christmas?"

She hesitated. "Yes, Brendan; before Christmas."

Clane sat back and glared at her in alarm and annoyance. "We hope." he added swiftly, changing his expression to a smile as he addressed his son.

Brendan's heart sank. "I've been stuck in here two months now."

"I wish you didn't have to be, Bren." said Clane. "It's the government who want to keep you here... I don't know why; Morgellons can't be catching otherwise the family would all have it, and we haven't had a spot."

"It's because it's unknown." said Gina. "It could be something the Roswell aliens had in their bodies or whatnot."

"It could be at risk of infecting the whole earth." put in Clane.

Brendan forced himself to nod. At the end of the visit, his mother once again kissed him through the event horizon of the containment pane and then Brendan walked around the limits of his compound, deep in thought. The sealed enclave that he had been in, his whole world since September, consisted of a dozen rooms with thin corridors between them. It was about the size of his elementary school. Nothing came in or went out without being thoroughly vetted and processed. Air, food, water, sewage; all were filtered, distilled, irradiated, disinfected, scanned, sealed and burned. The containment facility had been built at Fort Detrick as a contingency in the pre-Disclosure age to provide a place to care for patients in the event of an outbreak of a new disease. Now, in the post-Disclosure world, this had finally happened. Brendan had arrived there direct from when he had been apprehended by Dr Pearson and his colleagues in the Volta Union. They had driven him to an airport where a fixed-wing jet aircraft of the VU air forces was idling. This had flown directly to Andrews Army Air Field and from there he was taken to Fort

Detrick in a sealed van. He had been alone for the first few days, but then had been joined by a handful of other youths, aged about eight to sixteen. Dozens more joined them in the following two weeks until the compound was full. Since then nothing had changed. Brendan secretly feared he might never be allowed to leave and would have to live the rest of his life in this bubble.

The following morning was a Saturday and Brendan received a visit from Kerry, a young woman who was friends with Siobhan. She was one of a number of people who had been born in secret government facilities and had been grown through genetic engineering. It gave her strange facial features, although Brendan was now used to them. "It'll be alright, Brendan." she told him in her peculiar voice with its off-British accent. "You'll be out of here soon."

"How can you be so sure, Kerry?"

"I just know." She shrugged. It was typical of her. She seemed to have inexplicable insights like this all the time. Therefore Brendan's surprise was somewhat truncated when the following morning after breakfast he felt his ears pop. The other children all looked up; they must also have sensed the sudden change in air pressure. A man they'd never seen before walked into the room. After two months of isolation a newcomer caused as much astonishment as the appearance of a ghost. The man was middle aged and dressed in an army uniform. "Okay, kids." he said. "Quarantine is lifted; you're free to go. We've called your parents and they're on their way to pick you up." Brendan walked out into the corridor in a daze. The pressure door which made up the main entrance was open. It had been like part of the wall for the last nine weeks after being shut behind him when he arrived. He felt like it was the hidden door to a secret passage. Fresh, cold air hit him in the face and made him gasp. He walked down a passageway where a hundred smells flooded his nose. A door leading to the outside was ahead and he opened it. Beyond it was the open air. He felt dizzy and terrified at the vertiginous sight of the blue sky above him. An infinity of space lay above his head and he felt he might fall off the surface of the earth and plummet up into it at any moment. The light November breeze buffeted him like a hurricane; birdsong rattled his skull and his skin puckered from the chill. The buildings of Fort Detrick lay around him as huge and distant as planets in space. Behind him he heard an anguished wail. He walked back inside and heard the sound again; it was coming from the containment facility. He walked up to the pressure door and looked it; he didn't dare step through from subconscious fear that it would close behind him again. One of his friends, an eleven-year-old Canadian boy called Farid, was lying on the floor kicking and screaming. He was clutching the leg of one of the dining tables, which was screwed down to the floor. "I'm not leaving!" he wept. "I can't leave!... Go away and let me stay here!"

The embrace of Brendan's parents was the most sensual experience of his life. He cried in his mother's arms, and his father's arms. The touch of their skin and the smell of their bodies were intoxicating. He had not felt such intense love for them since he was ten years younger. As the family drove out of the gates of Fort Detrick in their ground car a large number of news reporters were there; TV cameras followed them as they turned off the drive. "What's going on?" asked Brendan. "Why have we been let out now?"

"The government have found out the truth about Morgellons." answered Clane.

"Can it be cured then?" asked Brendan hopefully.

"Yup, although it's not a medical procedure."

"How come?"

"Because Morgellons is not a disease, as such, it's something that's been put into the world."

Brendan frowned.

"There's a news special on TV tonight all about it." said his mother, sensing her son's confusion. "It turns out there was more to the chemtrails than we thought."

Brendan knew about chemtrails from his classes at school. Before Disclosure the Illuminati had filled the earth's atmosphere with toxic vapour to keep their true reptilian form hidden from human perception. The post-Disclosure chemtrail programme, what some people called "lifetrails", were a continuation of that, but only so that the earth didn't suffer a shock from it ending too abruptly. They were being reduced slowly, year by year.

"The chemtrails served another purpose too." said Clane. "They contained a new kind of microbe that the Loomies planned to infect every living thing on earth with. It's something they had bred in their laboratories underground, like the ones at Area 51."

"Like germs?" asked Brendan.

"Kind of." Gina picked up the narrative as if she and her husband had been rehearsing it. "But this was a new form of life, not like any living on earth today. It's more like something from another planet... Maybe it is. It could be a germ that came down with one of the crashed flying saucers. That's where they got it from."

"It doesn't really matter where it's from." continued Clane. "The Loomies decided to use it on us."

"Why?" asked Brendan.

"Nobody knows. We're going through their classified documents on the subject; so far we haven't found anything relating to a motive."

"So... I've caught this disease."

"No, we all have."

The car was standing at traffic lights. Both his parents looked over their shoulders at him from the front seats. Their faces wore the same sombre expression. Brendan realized that they were very frightened. "What do you mean 'we all have'?"

They hesitated; the traffic started moving again. "It's inside us all." said Clane. "The coloured fibres, the bits of glass, the metallic structures. We've all been infected... everybody who has been tested so far that is."

"I did the wine test." said Gina. "It's a way of checking for it at home. You take a sip of red wine and wash it round your mouth; then you spit it into a dish and the Morgellons strands appear... They did. It's been found in animals too; pets, farm livestock, wild animals. It's in plants too; it's in everything. This is the opposite of normal diseases; usually most people don't have them and those that do experience symptoms. With Morgellons it's the other way round. Everybody has it and doesn't know and those who get sick, like you did, Brendan; they're the ones whose immune system is fighting back against it. You developed your skin problems because your body is rejecting the infection... You're one of the lucky ones." She chuckled ironically.

Clane remained serious. "The reason you've been let out is because the government have found an antidote. Once we understood the project the Illuminati were undertaking we began work on a cure based on the same technology. It wasn't easy; we've had to create our own form of... 'pseudo-life' they call it. One that destroys the Illuminati pseudo-life and then destroys itself afterwards. We've had to back-engineer their medicine in the same way we've back-engineered their machinery... The TV special tonight will explain everything."

"So what's going to happen to me?" asked Brendan. "Are the doctors planning on injecting this... pseudo-life into me?"

"No. It's a bit more complicated than that. They have to inject it into all of us; into everything. Remember, all life on earth has been contaminated by this Illuminati pseudo-life."

"How can they do that?"

"By renewing the lifetrail programme... The pre-Disclosure chemtrail programme was the delivery method for the pseudo-life, so we must now use the same method to deliver the antidote."

"Will that cure my Morgellons?"

"Eventually."

"It could take a long time." said Gina.

"When it clears up that will probably be a sign that the lifetrails are working." added Clane brightly. He then added pensively: "Also, this kind of new tech could result in a breakthrough in medical advancement. Science is morally neutral; it can be used for either good or bad, depending on who's using it..."

Brendan looked out of the car window up at the sky. The blue firmament above the fluffy clouds was crosshatched with white lines. He could just make out the black specks of the aircraft depositing the haze of nourishment thousands of feet above him. He reached under his collar to feel his shoulder and his fingers rubbed against the plaster the doctors had put over his original Morgellons lesion, from behind the safety glass with their gloves. It began to itch again.

Chapter 7

Brendan was dozing and dreams began blending with his waking thoughts. A scene from his memory played out in his head. It was from three years earlier when he had just been released from the quarantine centre at Fort Detrick. He was watching his Canadian friend, Farid, kicking and yelling as the staff tried to remove him from the compound. *"I'm not leaving! I can't leave! Go away and let me stay here!"* Brendan jerked fully awake as he felt a hand on his shoulder. He looked up to see Crocker frowning at him from under the peak of his hardhat. He smiled apologetically and the old Bahamian smiled back. Brendan made a show of gazing very attentively at the panel of gauges of which it was his job to monitor. He had already been reprimanded for dropping off to sleep on duty once before. Crocker's full name was Beasley Alvin Crocker, but he insisted on always being addressed as Crocker, even by Brendan who was so much younger than him. Brendan adjusted his earmuffs and mopped the sweat off his cheeks as it dripped down from under his own hardhat. Even after almost two weeks he had not acclimatized to the temperature in the ship's engine room. An hour later there was a change of watch and another technician came to relieve Crocker and what the ship's company insisted on calling "the cabin boy". Brendan didn't mind the nickname; it made him feel like he belonged to the crew. He and Crocker went to the mess for a cup of coffee and then took a stroll on deck. A warm Pacific breeze was blowing and the ship's flag snapped at the top of its mast; the flag of the League of the World Earth Healing Organization complete with its aphorism "*IT'S NOT TOO LATE*". A hint of blue still washed through the mesh of lifetrails in the sky. The sun was a dimmed blob of yellow haze behind the vapour. Brendan still had not got used to this new kind of daylight even though it was now normal all over the world since the lifetrail operations had increased. "Dunno how long this will go on for." muttered Crocker, as if reading Brendan's thoughts. His black face creased into a scowl as he looked up at the heavens through his thick glasses. "The Loh-Wee-Oh keeps all its details to itself."

"Thirty or forty years I hear." Brendan copied his dour tone. He reached under his shirt and felt his most recent Morgellons lesion. It was almost healed; it had stopped itching and was covered with a thick, comfortable scab. His condition had improved slowly but steadily over the years. "I'm better already. Isn't that a sign that it's worked already?"

"On the surface it looks like it, but... Ah, I guess they have to drag it out by its deepest roots to make sure the whole weed is gone." replied Crocker with one of his usual metaphors.

Brendan nodded. The deck of the LoWS *Belleau Wood*, formerly USS *Belleau Wood*, was a flat oblong with a superstructure starboard side amidships, revealing the ship's original purpose as a light aircraft carrier. It had been refitted for its current purpose and the flight deck was now covered with a huge mound lashed down under a tarpaulin. The mound consisted of hundreds of tons of plastic litter that had been gathered from the sea. The storage spaces below decks were stocked with more of the rubbish. *Belleau Wood*'s mission was to help clean up what had become known as the "Great Pacific Garbage Patch". There were half a dozen of such patches in the world's oceans. They were caused by plastic flotsam dropped into the sea being washed by ocean currents until they gathered in the centre of an orbiting gyre current to create a vast floating slurry of rubbish that, left to its own devices, would take centuries to break down. In the meantime they caused a terrible hazard to wildlife and leached toxic chemicals into the food chain. As part of the Dubai Treaty of 1960, the League of the World Earth Healing Organization had begun an operation to cleanse the oceans of these millions of tons of discarded plastic fragments, from microscopic slivers to large items such as beer crates and fishing nets. The rubbish was gathered by a series of long traps called slat-booms that were spread out like artificial islands in the current. These were secured in place by sea-anchors two thousand feet deep while the fast moving gyre of the upper water column flowed through nets secured to the crescent-shaped booms. Here the plastic waste could be gathered and collected by ships. *Belleau Wood* had spent the previous two weeks visiting each of the booms and scooping up the captured rubbish. She would then transport it to the shore where it could be safely and cleanly disposed of. As a tenth grade high school student, Brendan was given the option of a vocational holiday during the summer break and had eagerly signed up with the LoWEHO's ocean cleanup team. When he joined the crew of the LoWS *Belleau Wood* his first response was deep disappointment and frustration. One of the reasons he wanted to go to sea was to work with Schauberger coils, the principle post-Disclosure marine engine. He had assumed without checking in advance that the LoWEHO would be using a shiny new Schauberger-powered vessel straight off the slipway; he never imagined they would convert some old US Navy rust-bucket for such an important task. He had fallen in love with Schauberger's designs since his visit to the Pismo Beach waterworks and wanted nothing more than to work with them. Yet as soon as he stepped aboard *Belleau Wood* he felt his spirits rise. He was introduced to Crocker, who supervised him for the entire voyage, and the two of them developed an immediate rapport. Crocker was the head artificer of the engine room today, but he had also been with the ship since she was built. He had been her chief engineer since her launch and sailed with her all through World War II. After she was decommissioned he had been part of the preservation team who helped maintain her; they originally planned to turn her into a floating museum. When the old aircraft carrier was sold to the League of the World he had worked in the yards while they refitted her and now returned to sea with her for her new mission. On Brendan's first day aboard, while the ship was moored in San Diego, Crocker had given him a complete tour of the vessel. The old man became sombre as they walked to the aft of the flight deck. He pointed to a patch of steel which was a slightly different colour to the rest; and lines of irregular welding were clearly visible. "This was where we fixed her after the attack." he explained. "We were hit by a kamikaze in forty-four. He struck us here while our group was patrolling east of Leyte. Ninety-two men died." He began weeping. Even after almost twenty-five years, the heartache of that moment had not left him. Brendan put a hand on his shoulder and comforted the man he had only just met. Over the next few days Crocker diligently and passionately educated his young charge in the wonders of *Belleau Wood*'s antiquated steam turbines. The ship had a hefty set of four trains that filled the cavernous engine rooms.

To Brendan's surprise he soon began to understand the old man's enthusiasm. The engines had been slightly modernized, some of the controls and instrumentation had been upgraded; but the pipes, pressurizers, boilers and condensers were in their original 1940's form. He stood rapt while Crocker and his team started up the trains, one at a time; lighting the boilers, opening the throttles, warming the turbogenerators, tuning the array of pumps, impellors, fuel lines, reduction gears, telegraphs and servomotors. When the engines were up and running they had the capacity to deliver ten thousand horsepower to the four propeller shafts; this could drive the huge vessel at thirty-two knots. "That would never be allowed these days." lamented Crocker wistfully. "I do wish, one day far out at sea, the skipper would really open her; that would be fun." As the ship got underway and departed San Diego, the only sensation the engineers had that told them they had put to sea was the rocking motion of the decks. Brendan thought for a moment whether he would rather have been topside, watching the departure with his own eyes, but then decided that he wouldn't have missed being in the engine room for the world. Now it was two weeks later and the following day the ship would return to its berth at San Diego. Then Brendan's stint aboard would be over. This thought saddened him. He had become accustomed to life on the waves with *Belleau Wood* and her crew. It would be particularly difficult to part with Crocker; the old sailor had become a surrogate father to him. However as soon as the ship was close enough to land to pick up a roam signal Brendan received a friendly text from Heather McManus and that cheered him up.

He was standing on the forecastle watching the unbroken line of the horizon dissolve into the jagged headlands of the southern California coast when he heard some commotion behind him. Some of the crew were gathered round the berm of rubbish lying across the deck. He walked over. "What's going on?" The men were all staring hard at a section of the cargo that poked out from underneath the tarpaulin.

"Look." One of them pointed at a clump of rotten shopping bags. There was a patch of oil on it that glistened in the sunlight. It looked as if somebody had spilled it onto the clump from a can.

"What about it?"

"It's moving."

"Eh?" Sure enough the oil was changing shape and flowing upwards against the force of gravity; it looked like an inverted film of a natural downward flow.

"What the hell is that?"

"Dunno." A few minutes later one of the officers came over to see what was going on. There was not much time to deliberate because the ship was nearing San Diego and so he ordered everybody to their harbour stations. After the ship docked Brendan was torn by two separate emotions as he said goodbye to Crocker and his other friends in the crew of *Belleau Wood*'s company. The crew assembled to say farewell and Crocker embraced him. The captain shook his hand and wished him luck. At that moment Brendan had every intention of dropping out of high school and joining the LoWEHO as an ordinary seaman, and he said as much. "Wait and see how you feel in a year or two, Brendan." said the captain with an affectionate grin. His other emotion ripped into his being as he descended the gangway, sparing him the full anguish of his parting. It was the text from Heather that he had yet to reply to. It filled him with excitement. As he walked across the quay away from the ship he looked over his shoulder when he heard raised voices. A group of people dressed in hazmat clothing were running aboard the ship. He wondered if it was something to do with the strange moving oil that had appeared on some of the plastic rubbish, but the images of Heather in his mind consumed his thoughts and he did not look back again.

Brendan walked along the seafront boulevard of San Diego to Lindbergh Field where fixed-wing airliners still departed regularly, although this service had greatly reduced now that so many people had flyers. He caught a plane for Detroit and was pleased to see it was one of the older and faster jets, not a newer propeller-driven one with Digby Carrousel engines. It was understandable that airlines were keen to introduce Digby-powered aeroplanes because they needed no fuel and so could compete economically with antigravity aircraft, but they were achingly slow by modern standards; their cruise speed being barely a third of a jet airliner. However they appealed to the growing market of traditionalists, mostly elderly retired people, who enjoyed long journeys and were unnerved by the rapidity of modern travel. A few people looked at Brendan curiously; it was unusual to see a boy his age, fifteen, travelling alone. Their gazes thrilled Brendan and made him feel grown up. The jet touched down seven hours later at Detroit Metro Airport and the passengers decamped. Siobhan was not in the arrivals hall to meet him as she promised, but when he switched on his roam there was a text from her: "*Bren, I'm at the GM building. Take a cab.*" Luckily he had enough cash for the seventeen mile journey. He felt annoyed at his sister for neglecting him like that, but had become used to it; she had been behaving strangely over the last few weeks. It was a moist August day and light rain was falling in waves between dry lighter spells. The headquarters of General Motors was a mighty cluster of interlinked skyscrapers on the riverside directly facing Windsor, Canada; as if the United States were bragging at its more modest northern neighbour. As the taxi pulled up, Brendan saw that there was a large crowd of people on a side street beside the complex. Police bollards had closed the road. A column of about twenty shiny new cars had been parked along the road and the people were walking around them and examining them; some were dressed in formal suits. There were a few television cameras and news reporters among them and one of them was Siobhan. She had a stills camera and was taking photographs of the scene. She waved and smiled as she saw her brother. "Hi, Brendan." She kissed his cheek.

"What's going on here?"

"These are all Chevy Malibus; the last of their line."

"Why the big party." Brendan gestured at all the people.

"These cars are IC's, the last IC's to be made anywhere in the world."

"Really?"

"Yeah. It's kind of the end of an era. From now on only Digbies and flyers will be produced."

Brendan approached the Chevrolets. The one at the front had its bonnet open and, as always, Brendan felt the urge to see its engine. He looked down under the bonnet; there were caps on the spark plugs and the camshafts, but he knew what lay beneath them. He quickly found the radiator, the lubrication oil tank, the fan, the carburettor. Maybe it was the time he had spent on board the old ship, but he had developed sentimental feelings for old and obsolete machines. He overheard one of the engineers talking nearby and his words were reassuring: "I'm sure internal combustion engines will continue to be made. There's always a market for craftsmen who like traditional engineering and want to maintain it. Hell, there are guys even still building tall sailing ships! All today means is GM will no longer mass-produce them..."

Siobhan beckoned Brendan over. "I have to pick the twins up from kindergarten. Want to join me?"

"Yeah sure."

They flew to Maryland in silence for the first part of the twenty minute journey. As Siobhan slowed her flyer during its descent she said spontaneously: "I'm thinking of writing a book."

"Hey cool." answered Brendan. "What about?"

"Something real. I don't want to write a novel. I am a journalist not a fiction writer. And now the twins are in school I've got a lot more spare time, even though I've gone back to work."

"What's the real story you want to write about?"

She paused and then spoke awkwardly. "What if I were to tell you... that the MFO's are abducting people?"

"Abducting?... you mean like kidnapping them?"

Siobhan nodded. "Not permanently... well not very often permanently... usually only for short periods, a few hours; after which they return the people to where they found them."

"Are you sure?"

"Yes, I've looked into all kinds of psychological explanations for what the abductees report and none of it fits. That's what my book will be about."

"But you've never written a book before."

She chuckled. "Neither has anybody before they write their first book."

"Do you know how to do it?"

She shrugged. "I've been writing news articles all my life; shouldn't be too hard to learn to write something a bit longer."

He paused as the flyer slowed down above the rooftops of Rockville. "What's it like to be abducted by an MFO."

"Well, the aliens appear, usually when you're in bed; and you can't move, can't escape them... What's going on?" She leaned forward and stared out of the windscreen as the school came into view. "They're out early." The playground outside the elementary school was full of frolicking children. Their parents stood in a line beside the gate to meet them; flyers circled the building like wasps. "Shit! Kindergarten's not supposed to end for another five minutes." She hastily landed and they trotted over to the school gate. "Where are they? I can't see Will and Coll." Siobhan became seriously worried and left Brendan's side to question the other parents. "Excuse me, have you seen my children?" she asked several of them. Then she then ran over to one of the teachers and they had a conversation which Brendan was too far away to hear. Then Siobhan raised her voice. "You did *what*!?... Jesus H Christ, I'm their mother!"

The teacher appeared to be protesting her innocence in a calmer tone.

"I don't care! You had no way of knowing who she was! You should never hand my children over to anybody except me! Only *me*! Do you understand, goddamnit!?" Siobhan then whipped out her roam and yelled something inaudible down it. Then she marched back to the gate. "Bren, get in the flyer; we're going home now!"

Siobhan's face was pink with rage and she flew too fast on the thirty-second hop from the school to their home. Brendan knew a big row was coming. This disappointed him because he had missed his parents while he was away at sea and was anticipating a cheery reunion. As soon as the flyer landed, William and Colleen ran out to greet their mother. Gina Quilley stood between them smiling and waving at Brendan. Her expression changed as she saw her daughter marching towards her. Siobhan turned to Brendan and gave him a silent glare that he understood immediately. He stayed out of the house and sat in the garden. Clane took the twins down the road to the park with a look on his face that was similar to how Brendan felt. The shrilling tirades of Siobhan and her mother echoed through the open lounge windows. Brendan was not afraid it would result in physical violence; but by the end of the argument, which would be in about quarter of an hour, both women would be in tears and would not speak to each other for at least five days. The meal that evening was as tense as a bowstring; Siobhan and her mother sat at opposite ends of the table ignoring each other. Clane made a pretence of talking cheerfully and Brendan tried to help him. Over the course of the afternoon he had found out from his father what the dispute was all about. Gina had picked up William and Colleen from school and took them home. This was literally two minutes before Siobhan and Brendan had landed. However she had not asked Siobhan's permission to do this and had not informed her by roam that she was doing so.

Just before he went to bed he saw Siobhan sitting still and silent in the empty kitchen. He went up to her. "Are you okay now, Siobhan?" he asked.

She nodded sardonically. "Maybe I should have kept the apartment."

He put his arm around her shoulder. He was about the same size as her now.

"Families!" she hissed and tittered. "We all need them, but... at the same time..." She left the rest of the sentence unsaid.

....

Brendan woke in the middle of the night to find Siobhan tapping his shoulder. "Brendan." she whispered. "Wake up."

"What?"

"Get dressed. I need your help. And be quiet! Don't wake up mom and dad."

Brendan was not still quite awake as he pulled on his trousers and tied his shoelaces. He was not alert enough to question what his elder sister wanted him to do. She opened his bedroom door and beckoned him, then putting her finger on her lips to remind him to remain silent. William and Colleen were standing on the landing half asleep. They were still in their pyjamas and had blankets wrapped round their bodies. Siobhan led them all downstairs; she tip-toed as she walked. She opened the door to the garage and ushered them through. As soon as the twins were on the back seat of the flyer they flopped down and went back to sleep with the speed that only a small child can. The door to the garage was electric and folded upwards to open so it made some unavoidable noise. Siobhan gritted her teeth as it hummed. Brendan sat down in the front passenger seat and waited. As soon as the door was open Siobhan sat in the drivers' seat and started the engine. The flyer glided out of the garage and hurtled upwards into the sky. "Siobhan, what's going on?" asked Brendan. He looked at the glowing dashboard clock; it said twelve-fifty-five AM.

His sister looked sad. Her face was fresh and she clearly had not slept that night. "I'm not going to let mom take Will and Coll away from me."

"Take them away? What are you talking about?"

"That's what she's trying to do."

"No, surely not!"

"Then explain her behaviour! What she did today!"

Brendan didn't respond.

"Mom snatched my children from school! She flew in just before I did and took them home. She didn't tell me on purpose. She didn't tell me because she wanted to scare me. She wanted to show me that she has control over Will and Coll! It was an exercise of power!... For a few minutes I thought I had lost my children! I was scared some fucking madman had got hold of them!"

"Really?"

"It happens!... And mom *wanted* me to think that!"

He hesitated fearfully. "You hate mom don't you?"

She looked painfully at him. "Yes. I can't possibly feel anything else for somebody who treats me like this. Nobody could. The rules aren't different just 'cos she's my mom... She hates me far more than I hate her."

Brendan looked out of the window. The lights of the cities beneath them lessened abruptly as they passed over the River Mississippi. "Where are we going?"

"Australia."

"Australia!?"

"Yes... I need advice from... from Julian."

"Will and Coll's dad?"

"Yes... He needs to see them too. I'm not sure he even knows they exist. I've tried to contact him and gotten no reply. He may not even know he's a father... and Will and Coll need to meet their daddy."

"Why do you need my help?"

"Because... I might need you to give a message to mom and dad for me... if we don't come home."

His heart dropped out of his chest. "You mean... you're leaving us?"

In the dim lights of the dashboard he saw her eyes become more reflective as they filled with tears. "I might have to, for Will and Coll's sake."

The world below became completely dark as they headed out over the Pacific Ocean. A while later the horizon ahead began to glow. The sun rose and shone through the windscreen; Siobhan and Brendan lowered the sunshades. William and Colleen continued to sleep peacefully. When a phone-call alert rang out from the dashboard application it made everybody in the flyer jump. "Who is it?" asked Brendan.

"Dad!" She looked over her shoulder out of the back window.

"Are you going to answer it?"

"No!... He must have heard us leave. He might be following us." She pushed the throttle forward to increase the flyer's speed. A coastline appeared ahead and Siobhan began to bring the vehicle lower. It was early evening in eastern Australia; the journey had taken them just under two hours. A light green landscape cruised past beneath the chassis. It was a fine evening with high light cloud. Suddenly there was a loud alarm from the navigation panel. "Shit!"

"What's up?"

"It says we're entering restricted airspace... There's an emergency shortwave radio channel here and it says I've got to call it immediately."

"What happens if you don't?"

"Don't know. They might shoot us down."

Brendan gulped.

She pressed the console. "Hello, SRA Air Command, this is Siobhan Quilley from the United States of America. I have an urgent personal message for Julian Spencer, an official of the SRA government. I request permission to land in Canberra and be given an audience with him."

There was a pause of over a minute then a male voice with a peculiar accent came on the speakers: "United States aircraft, this is SRA Air Command. Permission granted. Proceed on course two-six-nine for thirty-two miles until you are contacted by your escorts. Maintain current altitude and speed. Do not deviate from this flight plan."

She grinned and sighed with relief. "Understood." A few minutes later two helicopters approached them from the north. They banked behind the flyer and accelerated until they took position on either flank. Siobhan followed them cautiously. They looked like military gunships and were probably armed. Brendan suddenly realized that with all the haste and anxiety of the last twelve hours he had forgotten about his text from Heather. He took out his roam but it could pick up no signal. Below them was a city of white buildings all arranged in the form of a new town; an observably planned road layout of circles, hexagons and straight lines. The helicopters stooped downwards and Siobhan pushed the pitch lever forward on the flyer to mimic their actions. The two gunships came to rest on a concrete apron, touching down simultaneously like a well rehearsed dance pair. Siobhan took the hint and brought the flyer down between them. As she shut down the spinning disk engines a posse of five men walked swiftly over towards the flyer. They were badly dressed and rough looking; and they were all heavily armed. Yet they carried their rifles in slings across their chests and their sidearms in buttoned holsters; and they had smiles on their faces. Siobhan roused the twins and the family stepped out of the flyer. "Gentlemen." said Siobhan. "I'm Siobhan Quilley. I need to speak urgently to Julian Spencer."

"Come with us, luv." one of them replied and they pointed towards a minibus that was parked at the edge of the apron. Siobhan, Brendan and the twins sat on the back seats of the minibus while the armed men sat in front of them. One of them took the driver's seat and started the rumbling IC engine. Brendan noticed the vibration immediately; it was quite palpable, as if the engine was in poor condition. Indeed a cloud of grey smoke blew over the vehicle from the exhaust pipe. Brendan was about to tell the man sitting nearest to him that he had a leaking cylinder gasket, but instinctively stopped himself. Even though the men had been friendly so far they still had guns. "These guys remind me of Roger's Raiders." whispered Siobhan.

"Who?"

"Some men I knew at college."

The minibus drove down a long straight road with trees on either side. Eventually they entered a nearly spaced-out city with low-lying white buildings and grassy public areas between them. Some of the buildings were more modern and made of large square blocks of undressed concrete, an architectural style that had become popular in the 1960's. Despite being modern, the city had a dishevelled ambiance. The windows were all grimy, the grass was overgrown and full of weeds, litter blew along the pavements in the breeze. The minibus bumped over potholes several times. The road was busy with cars and trucks, but these were also in a poor state of maintenance and were all IC's. Rust streaks and black road dust covered the vehicles. A lot of them were smoking too and this created a stench that was everywhere in the city. They came to a major junction and a traffic jam built up behind some red lights. The motorists were impatient and sounded their horns. They cursed the other drivers whom they blamed for the slow movement of the traffic. "Get out of the way, you fucken drongo!" one of them yelled.

"You wait your turn, stupid cunt!" the other responded, raising his middle finger out of the window. Eventually the queue of cars shuffled forward and they entered a roundabout. After they had turned off it they crossed a wide bridge over a large river or lake. The shores of the lake were parkland, but some of it appeared to have been turned into small allotments. People were walking back and forth digging and hoeing patches of soil. The sun was setting behind distant hills. The minibus reached the other side and then turned right onto a driveway through a copse of trees. The drive ended outside a sprawling, stripped neoclassical building. Its walls were white, but like everything else in the city, it was faded and neglected. A few of the windows were broken. A polished metal signboard sported the words: *Parliament of the Socialist Republic of Australia*. A pole next to it displayed a bright red flag with a yellow five-pointed star on the left side and five smaller stars on the right arranged like the constellation *Crux Australis*. A number of people, mostly male, were clustered around the entrance to the building in a casual manner, like teenagers on a street corner. Everybody was dressed in a similar way to their escorts. Despite this being a seat of government, Brendan couldn't see anybody wearing a suit or uniform. The closest to a uniform were military berets with red star badges that a couple of them wore. Siobhan tittered as they left the minibus and walked up the pathway to the entrance. "Just come back from an office outing?" she muttered. They had to weave round some cars that were parked haphazardly across the driveway. Brendan noticed that they had not yet seen a flyer. The city seemed to consist entirely of ground vehicles. A few aircraft had passed over their heads, but these were all helicopters or fixed-wings. Also there were no lifetrails at all and the sky was a beautiful deep blue that he had not seen for years at home; it eased the squalor of the urban landscape around him. "Hey, Bruce!" yelled the minibus driver. "Is the boss in?"

"Yeah, he's in Central at the mo, I think." The man replying had a huge filthy beard and a leather sunhat on his head. For some reason the hat had a set of corks suspended from strings at regular intervals around the edge of the brim. "Who are these folks?"

"Yanks. They just flew here."

"Hmm." Bruce glared at them curiously through his plastic sunglasses.

Colleen and William stared back at him fearfully, clutching each of their mother's arms.

The interior of the parliament building was also cluttered and grubby. Cardboard boxes of books, files and folders were piled up against the walls. Several waste paper baskets were overflowing. There was a patio door leading to a courtyard where another group of people were cooking meat on a barbecue. Brendan and his family were taken down a corridor to a door labelled *Central Committee Meeting Room* and his escorts went in without knocking. The centrepiece of the room was a broad conference table with a red leather top; however the top was almost completely obscured by ashtrays, empty beer cans, piles of papers, pens and older generation matchbook computers. The place smelled of cigarettes and coffee, and there were stained mugs dotted around. Many of the papers had brown rings on them, denoting the previous locations the mugs had been placed. Along with the mandatory piles of cardboard boxes against their skirting, the walls had gilt framed photographs, portraits of people. Brendan recognized two of them as Vladimir Lenin and Karl Marx. The windows were open and fresh air mixed with the chaotic miasma of administration. The light curtains rustled in the breeze. About half the seats at the table were filled and Brendan saw his sister scan the faces nervously, hoping to find the man she was looking for, but he wasn't there. A middle-aged man sitting at the head of the table got to his feet. Even by the standards of the Australian parliament, which eschewed formal office wear, this man was dishevelled. He was wearing a string vest, flip-flops and cut-off jeans. "G'day." he said in a nasal voice and the strange accent that everybody else in Australia spoke. "My name's John Pankhurst and I am the Prime Minister."

"Prime Minister." Siobhan nodded at him uncomfortably. "I'd like to speak to Julian Spencer please."

"I'm afraid Julian is not here."

"Where is he?"

"I don't know." he smiled. "Can I get you anything? Tea, coffee? We don't often have foreign guests these days."

A young woman to the Prime Minister's right stood up and reached behind her where a refrigerator stood. She brought out two cans and offered one to Brendan. "Wanna beer, mate?" She smiled at him sweetly. She had blonde hair shaved at the sides and large circular earrings.

Brendan took it, but his sister immediately snatched it out of his hand and put it down on the table.

"Stacey, he's just a kid." scolded Pankhurst.

"He's old enough to start I reckon." She winked at Brendan flirtatiously.

"Mr Prime Minister!" interrupted Siobhan. "I need to speak to Julian as soon as possible."

"Why?"

Siobhan pushed William and Colleen forward. "These are his children!... I've tried to contact him directly; I've sent him

E-grams, I've tried to phone him, I've mailed letters here to be passed to him and he has not replied... What's so funny?"

The officials around the table were chuckling and exchanging glances as if sharing a private joke.

"What's so funny?" Siobhan repeated in a more irritable tone.

"We're just wondering what took you so long and why you're the only one in the queue." answered Pankhurst in a mocking tone. His colleagues all laughed loudly.

"What do you mean?" Siobhan's lip trembled as she spoke.

"It's just that we have no doubt Julian has plenty of kids; he's got them all over the world and he knows nothing about any of them."

Siobhan didn't reply. Her cheeked bloomed and she blinked back tears.

"Julian's got a bit of a reputation with the ladies. He likes to put it around a lot. He's a good-looking young guy, posh Pommie accent; the girls really go for that."

Stacey guffawed. "All in the service of fraternal comradeship of course."

Brendan felt the pain of sympathy as he looked at his sister struggling not to weep. William and Colleen were still grasping their mother's arms for dear life and hiding their faces in her blouse.

Pankhurst and Stacey softened as they detected her distress. "No drama though." The Prime Minister pointed at the twins. "We're not saying that he wouldn't be interested to meet these two little 'uns. He's a principled man; he would definitely take care of them."

"We would never have achieved the revolution without him." said another man on the far side of the table. "He risked everything for us. He's a hero of the SRA."

Pankhurst and Stacey looked daggers at him. There were awkward glances around the table, as if the speaker had breached a taboo subject. "He's still a fucken Trot." growled another voice.

"Do any of you know where I can find him?" butted in Siobhan impatiently.

There was a long silence and the officials looked sheepish.

"We're not sure." said the Prime Minister. "He left us last year."

"Left you for where?"

"Last we heard of him he was in India. He went there to work with his mate Ernesto Guevara."

"It's 'cos he a Trot." added Stacey.

"A what?" Siobhan frowned.

She rolled her eyes. "A Trotskyist. A tendency that follows different theory to us."

"We're Marxist-Leninists of the Third International." explained Pankhurst. "However there are a minority of Marxists who split from us and decided to follow the theories of Leon Trotsky."

"Wasn't he killed?" asked Siobhan. "Somebody hacked him with an ice pick."

"Yes, Soviet intelligence killed him in Mexico in 1940, but by then he had spawned a number of supporters, a series of tendencies and parties around the world. They're the Fourth International and Julian was a part of that. This made it inevitable that though he supported the Australian revvo, once we formed the workers state here, the honeymoon ended. He had very different notions about the next step... It's hard to explain if you're not familiar with socialist theory, but it meant he didn't want to stay in Australia and help establish the SRA, he had to move on to another place and start a new revvo. For him the revolution can't succeed unless it's immediately backed up globally. We, on the other hand, think a good local example can set the ball rolling for a longer process to the objective we all support."

"Mind you." added Stacey. "Julian's not an orthodox Trot either; he's a tad post-Luxemburgist too."

Siobhan nodded. "I remember the meetings he used to drag me to when he was in college... So when did you last hear from him?"

For the first time Pankhurst looked completely empathetic. "Back in February. He and Ernesto had made contact with the BSA, an Indian underground militia. Since then we haven't heard a snifter. He could be fighting with any of the numerous direct action cells in India, or beyond."

"I see." Siobhan replied quietly.

Pankhurst paused. "I got to be honest, I don't know how he would take to you. He's become very anti-American."

"He always has been."

"Yeah, but he's got a lot more strident lately. That's got a lot to do with your new president, Buckley." His face screwed up with hostility as he uttered the name. There were hateful mutterings from the other officials. "That mongrel Buckley has repealed President King's isolationist strategy and wants to try and throttle us. This is why he has just raised import tariffs on all Australian goods. He wants to build this up to a full trade embargo, maybe even war." He grinned as he saw Siobhan's dismal expression. "Not your fault, luv. You may be a Yank, but we don't blame you. You can't help what country you were born into. Julian is a lot more hard-line in that respect than us but. He actually told me once 'I hate all Yanks! I'd like to shoot them all!' See what I mean?"

"I still want to see him." sniffed Siobhan. "I want to stand in front of him, with our children, and try to talk to him."

The telephone rang on the table and Pankhurst picked it up. "Hello?... Yeah... What, not another one?... A Yank too?... Okay, let him land." He put down the receiver. "It seems we have another American aircraft approaching."

Brendan gasped. "Dad!"

"It's our father." said Siobhan. "He's followed us here... Don't hurt him!"

"We won't." said Pankhurst. "We'll just escort him down and bring him here like we did with you."

When Clane Quilley arrived at Parliament House, Siobhan and Brendan were sitting on deckchairs in the courtyard where the barbecue was still in progress. William and Colleen were playing around a large tree. As soon as Clane stepped through the patio doors, a can of lager was thrust into his hand. He opened it and sipped without thinking as he stared at his daughter and son. "Siobhan... Brendan."

"Hi, dad." Siobhan looked at her feet.

"So... what's going on?"

"I had to get away. I had to get Will and Coll away."

"From us?"

She paused painfully. "From mom."

"Are you going to come home?"

155

Siobhan looked at Brendan. "There's no point staying here now."

"You were looking for Julian weren't you?"

She nodded. "He's not here... So I'm ready to come back to the United States... but I can't live at home any more. I need my apartment back."

Clane bowed his head sadly. "Siobhan... your mom... she's not in her right mind still. She doesn't mean any harm."

"But she *does* harm! She *does* harm, dad!... It doesn't matter what she means or what she intends, or what her mind's like! I don't care about that. What I care about is the effect her behaviour has on me and my children. Whatever she means or intends does nothing to change that effect."

Clane hesitated and breathed deeply. "What if I stop her?"

Siobhan gasped. "Are you serious!?"

He nodded. "I'll put a stop to this! It has to end. What she's doing to you is not right... And I'm sorry I didn't do anything about it sooner. I'll fight your corner with you, Siobhan."

Siobhan gaped, as if failing to believe what she was hearing. "Really?... But what about you and mom? I don't want her to hate you too."

"Mom will not hate me. Mom will love me even more because she'll respect me."

Siobhan stood up and put down her can of beer and half-eaten hamburger. She walked over to her father and threw her arms around him, crying profusely and openly.

Chapter 8

The suburban streets were upholstered with snow. Siobhan switched the flyer to ground-hugging mode so it could slip in behind the ground vehicles rolling through the bright, white powdery fall. "It hasn't changed much." said Siobhan from the driver's seat.

Brendan watched her from the front passenger seat. He knew that it was difficult for her to come here. She had told him all about her relationship with Julian, about how she had spent time with him here in Portsmouth, New Hampshire. The streets were classic blocks, the houses were all detached and with wooden walls. They had shallow roofs and tall chimneys. "What's the name of these people again?" Brendan asked.

"Mr and Mrs Hill. I've spoken to them on the phone a few times and they're quite keen to tell their story."

"And they have actually been... abducted by..."

"Aliens? Yes, I believe so."

"Is what they say going to be a part of your book?"

She paused. "Probably." Siobhan checked the sat-director and stared hard at the doorways of the houses to read the numbers. "Here we are." They parked outside the house, which was architecturally typical for the town, and stepped out into the cold. They trudged up the garden path and rang the doorbell. A dog barked at the sound and a voice came from inside: "Quiet, Delsey!" The door was answered by a smartly-dressed black man with wide, sensitive eyes and a high forehead. "Good morning." said Siobhan. "Are Mr and Mrs Hill in; they're expecting us?"

"I am Mr Hill. Are you Miss Quilley?"

"Yes."

"Come in quickly please."

The home was clean and well-kept. A white woman with thin black hair approached and introduced herself as Mrs Hill. "Are you married?" asked Brendan before he could stop himself. He had never seen a Negro and Caucasian couple and it struck him as strange. Siobhan nudged him irritably.

Mrs Hill sighed with a mixture of annoyance and amusement. "Yes, young sir. Barney and I are married. It might not be legally recognized in every state yet, but it is here in New Hampshire where we live."

"I must apologize for my younger brother, Mrs Hill." said Siobhan tensely. "I told you he would be coming with me."

"That's quite alright, Miss Quilley; and do please call me Betty." The couple led their visitors through to the lounge and made them tea. Siobhan set her slate on the table and set up her microphone. The Hills sat at opposite them on a settee. "So, Betty and Barney, what happened to you?"

Three hours later Siobhan and Brendan flew home. "I can't believe it." said Brendan. "The aliens are still here. They keep visiting us... They even take us away."

Siobhan nodded. "It looks very much like it." She dropped Brendan at Heather's house. Brendan glowed with delight as he looked into Heather's eyes, like he always did. They went out to escape the prying eyes of Heather's family, even though it was a cold day. He walked hand-in-hand with his girlfriend along the icy streets of Rockville. He still could hardly believe that he had a girlfriend. He and Heather had been dating for six months; half an entire year. When teatime arrived and it started to get dark he walked Heather home and they kissed on the corner, out of sight of her house, before walking to the front door. Heather's mother greeted them with a knowing look; maybe it was his flushed cheeks.

The moment Brendan stepped into his own home he knew his mother and Siobhan had had another argument. Everything was outwardly normal. Gina was in the kitchen stirring a pot; she greeted him with a smile. Siobhan was hunched over her matchbook on the dining table in the lounge while William and Colleen watched television, singing along to some music in a children's programme. What was it that gave it away? It was almost like a smell in the air. When his father came home and they ate dinner, the table felt as if it were on fire. When Siobhan put the twins to bed Brendan was in his room. Siobhan quietly knocked on the door, as if she didn't want anybody else in the house to hear her. "Brendan." she whispered. "I've got to visit another abductee next weekend. Would you like to come with me again?"

"Yeah sure." He had enjoyed his visit to Betty and Barney Hill that morning. It was exciting to visit new places and spend time with his elder sister. He understood that he needed time with Siobhan away from their mother.

"It will involve an overnight stay." she added. She had a quizzical expression on face.

"Cool."

The following Saturday Brendan woke up early and excited. His parents spent breakfast talking to his grandparents on the phone about some major event that he never grasped. When he and his sister got into the flyer, Siobhan looked nervous and embarrassed. They took off and turned east. "Where are we going?" asked Brendan.

She paused. "The Volta Union."

"Where Dave lives."

"Yes... I've got a confession to make, Bren."

"What?"

"Dave is the person we're going to visit."

A pit of implications and contradictions opened up before him. "Why?"

His sister looked at him awkwardly. "I'm sorry I never told you before, Bren. I couldn't. Dave's family contacted me a few months ago in the strictest confidence... Dave is an abductee and so is his mom."

Brendan paused and then nodded.

As the flyer came into land on the roof pad of Dave's house the family were standing there to greet them as usual; but this time they were not lively and smiling, they were subdued and nervous. Dr Pearson made them all drinks while his wife escorted them to the conservatory. "Thank you for inviting us, Linda." said Siobhan, and for letting me bring Brendan."

She nodded and forced a smile. "You're welcome, and I appreciate you doing this, writing your book and stuff."

Brendan met Dave's eyes, but his old friend looked uneasy and standoffish. Brendan felt disturbed and a little hurt by the lack of his usual intimacy, as if Dave had suddenly relegated him to the level of a stranger and they were meeting for the first time. His brother Michael sat next to him; their knees and shoulders touching.

Siobhan reached forward and switched on the audio recorder that she had placed on the coffee table.

Dave's mother's mouth trembled as she spoke. "I'm going to tell you the truth about our family. This is something I've never told anybody before."

Her husband brought in a tray of glasses and sat down beside his wife. He looked embarrassed.

Linda Pearson continued. "I was born in Philadelphia in 1928. Everybody thought I was just an ordinary girl, but I was hiding a secret... They've been coming for me my whole life. Often when I'm in bed, but sometimes when I'm awake, just walking along the street or driving in my car... And when my boys were born, I found out they were taking David as well."

"What do they look like, Linda?" asked Siobhan.

She shivered. "Very like the ones which came down at Roswell, but... not quite. They're small, five feet tall or so. They have big black eyes and thin lips. Smooth grey skin. They're skinny and spindly, not robust at all."

"Can you describe a typical encounter with these beings?"

"They just appear in front of me, out of a blast of bright light. I then lose consciousness... The most common thing they do is... examine me. I find myself in a room that's a bit like a hospital. I'm lying on a table, like an operating table. These things are standing round me in a circle like doctors... I can't move! I can't remember how I got there!" She dabbed her eyes with a tissue and her husband squeezed her hand. "They... have these tools and they stick them into me. It's really hurts! They take blood from me and they... penetrate my belly and take my ova... I know because..." She broke down. "They sometimes show me my... my children! Children they've made with my ova!"

The family were all wincing as if in physical pain. "This is really tough for us all." Dr Pearson added as he comforted his wife. "When I found out about this, Linda and I had been married for two months. I... reacted badly, and I'm not proud of myself. It took me a long time to come to terms with what was happening to my family. At first I didn't believe her. I persuaded her to seek help from a psychiatrist."

"And I did." his wife swiftly added. "I felt it was the right thing to do and I owed it to Terry... The psychiatrist couldn't find anything wrong with me." She paused and exchanged a glance with her husband. "That was when we found out about the boys."

Michael shuddered.

"They took Michael once and never came back, but David... They take him all the time."

Siobhan turned to Dave, a boy Brendan's age. He stared at the ground and his eyes twitched as if he were fighting back tears. "How often to they come for you, David?" she asked.

"About every week or so."

"And how long has this been happening to you?"

"As long as I can remember. I thought it was normal."

Linda interjected: "Weird things used to happen when he was a little baby. Like we'd put him in his cot and when we came back he'd be on the floor at the other side of the room. As soon as he learned to talk he used to tell us about the... He used to call them *quees*. It became a bit of a family joke. David and his quees... but we found out the quees were real and they were the same beings that come for me."

"What does a quee look like, Dave?" asked Siobhan.

Night fell. Because of the time difference Siobhan and Brendan were still alert; it was mid afternoon on the US east coast to which their circadian rhythm was synchronized. Siobhan showed Brendan how to set up the cameras and microphones in all the rooms in the house. She had other instruments in her toolbox, including a thermometer and a device for detecting electromagnetic fields. When everything was ready they said goodnight to the family and returned to the flyer. They moved to a quiet parking space on the street about a hundred yards away from the house and Siobhan opened her matchbook on a bracket attached to the dashboard. It displayed a visual field from the cameras as well as readouts from all the other instruments. A row of sound waves scrolled across a box at the bottom indicating the normal noises from the house. "Will the aliens come if they know we're watching out for them?" asked Brendan.

Siobhan shrugged. "I don't know. Hopefully they will." An hour passed, then two. The family went to bed one by one. The house became dark and the cameras switched to thermal imaging mode. They showed Terry and Linda in their double bed in one frame and two other frames showing Michael and Dave in theirs. They lay still under their covers, occasionally fidgeting or rolling over. The grey shapes of the Pearson's cats, dark cream in the infrared, skulked down a corridor. Brendan became bored and began watching his own matchbook, using earphones to avoid disturbing his sister. He was watching a music video on the YourScreen sharing Meshboard, one by an almost unknown band from Liverpool, England called *The Beatles*, when his sister said something that he missed. He took out his earphones. "What was that?"

"I thought I heard something." she said quietly. "Not sure if it's significant. Everything seems normal in the house... We can listen to it on the recording."

"Right." Brendan nodded.

There was a long silence. "It's interesting that both Linda and Dave are abductees." said Siobhan. "I've found evidence that it often runs in families."

"Why's that?"

"Don't know."

"There's a lot of 'don't knows' in this business isn't there?"

"I guess. This is something very new."

"You mean the aliens have only just started abducting us?"

"No, I mean that it's never been publicized before. The aliens have been abducting us for as long as I've so far looked back. I've had E-grams from really old people who tell me they've been taken their whole lives. There are legends from centuries ago that sound a bit like alien abductions, except people use words like 'being spirited away by the fairies' instead of 'aliens'. From what I can see there's no beginning to this in any records. People have probably been snatched away by aliens since prehistoric times."

Brendan sighed. "I wonder who they are and why do they do it."

She nodded. "Me too."

Brendan became curious about the subject and started searching for YourScreen videos about aliens. He came across an interesting talk by an US Air Force Officer called Captain Robert Salas talking about how he was part of a nuclear missile launch crew and one day, three years earlier, aliens appeared outside his bunker and shut down the missiles in their silos. When the video had ended, Brendan said: "I'm glad they leave us alone."

Siobhan looked down. Her face was half-illuminated by the carotene glow of the streetlights. Her lips were hidden by shadow as she spoke. "I'm not so sure. Maybe they could do our family some good." Her voice was monotone and low, almost a growl.

Brendan could feel her resentment; it was like a black hole of malice sucking everything in. "Er... mom..."

"Mom and I have hardly spoken since that day at the school." Siobhan answered quickly. "That's five months."

Brendan had not heard his sister and mother talking, but wondered if they did so when he was not present.

"The thing is, I said some things to her that day that can't be forgiven or forgotten. There's no going back. It's toothpaste we'll never get back in the tube... I was just so angry. She'd effectively kidnapped my children!"

Brendan recalled the volcanic argument between his sister and mother in August the previous year following Gina picking up William and Colleen from school.

"You know the proverb 'Sticks and stones can break my bones but words cannot hurt me'? It's wrong. It should read: '... but words can break my heart'. That's what I did. I broke mom's heart."

"What words did you say?"

Siobhan shivered. "I told her... what really happened to Millicent."

"What do you mean?" He had a few memories of Millicent. She was an old Scottish lady who took over the family while his father was in hospital following his stroke a few years earlier; however these memories were slippery and confused. The name Millicent Arbroath-Laird was quite notorious in the media because she was on the list of individuals wanted for questioning by the Kennedy Commission, the US government's investigation into the covert Illuminati occupation of the country and the world beyond. She had disappeared in 1962 shortly before R-Day, when the human disguise of the reptilians failed and they were exposed for the entire world to see.

"Millicent is dead."

"Are you sure?"

She chuckled good-naturedly. "Reasonably certain, seeing

as I killed her myself."

Brendan felt his body freeze, his lungs were momentarily paralyzed before he gasped. "You... killed Millicent?"

"Yes."

His sister had killed somebody; not just anybody, but a person who had been as close to her as family. "But that means you're... a murderer."

Siobhan hesitated and then nodded. "I suppose I am... But... it was just before R-Day. It was a war. Can killing an enemy in war be called murder? That would make all soldiers murderers."

"But she was... an old lady."

"So?"

"How did it happen?" Brendan still pondered whether she was making this up.

"I came across her in the Denver airport underground base. Have you been to the museum there?"

"Yes, they took us there in Grade Six."

"That's where I killed her. I... didn't just shoot her either... I blew her to pieces with a grenade. I pulled the pin and shoved it up her ass."

"What!?"

Siobhan shuddered and nodded wordlessly.

"Why?"

"I was so angry. I surprised *myself* you know. It took me a long time to process what I'd done. I didn't feel guilty at first; during R-Day there was just no time. Everybody was simply doing what had to be done." She moved her head slightly so more light shone on it. "She was an evil woman, Brendan. You know what she did to you?"

He nodded and doing so gave him a wave of emotional pain.

"She was working for the Illuminati to destroy the world, and she wanted our family to help her. Is it really bad to put an end to such a destructive life? What if I'd let her live? She'd have been free to carry on. Possibly she'd have found a way to ruin R-Day. She was very intelligent... So I wasted the old sow. I then deleted the video of it from YourScreen."

"Did you tell Jack what you'd done?"

"No. That's why Millicent is still on his 'wanted' list. I've only told one other person before you... and that was mom."

"Why did you tell mom?"

Siobhan paused. "She was so mad at me. She was yelling at me, shrieking in my ear. Her face was red and her mouth was inches from me. Veins bursting out of her skull. She was screaming that I wasn't fit to be a mother, that she was more Coll and Will's mother than I was and I was more like their older sister, that she wished I'd let her adopt them, that she would go to court and get custody of them... Every word she uttered was intended to wound me as deeply as possible. I wanted to wound her back."

"So you told her you'd killed Millicent?"

"Yeah. I told her everything. I added a few things too, stuff that wasn't true, just to rub salt in. I told her I'd enjoyed it. I told her I'd danced for joy on top of her corpse."

"What did mom do then?"

"She just gaped at me. Didn't say a word. She shivered; I thought she might faint... I realized straight away I shouldn't have said what I did, but it was too late. We've hardly spoken since. She won't even look at me... Maybe there's a part of me that needed to say it, to tell somebody. I think deep down I'm shocked at myself, for being so violent. I didn't know I was capable of anything like that and I wanted to share it with somebody. It shouldn't have been mom though and it shouldn't have been like that."

"Maybe you should tell Jack."

"Why?"

"Well, he has the FBI out looking for her. If he knows she's dead it will save them the bother."

"I guess so... Mind you he's not looking for her specifically; she's just on a list of hundreds of names that are being sought after together. Taking one name off that list will make a negligible difference to their manhunt. Also, I might face some kind of charge."

"Murder?"

"No, at least not in the civilian sense. It was war, like I said. Thousands of people got killed. I just might be in trouble for not reporting her death sooner. I guess what I did might get some lawyer to consider it a war crime. I'd have to answer some tough questions. No, let the world think she's vanished.

A lot of those other vanished people will never be found anyway. Most of them are probably dead by now."

Brendan went to the house to go to the toilet then came back to the car and let Siobhan do the same. He watched his sister on the CCTV monitor walking through the corridors of the house, a white ghostly shape on the infrared and image intensifier. He lay back in the passenger seat and dozed while Siobhan stayed alert, staring at the monitor. When he woke up, the sky was lighter and birds were singing from the trees. "The family are waking up now." Siobhan said.

"Did any of them get abducted?"

"No. However, I'll go through the recordings and we may pick up something interesting." She yawned. "I need a bit of sleep before we go home." She and Brendan joined the Pearsons for breakfast. Their conversation was casual and more normal than it had been the afternoon before. Brendan was pleased to find that Dave and Michael acted as they usually did when they were together as friends. Siobhan left the table before the others to have a nap in the guest room. Brendan also felt sleepy and was glad that day was Sunday and he didn't have to go to school. The sound of church bells from the town filled the air, reverberating in from the garden so when that melodious jingle was mixed with another noise they noticed immediately and all looked up. It was coming from the front of the house. It alerted them all because the area was normally very quiet. They got up and rushed to the lounge where the window overlooked the street. A large black van had parked outside and a number of tough-looking suited men were strutting purposefully up the garden path. Dr Pearson went to the front door and opened it before they rang the doorbell. "Who are you?" he asked.

Brendan looked through the lounge door and saw one of the men produce an identity card. "Dr Terrence Pearson? Kwazi Okonokye, National Investigations Agency. May I come in?"

Peterson instinctively stood to one side and let him enter, together with three or four of his colleagues. The big black men filled the space with their bulk. "What's going on?" asked the doctor fearfully.

The leader was middle aged with heavy eyelids and a sparse

neatly trimmed beard. "It has come to our attention that you and your family have been experiencing alien abductions. We have come to investigate."

Pearson gasped. "What!?... Siobhan!"

Siobhan was running down the stairs, woken by the commotion, fastening the belt of her skirt. "Terry?"

"Did you tell them?" he demanded with a scowl.

"No! I swear I never told anybody. I wouldn't do that."

Pearson turned back to the agent. "How do you know about this?"

"I'm not in a position to explain that to you at present, Dr Pearson." the man replied woodenly. "There have been many reports of alien abduction right across the VU and the government is taking action. We request that you cooperate with us in our investigations."

The Pearson family stood in a cluster, staring with dread at the bureaucratic invaders. There was more noise outside. Brendan looked out of the front door and saw three more vehicles pull up in the street. These were of different colours and the people who stepped out were more casually dressed. They had cameras in their hands and began taking photographs of their surroundings. Siobhan looked at them knowingly and said: "Oh no!"

"Who are they?" asked Linda.

"News reporters."

The following half an hour was totally chaotic. Terry and Linda Pearson argued with both the government agents and journalists, the agents argued with the journalists and Siobhan had a particularly heated exchange with one of the reporters, a white man with a smug Canadian accent. Brendan eavesdropped and gathered that the man was also writing a book on alien abductions and Siobhan felt put down by this. She had assumed up till now that she was a sole pioneer enjoying an exclusive, but now she found out she was just one of several people researching the subject and at least one other person was planning to publish a book. What's more this new rival was working on a commission from a major New York imprint whereas Siobhan was freelance and funding her project herself. This would inevitably mean that her book would be marketed less widely and may well be completely eclipsed by its A-list corporate competitor. This was a very humbling and unsettling revelation for her. The tussle only ended when Siobhan took a call on her roam. Brendan was standing a few feet away from her and watched her face as she spoke. Her expression changed instantly from anger to dismay. "What?... Oh my God!... Where?..."

He knew something was badly wrong. "Siobhan, who is it?"

She lowered the instrument. Her face was ashen. "We have to go home, Bren; right now."

"What's wrong?"

"It's grandpa."

....

Siobhan drove the flyer eastwards across the Atlantic Ocean at full power. The morning sun disappeared behind them and it became night again in the strange time machine effect of antigravity travel. She spent the whole journey talking on the telephone to her father, learning as much as she could about the crisis that had just exploded in the family. The light-speckled coastline of Long Island rose in front of them and they descended towards a pool of light on the eastern headland. "Can you see us now?" Siobhan asked into the hands-free phone. "Yes... The police must have switched the lights on." There was a large crowd of people in the courtyard of the Montauk Museum. A trio of police cars were parked in a corner, the red lights on their roofs rotating slowly. Siobhan eased the flyer down beside them and she and Brendan jumped out. Their father ran towards them. He was deeply distressed, but calm. A senior police officer was beside them. He said: "We have just called somebody from the National Cult Support Centre and he's on the way. We're hoping now you two are here it might help. Come with me quickly!" He led them over to the radar tower; the old structure was lit up by police spotlights and the museum's own lighting. Before they went in, Brendan saw Susannah and his grandmother walking beside the doorway; they were both being led away by a policewoman, weeping profusely in each other's arms. The family climbed up the stairs inside the tower until they emerged through a trapdoor onto the roof. The huge reflector antenna loomed over them like a pair of rusty batwings.

Brendan suddenly felt precarious. The roof of the radar tower was a flat square about seventy feet along each side made of steel plates. There were no railings or parapet at the perimeter. Unlike the antenna itself the roof space had been cleaned of rust and the metallic floor was black and rough. A gaggle of policemen stood in the middle around the antenna mounting. One of them seized Siobhan's shoulder as she dashed forward. "No! Don't go near him!" he hissed at her. Siobhan had been trying to approach a man standing at the edge of the roof with his back towards the centre. He turned his head slightly as he heard her and Brendan saw his face. It was his grandfather. "Dad." said Brendan's father. "Siobhan and Brendan are here to see you."

He looked over his shoulder again. For Brendan it was like seeing his grandfather for the first time, even though he was so familiar to him. Arthur Quilley was an average sized man, but he looked smaller; his back was hunched and the left side of his body was slumped over as if injured. His head was bald and wrinkled with a few wispy patches of white hair which were rippling in the early morning breeze. "I'm sorry Siobhan, Brendan." he muttered. "I didn't want you to see this."

"See what?" asked Siobhan fearfully.

Arthur moved his feet forward slightly so that his toes were hanging over the edge of the roof.

"Dad." Clane implored. "Please step back! Walk over towards us! Whatever is wrong, we can talk it over. We can find a solution."

"There is no solution. He's dead." There were tears in his voice.

"Dad..." Clane bit his nails. "You found out a man has died. I'm sorry about that; it's a sad thing, but everybody dies eventually. It's not the end of the world."

"I found out Karl Dennison has died." he retorted. "The world *has* ended for me."

"No it hasn't, dad. You are still alive. You have a family that loves you. You have a life to lead."

"A life without Karl Dennison is not a life at all. It is a living death."

"Dad!... For God's sake!"

"Clane, you don't understand the glory... the majesty!... of Karl Dennison!

"But you haven't seen him for seven years!"

"Yes!... Seven years! Seven long years!... Sitting by the telephone, waiting for it to ring! Years and years of waiting! Waiting for him to turn his beautiful countenance towards me again!... And then, last night, Susannah's car pulls up outside our house. I thought she had brought Karl Dennison back to me, but then she tells me..." He roared in anguish. "AHHH! He is dead!"

Clane paused. "I'm sorry you had to find out this way, dad. Karl is dead, yes; but he was bound to die eventually. You knew that... This is not a reason to end your own life. Do you think Karl would want you to die with him?"

He nodded. "Yes, because he knew I lived for him... and I knew he knew that, and he knew I knew he knew that."

Clane screwed up his face. "The man was scum, dad. He abused me! He abused me physically and emotionally!"

"Don't you realize, Clane? He had a *right* to abuse you. I couldn't stop him! I couldn't stop him because... HE... WAS... MY... GOD!" He turned his head to look down at the ground. "Clane, there's nothing more to say now except... I'm sorry. I'm so very sorry." Arthur Quilley leaned forward slowly and peacefully, like a man leaning against the bar of a pub after a long day at work. His forward motion continued until he vanished below the edge of the roof. The crowd on the ground below screamed.

"DAD!" Clane leapt forward. Two policemen prevented him rushing forward too close to the edge of the roof. "Oh God, no!" Clane pulled back from them and bolted towards the trapdoor. Siobhan and Brendan followed him as he pounded down the stairwell and out through the door. A crowd of paramedics were surrounding Arthur where he lay on the concrete courtyard at the base of the radar tower. A row of policemen prevented Clane approaching his father. "Dad!" Clane cried.

One of the paramedics stood up and walked over. He shook his head. "Mr Quilley, I'm very sorry. There's nothing we can do."

Chapter 9

Brendan strolled through the underground shopping centre at a leisurely pace. He was relaxed and enjoying the feeling of having a distinct destination, but knowing he had more than enough time to get there. He walked into a department store. The staff were taking down the Christmas decorations as part of the general post-festive anticlimax that was characteristic of New York City. This shop was also playing normal background music instead of Christmas carols. The tune being played was actually a beautiful one and Brendan listened as he browsed the shelves. It was part of a new style that was very popular at the time called Sixty-Tronica. It was sad that he didn't know the title or composer of the piece and so would probably never hear it again. He knew he could approach the shop's staff and asked for details of their playlist, but felt embarrassed to do so. Instead he just stood still and enjoyed it. When the track ended he left the shop and took the lift to ground level. He emerged into the sharp winter morning sunlight at East 97th Street and walked along the pavement towards Central Park. He could already see the frightener looming over the bare spiky trees. It looked as if an ocean liner had been lifted from the sea and dropped into the middle of Manhattan. The massive aircraft was over eight hundred feet long and closely resembled a passenger ship; it had a white hull with rows of windows. A crowd was in the park watching it. Many local people still remembered what happened fifty miles away in Lakehurst, New Jersey thirty-two years earlier. An aircraft of similar size exploded on landing killing thirty-six people. However the frightener was very different in design to the *Hindenburg* airship. Instead of huge sacs of inflammable hydrogen gas, this new aircraft was held aloft by ten antigravity spinning disks; a far larger equivalent of those inside a family flyer. It was solemnly christened AV *Disclosure*, a special name indicating that this was a special frightener. Brendan quickly studied the Meshpedia page for the craft on his roam and found out that the AV prefix stood for "aerial vessel"; AV *Disclosure* had been one of the first launched. His family were waiting beside the frightener at the foot of the gangway with the other passengers. His father and mother, Siobhan, William and Colleen. Heather had joined them and she kissed Brendan's cold cheek with her warm lips. Kerry was there too. The young alien hybrid was not biologically related to them of course, but had been spending more and more time with the Quilleys over the last year.

Everybody was in good spirits, wrapped up in heavy clothes against the cold. A steward came down the gangway and checked their tickets, and then they were allowed to embark. Brendan and Heather had booked a large stateroom as part of the VIP status of his father. It had wide portholes that were slanted downwards to give a magnificent view of the ground. The frightener did not have a pressurized interior like a jet airliner and so was limited in altitude. For this reason it also could not move as fast as a smaller flyer. Frightener travel had become popular in recent years despite its slowness, or perhaps because of it. The speed of antigravity travel had made some people feel uncomfortable; they felt that the world itself had shrunk as a result. There was therefore now a booming market for aircraft that drifted along at a fast walking pace and did not rise above the world until it became invisible. Some new frighteners were even driven by sails. There was an open promenade along the top of the frightener where most of the passengers gathered to watch the takeoff. Brendan felt precarious for a moment, but recovered quickly. There was a chest-high parapet to prevent passengers from falling off. Social media was buzzing with multiple photographs and posts swirling around WorldMesh. There was a stern reprimand from the aircraft's owners when a crewmember used the word "frightener" in a comment; these vessels were officially called "sky-ships" and all employees were obliged to use the proper term. Brendan rolled his eyes at such a pernickety correction. Nobody knew where the neologism had come from, they weren't generally thought to be frightening things; but he did not know a single person who called them anything but frighteners. As the *Disclosure* lifted into the air there was no vibration or sense of motion. The only sound was the gentle humming of the antigravity drives, like a low-pitched musical bees' nest. The tops of New York's skyscrapers became visible as the observation deck rose above their level. Soon the whole of Central Park was laid out below them like a cricket pitch. The frightener eased forward as it soared, its keel was completely level the whole time. An echoing announcement came over the public address from the captain announcing that they were cruising at an altitude of four thousand feet and at a speed of ten miles-per-hour. The aircraft flew northeast along Manhattan. Its grey shadow flitted along the shore of the River Hudson. The urbanized areas of New York City's suburbs petered out to be replaced by crystallized winter countryside as the frightener travelled upstate. A delicious meal was served to the passengers in the dining room, but Brendan ate it as speedily as he could. He loathed every moment away from the experience of riding like a bird on the outdoor observation deck. He was bitterly cold, but didn't care. He felt invigorated by the icy wind whipping through his hair. At one point he heard church bells ringing in a town underneath. He marvelled at the science that allowed him to have this experience and, despite the view, wished he were in the engine room below decks.

By the time the *Disclosure* reached its destination night had fallen. It landed in another field at a small town called Dover in the Green Mountain region of Vermont. The passengers were shown to a sumptuous ski lodge where they were again served another delectable meal. "Aren't great days great?" said Clane cheerily as he tucked into his Irish stew.

"Are they that great?" Gina responded with semi-mock-dubiousness.

"Yes!" he answered playfully and gave a litany of all the reasons to be optimistic. "The economy is booming! We haven't had a stock market crash for four years. The wars around the world are calming down; even England is stabilizing."

"What about the communists?" asked Siobhan.

Clane waved his hands dismissively. "Oh, they'll see the light eventually. They'll probably reform into social democracies in a few years. They'll know it makes sense. I really think the decade to come will be far better than the decade we're leaving."

"I hope so." said another passenger, a man they had been talking to during the journey from New York.

"I know so! This could even be the start of the post-Disclosure equilibrium."

"What's that?" asked Brendan.

"Something I read yesterday in *The Washington Post* by John Fields; you know, the guy who presents *History Today*. He put out this dynamite piece called '23 Years' because it's the twenty-third year since Disclosure. He said that basically all the problems caused by the Disclosure revolution have now been addressed and fixed, and as a result we can now reap the benefits of Disclosure itself without having the burden of its drawbacks... He quotes me five times in it." Clane winked arrogantly. "We have the new tech well on the way to full development and integration. We're delving further and further down into the Illuminati files every day and we'll probably be at the bottom within twelve years or so. There are already development proposals for this 'post-new tech' you might have heard about."

"I've heard the phrase." said Siobhan.

He lowered his voice. "Well I can't say too much now, but this promises to be incredible even by the standards of what we've seen so far. It's largely to do with the medical field."

"I'll pass judgement when I've seen it, dad." said Siobhan with a half-smile.

"The point of all this is that we might be emerging out of the transitional period between the pre and post-Disclosure worlds. Fields quotes Winston Churchill's phrase 'the end of the beginning'; the beginning being that of the pre-post-Disclosure equilibrium."

"Pre-post-Disclosure equilibrium." Brendan repeated to feel what the words were like on his tongue.

"Brendan, you know about the three forms of equilibrium, don't you?"

"Of course, dad. It's basic stuff, Newton's second law. I am going for my high school diploma in physics and chemistry remember?"

"I know, son." He bowed his head apologetically. "Perhaps you could explain."

Brendan smiled at him warmly. "There are three states of equilibrium best illustrated by imagining a ball rolling along a surface. Unstable equilibrium is a state in which the ball is perched on the point of a cone or dome, or a similar structure. It is only in equilibrium because it is perfectly balanced; the forces are equal on both halves and it is touching the surface on its exact centre of gravity; but the tiniest nudge either way and the equilibrium is destroyed and the ball falls off. Neutral equilibrium is a ball lying on a flat surface. It stays still until it is pushed and when it is pushed it moves, but then it simply slows down and stops due to the resistance of friction. It then returns to equilibrium in a different part of the surface. Stable equilibrium is a state like a ball lying at the bottom of a bowl with steep sides. You can push it and it moves, but then it returns to its original point of equilibrium."

"And John Fields has turned this into a metaphor for politics. He claims we are now in a stable equilibrium. Every force that pushes us out of it does nothing to change the long-term state; we just return to equilibrium like the ball in the bowl. Up till now society has been a combination of neutral and unstable equilibriums, but now, for the first time ever we have stable equilibrium. Instability is the cause of all civilization's problems, with the exception of natural disasters like earthquakes and hurricanes. Instability is generated by scarcity, therefore in a world of universal abundance there can be no scarcity, and therefore no instability; equilibrium! This can only spread over the entire world and once it's done, it will last forever."

Siobhan frowned. "Wait a minute, dad. Are you talking about... utopia?" Her mouth twisted.

Clane blushed and hesitated. "Is it such a dirty word?"

"It's a word that has spawned quests that ended in extraordinary evils. There have been people through all of history who have believed that they have the key to create heaven on earth because of some religious belief or some revelatory political philosophy. What has always resulted is more like hell. What makes you any different?"

"Because this time what we're doing is based on science, not politics."

"Does that make you somehow immune?"

Clane paused. He looked uncomfortable. "Siobhan... I would never be part of anything that would result in hell on earth. I just want to see a better world than the one we've had all our life and I'm happy that we seem to be heading towards one which is better. Is that so bad? Are you saying I should try to resist that?"

Siobhan didn't answer. She looked awkward now, as if she regretted what she'd just said. Everybody else around the table was subdued by the tension between father and daughter. "No, dad... It's just that it may turn out not to be as simple as you think. You haven't mentioned one fundamental difference between the world before and after Disclosure."

"What's that?"

"It's not just us now. Up till now we've only ever seen the world as a planet with humans on it, an oasis of life in an infinite cosmic desert. Now we know we are just one little unit of a universe teaming with life. We can't make assumptions about the future of human civilization without taking into consideration reality. That's what mainstream politics is still failing to get to grips with."

"That's because the aliens generally ignore us. They fly down here now and again, occasionally they crash their craft, but really they act like we're not here. Why shouldn't we return the favour?"

"They do not though, dad."

He chuckled. "Oh, you mean the abductions."

"Yes. Why, do you think they're funny?"

"No, it's just..."

"Do you believe they're real?"

"Of course. We have lots of DOD formerly classified documentation about it."

"And you'll be hearing a lot more about it very soon." Siobhan's book was due to be launched the following month. A number of governments around the world had published several reports and set up official inquiries into the abduction phenomenon. "You can't call this ignoring, dad... You used to be the kind of person who would understand that. I think maybe you've been working in Washington for too long."

In the silence everybody looked at Kerry. She was as calm as always, quietly eating her meal. She had not spoken so far. Brendan guessed that everybody was thinking the same; her very existence was a contradiction to what Clane had just said. Her body was partly extraterrestrial. As he watched, she picked up a hunk of food with her fork and placed it in her mouth between her thin lips. She dabbed the pale skin at the sides of her mouth with a napkin. Her nose was small and recessed, like an East Asian's, but her eyes were very large and a bright dark blue. Her hair was thick and sandy; pure golden blonde in colour. Apart from that she looked no different to a natural human being; for example her hands were completely normal. Over the previous year Kerry had definitely become a part of the family in all but name. Siobhan had once told Brendan that she regarded Kerry as a younger sister. She and Siobhan had met in 1958 during the second invasion of Area 51. Kerry had lived her whole life deep within the underground laboratory, only being allowed out onto the surface as a rare treat. Kerry had no family; her surrogate guardians had disappeared just before the invasion. They had abandoned her and all the other hybrid children. She was taken to the Walter Reed National Military Medical Centre in Bethesda, Maryland and kept on a secure ward. It was like a prison for her; she was constantly examined by doctors without her consent and not allowed out of this solitary confinement situation. She was also saddened by the dispassionate departure of her surrogate parents, and she knew now that they were not her real parents and were only doing their job in looking after her. Did they ever really care about her? Kerry had some amazing abilities that had previously been called psychic, something mainstream public science had only started taking seriously since Disclosure. They allowed her to disable temporarily the security staff guarding her and allow her to escape. She used the same technique to find help and was quickly located and picked up by John F Kennedy's underground rebels who were already by that time planning a coup against the unlawful government of President Henry Dealey. Many books had already been written about that. She had lived with them for four years until R-Day when the reptilian Illuminati overlords were exposed for what they really were. Since then she had had no permanent home. She had stayed with friends from the former underground and also slept in the dormitories of one of the many hostels that had been hastily built after R-Day. There was a whole nation of orphans and homeless adults, both human and quasi-human, who had been thrown into the society of the surface world since the fall of the New World Order. These were the survivors of the atrocious scientific projects the Illuminati had been carrying out deep in the earth's crust. Some had also been bred for Satanic rituals and had been saved from being killed in this manner. They needed housing quickly; therefore the hostels were mostly temporary prefabricated buildings or even just tents. They were usually overcrowded and uncomfortable. Many of the residents were suffering from mental trauma and physical illness, and so they did not make healthy companions. Therefore Kerry was very happy to have grown closer and closer to the Quilley family to the point where they gave her a place to live. She was working fulltime for an agency that tried to arrange family adoptions for the millions of children in the hostels and proper accommodation and employment for the adults.

Gina now spoke out to try and resuscitate the pleasant and carefree interaction with which they had begun their dinner. "So, Siobhan; you think you're dad's been working too long in Washington do you?" She gave everybody a mischievous grin. "Well, we've got news for you!" She looked at her husband, giving him his cue.

"Yes indeed." he responded, continuing in her theatrical style. "I have an announcement to make. I am retiring."

Siobhan applauded. "Way to go, dad!"

"You've been talking about it for long enough." added Brendan.

"I have indeed, in fact I hoped I could get out in sixty-seven after Martin lost, but... well... one thing led to another and... this and that got in the way." He shrugged and looked at them as if to ask for their tacit understanding. "Anyway, I have submitted my resignation to President Buckley and he has replied with his acceptance, thanking me for my service and wishing me well."

The cheers of well-wishing spread to the other tables; many other passengers had overheard him. Some of them had their roams out and were taking furtive photographs of the family and texting furiously, wanting to be the first to break the news on social media. It reminded Brendan that his father still occupied a status of moderate renown. The dinner table family conversation had suddenly transformed into an impromptu press conference.

"Buckley asked me to reconsider." continued Clane. "As you know this is an election year and he wanted me to campaign with him. I declined. Even if I was the campaigning sort, I just feel I'm no longer needed. In fact I wouldn't be surprised if Bill just disbands my department. As I've been saying all evening, Disclosure is finished. The job is done. I don't believe we need a Secretary for Disclosure Affairs; I'll probably go down in history as the first to hold that that office and the last."

"What do you plan to do next, Mr Quilley?" shouted a woman on a table across the room.

"My wife Gina and I will be moving to the Gold Coast of west Africa where we will make ourselves a new home."

There was another approving exclamation from the diners. After that the meal went back to normal. Brendan got up to go to the lavatory and walked past a table where three men were sitting. "*Utopia*?" one of them asked. "What's that?"

Brendan instinctively stopped to eavesdrop. He bent down and pretended to tie his shoelace.

"It means a perfect world, a paradise." said a second man.

"Sounds fine to me." said the third man. "If that's where we're heading, sign me up!"

"But wouldn't we get a bit bored?" asked the first man.

"No way; I'll find plenty to do. I'll play golf and computer games all day, man."

"But wouldn't that wear off after a bit? I mean... I don't like a world where lots of shit happens, but problems can be good. They give us something to get our teeth into, that gives us something to strive for."

Brendan had to stand up and carry on walking to prevent the men becoming suspicious of him. However he logged the points he had heard in his mind with an uncanny feeling that they would become relevant in the future. Just before he was out of earshot he heard the first man say: "We might have to bring back violent sports, I mean gladiator stuff; mortal combat."

....

It was eleven-thirty PM. All the people who had travelled to the Green Mountain area in the frightener and had dined at the ski lodge donned their outdoor clothing and set off for the short walk to the observation area. Brendan moved stiffly in his parka and insulated trousers. His boots crackled deliciously in the powdery snow; snow that was pure ice and had never known melting temperatures, snow for which water was as alien as sand in a desert. Dry, but potential moisture; there when needed. The scrunching noise of multiple footsteps in the ankle-deep snow filled the frigid air around him. His own breathing filled his ears because they were covered by his woolly hat. The sky was mostly clear with a few clouds, matt black on the shiny black of the sky, like a badly painted ceiling. The sparks of stars peeked through the coat, like static arcs of welding. Around them were the spiky ghosts of trees. The procession of people were like mobile snowmen in their wrappings. Their guide was directing them to a spot where a gap in the trees showed a magnificent view over a wide shallow valley. It was hard to tell at night, but Brendan felt he could see for miles. Above the horizon were some featureless rounded peaks. "Ladies and gentlemen." called the guide. "It is five minutes to midnight. The display will begin on the stroke." People began chattering excitedly. Some were watching the TV broadcast from Times Square on their roams. "Why don't they just go there instead?" muttered an irritated voice next to Brendan. Brendan also felt that the lighted squares of roam screens among the crowds ruined the atmosphere. He assumed everybody had come on this expedition to have a different New Year experience to the average one. "Twenty seconds, ladies and gentlemen!" called the guide and a few seconds later began the countdown which everybody followed in unison: "Ten... nine... eight... seven... six... five... four... three... two... one... ZERO! Happy New Year!" A glow-worm line of dim light appeared in the valley below, an almost imperceptible web of different coloured darkness. Within seconds it grew to a mesh of white luminescence that was almost blinding in Brendan's night vision. The people waved their arms in the air in delight and gave off "Ooh's!" and "Aah's!" like spectators at a fireworks display. The guide spoke above them again: "Ladies and gentlemen it is now 1970, a new year and a new decade! Happy New Year!" He then broke into a rendition of *Auld Lang Syne* which everybody joined in with, linking opposite arms in the traditional way. The lace of light in the valley burned for a few more seconds then faded slowly over about twenty seconds until the scene returned to its original darkness; but the pattern of light remained on Brendan's retina as an imprint of purple. The illuminations were created by a synchronized demolition of multiple electric pylons. Now so many towns, cities and private houses had their own free energy generators much of the national grid was being dismantled. Up until Disclosure, electricity was delivered by a network of huge electrical circuits spanning thousands of miles of copper wires, charged at certain points by power stations fuelled by coal, gas or nuclear fission reactors. Most of these wires were looped across the countryside, suspended above the ground by steel lattice pylons. These pylons were being demolished and the metal recycled. Some were cut apart slowly with saws, but some were being pulled down in one go with thermite charges, the method wrongly promoted by pre-R-Day disinformation artists as the cause of the Empire State Building's demise. These disintegrations were spectacular; the thermite sparkled and blazed like a firework, therefore it had become a new kind of entertainment to carry out mass thermite demolitions of entire rows of pylons at night. These displays always drew masses of onlookers. This New Year special in Vermont was the largest yet.

The cluster of people stood around chatting for a few minutes then diffused slowly back down the trail to the ski lodge. The frightener was parked next to it. All its windows showed lights. It looked as if it was in the sea and the lodge was on a dockside. They embarked and retired to their cabins for the night flight back to New York City. Brendan and Heather lay together in their cabin's king-sized bed. They talked quietly about the future, marvelling at the prospect of a brand new decade, enhancing the general "new beginning" and "we all get the chance to start again" feeling that accompanies every new calendar year. It was now January the 1st 1970, a Thursday. This Thursday was the first time anybody wrote nineteen-seventy-something on a date entry instead of nineteen-sixty-something; an act that would henceforth become the norm for the next ten years. By the end of the decade what would have happened? How would things have changed? Heather kissed Brendan's cheek. "Got any New Year's resolutions, baby?" she asked.

He paused and then chuckled. "I've not thought of any yet... but I will by New Year's Eve!"

....

Brendan wandered slowly through Rock Creek Park. It was reasonably warm, but wet. A light rain fell, dampening his hair. Despite his comfort, he felt a foreboding chill in the air and wondered if it was just his imagination. It was a Saturday, the beginning of the spring break from school, a week before Easter. Then he would begin the final term of his junior year in senior high school. He had been going for walks alone in the area more and more often in the last few months, just to think quietly. There was peace here; just the singing of birds and the rustling of the wind in the trees. Some of the trees were in early blossom and the sight delighted his eyes. The only disturbance was the occasional overpass of a flyer, but the gentle musical buzzing of flyer engines did not spoil, indeed almost enhanced, the natural purity of Rock Creek; very different from IC or Digby car engines on nearby roads that had slowly and steadily diminished since flyer travel grew in popularity. He hadn't been heading in any particular direction on his stroll so when he came across the clearing he suddenly jerked to a halt. He was in the clearing with the open patch of grass and rows of logs put there to act as benches. This was where he had last seen the Indian, years ago when he had been a child. He had not thought about the Indian or Boggin for a long time. There were three thick logs arranged in a row on the north side of the glade. Brendan sat down on the first one, where he had sat back then. He didn't think of himself as a child anymore even though it had only been seven years earlier. He suddenly noticed that the third log along had been replaced with a new one; the original one must have become rotten. He sat down on the first long and looked at the ground. He had sat here, aged ten, and spoken for a few minutes, just a few precious minutes, with the Indian. It surely must have been real. Brendan ran through the incident in his mind. Yes, memory was not perfect, but this felt as real as any other memory in his head. Could it really have been nothing more than a childish fantasy? Even Siobhan had dismissed it thus, but Siobhan could be wrong, couldn't she? He ran his hands over the bark of the log. It was dry and cracked in death, a few mushrooms sprouted through the cracks and beetles crawled over its rugged surface.

He looked up at the afternoon sky, if you could call it a sky. A few gaps had appeared between the natural clouds and beyond them, high above them, was the ubiquitous haze of lifetrail altostratus. The organic blue of the sky was invisible and would remain so completely for the next five years. It would be a difficult half decade. All vegetation on the planet would be degraded through the decrease in sunlight. Dutch elm disease and similar fungal infections were becoming endemic in trees across the world. Forests were going to die. This would have an inevitable knock-on effect on the rest of the ecosystem. Brendan hadn't realized what a difference it would make. He had not voted in the global referendum the previous November because he was too young; and all his family had abstained, as had about half the eligible population. It was such an important choice that the League of the World Earth Healing Organization had decided to give the decision to the human race. It was the biggest election in history. Not all nationalities were given the opportunity to vote, thanks to the boycott by the Socialist Republic of Australia and all its allies. For them the whole concept was "Fascist, pseudoscientific, science fiction crap! Anti-Semitic garbage!". The Red Bloc had uniformly and staunchly refused to allow lifetrailing operations over their territories and all attempts to persuade them otherwise had been rebutted. This only aggravated the underlying problem. The prospectus for atmospheric lifetrailing had to take into account that a quarter of the earth's land surface could not currently be directly sprayed upon. The referendum took place over the course of an entire week. Such a huge poll had never been done in the history of the world; almost a billion people came to polling stations to vote. The choice had been binary and comprehensive: The LoWEHO calculated that with the early 1960's level of lifetrailing, the operation would have had to continue for about thirty years. However a very intensive five-year programme might have the same results. The former choice involved up to ninety-five percent of natural sunlight being preserved, but it would need to continue until the end of the twentieth century. The latter would only last for five years, but during that time the planet earth would suffer a fifty percent drop in surface insolation. The earth would have to endure five years of twilight. Average global temperatures would plunge three degrees or more which would shorten summers, make winters harsher and devastate agriculture across the world. It would be a manmade mini-ice age. The biosphere would reel from the blow for many decades afterwards. Earthquakes and volcanic disasters would almost certainly increase as the natural electrogravitational rhythm of the planet was wrenched so sharply onto a new beat. It truly was the chemotherapy against the Illuminati cancer. On the other hand, it was a short, sharp shock as opposed to the long drawn-out soft-kill alternative which could have equally dire side effects over a far longer period of time. After five years, all lifetrailing would cease and the sapphire heavens would return allowing nature to recover. The votes were counted tensely and with much drama at the LoW's headquarters in Cairo, Egypt. The options where christened simply "short" or "long" by the media (The delegates from the Red Bloc were sternly informed by the Secretary-General that had their countries cooperated then the time periods would have been three and twenty years respectively, instead of five and thirty). The results were close: Short- fifty-two percent; Long- forty-eight percent. The concentrated five-year lifetrail project had commenced a week ago on the first day of March.

Brendan continued to look around him, almost expecting the Indian to appear, wondering what he would do if the Indian did. Then he stood up and walked on down the pathway to Parklawn Valley. After a hundred yards or so he pulled up short with a shock. There was a man lying in the bracken completely still between two trees a couple of dozen yards away. He was dressed in a brown jacket. Brendan instinctively dashed off the path into the undergrowth, vaulting over branches. As soon as he was within ten yards he realized that it was not a man but a deer. He leaned over it. Its pelt had resembled human clothing from a distance. The corpse of the deer lay on its right side. It must have died very recently because there was no decomposition. It was completely intact except for a number of very precise and extreme injuries. Its left eye was missing; it had been extracted from its socket as if by a surgeon with a totally circular incision. Its lower left jaw had been stripped of all flesh, totally and within a very defined segment. Outside the area its skin and subcutaneous muscle was fresh and unspoiled; inside there was nothing but dry white bone, as if the mandible of another deer that died years ago had been shoved into its skull. Brendan straightened up and backed away. He trembled. The injuries this animal showed were exactly those the public information films on television had been warning everybody about for the last couple of years. He forced himself to remain calm and took out his roam. He knew which number to ring because the films had delivered a mnemonic jingle that had permeated popular culture: *Oh-one-seventy-two-forty-two-six.* Somebody answered immediately: "Hello USDA Mute Squad."

"Hello, I think I've found one of the animals you talk about on TV."

"Right, give me your name and location."

Within ten minutes three flyers were swooping down towards him. A group of businesslike people stepped out and got to work immediately, removing the body and examining the area. One of them, a woman in a white boiler suit, escorted Brendan to the back of one of the vehicles where she asked him a number of questions: "Have you seen any bright lights in the sky today?... Did you see any strange flyers or other aircraft?... Have you seen any unusual people in this area?..." Some of the people in the team were clearly reporters who took multiple photographs of the scene and asked Brendan similar questions to the USDA woman. After an hour of cross-examination he was allowed to pass. Two of the reporters accompanied him for a while asking him further questions, but eventually they thanked him and walked back to their flyers. Brendan came to a junction and changed direction in order to exit the park as soon as possible. He walked quickly, feeling vulnerable. He had seen the documentaries on television of course; everybody had. More and more animal cadavers had been turning up with the same mutilations Brendan had observed on the deer. Along with the jaw strip and eye removal many of the cases involved the draining of blood, causing the tabloid press to nickname the hypothetical perpetrator "Dracula". Very often genitalia were taken and the rectum cored out. The injuries were as precise as if performed by surgery. The targets of these sinister killings were farm animals, wild animals, pets and marine mammals like seals and dolphins. There were reports of such incidents dating right back to the beginning of the records, but since Disclosure it had been revealed that the government had been secretly concerned about it since the 1920's. However, now they had to deal with it overtly. In February the National Farmers Union had marched through Washington DC to demand action from the White House. President Buckley's Secretary of Agriculture had met with their committee and arranged a compensation package that would be easily passed though Congress, but said nothing about a solution to the underlying cause. Clane had laughed sardonically. "What can they do?" There was some relief in his laughter because he had retired the previous week. His successor in the Department of Disclosure Affairs was a thin young man named Gerston Baskerville who had previously been a junior assistant secretary in the Department of the Interior. "His face turned white at the handover ceremony." Clane chuckled. "The first folder I handed him was one about the animal mutilations. Thank God it's not my problem any more! I think I unintentionally smirked a bit as I said: 'Good luck, kid.' and walked out of the office for the last time." The mutilations phenomenon was one that concerned both Disclosure and Agriculture because there was a pattern to the attacks related to the specialities of both departments. They tended to come in waves and certain areas were targeted for certain periods of times. Sightings reports of MFO's increased considerably when and where these waves were in progress. This made it likely that aliens were doing it; they were snatching animals out of fields and woodland and returning them dead with parts of their bodies missing. Why? Theories abounded; from scientific vivisection to DNA harvesting to the aliens' sexual proclivities. None of them made any sense. "If they wanted DNA they could get it by plucking off a hair." Brendan's father had said, his brow furrowed in confusion. The farmers' protest was only the start of a more widespread public restlessness. There had been an outcry a few weeks ago when a human body had been found in Mexico of a missing woman. The injuries were the same as those found on the cattle and other animals. A chill descended on the world. A wide variety of animal species had been targeted by the mutilators, but there had previously been an unspoken assumption that *Homo sapiens* was being passed over. Now that assumption was shattered and it became clear that whoever, or *what*ever, the perpetrators were, they did not regard human beings as anything exceptional or worthy of a respect not shown to other beasts. They were just one more breed of two-legged ground-ape. Why? Did we think we were somehow special? The abductees appeared to be the lucky ones because they were returned alive and in one piece. The president had had numerous meetings with the FBI and Department of Defence over the matter and there was talk of a "space force" being established to protect America from extraterrestrial violations. Although somebody in the White House Press Room had inevitably asked: "What tactics could this hypothetical 'space force' employ against this threat?" The president had paused...

Brendan was relieved to reach a street leading off from the park. The mutilations almost always happened in isolated areas to lone individuals, hikers in the wilderness or teenagers walking through a wood. The fact that these events happened together in multiples in a specific place and time made him wonder if "Dracula" was still about. Once he felt cement under his feet and saw other people walking along the pavement, he relaxed. When he got home his mother ran out into the hallway with a mixture of excitement and relief. "Brendan honey, are you okay?"

"Fine, mom."

"You've been on TV."

"Already? Jeez, that was quick. Yeah, I found a mute up Parkdown way. A deer. Some reporters came along with the DoA and asked me some questions."

Gina sighed. "Oh God, I hope this isn't the start of more... Stay away from Rock Creek till it all dies down."

"Watch out! Drac's about!" Brendan laughed and went upstairs to his bedroom. His mother did not join in his merriment. He switched on his desktop computer with the intention of knocking out some revision. As always, the material on WorldMesh distracted him. He answered some E-grams and social media comments then saw a pop-up of a news story about something else he had been personally involved in. He shook his head in bemusement. "How come our family always ends up doing things that get in the news?" he muttered to himself. After a brief moment of intrigue, he hadn't thought any more about the strange black substance he had found while collecting marine litter aboard the LoWS *Belleau Wood*. Since then it had attracted a lot of media attention because it was a major mystery and the government had got involved with containing and studying the substance the ship had discovered. It was officially called "sentient oil", but the media had quickly adopted the moniker "black goo". At first there were fears that it was a product of the pre-Disclosure chemtrail programme like Morgellons disease, which would have complicated the lifetrail referendum; but the latest research indicated that it was not. It was in fact not man-made at all. There were no further answers at that time; even the secret documents from the Illuminati's vaults, or rather those so far analyzed, did not mention it.

As Brendan studied, he realized that he would certainly graduate at the end of the year. His knowledge about his subjects put him beyond confidence. He was as likely to fail as he would if somebody asked him to count from one to ten. He had even already applied to a few local specialist graduate schools. He was still confined to the pure sciences, majoring in physics with a minor in chemistry and mathematics; the perfect combination for continuing his studies in engineering. He was going to graduate and he was going to graduate very high. To be an engineer; his dream. He wanted that with all his heart. He sat back in his chair and stretched his feet out beneath his desk. For the first time he considered his future as a realistic perspective, devoid of the thought experiments that these notions inevitably were to a younger pupil. It wasn't hypothetical anymore; it was his immediate future. He started browsing the Mesh to find opportunities; which were considerable considering his school prospects. The most prestigious circles of higher education lay spread out before him; the Massachusetts Institute of Technology, Virginia Tech, Battelle, Texas A and M, UC Berkeley. He had previously discussed these opportunities with his father. The advice he had received was positive: "The world is your oyster, Bren. I'm so proud of you, my intelligent son! You're doing so well no college on earth would refuse you."

Brendan glowed under the approval of his father. "I was thinking of maybe even Oxford or Cambridge."

Clane shrugged. "Hmm, the political situation in England is still pretty dodgy."

"But Oxbridge has completely reopened."

"Yeah, for about the tenth time since 1950! It may well close again before you complete a year. No, son. Keep it stateside."

He hesitated. "Maybe Berkeley; they're leading the world in Schauberger systems."

"Don't go to Berkeley, Bren; it's a nest of commies!"

"Then where, dad?"

Clane paused, and then his face lit up. "Hey, try for Annapolis!"

"The naval academy? Are you serious?"

"Absolutely. It's just down the road; you'd be close to home."

"But... you're saying I'd have to join the military."

"Well, of course. You'd have to do your two-for-seven, as they say."

"Dad, I don't want to join the military."

"Why not? It's a good career; you get everything paid for you. You never have to worry about healthcare bills or school funds and stuff."

"But... I might have to kill people."

Clane shrugged. "Sometimes that's the only way to keep America safe." He laughed. "But come on! There's hardly going to be a war now, is there? Who is there left to fight? Germany and Russia? Those days are over. And besides, they pay all your tuition fees and the rest. You get board and lodging, your three squares a day. No civilian university provides that unless you pay out through the nose."

Brendan looked at his father's smiling face. The money issue was irrelevant, Brendan knew that. He hadn't admitted it, but Clane was actually very rich. He had just retired on a senior federal government official's pension on top of other incomes and savings he had, which would basically mean that it would be the generation of William and Colleen's grandchildren before there was any possibility of the Quilley family having to worry about money again. The scrimping and saving for a child's college fund that most parents had to go through was incomprehensible to Clane's brood. Clane could afford to send his son through any academic course on earth and not feel it more than the turning of small change. "Dad, why do you want so much for me to go to Annapolis?"

His father looked slightly embarrassed, probably guessing his son's thoughts. "Well... okay, I'd like to see you do it for my own sake. You see, I went through the war. I was enlisted; I never even considered OCS... and I would enjoy seeing my son become an officer in the US Navy. To me it would look to me like a natural progression."

"Yes, dad; but this is my life not yours." Brendan regretted the remark as soon as he'd said it; it sounded unduly harsh.

However Clane nodded his head in an understanding manner. "I know, Bren; and I'm sorry."

That afternoon Brendan travelled to Annapolis on his motorflyer. His mother had bought him the vehicle a month ago and he loved using it. It was a small two-disk antigravity craft that resembled a motorcycle or bicycle without wheels. It could only carry a single occupant who sat on a pillion seat with their legs astride the airframe. The pilot was not enclosed as they would be in a larger flyer so they had to wear warm clothing when flying at high altitude; and a safety belt across their lap was necessary to prevent them falling off. He landed in the city centre near the Maryland capitol and walked along the redbrick streets to the naval academy. The main gate was set between imposing white walls with the gilded lettering: "*UNITED STATES NAVAL ACADEMY-FOUNDED 1845*" set on one side of the decorated iron grid of the barrier. To his right, the ivory dome of the college chapel loomed over the outside streets in a swaggering and superior manner. Beyond the gates a road stretched away into the sacred and inaccessible holies of the academy. A row of students in immaculate uniform were marching in tight formation while a drill instructor shouted orders at them. A large group of people were watching through the gate; the majority were women.

Brendan stood and thought about how the military was actually a form of religion. He had never voiced these thoughts because he knew they were taboo, even in the post-Disclosure world. Of course it was perfectly correct to respect a person who does a difficult and dangerous job, but the adoration for the armed forces went beyond that. There were many other jobs in which those doing it had to face danger. Brendan went to his local library and looked up the statistics in *The American and Canadian Almanac 1969*. The most dangerous job you could do was to be a fisherman, yet there were no fisherman's memorials in the middle of big cities. There were other dangerous occupations named below fisherman, a coal miner, oil rig worker, fireman, deep sea diver. Oddly enough general military service did not even make the top ten. So where did the military religion come from? And there was no doubt it existed. Soldiers were seen almost as a higher species, tomorrow people, supermen; like the queen bees were above the drones. Brendan chuckled at the thought that humans were behaving like insects; maybe that's why the aliens abducted and mutilated them without a qualm. There was even the word *civilian* to describe people not in the military. On reflection Brendan considered this bizarre. Civilian and military people had the same number of arms and legs; both had a heart, lungs and a liver. Why did you need a separate word for a person who, when it comes to sheer facts, simply does a different job? Why was it that if a soldier was in the news for a non-military reason then their status as a soldier would always be alluded to, even if it was completely irrelevant to the story? For example, there was a famous singer-songwriter in the pop charts at that time who used to be an officer in the US Army. No article or interview about that singer in any music journal had so far failed to address the fact that he used to be an army officer. However at the same time there was another singer who used to be a hospital porter in Chicago before achieving musical success. Why was it that almost no journalistic literature about that second singer referred to his former life as a hospital porter?

In the same vein, a man had recently rescued a group of pensioners from a burning building in Maine and every single news report about the incident declared the information that he was an army sergeant. But how often did you see the headline: *Insurance Broker Chases Off Mugger* or *Painter and Decorator Saves Child From Flood*? And what effect did this have on the soldiers themselves? The answer was obvious to anybody who lived near Annapolis, as Brendan did, as well as Washington DC. Being told that they were gods, they believed that they were gods. Brendan had seen them in cafes and on buses, going up to strangers to be complimented. They strutted around like touring celebrities. They were so used to being publicly venerated that they expected it and demanded it from everybody. Occasionally soldiers would encounter hostility, usually from other young men. Often this would escalate to physical fights breaking out in bars and nightclubs. The soldiers actually enjoyed this reaction because they knew deep down it was only inspired by envy. The civilian men resented the soldiers for their social status, their attractiveness to women and the many other extraordinary rewards of military service. The one thing military men could not abide from civilians was indifference. Those whose who were neither hostile nor adulatory. The people who refused to be "squaddie struck" and treated the soldiers like everybody else, politely and apathetically, apparently unaware of their eminence. Brendan's father had told him about an incident that happened to him in 1955 when he had visited London. He had been challenged by a group of soldiers in a pub merely because he was not looking at them. From trawling the darker and angrier Meshboards on the subject, Brendan could see that some of the hostile elements were learning this lesson and deliberately feigning indifference when in the company of soldiers as a terrifying new weapon in the war against the military; or else was that just their own sense of inadequacy?

Brendan watched the midshipmen inside the academy quickstepping away and realized something that he had asked himself as a small child. Why do young men sign up so eagerly for the armed forces, possibly to kill and die in wars; even in pre-Disclosure times when many of those wars were neither just nor patriotic? Now he was old enough to understand that the answer was self-explanatory. Despite himself, Brendan sympathized completely and felt that same desire too. Perhaps it was something natural and unavoidable to the masculine mind, as essential as breathing. He went up to the guardhouse and asked for a prospectus.

....

Of course Clane was overjoyed that Brendan had decided to apply for The United States Naval Academy. He insisted on driving his son to his appointment with the admissions board. They took the ground car for the half-hour drive to Annapolis. He talked almost non-stop for the entire journey, filling Brendan's head with advice. "Remember, keep showing them you are of good moral character..." He also told his son what to expect. "You have to wear a crackerjack uniform for your first year; it's an ugly thing with a neckerchief. They call you a 'plebe' too which is really derogatory; but it's all done to build your character. It toughens you up... But if you get through your first year they give you this nice tunic with a double row of buttons... Also you can make a good impression by calling the floor a 'deck' and the walls 'bulkheads'. I know that's maritime terminology, but at the academy they talk like that even about buildings on land."

"But, dad." Brendan reminded him three or four times during the conversation. "You've never been to Annapolis. You were never an officer."

"I know, son; but you pick things up in the service. I learned from the officers who had been there."

They were admitted at the main gate and drove along the wide straight internal streets of the USNA, past many glorious aristocratic stone buildings to a carpark outside a more modern building. Brendan insisted his father wait in the car, to which Clane reluctantly agreed. Brendan entered one of the more modern structures of the academy, dressed in his Sunday best, trying to look confident. He announced his presence to a female midshipman at reception and waited in a velvet chair, bolt upright and clutching his application papers, waiting to be called in for the interview. After ten minutes, the receptionist directed him into a doorway behind her desk and he was greeted by three men in uniform sitting behind a table. A small solitary chair was placed in the middle of the room facing them where Brendan was asked to sit. The interview did not last long. The men asked him about his studies and achievements at school. They wanted to know if he played sports and asked him a few questions about his personal life. Brendan told them about Heather and the interviewers asked whether he planned to marry her. Brendan said no, knowing that he had to be a bachelor to enter the academy. Then they thanked him and the appointment was over; however, one of the men offered to take Brendan on a tour of the USNA campus and he agreed. His interviewer-cum-guide was a grey-haired kindly man called Commander Leach who was also keen for his father to attend; so Brendan went to the car to collect him. As they walked around the grand, clean college with its shiny stone oblong buildings and its neatly-trimmed shrubberies, it became obvious that this tour was a courtesy not normally extended to preliminary applicants. Commander Leach treated Clane very reverently and asked him many questions about MFO's and the new tech. Clane kept catching Brendan's eye to smile and give him a cheery look. On the drive home Brendan's father was very optimistic. "It's a foregone conclusion, son. They want you more than you want them; it's obvious." He was right of course. Brendan was the son of "Mr Disclosure" himself and Commander Leach in particular was a true enthusiast for Disclosure. Therefore Brendan was not surprised when a few days later a package arrived in the post, with an accompanying E-gram, announcing that he was to sit the USNA's entrance examination. This he would take concurrently with his standard high school Scholastic Assessment Test and the marks he achieved in both would be combined into a final grade for his Annapolis application. If he passed that, along with the medical and fitness tests, and if a Member of the US Congress sponsored him, he would be able to enrol at the US Naval Academy in June of 1971, just a month after he'd finished school. Brendan sat back in his chair after reading through the documents he'd been sent. He put his hands behind his head and sighed deeply. His future suddenly appeared vertiginous, both frightening and thrilling. He had just over a year of normality left, and then he would be thrown headfirst into the deep end of the adult world.

Chapter 10

Brendan and Heather went to bed early. They were at Heather's house and her parents were away for the weekend. They kissed, made love, talked, watched a movie on television and generally savoured each other's company. They discussed the future. Heather had also graduated, in English and history. After the summer she would be heading for Arkansas to study at the state university. Brendan set his alarm clock for five thirty in the morning. Heather awoke with him and they ate breakfast together with the early morning gloom flooding into the kitchen windows. The kissed passionately on the doorstep; they would not see each other again for at least three months. Then Brendan hoisted his rucksack onto one shoulder. He was taking very few personal possessions with him. He waved to Heather as he walked down the garden path and blew her a kiss as he turned the corner of the street. The air was chilly, but the clear sky foretold a pleasant summer day ahead. He caught one bus into Washington DC and changed for Annapolis. The second bus dropped him off a few blocks from the US Naval Academy. He drank a cup of coffee in a cafe and then walked along the pavement to the creamy walls of the campus. He paused outside the main gate, once again admiring the fine architecture. The green open spaces and obtrusive structures within the gate were quietened for the holiday. They calmly awaited the fresh influx of midshipmen that would arrive shortly. Brendan walked back and forth in front of the gate. He thought about where his life was going, the decisions he had made over the previous twelve months, and what his future might have been like if he had made different decisions. He looked at his watch; it was time to catch another bus. He turned his back on the United States Naval Academy and walked away.

The speed-frightener looked like a flying saucer. It was disk shaped and about a hundred feet in diameter. Brendan boarded the antigravity craft with all the other passengers at a terminal built into the roof of the new Inner Harbour Convention Center in Baltimore. Inside the frightener the seats were arranged in concentric circles like a small theatre and the pilot sat in a blister cockpit above the main disk. There were windows behind the seats along the rim, but these provided light and no view. The buzzing of the engines started and the light changed, indicating that they were now airborne. A stewardess served them with tea and coffee. Brendan sipped his and thumbed through the giveaway magazine until the frightener came into land after an hour and ten minutes flying time. He followed the queue of passengers exiting the aircraft and emerged into very different sunlight, that of late afternoon. A signboard was hung above the gangway saying: "*Welcome to Ireland- Céad Míle Fáilte.*" He lined up at the customs desk and had his passport checked. He only carried minimal personal luggage. He stepped out of the frightener terminal onto the streets of central Dublin and was immediately assailed by multiple sights, sounds and smells. A strange feeling came over him. He walked a few hundred yards and found himself at Arran Quay. A lot of building work had been done since he had last seen it, but it was still unmistakable. Brendan had been born in Dublin and some of his earliest memories were of the city. It felt apt that he had come back to his birthplace the moment before he came of age. He went to the railway station and had to resist the urge to take the urban service down to Greystones and visit his old house. Instead he got on a train for Drogheda. From the station it was a short ride on a ground bus to his destination. He saw it before the bus pulled up to the correct stop. A large flag fluttered at the top of a pole sporting the emblem of Seaguard, a blue circle on a white background with three lines of marine waves inside it. The bus drove away with the whine of its Digby Carrousel and Brendan paused with trepidation. The facility did not look welcoming. It was protected by an eight foot chicken wire fence topped with a reel of barbed wire and inside it were a number of low white and red coloured buildings laid out haphazardly, as if the site had been designed by multiple architects over a long period of time. Its name was on a large sign: "*Seaguard Inc Training Dept- Drogheda*". The gates were crude metal grids which slid on an oily steel track; a stark contrast to the polished marble grandeur of Annapolis. There were numerous warning signs by the gate for security and safety as well as a promotional billboard showing photographs of ships and the slogan: "*Your Career with Seaguard Starts Here*".

Brendan was not alone; a large knot of young men stood

outside the gate. Some had parents with them who had brought them to the training facility. He exchanged embarrassed and fearful glances with them all, as if they had all just been delivered together to a prison by a Black Maria. He walked past them and approached the sentry box at the gate where a security guard stood as if waiting for him. He smiled in a friendly and knowing manner. "Good evening."

"Good evening. I'm Brendan Quilley." He handed the man his appointment documents.

He smiled sympathetically. "Over there, Mr Quilley; in through that doorway."

Brendan walked over to where the man directed and entered a large room with a low ceiling and rows of chairs. Two more uniformed men checked his papers at a desk and then told him to sit on one of the seats. They took his luggage and put it into a cupboard. There were a few more recruits waiting there, their arms pressed to their sides with tension. Brendan sat next to a boy of about eighteen, his own age, with a thin face and red hair. They glanced at each other, but did not speak. Over the next twenty minutes more and more boys came in took their place in the room until there were about fifty people filling every seat. Eventually one of the men at the desk stood up and walked to the front of the room facing their chairs. "Good evening, gentlemen." He spoke in a deep, penetrating voice that was clearly accustomed for shouting and felt uncomfortable using the normal volume of speech. He had a large and intimidating frame inside its blue uniform; muscular arms and a thick neck. His crew-cut hair was topped with a blue beret. "My name is Training Sergeant Bayrooth." he said in an English accent. "And from this moment onwards you will do everything I say, understood?"

The crowd muttered a disorganized and informal affirmative.

"'Yes, *sir*'!" he yelled.

"Yes sir!" they all immediately copied.

"Right!... All of you get to your feet and form a line. Walk through that door on the far side."

Brendan did so and was shocked to see a row of seven barbers' chairs lined across the floor of the neighbouring room. Some of the other boys muttered in confusion.

"Take your clothes off." commanded Training Sergeant Bayrooth.

The boys looked blankly at him.

"TAKE YOUR CLOTHES OFF!" he repeated with a yell that rattled Brendan's ears. He hastily tugged off his jacket and jumper and then undid his trousers, which was not easy because his hands were trembling. Some of the others were slightly ahead of him and stood there in their underpants.

"No! All your clothes!" Bayrooth qualified.

Brendan's skin felt cold and vulnerable as he stood there naked, like a peeled grape.

Bayrooth pushed his shoulder, forcing him towards one of the barbers' chairs. "You, get in that chair!... And you, you, you, you, you and you!" As soon as Brendan had taken a seat a group of people wearing white jackets walked in from a side door carrying electric hair clippers. Brendan gulped as he noticed two of them were women. He blushed and became acutely aware of his nakedness, but the woman who approached him did not look at his body or speak to him. She kept her gaze neutral and fixed on what she was doing as she applied the blade of the clippers to his head. His skull buzzed and his scalp tickled as the clippers tore at his hair. Lock after lock fell to his bare shoulders and from there onto the floor. A few minutes later he stood up, completely bald, and followed another instructor's directions into a third room at the same time as Training Sergeant Bayrooth noisily selected a second handful of recruits for his shearing pen. The third room was a large shower stall where he and the other boys who had just lost their hair were sprayed with piping hot high-pressure water from the ceiling heads. At the far end they took towels from a pile and dried themselves. There were more instructors there, as if they were all part of a production line. One of them handed Brendan underwear of the correct size and he was ordered to stand next to the others in a row. After another ten minutes all fifty of the newbies were there in blue vests and boxer shorts. Bayrooth emerged from a door at the far end; presumably he had walked round outside the building. "Right then!" he barked. "You boys constitute Training Company 71D. This is your colour." He pointed to a flag hanging from a pole at an oblique angle. It was blue and simply had "*71D*" embroidered on it. Brendan guessed that the "71" referred to the current year, 1971; and presumably there were at least three other training companies, A, B and C.

After that, all the boys were issued with a kit that consisted of various uniforms, toiletries and bedclothes. None were allowed to keep their personal effects. Bayrooth led them to a dormitory with multiple rows of bunk beds and showed them how to store their clothing in the adjoining footlockers and how to make the beds. He folded the sheets neatly like a paper envelope under the mattress. "These are hospital corners." he said. "We call them that because if you don't do them properly I'll put you in hospital." He chuckled. Nobody else laughed. After they had all made their beds to the Training Sergeant's satisfaction, which took a long time and a lot of sore eardrums, he showed them how to stand to attention, salute and gave them a few more basic instructions in Seaguard's protocol. They wrote nametags that they attached to all their equipment. By now the sun was low in the sky outside the windows of the dormitory. Brendan glanced at the clock on the wall: eight-fifty PM. "Right." Bayrooth said. "Lights out in ten minutes. I strongly recommend you get as much sleep as possible."

Brendan lay in his bed. His shaved head felt strange against his pillow. He had a lower bunk and was staring at the springs and underside of the bed above him. Occasionally his bunkmate above would shift and the springs would creak. There had only been time for brief introductions with his fellow recruits before they were sent to bed like small children; the man above him was called Bill. Blinds had been lowered over the windows, but there was still enough light to see his surroundings once his eyes adjusted. He heard the sound of sniffing and plaintive sobs; a boy on a nearby bed was weeping. Brendan knew that the next three months would be very difficult for him, but it would be worth it.

....

"WAKE UP! GET OUT OF BED!"

Brendan shot bolt upright in bed, his dreams still running through his head, blending with reality as a hypnopompic melange. The lights in the dormitory were on. Training Sergeant Bayrooth had just wrenched the covers off his bed and Bill's; and he was moving on to the next bunk. Brendan was on his feet; his eyes were still half-closed. He stood to attention at the foot of the bed the way he'd been taught the previous evening. He felt as if he hadn't slept at all, although he had; despite it taking him a couple of hours to drop off properly. The boys were all stood to in front of their bunks within a minute. Bayrooth ordered them to dress in their utility uniforms and follow him. He led them outside onto a sports field. It was twilight; at that time of year in Ireland this meant that it was around four to five in the morning, although Brendan had not had time to look at the clock. The air was chilly and damp. Stars were mushy blotches behind the lifetrails in the purple sky. The dawn was a bright smudge to the east over the sea. The recruits jogged around the field and along the banks of the River Boyne; the Seaguard facility was on the northern County Louth side. Bayrooth made them do a series of callisthenics, press-ups, sit-ups and star jumps. After that they were allowed breakfast. Brendan sat on a bench eating toast, eggs and baked beans off a metal tray alongside his opposite numbers. All of them were too tired and hungry to talk. Brendan contemplated as he ate; what had brought him to where he was at that moment.

His father had been disappointed when Brendan told him he was not going to Annapolis. Brendan had explained his reasons to him and he had nodded his head in reluctant agreement. The US Naval Academy was too constrictive in its curriculum. He would have been forced onto a course that would have meant repeating a lot of what he had learnt already at school and in his own private studies. He did feel the call of duty and desired the status of the military, although he had tried to integrate that desire; however his principle goal was to become a new tech engineer. He had done a lot of research and had discussed this with his father. It was an uncomfortable fact, especially for his father, but it was the truth. The United States Navy was radically downsizing. They called it "restructuring", but that was just a euphemism. The USA, along with most other major world nations, had signed up to the League of the World's External Defence Pact of 1961. This was a renewal and reinforcement of the Kellogg-Briand Pact of 1928, an agreement that effectively outlawed all wars except under specific circumstances; namely repelling the direct physical assault of a country's territory, state assets or citizens. This would change the word "defence" from its Orwellian to its literal meaning. The Kellog-Briand Pact had been drafted and passed during the cooling off period following the horrors of the Great War which traumatized the earth. The post-war pre-Disclosure realpolitik had undone the pact and led to World War II; but today, in a post-Disclosure World, it was now being taken more seriously. Therefore the US Navy was being transformed into a force primarily aimed at warding off armed invaders of the American coasts. Seeing that the United States was one of the most geographically secure nations on earth; with a shining sea on each side and very large allied countries, Canada and Mexico, on its two land borders, maritime protection was extraordinarily easy. Therefore the future of the US Navy involved the scrapping of most of its assets. No new aircraft carriers had been built since the end of World War II. The nuclear submarine programme had been shelved; and this decision was made even before it had been revealed that the new tech made dirty and dangerous nuclear fission power obsolete. The US Navy was looking more and more like a souped-up version of the US Coast Guard; and indeed there were currently calls in congress to merge the two services. In technical terms, which are what interested Brendan, this meant that the Navy was currently prioritizing maintenance of its commissioned smaller ships, the frigates and destroyers. Its future stratagem eventually involved building more ships that were similar, and as conservative as the Navy's reputation, with a displacement less than four thousand tons and powered by boring old IC gas turbines, reciprocating engines or Digby Carrousels. If Brendan had graduated from Annapolis he would have been faced with being part of the jostling bottleneck that was the shrinking officer corps. If he wasn't simply made redundant, which was far more likely, he would have had to spend five years working with engines he really didn't want to. The best he could hope for would be a placement on one of the old nuclear fission submarines; whose engines were a type of steam turbine. It would have given him a happy reminiscence of his days on the old *Belleau Wood*, but done nothing to lead him to his ambition. It seemed like a dead-end, but then a getaway car drove up. Despite the 1961 pact, naturally many nations still harboured the desire to coerce their influence on the geopolitical stage; but they could not use their armed forces to do so. Therefore they went looking for a legal loophole and soon found one: mercenaries. Over the last decade many private companies had sprung up that provided the same service that long-distance large scale military forces used to. These would often be employed by state or corporate actors to intervene in foreign affairs in place of their own national assets. The LoW forbade them from using their own militaries, but sending in a few "civilian contractors" was absolutely fine. Seaguard was by far the largest of these contractors, along with its newer sister companies Landguard and Airguard. Seaguard was nothing less than a completely private blue water navy. Its fleet consisted of five aircraft carriers, seven capital cruiser-type ships, thirty-four smaller surface combatants such as destroyers and frigates, fourteen submarines, twenty-two littoral combat ships, seven amphibious assault ships and numerous other supporting vessels. There were ten Seaguard bases all over the globe and its annual turnover was over five billion US dollars.

Interestingly Seaguard was a workers' cooperative. Its employees did not receive wages in the conventional way; instead they all owned a share in the company from which they derived their earnings, called a "lay". This was split into fixed monthly instalments so that it resembled a salary for practical purposes; however at the end of the financial year, late March, all shareholders received any additional profits as a lump sum. This was called a "capital dividend" and it could be quite considerable. The number of workers' cooperatives had exploded in recent years and so this eventuality was becoming an annual celebration; "Cap Div Day". Retailers treated this in the same way they did Christmas, carrying out advertising campaigns and special offers so that co-op members could be persuaded to part with their sudden bonuses. Along with their shares and capital dividend, workers' co-op members were awarded increments for rank and bonuses for additional services. The payroll system was Byzantine in its complexity, but the upshot was that people in co-ops had a higher income than those who simply took a wage in a conventional business. Co-ops were more profitable, more productive and more efficient. A few co-op members in the early days of the scheme sold their shares in exchange for cash and a salary contract; they ended up regretting it and were desperately trying to buy their shares back or join other co-ops. It was a system that was inheriting the earth. In fact, at that time almost everybody was trying to get onto the workers' cooperative ladder. Part of the success of the co-op revolution was down to the fact that its members were more dedicated and motivated than those who were simply spoon-fed a wage. As equal shareholders they were actively involved in the running of the business, not simply working there. For example, Seaguard had a standard military unified chain of command. Operations were led by somebody called Admiral Jonathan Pierce and he had an officer class beneath him, and below them a hierarchy of non-commissioned ratings. However all operatives from Admiral Pierce down to new recruits like Brendan were governed by a board of executives which they elected. These executives might be members of the Seaguard co-op or they might simply be employees of the shareholders, i.e. the Seaguard staff.

The philosophical godmother of the movement that created this new form of commerce was a writer called Ayn Rand. She had done speaking tours of schools and universities and had spoken the previous year at Brendan's high school in Rockville. She was a crusty lady with a strong Russian accent who had become famous over the last few decades for a series of allegorical novels she had penned. Brendan bought her latest one, *Atlas Shrugged*, that she had published thirteen years earlier. It was a whopping doorstep of a volume, over a thousand pages long. He had not had time to read it, but intended to do so because its plot involved the discovery of new tech in a way different to how it actually happened. Rand had been given the informal seal of approval by the Buckley administration where she was hired as an outside adviser. After Buckley's re-election she had taken a minor role in the Department of the Treasury, but her true purpose was to talk and write, to disseminate her ideas to the population.

All these facts were abstract to Brendan. He cared about

nothing except engines. He was joining an organization which embraced the new tech with a passionate vigour. It was only a matter of time before he was finally working with it. He cleaned his breakfast dish and returned it to the service counter. After breakfast the recruits were given a lecture in what resembled a school classroom without the desks. The rows of seats had a large gap between them. Brendan wondered what this was for until he realized that it was a space where Training Sergeant Bayrooth could walk between the rows making sure the audience was paying attention and not falling asleep after their early rise. If any of the boys so much as yawned Bayrooth would stride up to them and poke them hard with a baton. The lecturer was an elderly administrator wearing a brown civilian suit who had come down from the company's headquarters in Dublin specially to talk to the new personnel. He told them about the history of Seaguard, details about the structure of the company and advice for his audience's careers. Brendan forced his head upright and his eyes to the front despite the face that his eyelids felt as if they had breezeblocks attached to them. He was almost grateful when he received the baton on his nape because it destroyed his agonizing drowsiness. The activities during the rest of the day banished it for good. As soon as the lecture was over the boys were marched outdoors again and across the grounds. They jogged in strict file; Brendan and Bill shoulder to shoulder with two more boys in front and two behind. The pacemaker at the front decided the speed and they all had to keep to it. Brendan's heart thudded in his gullet. He coughed and spluttered, bringing up phlegm and spittle. His breath felt red hot as it rushed in and out of his lungs. Just as the longing for rest passed through his head, he heard Bayrooth's voice in his ear: "Keep going, Quilley! Keep going!" It was as if the trainer could read his thoughts. Keep going he did until eventually, blissfully, the double line of recruits was ordered to stop. They stood in a line, panting and wheezing. Brendan was upright with his hands at his sides as he'd been taught, but for him it felt like being in a luxurious bed. Bayrooth didn't speak for a few minutes, giving them all a chance to get their breath back. Then he pointed behind him and yelled "All aboard!". They were standing on a quay by the river where a large ship was moored. It was an old-fashioned tall ship with a high wooden hull and towering masts that loomed over the riverside. The Seaguard banner flew from an angled pole on its stern. The recruits stumbled up a gangplank onto its decks. Everything looked brand new and polished, and Brendan suspected that the ship was a modern replica rather than a preserved antique. "Get up the rigging!" commanded Bayrooth.

He was met by blank, frightened faces. "What?" mumbled one boy incredulously.

"I said get up that rigging!" repeated Bayrooth.

Brendan's stomach warped as he understood. He looked up at the lattice of ropes and pulleys with horror. Bayrooth started propelling the boys towards the rigging and they began climbing. Brendan waited in the line, feeling as if the gallows were ahead of him. His heart throbbed in terror. "Quilley; mainmast, fourth spar port." Brendan stepped up onto the platform where the rope ladders to the aerial hell began and gripped them with his quivering hands. He began scaling the wobbly hemp rungs. At first it was easy, like climbing a short stepladder, but after ten feet of so he began to feel the weight of the air below him and the oppressive force of gravity. The fittings and planks of the deck beneath were unnaturally small. He squeezed his eyes shut and gripped the ladder for dear life. "Keep going! Don't look down!" bellowed Bayrooth. Brendan went up another step, then another; he kept his gaze firmly on the ropes in front of him and forced the world underneath out of his mind. He narrowed his eyes on the top of the ladder so that he was blinkered to everything around him and focused on each step and change of handgrip. After a few more feet the climb became easier, as if he had reached the peak of acrophobia and pushed through it to a calmness beyond it. Eventually he came to a wooden platform built into the mast. He rolled onto it with relief, enjoying the sensation of a solid surface. There was no time to rest. An assistant trainer stood on the platform who was fitting the boys with safety harnesses. Brendan allowed him to wrap the belts around his waist and shoulders. This was connected to a line that ran beside the next leg of climbing. A second ladder sprouted from the platform, leading up into the heights of the ships rigging. Even though he was now much higher up, Brendan found this climb easier than the first. It was partly the safety line, but also the fact that the ground below was now so far away it appeared not to matter as much as it did when he was lower down. It was like a picture or television image. He was on the mainmast, the middle of the ship's three, and Bayrooth had ordered him to climb to the fourth spar; that meant he would be almost at the top of the five spar mast. When he reached the fitting where the spars were connected to the mast there was another smaller platform and a trainer transferred his safety line to the spar. Brendan then felt frightened again as he stepped onto a metal pole that was fitted to the spar below it that acted as a foothold. There was another pole built into the spar itself for his hands. He began inching out along the horizontal strut where two other recruits already stood. He was on the port, left hand, side of the ship and was suspended directly over the hard concrete wharf. He experienced a momentary return of the visceral fear of falling he had previously felt, but it passed over quickly. He was fairly safe. There was a solid footplate under his boots and a rod where he could easily hold on. He also had the safety line that would catch him if he slipped. If the spar had been set up at ground level he would have climbed onto it as casually as if ordered to walk down a street. The difference was all in his mind. He even began to enjoy the view. From where he stood he could see the green farmers' fields around the base and the muddy blue waters of the Boyne flowing through the marshes and out to sea. After a few more minutes the recruits were allowed to come down off the mast. Everybody looked cheerful as they lined up on the quay and Brendan felt a sense of achievement. They ate another meal and then there was another instruction session. Things were going smoothly and the mood of the group rose. If this was how the rest of the three months basic training would go then it shouldn't be too difficult. However, the moment the instruction session was over Training Sergeant Bayrooth pounded up to them and roared: "Get your lazy arses onto the parade ground now for some more PT!"

That PT session went on all afternoon. They ran, they marched, they did press-ups and sit-ups, and eventually they were forced to swim in the River Boyne fully clothed. Brendan had no sense of the passing of time, but it felt like days. When night finally fell he could barely believe it was the same day. At long last they stopped. He and the others were standing up to their calves in cold mud after tramping through the wetlands of the Boyne estuary for the last two hours. He shivered, his arms straight and his head up, struggling to maintain the poise. It must have been past midnight and he longed for Bayrooth to tell them finally that it was time for bed. These hopes were dashed when the trainer said: "We're not finished yet, lads. We have night time navigation to practice now."

There was a barely suppressed groan from the assembly.

"What's the matter, don't you like it?... You can quit if you want to. Anytime! All you have to do it stick your hand in the air and say 'Sir, I want to quit' and you can go straight back to barracks now. There'll be a nice hot dinner waiting for you, a warm bath, a soft cosy bed where you can sleep the clock round... Seaguard isn't for everybody. Not everybody has got what it takes! Come on! Any girly-men among you? Anybody miss their mummy?"

A boy to Brendan's right raised his hand. "Sir, I want to quit." He was crying with shame and embarrassment.

Bayrooth marched over to him. "Are you sure, Meadows?"

"Yes, sir."

Then to Brendan's amazement, Bayrooth held out his hand to the boy and they shook. "You did what you could, son. Well done for giving it a go. Corporal Gomez will escort you back to base." The tenderness with which Bayrooth spoke that last sentence was so uncharacteristic of him that everybody gasped. Meadows was led away by an assistant trainer while Bayrooth turned to the rest of them. "As for the rest of you, don't just stand there like a bunch of storks, get your legs moving! NOW! Left, right, left, right!..." It was almost two AM when they finally staggered into their dormitory. They stripped off and showered. Even then they couldn't sleep straight away. They had to make their beds with fresh linen first. Brendan was so exhausted that he began hearing voices in his ears and seeing faces in the creases of his folded blanket as his overdue dreams demanded his presence. He collapsed

onto the mattress and was asleep before the lights went out.
....

Brendan's powerful legs thrust through the water. He was running along the beach through the surf besides Bill and all his other friends. Saltwater splashed up over him, kicked up by his boots and those of the others. His trousers were soaked, but he didn't mind. His breathing was even, his muscles moved steadily, like the pistons in an IC engine. His body and mind had been toughened up. He enjoyed the view of the distant hills around him in Annascaul, County Kerry. He had visited some beautiful places over the last three months, especially during the last six weeks when the pace and format of his training had changed. He had hiked over the Curlew Mountains. It had been fun as well as picturesque. The troop had camped out in the wilderness and practiced living off the land by hunting, fishing and gathering edible plants or fungi. He had learned how to light a fire without matches, skin a rabbit, keep himself warm, treat wounds without proper medicine and a hundred other skills in the art of field-craft. He had also played a lot of sport, an activity that had only moderately interested him as a child. He had played soccer, rugby, boxing, Gaelic football and athletics. There had been numerous competitions against other recruit units at the base. It made him realize how insular the United States of America was in the sporting world. The most popular US sports of baseball and American football were virtually unknown beyond its borders. Seaguard was an Irish-based company and so that national culture considerably rubbed off on it. He had just one more week to endure and then he would pass out of phase one training. However, it was no longer a case of endurance. Brendan had become used to this lifestyle; he even enjoyed it. He could have happily gone on for another three months. The boys of Training Company 71D had originally numbered seventy but were now whittled down to thirty-nine, reorganized into three platoons. Many had quit and a few had been given medical discharges. Training Sergeant Bayrooth still barked and hollered at them, but his tone had eased slightly during the last third of their course. One subtle difference was that a month ago he had ordered them all to address him as "Training Sergeant" instead of "sir". This was one of many changes that had altered the atmosphere of their little community. He had made many friends and he had a feeling that he and Bill would be pals for life.

Eventually Bayrooth ordered them out of the sea and onto the beach; water dripped from their utilities and Brendan felt it squelching in his boots. A firing range had been set up on the beach and the trainees set up their weapons. Brendan managed to hit the centre of the target most times despite just finishing a long run. His kit had expanded as the course had worn on. He had been particularly inspired when he had been issued with armaments. The rifle was a Browning AR64 and was quite simple to use, even compared to the pistols his father had taught him to fire. Shooting the rifle was the easiest part; most of the instruction he'd received was about maintenance and safety. He had learned how to dismantle and clean it. He knew never to point it at anything he didn't want to shoot and to "clear" it after use; that is, remove all the ammunition. He had other items in his field kit as well that made him feel less of a recruit and more a proper operative (The word "soldier" could never be used for legal reasons). These included a combat dagger, a first aid kit, a compass and a pair of binoculars. His relationship with live firing had gone bad at one point. He had damaged his first rifle by fitting it together wrongly. When he fired, the weapon broke permanently and had to be scrapped. He was issued a new one, but Bayrooth punished him. The sentence had been carried out on this same beach three weeks ago. Brendan had been made to wade across a shallow stretch of water to a small sandbank. The water had risen up to his chest at its deepest. He had had to carry his new rifle over his head as he walked. "Hold your weapon high, Quilley!" Bayrooth warned him. "If it touches the water then you miss chow tonight!" Brendan's arms felt like fire and the rest of him felt like ice as he trudged through the freezing sea, but the thought of skipping a meal was even worse. Food had become an absolute necessity for all the trainees in terms of both nutrition and morale. Brendan had been far more proficient with his rifle ever since.

The passing out ceremony arrived the following Thursday and Brendan put on his full dress blues. He stood in front of a mirror for many minutes admiring himself in it. He and all the other training companies marched back and forth across the parade ground. There were spectator stands set up for their families and Brendan's were there, cheering him on. He watched his mother, father, Siobhan and the twins whenever he was facing in the right direction. The weather was warm and dry and everybody was smiling as they strode back and forth in unison. A dais of assembled dignitaries watched them including Seaguard officials and flag operatives. Brendan lined up with his classmates and a vice Admiral pinned a badge to their uniforms shaped like a silver sailing ship, the symbol of a qualified Seaguard sailor. When it was Brendan's turn he shook the officer's hand. "Well done, Seaman Quilley." He smiled.

"Thank you, sir."

Then Brendan walked over the stage to where Training Sergeant Bayrooth stood. They shook hands and the brutish drill instructor grinned. "Well done, Quilley. It's been a pleasure having you in the company."

"Thank you, Training Sergeant." He felt a sudden pang of almost filial love for Bayrooth. He had to blink rapidly to hold back tears. It was odd considering the continuous hazing that man had given him for the last three months. After the formalities were over the newly qualified sailors were allowed to mix with their families. There was much hugging and kissing all round. Multiple photographs were taken. It reminded Brendan of watching Siobhan graduate from university when he was a small child twelve years earlier. The one dampener on the jubilation was the absence of Heather. His beloved girlfriend had been booked for a crucial examination that very day and she was unable to avoid it. Therefore, as soon as he'd eaten the celebratory dinner with his family, he left the gathering.

He changed back into his original clothes, the ones in which he had arrived back in June. It felt like years ago. The clothes felt strange to wear. The trouser waist was too big, indicating that he had lost a lot of weight. He stepped out of the gates of the training camp and waited at the bus stop opposite. When he got off the bus in Drogheda he stood still for a moment in shock. He had entered the same world that he had left three months earlier, but it was like a distant planet. He couldn't get used to seeing people all wearing different clothes; there was nobody in uniform. Also some of the people were old and overweight. As he walked along the banks of the Boyne towards the station he saw some women. He stopped and stared. He had forgotten what women looked like; their hair, their clothes, the shape of their bodies, their faces, and the sound of their voices. He felt a sense of wonderment beyond the mere sexual. He had been so hot-housed by the intensity of Seaguard's training regime that it had institutionalized him. He had been living day and night on the base since mid-June. The only time he had even seen the outside world was when he went on expeditions and route marches. He checked himself when some of the women glared at him sharply for staring at them. He felt a bit guilty, for making them feel uncomfortable, but also because of a sense of loyalty towards Heather. The thought of his girlfriend made him quicken his pace as he strode towards the railway station. When he reached Dublin he caught the next speed-frightener to Baltimore and then went to his apartment to pick up his motorflyer. He ignored the dust and cobwebs that had accumulated in the quarter that the flat had been empty and sped off south toward Arkansas. Half an hour later, he landed in the carpark of the sprawling Jonesboro campus of Arkansas State University. He locked his motorflyer and headed into the main building where he knew the great hall would be. He saw a sign outside the hall with the words: "*Quiet please- exam in progress*", found a bench to sit on and waited. An hour later he heard people stirring in the hall. The students then rumbled out of the door, looking exhausted and worried. Heather was in the middle of them, neither one of the first nor last to leave. She saw Brendan and stopped in her tracks. She smiled and he smiled back. She pushed her way through the crowd and walked up to him. "Hi there, Brendan."

"Hi there, Heather."

How did it go?" she asked.

"Okay." he replied. "How did *it* go?" He nodded at the door to the hall.

She shrugged. "Pretty good; it wasn't too difficult. I feel confident." They paused for a moment then both began laughing at each other at the same time. The next moment they were in each other's arms, chuckling and weeping as they kissed.

Hours later, when they were both lying in bed, listening quietly to the sounds of Heather's accommodation block around them; Brendan turned to her instinctively, without any forethought or after any premeditated plan, and he said: "Will you marry me?"

....

Brendan had to make serious preparations for his two long motorflyer transits. He thought about taking public transport, but decided he needed solitude; he wanted time to think on the journey before reaching his destination. He packed his motorflyer panniers with a life-raft and distress beacon. Also four large plastic bottles of water and a tent. He had to worry about an emergency landing in both the ocean and desert. He had also fitted a hard Perspex windscreen to the front of the aircraft back in Rockville. Then he dressed for the journey. He felt strange donning a thick parka and kapok double layered trousers while standing in the carpark of Arkansas State University. It was a warm day of seventy-five degrees, typical for September in Dixie. He began sweating as he mounted the aircraft, but knew before long he would be glad of the thermal insulation he now wore. He put on his flying goggles, took off and headed east. His eardrums creaked as he ascended and he had to yawn every few seconds to clear them. He levelled off at ten thousand feet, just above the lower cloud layer. The Atlantic Ocean rolled under him after twenty minutes as he left North America just south of Chesapeake Bay and for the next ninety minutes his whole world was the sea blue beneath him and the hazy lifetrail-stained grey sky above. The golden glow of the Sahara Desert emerged over the horizon and he welcomed it, knowing it marked the impending end of his travel. There was a silver jagged line running from the coast inland across the sand; from his altitude of ten thousand feet it looked like a line of stitching. This was the Mauritania West African Waterworks Pipeline and Brendan followed it, admiring its shiny undulating perfection. He descended as he approached Tamale in the Volta Union and his navigation computer led him directly to his parents' home. The evening sun cast his shadow on the land below, a tiny dot zipping across the jungle and savannah, and then the streets of the city. He circled the house a few times, hoping the occupants would see him, and landed on the rooftop carpark next to his father's flyer. His mother and father came out to greet him. They had made him large dinner, even though all of them were still slightly full from the luncheon at Drogheda. The house they lived in was very similar to the Pearsons' except it was somewhat larger. Like their friends in Bawku, they had moved into a newly built suburb that was almost entirely populated by Western expatriates. After the meal they drank some wine and beer, and watched television. Brendan knew he had to tell them, but wanted to wait for the right moment. After a couple of drink rounds he knew that the right moment would never arrive, but he had to tell them at some point anyway; so he just did.

Clane slammed down his beer glass. "What?"

"I want to get married, dad."

"Who too?"

He chuckled. "Heather of course. Who did you think?"

There was a long silence, and then his mother said: "Honey, do you think that's wise?"

"What do you mean, mom?"

"You're very young."

"I'm eighteen! How old were you when you and dad got married?"

She paused and sighed. "Twenty-one."

"So that's just three years difference."

"Yes, but it's a big three years."

"Not these days, mom. Times have changed."

All through this conversation Brendan's father had been sitting silent, but a grin was slowly growing on his face. "This is fantastic!" he blurted out.

"Clane!" Brendan's mother snapped.

"No, Gina it is! Our son is getting married! It's wonderful."

"But he's just as boy!"

"He is not! He's grown up now."

"He's a teenager!"

"He's just passed basic training; he's a man! And Heather is a nice girl..."

The argument went on for a few more exchanges. Eventually Brendan intervened. "Look, it's not like we're going to jump the broom tomorrow. We haven't decided on a date yet and it's not something we can do for a couple of years. Heather's got college and I've got Power School."

Gina relaxed after hearing that. They talked about other subjects for several more hours before going to bed. As he was closing his bedroom door, Brendan overheard his mother talking to his father on the landing. "Who knows what could happen between now and then? They may decide not to go through with it; or he might meet somebody else." His father replied, but his words were inaudible. Brendan closed his door quietly. He knew that Clane held Heather in far higher esteem than his wife did. Gina had always displayed casual hostility towards her, even when she and Brendan were small children. Clane once told him that Gina and Heather's parents had had a major conflict over something long ago when they had first moved to Rockville, but he didn't go into details. Brendan slept badly, partly because he was sad about his mother's antipathy for the girl he loved, but also because of excitement.

In the morning he got up early and breakfasted with his parents. They bade each other a fond farewell and Brendan swung his leg over his motorflyer. He ascended above the African landscape and set a course due north along the Greenwich Meridian. When he reached the English Channel he turned northwest towards Ireland and the autopilot guided him toward Belfast and the Seaguard Power School, the company's engineering academy into which Brendan had enrolled. During their basic training, the recruits had to make choices about their future careers in Seaguard. After passing out, they would be sent for advanced training in a more specialized field; weapons, amphibious warfare, submarines, aviation, communications and a myriad of other trades. For Brendan the decision was a no-brainer; he would become a marine engineer. The new sailors were offered a month's leave after the end of phase one training, but Brendan had declined it. He wanted to start at Power School as soon as possible and an opening was available the very day after his qualification. He simply couldn't wait. Belfast was a fine city with neat buildings, clean red roofs and straight streets with right-angled junctions. It looked fresh and health today, with bright sunlight and the glitter of recent rainfall on the roads and pavements. It had originally been the capital of Northern Ireland and was today a thriving second city of the Irish Republic. The partition had fallen in 1962 soon after R-Day with the collapse of the United Kingdom. Today the region was fairly peaceful seeing that the Ulster Protestants had no Britain to remain united with. The new republics of England, Scotland and Wales had turned their backs on their former territory over the water. After a decade within a united Ireland the people on both sides of the divide had become accustomed to it. Another incentive for a new start was the fact that the R-ratio, that is the amount of the population who metamorphosed into reptilian form on R-Day, was the highest in the world. Over forty percent of the Northern Ireland's citizens had shape-shifted and then dropped dead when the SQEC particle accelerator in Canada had been destroyed. What was almost as shocking was that the forty percent consisted of both Protestants and Catholics in proportional levels.

The Power School was housed in a modern steel framed glass walled square structure that reminded Brendan of the newer parts of the naval academy in Annapolis. It was situated to the west of the city centre. He orbited it a few times at about a hundred feet to admire the campus and enjoy the anticipation of what was to come; then he landed in the carpark and stripped off his flight suit. He had his uniform on underneath and carried his kitbag towards the door that was marked "*Reception*". He announced his presence and waited on a bench until a thin young man with spectacles and a white coat, like a doctor's, approached from the end of a long corridor. "Mr Quilley?" he said as he came close and held out his hand. Brendan shook it. The man had called him "mister" instead of using his rank; this meant he was a specialist rather than an operative, a non-combatant employee of Seaguard. "I'm Dr McCauley." He had a strong Ulster accent. Something about his demeanour made Brendan uneasy. The slightly over-forced smile, the evasiveness of his eyes. He had bad news for Brendan.

"Dr McCauley. Good to meet you. I'm very much looking forward to studying here."

He paused awkwardly. "And we're looking forward to having you here as a student, Mr Quilley... but I'm afraid we can't enrol you today."

"What? Why?"

He sighed and handed Brendan a brown envelope. "I've been told to give you this."

Brendan ripped it open in a panic. Inside was a two page letter which he skimmed in a second, read more slowly and then a third time more slowly again. He groaned and screwed it up with both hands.

"I'm sorry, Mr Quilley. Naturally you'll be welcome back to Power School at a later date."

The letter was a deployment order. It informed him that he was to be loaned to Landguard, Seaguard's equivalent in the land warfare role, to assist in security operations in the United States of America. There was no duration in the details so Brendan didn't know how long this secondment would last. "What the fuck!?... Why!? What's all this about?"

McCauley shrugged. "I don't know."

"They *told* me I had been accepted at Power School! They *told* me goddamnit!"

McCauley made Brendan a cup of tea and let him use his office. Brendan called Seaguard's personnel administration and demanded to speak to whoever had arranged his detachment. After being transferred a few times and being put on hold for a long time, he spoke to a gruff and unsympathetic officer who informed him that his draft was not negotiable. Brendan was trapped. He had no choice. He was almost in tears as he shuffled out to the carpark and dressed again in his flight suit. He didn't look back and he drove his motorflyer into the air and headed west across the Atlantic.

....

Brendan was bored and thought of what kind of boredom it was. Tedium rather than monotony. The two were not exact synonyms and the former included an element of stress mixed in with the boredom. He was standing on Constitution Avenue in Washington DC. In front of him was the neoclassical facade of the National Art Gallery. It was cold and raining lightly; drips trickled down the visor of his helmet. The trailing end of the demonstration had just passed; about five thousand people covered in raincoats and carrying placards and banners, chanting angrily. A man was walking back and forth on the road in front of Brendan and his colleagues. He had dark greasy hair and was wearing a trenchcoat. There was a patch on the breast that said: "*Columbia Finance*". He grinned with yellow smokers' teeth at Brendan. "Good afternoon, young sir. Can I interest you in purchasing alien abduction insurance? We at Columbia Finance offer the lowest premiums, the biggest payouts. No interview with an MFOlogist is required..."

"No, thank you." Brendan interrupted curtly.

The salesman nodded, moved on to the next cop and repeated the question. This time he handed the officer a promotional leaflet. He was in the right place. The street protest Brendan was helping to manage was organized by a lobby group representing alien abductees. They were demanding assistance from the government as well as criminal injury compensation. The procession had been led by Betty Hill, the woman whose house Brendan had visited three years ago with Siobhan. Her husband Barney had died in 1969 and she was now the sole director of the AAACWS- the American Alien Abductee and Contactee Welfare Society which had four hundred thousand members. Brendan's job was to assist the local police in maintaining law and order during the march, which wasn't difficult because the abductees were a peaceful tendency. Eventually he heard the sound of a voice speaking through a megaphone in the distance. The demonstration had reached the end of its route on the National Mall and they were having a rally. Cheers rose from the crowd every now and again as the speaker addressed them. At the end of the rally the demonstration broke up and seeing that there were no counter-demonstrators to keep away from them, and there never would be since the skeptic movement had entirely collapsed, the police operation ended. Brendan said goodbye to the DC police he had been working with and headed for the Landguard hub, which consisted of a caravan parked on a street corner. He handed in his weapons and equipment and then checked his slate for further orders. There was an

E-gram: "*QUILLEY, Brendan 62481. Immediate. Proceed to Landguard base, Dallas Ft Worth TX.*" He sighed; it was another assignment, the third since his secondment had started in September. It was now November the 6th. He left the hub and walked to the railway station. He could have nipped there by flyer in forty-five minutes, but he preferred to take the train, even though it was an eighteen hour trip. His orders hadn't prohibited him from doing that. He loved rail travel. Trains were the nearest he could get to engineering at the moment. He loved the concept of the railways; energy and mass channelled so smoothly and efficiently down a steel conduit. It thrilled him. He sat in the dining coach and read his copy of Siobhan's book *Taken*. Despite her uneasiness, she had quickly found a publisher and the title had sold reasonably well. It had served as useful homework for the demonstration he had supervised that day. He spent the night on a couchette in a compartment with three other people. The rocking, rumbling and jerking of the coach over its rails was one of the most tranquillizing sensations he had ever felt. He slept deeply and calmly. He awoke to see dark clouds exactly like the ones he had left behind in Washington DC. Thanks to the intensive lifetrail schedule everywhere was having a damp cold autumn. He raised the window blind and saw that the train was rolling slowly through the suburbs of Dallas. When it pulled into the station Brendan walked up the platform with his kitbag and took a taxicab to the local Landguard base in Fort Worth. He ate a meal in the mess and then attended muster for his duties, being introduced to a dozen new strangers again, which seemed to be the norm during his current job. The unit to which he had been assigned drove in a bus to a Texas State Police station. The lieutenant in charge briefed the mixed team of mercenaries and police officers: "Right, we've got some trouble in Aurora, a little place up in Wise County..."

Brendan pricked up his ears. This was somewhere his father had told him about although he couldn't quite remember why. However, as the lieutenant explained, Brendan began to understand why his father was connected to the location. They were taken to Aurora on a convoy of buses. Over two hundred police and security assistants were aboard them, which was amazing considering the village itself only had about five hundred residents. Brendan couldn't conceive of why such serious social unrest had broken out in such a tiny rural settlement. Aurora was a sparse amalgamation of farms and country houses linked by straight untracked roads with bushes and clusters of trees in between. It sat astride Highway One-One-Four as if cut in half by the main road. The police buses turned left onto Cemetery Road and came across a double row of white vans parked on the verges. They were clean and new; on their sides and doors was the seal of the Department of Disclosure Affairs. Around the vehicles were standing a group of DoDA officers looking agitated. A gaggle of reporters were actively taking photographs and writing on slates. After they had decamped from the buses the police lieutenant briefed the state troopers and their aids. "Right, guys. This is the situation. The DoDA has an exhumation order for a grave in the local cemetery down this road. The ruling was issued last month at the North Texas US District Court. An appeal was turned down last week at both the Texas Supreme Court and the Texas Appellate Court. The DoDA are now here to exhume the grave, but the local people are blockading the cemetery. Our task it to remove that blockade and allow the DoDA to carry out their duties under the exhumation order. Use minimal force and only make arrests if necessary..." The cops then began marching down the road past the white vans. A reporter ran up to Brendan as he strode along. "Excuse me." he said in a Texan accent. He was a large man with glasses, a sunhat and a thick dark beard. "Jim Marrs, *Fort Worth Star-Telegram*. Can you tell me what the police intend to do here today?"

"No comment." responded Brendan immediately. He marched down the narrow track between well kept gardens and lawns until they arrived at the cemetery. A white metal fence surrounded the necropolis. Inside were the gravestones, all clean and all different shapes and sizes, and arranged in rows. Between them were trimmed baulks of grass, all lush and green like grass in Texas tended to be in autumn. There were aggressive warning signs by the gate giving a list of numerous everyday activities that were banned inside the cemetery, and a white painted steel arch over the gate with the words in black: *"Aurora Cemetery- est. 1861"*. A huge crowd of people were standing inside the white fence. They faced the oncoming phalanx of policemen with scowls and resolute stances. There were men, women and children. An elderly couple were near the gate propped up on walking sticks, clearly finding it difficult to remain upright. One woman was holding a small baby, her husband stood at her side holding the hands of two other children aged about four to six years. The police stopped suddenly with the thud of their hard boots.

"Good morning." called out the lieutenant. "I am Lt. Brady of Texas State Police. We're here to assist the US Department of Disclosure Affairs in their operation to remove one of the cadavers from a grave plot here. Please stand aside and allow them to do their jobs."

"No!" shouted a man from inside. "Nobody at rest is going to be disturbed in a grave at this cemetery! This is sacred ground. I am the chairman of the Aurora Cemetery Committee and this breaches every standard we have worked to maintain. We will not permit it!"

"Sir, we have an order from a US District Court enforcing..."

"I could care less what the damn Feds want for their business! This is a holy place that we, the townsfolk of Aurora, have struggled to preserve for over a hundred years! We have been honouring our fallen here for our entire history and we will not dishonour them now... So take your court order and shove it!"

"Sir, it is my understanding that the grave the DoDA with to exhume is not the final resting place for any resident in this town. The cadaver interred is that of an extraterrestrial being, is that not correct?"

"It makes no difference. The man died here in Aurora and was given a proper Christian burial here at the cemetery in Aurora. He is entitled to remain at rest for all time under the right of sepulchre laws in the State of Texas!"

"Sir, I'm afraid those laws include the provision for proper legal exhumation under licence, and the DoDA has that licence. Now, all of you, leave the cemetery and disperse to your home addresses. Do it now please, or we will have to employ the lawful use of force!"

There was an ugly scene. Brendan felt awful being a part of it. There was no violence; indeed most of the occupiers were not capable of serious violence, being too old or too young or female. He and the other Landguard operatives, together with the Texas state troopers, frogmarched the people one-by-one out of the cemetery and down the lane to a holding area where they were arrested. Some of them had to be handcuffed. They protested verbally, sometimes clutching at tree branches and fence posts to try and anchor themselves in place. It took almost two hours, then eventually the cemetery was empty and Brendan too his place by the fence as the law enforcers formed a human chain around the graveyard. A group of DoDA personnel walked seriously down the road from the vans and in through the gate. They were all wearing white nuclear, biological and chemical protection suits with hoods and masks. Four of them carried a steel box the size and shape of a coffin. More of them arrived with a set of gardening tools. They set up a large plastic tent underneath one of the trees. A few hours later four of them re-emerged carrying the steel box. Despite their hazmat suits, Brendan could tell by their body movements that they felt nervous about what they had found. When he was relieved of duty and returned to the Fort Worth Landguard base to relax he read about it on his slate. Jim Marrs, the reporter who had questioned him, had written a long article in the *Fort Worth Star-Telegram* about the day's events. The DoDA's interest in the grave came from the story that it contained the body of an alien. In 1897 a strange aircraft had crashed at Aurora and the body of a biological occupant had been retrieved and buried in the cemetery. It was similar to the Roswell Incident only fifty years before. The DoDA was investigating all events of an extraterrestrial nature under an open and public commission.

Tired of the news and almost ready for bed, Brendan logged onto SeaguardMesh, the company's private computer network, and opened his E-grams. He had one that made him sit up: "*QUILLEY, Brendan 62481. Flash. You are relieved of detachment to Landguard. Proceed ASPC to Seaguard Power School in Belfast, Ireland.*" Brendan read the E-gram several times, hoping he was not dreaming. The last two months of his miserable duties melted away in his memory like ice cubes in hot water. Everybody in the mess jumped in shock as Brendan leapt to his feet and whooped for joy.

Chapter 11

"Stand blue watch." came a voice from the loudspeaker on the overhead. Brendan looked up from the control panel and yawned. That pipe meant that he was now off duty for the next six hours. The technicians around him stood up as the new watchstanders walked into the engine room carrying fresh mugs of coffee and buttoning up their boiler suits. "Good morning, sir." said Chief Artificer Marvin Hollinshead to him as he greeted the departing watch.

"Morning, Marvin." replied Brendan. He knew that proper protocol would be for him to address the technician by his surname alone, but he found that too strange. Ashore it would be obligatory, but at sea this was one of the many regulations of which the bending, or even breaking, was tolerated. Brendan was only twenty-one years old while Hollinshead was forty-four. It felt almost theatrically strange to be addressed as 'sir' by a man so much older. Brendan was an officer and had been since his commission three months earlier when he had ascended from Senior Cadet Quilley to Sub-Lieutenant Quilley. This single step up the hierarchy came with a massive cultural jolt. He had to leave his bunk in the general berthing section and move to a stateroom which he shared with two other officers. His laundry and other housekeeping were done for him by a steward and he ate all his meals in the wardroom instead of the rated mess. As with Hollinshead, the way the crew spoke to him changed. The most uncomfortable part of this transformation was when the crew were informally socializing. A week earlier they had put in at Jakarta for shore leave and he had been subtly informed that he would be expected to accompany the ship's other officers to the opera house. He was very disappointed because he was hoping to spend the evening at the racetrack with his usual friends among the ratings. So instead he endured hours sitting in his dress whites watching Mozart's *The Marriage of Figaro* with the captain and tactics officer sitting on either side of him, neither of whom he particularly liked. He didn't speak any Italian other than the usual English loanwords like "spaghetti" and so could not understand the performance. Afterwards they went to a grand restaurant. Brendan had a very upmarket meal, but he didn't enjoy it much. He longed to be with his old friends trawling the taverns, nightclubs and fast-food joints, addressing his friends by their first name. Instead he had to dine with the other officers who always called each other "Mr..." whoever. At least at sea he was still reasonably free to mingle naturally and behave like a normal human being.

"You have the engine, Marvin." he said to Hollinshead after a brief report, formally handing over the watch to his colleague.

"I have the engine, sir. You may stand relieved." The new watchstanders got to work while the old ones wearily trooped out of the engine room to the mess or their bunks. Brendan did not leave immediately. He wanted to have one last walk around the engine room.

Brendan was sleepy and hungry, but his excitement still had the power to raise him above his bodily needs. He had only qualified to command a watch in the engine room a week earlier and since then he had stood five stints in charge of the ship's power-plant and propulsion system. These six-hour periods of time were a dream come true for him. He was almost disappointed when his watch came to an end, allowing him finally to eat and to sleep. The engine room of this ship was very different from the one inside the LoWS *Belleau Wood*. Firstly it was far quieter. In place of the shriek of the turbines and the roar of pump motors was the serene rustle of seawater running through pipes. The engineers did not even need earmuffs. It was also much cooler with no boilers, hot gas channels or steam pipes. There was very little need for lubrication oil, so the engineers did not have to endure, or enjoy, the smell and stains which were one of the pleasures or hardships of their trade. It was a shirtsleeve environment. Unlike most ships' engine rooms which are usually situated aft, this one filled the entire lower decks of the vessel from stem to stern. Its principle hardware consisted of two large bore pipes that ran from intakes at the bow to outflow vents at the stern, both well below the waterline. These functioned rather like a jet engine, except it was water that was sucked in at the front and blown out of the back instead of air. From a military point of view this made the ship far more stealthy because the engine was very quiet compared to a conventional reciprocating engine. The latter produced vibrations and was driven by noisy screw propellers, making it easy to locate by an enemy using hydrophones. Brendan's ship was like a silent shark, gently undulating its way through the ocean. The pipes led from the intakes at the prow to a refrigeration system that cooled the water to the right temperature, about two and a half degrees Celsius; this was then channelled into an "implosion vortex chamber" which consisted of a double helix of inwardly spiralling pipes of carefully measured dimensions. At this point, energy was released and the water was then thrust aft and out of the ship at an accelerated rate providing propulsion for the vessel. The energy came from a zero point release process within the water itself and it required no fuel. It was free energy. Brendan had first been introduced to the concept when he had visited the waterworks at Pismo Beach as a child and had been hooked on it ever since. The technology had been invented by an Austrian forester called Viktor Schauberger forty years earlier. He had found that fish swimming in a river can power themselves using their gills instead of their fins. He had created from this his machine, the "Trout Turbine". He had been forced to work for the Nazis against his will when they annexed Austria and he helped design the "Haunebu" flying saucers. He died in 1958 unrecognized and unappreciated... until Disclosure. The Schauberger-designed engines of the ship were not only very quiet, they were comparatively simple. There were no large moving parts at all and the most complicated pieces of machinery were actually the pumps in the seawater cooling stage. There was a fairly complicated volume throttle to adjust the ship's speed, but apart from that the engine was very minimalist. This made it very easy to maintain. Only four crewmembers at a time were needed in the engine room during normal steaming routine. Their principle tasks were to monitor the temperature of the seawater inside the system to prevent a "thermal stall", when a pocket of warmer water was caught inside the engine jamming it. The structure of water flow inside the vortex implosion chamber was also very important. Sometimes this was disrupted by solid objects such as fish, driftwood, seaweed and other foreign bodies being sucked into the engines; it could also change according to the salinity and other chemical changes to the seawater. There was an array of auxiliary systems powered by the main drive, principally the electricity generators. The intakes had pumps to drive seawater into the engines at low speeds, but when the ship was making more than ten or eleven knots these could be switched off and water flowed in effortlessly by a ram effect. The efficiency of the intakes was dependent on water temperature. In the hot tropical seas this was lower, but in colder seas it was higher. In polar waters it was even necessary to use a heater to bring the water up to the ideal temperature for implosion.

Eventually Brendan was ready to say goodbye to the engines for another twelve hours. He also got the impression that Hollinshead was irritated by Brendan's habit of hanging around in the engine room when he was off duty. During the watch, the space was Hollinshead's domain and the young sub-lieutenant was invading it. Brendan was trying to break the habit. He nodded apologetically to the older rating as he exited the hatch and climbed the stairway to the rest of the ship. He stepped out onto the open deck for a breath of fresh air. It was dawn on the Andaman Sea and the weather was calm and bright. The sun was glinting on the horizon and the hiss of the ship's hull cutting the water filled his ears. He leaned over the rail and admired the lines of the craft. His ship was called Seaguard *Heather* and Brendan found it both amusing and comforting to be aboard a ship with the same name as his wife. *Heather* was one of the seven ships of the *Shamrock*-class. They displaced five thousand tons and were the principle frigates of the Seaguard fleet. He was on the port side and looked forward to his right at the gun turret and missile launchers on the prow. When he turned his head aft he could see the air platform where the ships two anti-submarine flyers took off and landed. He was finally ready to rest. He ate breakfast and retired to his stateroom. He knew he would not be able to relax for the entire twelve hours until he was due back in the engine room. Everybody aboard the ship had more than one job and could be called to do anything at anytime; therefore taking every opportunity to sleep was essential. He collapsed into his bunk fully clothed in his boiler suit and fell into slumber instantaneously as usual.

He was woken soon after ten AM by a pipe on his personal voicelink, a small communicator that resembled a roamphone. "Four hours sleep." he muttered as he rolled out onto the deck. "Not bad." All the officers were summoned to the wardroom for a briefing by the captain. Seaguard *Heather* had been given orders for an amphibious operation. They were sailing through the Mergui Islands off the coast of Burma heading towards Bentinck Island. Intelligence sources had indicated that there was somebody living there who was wanted by the League of the World's Disclosure and Reconciliation Organization. They had orders to land on the island and arrest the suspect. Brendan's job was to lead the landing party. He went to prepare the launch with a group of six sailors. They dressed in landing fatigues, helmets and flak jackets. They armed themselves with a variety of weapons and then inflated the rubber sidewalls of the launch. Brendan tested the Digby-powered outboard motor and attached it to the launch. By the time they were ready, the ship had arrived. It was crawling along at bare steerageway, about two knots. A few miles away the skyline was dominated by a row of steep and high triangular hills completely covered in bright green forest, the deep green of a tropical rain forest which was a distinctly different shade to the temperate broadleaf and coniferous forests that Brendan was used to. The landing party climbed aboard the launch and it was lowered into the sea by a crane. The pilot started the motor and they powered away from Seaguard *Heather* towards land. Brendan looked back the ship; a number of the crew were standing on the open decks watching them.

The target shoreline was on a smaller island just off the coast of the Bentinck mainland, as if it had once been a peninsula that had detached itself. The island was about two miles long and its land rose to a wooded crest a good few hundred feet above the coast. The suspect was supposed to be living on the eastern side of the island so the ship had approached from the west in order not to alert them. The dramatic geography of the island helped that concealment. The boat bumped and rocked through the surf until it arrived at the clean beach of the shore. The sailors had their rifles at the ready even though the island was thought to be uninhabited apart from the suspect. Nobody was in sight. The beach was covered in pieces of flotsam and dry seaweed. There were no footprints in the sand. "Get the launch undercover!" ordered Brendan. They carried the boat up the beach and left it under an overhanging branch of a tree so that it was hidden from anybody inland. Then they began walking up the hard slope of the island, hacking away the undergrowth with machetes to create a rough temporary path. The air was stifling. Brendan found that at sea there was always a freshness and chill to the air regardless of the climactic zone he was in, but on land it was totally different. The island's trees provided a lot of shade, but it was still very hot and humid. He sweated like a showerhead. The jungle scent crowded his nose, and the rattle of birdsong and chattering monkeys surrounded them. Flies buzzed intrusively around his head. They used a map and satellite images to guide them. Eventually they reached the ridge and could see downhill to the eastern side of the island. The highest point of the island was marked by a crude wall of rotten cement surrounding a shallow earthy pit. Inside them were the rusty remains of metallic objects that looked like mortar launchers. Brendan knew that this was the remains of a Japanese dugout left over from World War II. The mood of the sailors became grave as they approached the target location. They kept their heads low and peeped cautiously out from between bushes, treading silently. The suspect was said to be solitary, but the sailors did not yet know how much of a resistance they would make. There was a building ahead, a large bungalow with a long verandah. Beside it were a collection of small sheds. The sailors crouched at the edge of the clearing in which the buildings stood. At a signal from Brendan three of them ran forward towards the front door while three more took up positions at the back of the house in case the suspect made a run for it in that direction. Brendan knocked on the door with his fist. "Melanie O'Conner! Open the door!" He thumped again. "Open the door, Melanie O'Connor! You are under arrest!"

There was the noise of footsteps from inside the bungalow, easily audible through the thin walls which were laced with green mould. The latch clicked and the doorknob turned. The door was not locked; and Brendan wondered why this had not occurred to him seeing as that the house was so remote and inaccessible. It squeaked open and a face appeared. "So you're here at last." said a calm voice.

Melanie O'Connor did not resist arrest at all. She held her arms out willingly for the handcuffs and listened politely as Brendan read out the arrest warrant. She stood tall in a dignified and fearless manner as the six aggressive men apprehended her. She was tall and very thin, almost emaciated. She had long thin grey hair that looked as if it had not been cut for a while. She was wearing a tattered dress that had once been white but was now a dirty grey. Its hem and cuffs were ragged. She had a bony face with a very prominent chin, but the most striking part of her physiognomy was her eyes. They were bright blue and very wide. Even though she was clearly quite elderly, Melanie O'Connor's eyes looked like those of a much younger woman. However they were strangely lifeless, devoid of depth. They looked as if they had been painted onto her face. Her home was bare except for some basic furniture. She had a water distiller and a free energy generator, to provide power. She had several computers and a satellite antenna through which she was obviously keeping in touch with the outside world. This might explain why she was unsurprised at being arrested; her name had been circulated in the media for many years. Despite her undernourished manifestation it appeared she had been eating well. There were saucepans and other eating utensils in the kitchen sink waiting to be washed up. The sheds surrounding her house were packed with stocks of canned food and other groceries that were only partly consumed. Brendan estimated she could have holed out there for another five years if she'd had to. At first O'Connor only spoke to confirm her name, but then turned to Brendan. "You say you're Brendan Quilley?" She had an educated Anglo-Irish accent. "Aren't you the son of Clane Quilley?"

"What of it?" responded Brendan evasively, remembering that he had to play the role of policeman.

"I'll need your father to testify at my trial."

"Eh? What are you talking about?"

"My lawyer will be in touch." She looked at him over her shoulder as the sailors led her away up the hillside towards the beach.

....

Seaguard *Heather* was steaming away from the Mergui archipelago as fast as possible to clear the datum following the apprehension of Melanie O'Connor. Once the ship was out of sight of land, the captain ordered the vessel to stop in order to reward the crew for a job well done. It was four-thirty PM and the sun was dropping towards the horizon. All off-watch crew stripped off their clothes and dived into the sea for a deep water swim. The crew was all male and there was no shame in their bodies. It was an almost primeval sense of brotherhood, as if they had become a litter for a creature from a species that has multiple births. They rolled in the sea like children in a bath. Brendan stood on the gunwales thirty feet above the waves, completely naked, brimming over with a sense of fun. He jumped; there was a rush of air and then a rush of water filling his eyes, nose and ears. He clawed his way up to the surface and breached like a dolphin, whooping, gasping and spitting brine. The sea was tepid; almost body temperature, like amniotic fluid. He had a sense of contentment so deep that it crossed his mind that it might be a subconscious memory of his mother's womb.

Someone on the deck above threw down a beach ball and an unceremonious game of water polo broke out. Brendan took part eagerly until a blast of air and water burst out of the sea. A spout of white spume rose above them and drops of hot water showered down on them. "Whale!" somebody yelled. Brendan looked at where the spout had come from, treading water to see over the waves. A hundred feet away the waters parted and a dark bluish-grey hump rose up, drips trickling off its greasy surface. It rolled forward like a vast snake and vanished briefly. It then remerged with another blast of foggy steam from a complex blowhole on the top of the hump. Then a huge tail lifted up above the water, like a fish's only horizontal; about twelve to fifteen feet from tip to tip. It cast a shadow over the swimming humans as if an aeroplane had just appeared in the air. It paused erect for a few seconds, like an angel spreading its wings, and then it slid through the surface into the depths so smoothly it barely made a ripple. Brendan stared in wonder. The other sailors were chattering excitedly, swimming closer to the marine behemoth that had emerged in their presence. "It's probably curious." said one. "It's come over to see what we're doing."

"It's a blue whale!" called another man. "The biggest whale of all; even bigger than other whales and they're all really big."

"It's perfectly safe." said somebody to a man who was nervous. "It's the largest beast that ever lived, but it's gentle as a lamb. It only eats tiny shrimps and it's got no teeth in its mouth."

Brendan called up to a friend of his on the ship: "Hey, Del; has anybody got a pair of goggles?" His friend threw down a pair of swimming goggles and Brendan put them on. He ducked under the surface and was surrounded by the maritime sheen of the ocean. The sounds of waves were cut out and the voices of his crewmates were muffled and muted. The whale's body was a black wall in front of him. He kicked himself closer and closer until he could reach out and touch its skin. It felt rubbery and slightly oily. He ran his knuckles along its flank as he paddled along until the creatures left eye appeared. It was deep-set and dark beneath a thick, powerful lid. Brendan couldn't tell its iris and pupil apart. He gazed into the slate blue cornea and the eye gazed back. Then the massive eyelid blinked and the whale pushed itself onwards. Brendan's lungs were aching from holding his breath so he surfaced and gasped. The noises of the world above the sea returned; the talking of the crew, the hissing of the waves, the rushing of the breeze. Brendan noticed them as if hearing them for the first time. The whale slowly glided away, its tail rose into the air one more time as if it were waving goodbye.

"Are you alright, Mr Quilley?" the captain asked him at dinner in the wardroom that evening.

"Yes, sir." he nodded.

"You're very quiet." Brendan realized that his strange mood had quickly been noticed by his shipmates. In the intimate closed society of the underway Seaguard *Heather*, there was an almost telepathic link between them. Since the swim in the sea that afternoon he had been consumed by very strange thoughts and emotions. He felt as if he had suddenly emerged in a new environment; everything around him had lost its familiarity and it was as if he were seeing everything for the first time. His body felt ungainly and clumsy. When he breathed, the air felt too dry and he noticed subtle and minor smells that he had ignored before. Every time he closed his eyes he could see the calm gaze of the whale's eye. It almost was as if the whale had spoken to him, but that he hadn't quite heard the words or they were in a language he couldn't speak. Over the last few hours he had done his job normally. Melanie O'Conner had been taken to the ship's brig. The small cell was normally used for storage when the ship had no prisoners, which was almost all the time. These had been hastily moved to make room for her. Two hours later a flyer from the aircraft carrier Seaguard *Munster* had arrived on *Heather*'s landing pad. Brendan and three sailors led her up onto the deck. The flyer then took off with her aboard in handcuffs. From *Munster* she would be flown to Fort Batten, Seaguard's operational headquarters in Dublin, where she would be handed over to the company's client, the state authorities, and formally charged. However, all through this procedure the whale and his interaction with it were never out of Brendan's mind.

....

The environment could not have been more different. Just a month earlier Seaguard *Heather* and her crew had been enjoying the tropical warmth of the Burmese coast and now they were on the other side of the world, steaming through the ice-speckled southern ocean. The refrigeration system on the engine induction had been deactivated and instead the heater had to be used to warm the seawater to the two-point-five degrees Celsius necessary for the Schauberger reaction. Its outside temperature was barely above freezing; freshwater that cold would have been solid ice. Brendan was on watch in the engine room where he was happiest. When he was down here in the bowels of the ship he was cut off from the confusion, complexity and strife of the outside world in the same way he was cut off from fresh air and sunlight. He was willing to trade the latter for the former any day. The engines responded predictably to commands; he understood them when he was baffled my almost everything else. He had not yet been briefed on the purpose of their current mission except that he knew something very strange was going on. When the ship had docked at Port Stanley in the Falkland Islands three days earlier the amphibious assault ship Seaguard *Finn McCool* had been there also. *Heather* had then been ordered to act as a destroyer escort for the *Finn McCool* as it sailed to Southern Thule. Brendan had difficulty finding Southern Thule on the navigation charts. It was a little trio of islands at the southern end of the South Sandwich chain, on the extremity of the Antarctic Peninsula. Each one was less than two miles across and extremely cold, windswept and barren. There was no soil, only rocks and ice; and nothing lived there except passing penguins. Therefore it made the *Heather* crew very inquisitive when they learned that *Finn McCool* had embarked an entire battalion of troops from the Seaguard Marines. There were also a large number of news reporters on both ships. "What is this? D-Day?" quipped Marvin Hollinshead. The three-day voyage had been fairly uneventful except that a reconnaissance aircraft from the Greater Bolivia Socialist Union had circled them a few times at a low altitude, obviously curious about activities of the evil superstitious capitalist imperialists. The Red Belt was worrying close and the GBSU had just declared war on Argentina; it was a tense and pessimistic time in that part of the world, especially since the GBSU now had nuclear weapons. An even greater threat was icebergs. Unlike the *Titanic* sixty-two years earlier, Seaguard *Heather* had the technology to scan the sea constantly with radar and sonar; but despite this the captain ordered a limit to her speed in case there was a chunk out there too small to be detected, but large enough to do damage to the hull.

When Brendan came off watch, it was dark and the pair of Seaguard warships was just a few miles from Southern Thule. They slowed to bare steerageway and tiptoed along the western coast. The captain gave all the officers a briefing and then all the off-duty officers went up on deck to watch. However there was nothing to see except utter blackness. Night had fallen and clouds covered the sky, both natural ones and lifetrails. No moon or stars shone. Neither ship was running with lights because it was important that they should not be seen from the shore. There was a habitat on the nearest island that might have had artificial lights on it, but it was on the far side of the land. The ships had approached from the opposite side of the island, as they had when landing on Bentinck Island the previous month. "It's like being inside an eight-ball." said the navigation officer perceptively. The frigid air ate into their parkas like acid. Luckily there was only a light wind; otherwise the sub-Antarctic cold would be unbearable. Brendan knew from the briefing that at that moment landing boats from *Finn McCool* were sailing towards the shore to deposit the marines. Eventually the officers got bored of staring into the darkness while shivering and chattering their teeth. Brendan went to bed. He got up at dawn for an extra watch on the bridge as junior officer-of-the-deck. His job was to assist the officer-of-the-deck, the man directing the ship's movements; which was a very easy job at that time because Seaguard *Heather* was sailing back and forth at dead slow speed. He watched the sky lighten and for the first time saw the view around them. They were two miles off the western coast of Southern Thule, an extinct volcanic cone completely white with ice and snow. Its peak was muffled by the low clouds. *Finn McCool* was matching their movements two hundred yards off their inside beam. Nothing happened through the hours of the morning and the crew chatted quietly to pass the time. Suddenly there was a cracking banging explosion, easily audible inside the ship's hull, like nearby thunder. Brendan looked out of the window towards the island and saw a column of smoke rising from Southern Thule. It formed into a mushroom shape, as if nuclear, and was thick and grey like wood smoke. It merged with the overcast. An hour later the landing boats set sail from the shore towards Seaguard *Finn McCool*. When all the men and craft were stowed aboard both ships powered up their engines and headed west. Southern Thule dropped below the horizon. Brendan was brimming over with curiosity, but he had to do another six hour watch below. It was the first time ever he looked forward to leaving the engine room.

After the watches changed, he leaped up the stairs to the wardroom where a dozen officers and stewards were clustered round the television screen. The news networks were all buzzing with what they called "the drama in the south". While Seaguard *Heather* and *Finn McCool* had been floating off the coast, the marines had landed on Southern

Thule and approached the settlement on the island, a base called *Il Nostro Sud* run by an organized crime syndicate. The TV news channel displayed a photograph of it from a few years previously. Its architecture was typical of polar bases, consisting of a row of bright red buildings elevated off the ground by metal piles. They were cylindrical and had small windows to conserve heat. The marines had surrounded the base and ordered the occupants to surrender. It turned out there were only fifteen people inside and they had few armaments. Being grossly outnumbered and outgunned, they did the sensible thing and agreed. At present they were locked in the brig aboard *Finn McCool*. The marines then laid explosive charges and blew the buildings sky high; that had been the explosion. Brendan looked at the size of the buildings, remembered the yield of the blast and thought that it had been somewhat excessive. However, that was certainly not the end of the story. The news programme played a clip of a video filmed by an embedded reporter following a squad of special forces operatives into a cave in the side of the mountain a short distance from *Il Nostro Sud*. She described her experience in a breathless excited New Zealand accent: *"There's light in here, but where is it coming from? We're moving further inside. The ceiling is very high. It looks as if this tunnel has been dug artificially. It's lined with what looks like blue ice, but the floor has a tread; it's not slippery... There's something ahead of us, some solid objects... My God! There are people down here... Not people!..."* Then she screamed in shock. The video showed a row of moving figures. At first Brendan thought that they were monkeys or apes, then that they were small people; but then he realized that they were something else entirely. They were small, with large heads and bright blue skin. They moved slowly and gracefully like ballet dancers. It was as if they had a local gravitational field around them that was lower than the earth's. Their penetrating black eyes stared into the camera lens from about fifty feet away... Then the video cut out. The programme returned to the studio and the news anchor looked shocked. *"These are preliminary reports. More information is coming soon, but..."*

"Did we just see aliens?" asked the chief engineer?

Brendan sat rooted to the spot. He knew what aliens looked

like, of course. The images of the numerous dead aliens in refrigerated caskets in the formerly secret underground bases were popular icons at that time. However, nobody had previously known what they looked like when alive. Most people assumed that if there were any alive then they were living on distant planets or an otherworld somewhere else. Nobody had suspected that there were living ET's at large on the earth. He looked at his colleagues. They were all struck dumb, their faces pale.

Everything happened very fast after that. A flyer arrived on *Finn McCool*'s flight deck containing a posse of intelligence analysts from the client, the League of the World. They marched quickly toward the hatch, eager to interrogate the gangsters who were manning the base on Southern Thule. There was no communication at all from the amphibious assault ship except basic navigation commands, but Brendan and his shipmates heard on the news that the special forces had captured some canisters of sentient oil, known colloquially as "the black goo". The gangsters had been on Southern Thule to mine the substance that existed in a huge deposit deep underneath Southern Thule. The reason for this was not currently understood.

Seaguard *Heather* steamed north. Her orders were to escort Seaguard *Finn McCool* to the company's principle naval base on the Bandon estuary in County Cork, Ireland. They were told to proceed with all dispatch. This would take almost two weeks. The intelligence officers wanted the fifteen Southern Thule occupants transferred by air immediately, but this would not be possible until the taskforce was well north of the equator because of the behaviour of Red Belt air forces. Aircraft from the GBSU and several socialist nations in Africa were almost always overhead. Sometimes they would descend to fly over the ships at a very low altitude, an obvious intimidation tactic. The underway routine went on as normal. Watches came and went; drills and exercises carried on as normal. Then one day when they had just crossed the equator, Brendan was supervising the helm on the bridge when the communications officer piped a report. "Ship, radio. I have intercepted flash traffic from *Finn Mac*."

"What does it say?" asked the officer-of-the-deck.

There was a pause. When the comms officer answered, his startled tone was detectable on the intercom. "They're asking Ops Command permission to... to jettison their cargo?"

"What!?" the OOD exclaimed. "I'm calling the skipper."

The captain of Seaguard *Heather* was a thickset man with a large brown beard. When he arrived on the bridge and heard the OOD's report he grabbed the radio telephone handset. "Put me through to *Finn Mac*!" he ordered. After a pause he said: "Sean, give me a report." He nodded as the other commander spoke. "Okay." Then he addressed the bridge crew. "*Finn Mac*'s master has asked Ops Command to jettison the sentient oil containers because they are leaking and the substance inside has 'come to life', whatever that means..."

"Captain!" interrupted the OOD. "*Finn Mac* is slowing." Brendan looked out of the side window of the bridge and, sure enough, the bow wave of their companion ship had lessened and the vessel had fallen behind.

"All stop." ordered the captain and the helm obeyed.

The ship went to action stations and Brendan was put in command of a standby rescue party. They prepared the launches and rigged out the davits ready to lower them. Boxes of additional life jackets were lifted out of lockers. They attempted to communicate with the ship they were escorting, but nobody was answering the radio now. Brendan lifted his binoculars and saw a large number of people on deck rushing around. Then he saw life-rafts inflate and drop into the sea. "Oh shit!" he exclaimed. "What are they doing? It looks like they're abandoning ship." Sure enough, a moment later an automated mayday signal was transmitted from Seaguard *Finn McCool*.

"Mr Quilley!" barked the captain. "Get your boats in the water and head over there. See if we can help."

"Aye aye, sir." Within three minutes the two rescue boats from Seaguard *Heather* were bounding over the waves of the open ocean towards their stricken companion. *Finn McCool* was an ugly and ungainly vessel, very boxy and flat. She was designed with a low and wide profile to minimize the draft, allowing her to sail in shallow waters near coasts. She had an abrupt and truncated stern where the giant ramp was lowered to deploy landing craft. It was down now as the landing craft were being prepared to act as makeshift lifeboats. "Ahoy there!" Brendan called out from the lead boat as it approached the ramp. The crew of *Finn McCool* looked like disturbed ants as they ran about the place, putting on life jackets and loading emergency supplies into the landing boats. They were clearly terrified, but were keeping their heads, acting out their training expertly. Brendan's launch came alongside the ramp and he stepped onto the deck of the other ship. As he did so the marines were lining up and boarding the landing boats one at a time. They had with them the prisoners from Southern Thule in handcuffs. There were fifteen men in all, easily recognizable because of their civilian clothing. They babbled urgently at their captors as they were frogmarched into one of the landing boats. "We warned you!" one of them yelled, a young man with an accent that sounded Russian, or from somewhere else in Eastern Europe. "We told you this would happen!"

Brendan walked up to him. "What do you mean?"

"The nano oil is inert below two degrees Celsius, but when it warms up it comes to life. It cannot be stopped!"

"Get a move on!" ordered a marine and shoved him hard in the shoulder. He disappeared inside the landing craft. Brendan radioed this information to *Heather*'s captain and the captain ordered his away team to investigate. There were fourteen sailors with Brendan and they crossed the landing bay dodging *Finn McCool*'s compliment who were all walking in the other direction. Brendan had the deck layout of the ship on his wrist-slate and he glanced at it from time to time as he led his team along passageways through the bowels of the vessel. "We really should be kitted in NBC." muttered the chief petty officer who was his second-in-command.

Brendan nodded in agreement. From what he had heard about the black goo, and how little was known about it, it would have been prudent to wear hazmat suits to protect themselves, but it was too late now. The rescue party arrived at the hatch to the storage room and peeked inside. There were a row of unmarked oil drums made of plain dull metal. On the left side of the room there were three drums that had been deliberately separated from the others. They had ragged ruptures in them, as if somebody had attacked them with a giant can-opener. Black viscous fluid was pouring out of them and was forming a smooth puddle on the floor. Unlike normal crude oil, this substance was odourless. The CPO chuckled contemptuously. "Is this all these guys are bolting from?"

"Wait!... Look!" Another sailor pointed at the far side of the room. There was a second door wide open. It was a few feet above floor level and a row of steel frame steps ran down from it. The steps and the bulkhead behind it were covered in the same black, slimy oil-like substance that covered the deck. "It's flowing into this compartment from somewhere else." said the CPO.

Brendan nodded, but then he looked again and did a double take. "Is it just me or is that stuff flowing upwards instead of downwards?"

"Yes, sir. It is." said the CPO.

"How the hell is it flowing uphill?" gasped Brendan.

Nobody replied. A shocked hush came over the group, a superstitious primeval dread at the sight of something that broke the rules of normal reality. Then a young sailor nearest the broken oil drums jumped back with a start. "Look!" He pointed with a trembling finger. The puddle on the deck was changing shape. It was extending a limb away from the vaguely oval shaped pool towards the group of men by the door. "It's heading towards us!... It's like it knows we're here!" The man's tone was a blend of terror and fascination.

Brendan was unable to react immediately. Nothing in his training had prepared him for this. He opened his mouth and his voice was numb. He coughed and tried again. "Retreat!" he ordered. "Everybody! Back to the boats now!"

The sailors needed no additional persuasion. They ran down the corridor as fast as they could towards the landing bay. Just before they turned a corner and were out of sight of the hatch, Brendan paused and looked back. The black goo was lapping over the threshold. By the time they were in the boats the ship was almost empty. Only a few life-rafts were left to launch and the crew were piling in supplies and dragging them to the ramp. Brendan's rescue party headed back to Seaguard *Heather* as fast as they could. There were a number of flyers overhead from the company's reconnaissance service; clearly word had got back to the operational headquarters and a major alert had been called. Once they were back on board the frigate they saw that some of the survivors from *Finn McCool* were there too, having nowhere else to go except wait in a life-raft. A recovery speed-frightener was on the way to pick up all the former occupants of the amphibious assault ship. Brendan stripped off his immersion suit and life jacket; then he headed to the bridge. The captain turned to him as soon as he walked in. "Well done, Mr Quilley." he said. "We've just had new orders. As soon as all the survivors are safely clear, we're to sink *Finn Mac*."

He gasped. "Sink her!?"

"Yes. It's because of the escape of the sentient oil. We don't know how dangerous it is so the most precautionary thing to do the ship put it in Davy Jones' locker."

A few hours later the recovery frightener appeared. It descended to sea level like a giant albatross and hovered over the water so that the life-rafts and landing craft could board it, then it took off for Fort Batten. The empty Seaguard *Finn McCool* was adrift, tipping in the waves without its engine to stabilize it. It was a very easy shot. The captain chose a single standard anti-ship torpedo. It ran out for just two minutes before detonating against the hull. The explosion caused a massive column of white foam to shoot hundreds of feet into the air. The shattered vessel settled down by the stern and slowly slid beneath the waves. It took about ten minutes to sink. Its prow rose into the air, water pouring out of its Schauberger intakes in white cataracts, then it was gone.

....

Brendan sat at the wardroom table with the communications officer, the weapons officer and the executive officer. They were all staring intently at the object on the tabletop. "Have you told the skipper you've got this?" asked the XO?

"Not yet." The weapons officer said.

"Well you're going to have to." he snapped.

"Aye, sir."

"How did you get it anyway?"

"One of the booties gave it to me when he came aboard." He used naval slang for a marine. He just held it out and I took it."

The object was a small pot made of thick glass. Its opening

was covered by a rubber stopper and a waxy plastic seal held it in place. Inside the jar was some black goo, about a quarter of a pint. It felt safe there, contained and isolated. The four men watched fascinated as its surface shifted as if it were being tipped, although it was sitting flat on the table and the sea was calm so the ship was hardly rolling. It rose on one side in the direction of Brendan, then returned to normal and did the same to the comms officer and again to the two others. It was aware of their presence and could detect them as if it had sense organs. The XO whistled. "Good grief! What the hell is it?"

"Nobody knows." said Brendan. "It might be ET or it might be something on this planet we never knew existed until now, although some appeared on a LoW ship I sailed on a few years ago."

"It must have something to do with those blue aliens." said Weapons.

"I wonder who they are." added Comms.

"What's it doing now?" asked Brendan. The glutinous black substance had formed a new shape inside its glass prison. Its surface formed a cone that then flattened in one direction like a ridge. The sides of the ridge touching the glass thickened, tapering towards the middle. A ripple started running through it; it looked like a straining muscle. A crack appeared in the glass side of the jar. The same idea occurred to all four officers at the same time and they recoiled back, struggling to stand up from their chairs. They were not fast enough to escape. There was a penetrating pop and the jar exploded as if hit with a bullet. The liquid inside had metamorphosed into a brace and broken the container it was trapped in. Fragments of glass and black drops flew everywhere. Brendan shut his eyes and mouth, but not before some of the oil got inside. He yelped and blinked in panic, spitting and rubbing his eyelids hard. When he could see again he saw that the oil was covering his body as if he were a mechanic on an old diesel engine and the other three were the same. They stood there stunned. There were hasty footsteps in the passageway outside and the wardroom door burst open. Three or four people entered, alerted by the sound of their voices. One of them was the captain. He took the entire scene in with a dropped jaw. "What the hell is going on here!?" he shouted.

The executive officer opened his mouth to answer, but then he noticed something else strange. The oil was disappearing. It was evaporating off every surface it had landed on. Tiny wisps of fume sizzled as the smears and splats shrunk and vanished like water on a hotplate. However, there was no fume coming from the oil on Brendan's body. It was not evaporating; it was being absorbed into his skin like handcream. He feverishly slapped at it, trying to rip it off his skin before it could sink in, but that was impossible. Within ten seconds all the sentient oil mess in the wardroom had gone. They were left standing in the room with nothing but clean pieces of broken glass there to indicate anything abnormal had taken place.

Chapter 12

"Keep periscope depth." ordered Brendan.

"Keep periscope depth aye, sir." replied the helmsman and adjusted his controls. The submarine tilted upwards. Brendan leaned slightly, well used to the angles the deck took as they changed depth. "Make turns for seven knots." He ordered. He was focused completely on his job as officer-of-the-deck aboard Seaguard *Foyle*, but his mind was split in two and the other half was a churning millrace of emotion. He was only able to function by keeping the two halves apart. He glanced at the bulkhead chronometer; it was just twenty-five minutes until the watch change. He had never felt so relieved. He didn't think he could maintain his professional poise for much longer. "Conn, sonar. Transients on Masters seven, eight and nine." came a voice in Brendan's earpiece.

"Report." commanded Brendan.

"I think they're releasing harpoons, sir."

"I'm coming through." The sonar room was a cubicle to the port of the control room through a soundproof screen door. Inside it the four sonar operators sat at their consoles, monitoring the displays that revealed the convoluted sonic landscape of the undersea world. "What is it, Ears?" asked Brendan.

The submarine's chief sonarman was named Wallace Keen, but everybody called him by his nickname, "Ears". He looked up and over his shoulder at the Officer-of-the-deck. "They're firing on the whales, sir." His mouth was a taught line between his earphones.

A blast of dizziness almost knocked Brendan off his feet. "Are you sure?"

Ears winced and put a hand to his left earphone. Then he nodded. "The whales are screaming, sir." He picked up a spare set of earphones and held them out to Brendan so that he could also listen.

Brendan jerked backwards as if the earphones had poisoned barbs. "I can't!" he hissed.

Ears looked at him sympathetically as Brendan backed out through the screen door.

Brendan felt the deck pitch under his feet as if the submarine were carrying out torpedo evasion manoeuvres. He staggered back to the conn, the platform in the centre of the control room from where he directed the undersea vessel. The junior officer-of-the-deck had raised the periscope and had his face pressed to the eyepiece. He stood aside as Brendan approached to let him use it. "We have visual contact on the whaling fleet, sir." he said.

Brendan was about to look through the instrument and then stopped. He shook his head. He tried to speak, but no sound came out.

The JOOD frowned in concern. "Are you alright, sir?"

Brendan collapsed into a chair by the navigation table. "Warm tubes two and three." he said. He didn't consciously utter the words. It was as if he had just heard somebody else say them.

"Come again?" replied the man at the weapons control panel.

"I said warm tubes two and three!" snapped Brendan in a much louder voice.

"Aye aye, sir." he answered tensely after a long pause.

"Mr Quilley sir." interjected the JOOD. "There are warshots in those tubes."

"I know, Mr Baker."

The crew on the weapons control panel began switching on the two anti-surface torpedoes loaded in the tubes in the bulbous prow of the submarine.

"Why are you warming them, sir?"

The captain strode into the control room. "What's going on?" he demanded. "Lieutenant Quilley! Why are you warming two torpedoes?"

Brendan looked up as his urgent face. "We have to do something, sir."

The captain's expression softened. Captain Vine was a thin elderly man who had been a Seaguard officer since the company had been founded. He had a long white beard and shoulder length white hair giving him a somewhat biblical appearance. "Mr Quilley, you're relieved. Go to your stateroom. I'll take the deck."

Once Brendan was in his cabin he fell onto the bunk in convulsions. He buried his face in his bolster, weeping and bellowing with anguish and rage. He had been reading up on everything to do with whales and related creatures ever since his experience while swimming with the whale off the Mergui islands a year earlier. One thing on the subject he could not bring himself to look into in any detail was whaling. He found the notion of killing or harming whales so utterly obscene that he could not bear it. In the same way he could not visit captive dolphins in tanks because of the emotional pain it caused him. It was strange because Brendan was not generally passionate about animal rights. He disliked cruelty to animals, as most people did, but it was not something that occupied his soul in the way it did dedicated animal rights activists. He was not a vegetarian and could happily sink his teeth into a burger or steak without a qualm related to the unfortunate cow that lost its life to provide that food. It was only when it came to the clade *Cetacea* that he was completely consumed with sentimentality.

After twenty minutes he had recovered enough to function. He went to the head and washed his face. He combed his hair and blinked a few times to try and clear his bloodshot eyes. Then he changed into a new set of submariner's overalls and left his stateroom. As always when he was suffering, Brendan found solace in his engines. Seaguard *Foyle* was his first submarine, apart from his week on the training boat. He had applied for the submarine division almost as afterthought from his promotion to lieutenant. He had been moved on from Seaguard *Heather* when qualifying as a senior engineer and been through a four month training programme at Fort Batten. It had involved a lot of swimming and floating in the escape simulator as well as academic study. At the end of this he had earned his submariners' "dolphins", a badge resembling pilot's wings that featured two dolphins and the Seaguard operations insignia. Predictably his father was ecstatic that his son had qualified in submarines, seeing as Clane had served in them during World War II. "Welcome to the world's most exclusive club, son!" he had chuckled and slapped Brendan's back. *Foyle* was a *Shannon*-class submarine which included all of the company's fourteen undersea vessels. It was driven by a twin Schauberger coil like *Heather*'s, but it was arranged differently and, like everything in a submarine, was far more compact. It gave *Foyle* unlimited underwater endurance, like the older nuclear submarines, but without the threat of radiation or the other practical, environmental and political problems of nuclear power. It was also far stealthier than those with the noisy machinery of a nuclear fission powerplant. Alternatively a few of the even older diesel-electric submarines were still in service with some navies. These were quieter, but they could only dive for a few hours before having to surface and recharge their batteries with a petroleum engine. This also meant they could not sail beneath thick ice. By 1975, nearly all new subs were Schauberger-powered except for a few small coastal patrol vessels that had large Digby Carrousels. As soon as Brendan had joined his first boat he knew that he had made an excellent decision. A lot of what he disliked about service aboard a surface ship ("skimmers" as the submariners called them) was happily absent in submarines. The snobbish barrier between the officers and ratings and the anal-retentive social etiquette during runs ashore were unknown in this new carefree culture he had adopted. He, as an officer, was perfectly entitled to visit racetracks and backstreet pubs with the most junior seaman. He could address that man by his first name and could in turn be called "Brendan" by him while off-duty. Brendan squeezed into the narrow space where the port intake pipe emerged in the engine room. He had with him an ultrasound scanner and his job was to check the steel pipes for any cracks or spots of rust.

Brendan did his job with due diligence, but never were the thoughts of his torment out of his mind. Three days earlier he had heard hunted whales screaming for the first and last time. He felt that if he ever heard that sound again he would climb into the escape trunk without an aqualung and open the sea-valve. The ethics of whaling had been under question for many decades due to the declining populations of hunted species as well as scientific research. It had previously been assumed that whales were little more than air-breathing fish, but it had since been revealed that they are highly intelligent and sensitive, perhaps even more so than the great apes. Along with this, the invention of plastics and petroleum extraction had reduced the market for whalebone and whale oil since the late nineteenth century, so vociferous calls to stamp out the practice grew during the first three quarters of the twentieth century. Nine months earlier, in June 1974, the International Whaling Commission had instituted a blanket ban on all whaling effective from the New Year. It was a carefully planned moratorium, organized with the help of the LoWEHO and several major governments. It included compensation deals being negotiated, purchasing or redesign funding for whaling ships and redeployment or adult training schemes for the whalers. However Iceland had rebelled against the ruling and announced it intended to continue full commercial whaling. The small mid-Atlantic island nation had survived Disclosure fairly well. Unlike most countries, it had successfully maintained its government and pre-Disclosure constitution throughout the transitional years and today had a booming economy. Its insistence on continuing its whaling industry began when it submitted an appeal to the International Whaling Commission based on the single exemption clause of the ban: one relating to aboriginal subsistence. Iceland had been hunting whales since the first Viking settlers landed there in the early middle ages and this was therefore a part of their traditional culture. They conveniently sidestepped the fact that they now invariably used modern whaling methods and never the rowing boats and hand-thrown harpoons their ancestors used to. The IWC had unanimously rejected their appeal. Therefore when Iceland defiantly sortied its entire whaling fleet on New Year's Day the authorities were compelled to act.

Brendan had just returned to work from Christmas leave. Seaguard *Foyle* was docked at her homeport, the Belgooly submarine base in County Cork, when the news broke that a joint IWC and LoWEHO mission had lodged a formal protest against the Icelandic government. Iceland had ignored it, which was when the mission contracted Seaguard to use force. *Foyle* had put to sea two weeks later on the eighteenth of January as part of the company's anti-whaling taskforce. Since then she had been patrolling the Atlantic Ocean between south-eastern Iceland and the Faeroe Islands where most of the whaling fleet were operating. She had spent that time monitoring the traffic and gathering data on whaling fleet manoeuvres while diplomatic attempts to resolve the crisis were pursued at the

LoW headquarters and the Icelandic embassies. So far no military action had been taken despite Iceland continuously presenting a consistently obstinate position. This impasse could not last forever.

After checking the pipes in the engine room, Brendan returned to his stateroom to sleep as well as he could for as long as he could. He was awoken by a telephone message at nine AM summoning him to the wardroom for a briefing. Time of day had little meaning in the depth of the ocean, but Brendan tried to maintain his circadian rhythm as much as possible within the irregular system of watches. He got out of bed and tiptoed out of his stateroom, being careful not to wake his sleeping bunkmate above him. In the wardroom, Captain Vine sat at the head of the table with five other officers in chairs beside him. They were all from weapons and tactical systems, which piqued Brendan's curiosity. "Mr Quilley." said the Captain deadpan. "Take a seat and then we are ready to begin."

Brendan did so. He looked at the faces of the other men, but they gave nothing away; their gaze was focused on their commanding officer.

Vine spoke concisely and dispassionately without preamble. "We've received new orders from Op's HQ based on instructions from our client. A last minute attempt by the Loh-Wee-Oh to persuade Iceland to cease whaling is underway. They have until twelve hundred hours UT to comply. If they haven't we will sink one of the catchers." He paused for effect.

Brendan felt his heart pound. The other officers either blanched or flushed. Seaguard submarines had never fired a shot in anger since the company was founded.

The captain continued. "If they do not alter course for port within sixty minutes of that action, we will destroy their factory ship... I would like Lieutenant Quilley to be attackie."

Brendan looked up sharply into Captain Vine's eyes. The old man's kind gaze and knowing tone of voice said more than any words could.

At eleven-thirty AM, Brendan stepped shakily into the control room. The battle stations gong was sounded and the crew took their positions. "I have the conn." he said.

"Lt Quilley has the conn." said the officer-of-the-deck and stepped down off the periscope platform to attend his own battle station at a fire control console.

Brendan was now in control of the entire submarine. As the attack instructor he would direct everything that happened during the operation to come. He experienced a moment of vertigo as if he were looking down off a cliff. He was overawed by the power he suddenly and temporarily possessed. "All ahead two-thirds. Keep periscope depth." he called out.

"All ahead two-thirds. Keep periscope depth aye, sir." The helmsman repeated his order.

"Warm tubes two and three."

"Warm tubes two and three aye, sir." confirmed the weapons officer.

"TMA, current status of Master six."

The target motion analyzer responded: "Course two-two-seven. Speed sixteen knots. Range twelve thousand yards, sir."

"Do Masters four and five concur?"

"Yes, sir. They are on a matching status."

"Very well." Brendan gulped. "Master six" was the nearest whaler and it was heading towards a pod of twenty-three Atlantic right whales about thirty nautical miles to the southwest. Two others were accompanying it. The whales were a family group and they included a few calves.

"Time!"

"Eleven fifty-five, sir." replied the yeoman.

Brendan knew the time as did everybody else; there was a bulkhead chronometer just a few feet away. However he wanted it stated so that the control room understood the nature of what they were doing. The three ships had five minutes to turn back. The minutes and seconds ticked down as *Foyle* rose from the ocean depths. The second hand rose one last time to the top of the face and passed it. The digital display flicked from eleven-fifty-nine to twelve o'clock. "Up periscope." commanded Brendan. The chrome pole in the centre of the command platform rose upwards until the lens mounting emerged out of its well. He pushed the handles down and peered into the eyepiece. The world above came into view and his darkness adjusted eyes were dazzled by sunlight. It was actually a grey overcast day, but it looked bright compared to the deckhead lamps. A light rain was falling and there was a thin surface fog. A wave washed over the lens and for a moment he saw the blue green of the sea before it passed and the dark cloudy sky and grey sea returned. Water dripped across his field of vision. The illuminated green crosshairs of the periscope swam in and out of focus and he blinked. Another surface mast was raised alongside the periscope which detected radar and other electromagnetic transmissions. A display on the periscope lens indicated that the ships were scanning the sea with search radar, but this was designed to pick up whales and would not detect the periscope. In the distance he could see Master six through the fog. His fingers found the magnification toggle and he zoomed in. He rotated the instrument slowly until the ship came into view. Master six was in front of him, as if he were swimming in the sea a few dozen yards away. Despite the light fog it was visible in every detail. It was a catcher of about two hundred tons. A modern whaling fleet consisted of a number of small fast vessels called catchers. These would track down the whales and kill them. Then the floating cadavers would be picked up by the factory ship, a larger and slower vessel of eight to ten thousand tons on board which much of the processing of the blubber, meat and bone would be done so that the finished commodities would be ready when the ship docked. The catcher Brendan now saw before him was steaming fast on its way to its helpless and unsuspecting prey. It was an ugly craft, as if its appearance was moulded by its purpose. It had a misshapen square aft superstructure and at the bow was a raised platform almost as tall as the superstructure. On it was mounted the harpoon cannon. This was a solid metal tube about eight feet long set on a pillar. As Brendan watched a sailor clad in yellow oilskins was loading a harpoon into the muzzle. He first pushed in the propellant charge, a cylinder of gunpowder, followed by the projectile, a long straight javelin with a wicked-looking barbed point. There was an ovoid black bulge just behind the tip which was a grenade of solid explosive mixed with steel fragments to act as shrapnel. It was designed to penetrate deep into the whale's body and detonate; this caused a huge wound that would bleed profusely. A whale's bloodstream is very vulnerable to injury and it is harder to staunch exsanguinations from it than with most other animals. A whale hit by this weapon usually bled to death with a few minutes. There was no danger to the crew; the whales could do nothing to fight back. The days of rowing boats, handheld harpoons and legs being bitten off, as described in Herman Melville's *Moby Dick*, were long gone. Brendan watched more men in foul weather gear pottering about on the catcher's deck, cheerfully going about their business. They stopped to chat occasionally. Brendan stared at them in fury and disbelief. He recalled a long poem about whales he had read a few months ago which described the crew of whaling ships as "blind dwarfs." He now nodded to himself silently.

Brendan stepped back and slapped the handles up. "Down periscope." he said, his voice cracked. The instrument slid back into its well. "No aspect change on Master six."

"Attackie." said another officer who was acting as Brendan's assistant, a pleasant Irishman called Lt. Gary Marsden. He also shared Brendan's stateroom.

"Mr Marsden?" he sighed.

"Our orders give us some leeway. The catchers will not reach the whale pod for another two hours. Maybe we should wait for a while; allow them a bit more time to reconsider. We can follow them and keep them in torpedo range..."

"No!" interrupted Brendan. "We start the attack now."

Marsden nodded calmly. "Aye aye, sir."

"Up periscope." Brendan had his hands out ready as the instrument rose. He snapped down the handles and once again acquired visual contact on the nearest catcher. "Master six is redesignated Target one. Target one bears... that! Range... that!" He pressed a button on the periscope handle that sent information about the visual signature of the target to the fire control system.

The TMA technician read out the information. As soon as enough was known about the target; its speed, course, range and other factors, they would know enough to release their weapons and be fairly sure of a bull's-eye. "Firing solution on Target one!"

"Very well. Make the weapons in tubes two and three ready in all respects."

"Flooding tubes and opening bow caps." said a weapons technician. The torpedo tubes were now exposed to the sea and the weapons inside were powered up and ready to be fired.

Brendan peeked again at the catcher. It was steaming along as before, completely oblivious to its impending demise. "Fire tubes two and three!"

"Shoot and vent!" There was a loud thud as a blast of high pressure air pushed the two torpedoes out of their tubes. Their engines started and they buzzed away through the sea towards the target like hounds seeking a fox. "Torpedoes from tubes two and three are running normally."

Brendan kept his eyes to the periscope listening as the crew in the control room read out numbers indicating the progress of the torpedoes on their seven mile journey through the ocean. Two of Seaguard *Foyle*'s anti-ship torpedoes had enough explosive yield to sink an ocean liner; the little whaler could never survive even a single warhead. He had used two just in case one of the weapons broke down.

"Target one acquired!" said the weapons officer. This meant that the torpedoes' sonar had detected the ship independently. Up until then the weapon's guidance computer had been steering them towards the vessel through a wire that the weapons trailed behind them to connect them to their mother ship. "Two hundred yards remaining... one hundred... fifty..."

The explosion was silent in the periscope viewfinder. The whaler erupted into a fountain of fire and water. A moment later the second torpedo struck and the severed fo'c'sle with its harpoon gun rose into the air spinning end over end until it fell into the water with a foamy splash. As the torpedoes impacted the crew broke out into a cheer. It was a stoic professional cheer, a celebration of victory, a job well done and the knowledge that they had made it into the Seaguard history books. "Conn, sonar! Loud explosion on the bearing of Target one!" superfluously reported the excited Ears Keen.

Brendan kept watching the spot where the torpedoes had detonated. When the sea calmed down there was nothing to see. The catcher had not sunk; it had been blown to pieces.

Brendan cheered too, but his cheer was different. He laughed manically like a man on drugs. He roared, he chuckled and he hooted. His joy was almost physical. It felt like an orgasm. The rational side of his mind eventually took hold after a few more seconds. "Alright." he gasped. "Target one has been destroyed. Down periscope. All ahead standard. Hard a starboard. Steer course zero-eight-zero. Keep six hundred feet... Once we have cleared the datum we will reacquire Masters four and five and see if they are retreating. If they are not we will attack the fleet's factory ship from long range. Load tubes two and three with anti-surface missiles."

....

The ship they had sunk was called the *Svarasson*. Her entire crew of thirteen had perished. The Icelandic government was up in arms about it. As Seaguard *Foyle* sailed away from the scene the other two catchers approached the location where the *Svarasson* had been hoping to pick up survivors. When none were found they both turned onto a reciprocal course and headed for their home port, as did the factory ship. No further deterrence was necessary. It took two hours of careful sonar scanning to be certain of the fleet's intentions. Weapons were loaded and warm in case they were needed. When the successful outcome was clear, Brendan secured battle stations and the boat went back to patrol routine. He felt drained of energy. As soon as he was free to, he retired to his stateroom and collapsed into his bunk. He stared up at the underside of Gary Marsden's berth breathing deeply with contentment. For the first time since leaving port he felt at peace. He hadn't realized how heavy the emotional burden was that he had been carrying until the moment it had been lifted. It was as if the prison door had opened, as if the curtains had parted and he could see daylight. What he had experienced when the torpedo impacted the whaling ship and fragmented it was something completely new. It was an ecstasy of a kind he had never before known. It was a mixture of a sudden sense of freedom and the projected happiness of seeing somebody he loved full of joy. It was the whales he loved of course. They were safe. Never again would the unspeakable acts of the whalers be inflicted on them; and it was all because of Brendan Quilley. He grinned with pride and stretched luxuriously across his mattress. However there was still an introspective element to himself that reprimanded him. He had just killed thirteen people. If he had hunted down and murdered thirteen people on the streets of New York and buried their bodies in shallow graves in the woods the media would call him a serial killer. Yet he was not. What he did was a legal act of war. The Icelandic government had broken international law. Every non-violent endeavour possible had been undertaken to persuade them to change their position. The Icelandic government knew that and the whaling industry knew that. The men on the catcher knew that they were carrying out a criminal act. They should have refused. They had been killed by a just and lawful use of force. Of course Brendan could never be a whaler; he would have committed suicide first, but if he had been he would have accepted the consequences of his actions, entered into with understanding. Those thirteen men only had themselves to blame.

Brendan rolled onto his side and stared at the lockers that were built into the opposite bulkhead. An unsettling new thought blotched his mind. He suddenly realized that what he had done today ran contrary to how he had been brought up. The true source of his psychological release was hate not love. The justification he had just cogitated could not dissolve the fact that he had enjoyed killing those whalers. He had not shrugged his shoulders and said: "Sorry about this, but..." or "Ah well, it's a rotten old job, but..." He had torpedoed the whaling ship with intense relish. He hated those men for what they were doing. The indifference with which they committed acts of barbarism against some of the most wonderful beasts on earth was so wholly other. This new emotion Brendan had experienced was watching the source and object of his hatred annihilated. He could never forgive the whalers and he didn't want to forgive them. He felt no need to. However, for his whole life he had been taken to church every Sunday by his parents and he knew that forgiveness was the cornerstone of Christian belief. It was the highest grace; and it was even mentioned in the Lord's Prayer: "...*forgive us our trespasses as we forgive those who trespass against us...*" This was put into more detail in the Gospel of St Luke: "...*Love your enemies. Do well to those who hate you, bless those who curse you, pray for those who abuse you. To one who strikes you on the cheek, turn the other cheek also for him to strike. From one who takes away your cloak do not withhold your tunic either. Give to everyone who begs from you, and from one who steals your property do not demand it back...*" Brendan had failed in his Christian duty to the ultimate extent. He had destroyed his enemies, those who abused the whales he loved. They struck his cheek and he turned around and beat both of theirs black and blue. He had punished his transgressors in the most extreme manner possible... And he felt no remorse, in fact he felt proud. He recalled his conversation with Siobhan a few years ago when she had told him how she had killed Dr Millicent Arbroath-Laird. He remembered her words: "*She was an evil woman, Brendan... She was working for the Illuminati to destroy the world, and she wanted our family to help her. Is it really bad to put an end to such a destructive life? What if I'd let her live?... I think deep down I'm shocked at myself for being so violent. I didn't know I was capable of anything like...*" Now Brendan was in the same position. It frightened him. He once again experienced the vertigo of staring over a precipice into an abyss.

Chapter 13

It was a Saturday morning. Brendan and Heather woke up to the alarm and looked at the clock. It was just before six AM. They arose from their bed and dressed without a word. The sky was dark quartz purple and there was a chill in the spring pre-dawn air as they stepped out of the door to their married quarters in Seaguard's Kilmacsimon barracks. As soon as their flyer had cleared the residential reservation they descended and switched to ground-hugging mode. They headed west, deliberately choosing the small country lanes and avoided the main road. The green fields and woods were shrouded ghosts in the gloaming. The tarmac of the road glittered in the headlights. They had one window open a crack; and the rush of the wind mixed with the buzzing of the vehicle's four antigravity discs was the only sound. After half an hour they arrived at their destination, Galley Head. They parked the flyer in a small carpark and stepped out. Already it was clear there was a difference. Brendan could see stars in the sky, a paint splattering of white light across the welkin. He breathed in deeply as if he could smell the light descending onto them. To their right stood a lighthouse, now deactivated, a squat white conical tower with a rotunda at the top. Its outline was visible against the stellar background. There were a few other people there, about a dozen. This was a slight disappointment; Brendan and Heather had come here specifically because they hoped to be alone. However after a few minutes they both warmed to their impromptu companions. They talked cheerily to each other. All of them were individuals or couples who had come to Galley Head to enjoy the moment privately; Brendan chuckled at that thought. Maybe it was this that made them a temporary band of friends. Most people around the globe had gone to the big street parties in the major cities of the world; Dublin, New York, Tokyo, St Petersburg, London, Calcutta. The centre of every global metropolis was a frenzy of carousing. The sky changed colour due to the approaching dawn, becoming lighter. Then a golden blotch above the sea on the eastern horizon announced the rising of the sun. Its upper limb sparked a line of yellow dawn across the ultramarine ocean. The stars dissolved like sugar in hot tea. For the first time in five years Brendan saw the deep magnificent blue of the natural sky. It was Saturday the first of March 1975; the intensive lifetrail programme was over. The last flight had sprayed its last drop of chemical the previous night.

Since it began in 1970 everybody knew that the end of it would be a day of worldwide celebration. People had almost become too used to a sky of brown muck, a sun that was never bright enough to dazzle; failed crops, dead forests, rampant fungus, earthquakes around the Pacific rim, blizzards and frost. On the other hand, Morgellons disease had been eradicated. Regular studies of the land, sea and air had been monitoring the levels of pseudo-life in the environment and it had shrunk to nothing, or at least it was below detectable levels. There had literally been no trace of it for eighteen months. The scientific surveys would continue for the foreseeable future to make sure the lifetrail programme had worked. It would be many decades before they knew for sure. If just one filament of pseudo-life had survived, anywhere in the world, it could multiply, regroup and begin the synthetic plague again. It was possible that by the early twenty-first century a new lifetrail programme might be required; but, for now, it was all over. Nature was home and free.

At about ten AM, Brendan and Heather went home and ate a late breakfast. They had planned to go and visit their families in the United States, but then Heather suddenly felt nauseous. She ran upstairs to the bathroom and threw up in the toilet. Brendan came in and stood over her, stroking her head as she kneeled with her head in the bowl. "Are you alright, honey?"

She nodded as she retched. Eventually she felt better and sat up. Brendan brought her a glass of grapefruit juice. She sipped slowly. "That's lovely; really freshens my mouth."

"Feeling better?"

"Yes. Sorry about that, Bren. I've not felt right for a few days. Maybe I should go and see the doc."

"Are you up to coming to see mom and dad?"

She paused. "Sorry, Bren. I think I'd better stay here."

"It's okay." he smiled at her. "Can't be helped. I'll tell them." Heather went and laid down on the settee. Brendan kissed her cheek and left.

The flyer trip across the Atlantic was visibly different

without the lifetrails. As the darkness fell again and the stars returned Brendan stared from the driving seat in wonder. He landed in Rockville after ninety minutes in the air. The local time was five AM and the family were still in bed. However his father-in-law was awake to greet him and let him into the house. He dozed in the McManus lounge until enough light was in the windows to rouse him and he watched the sun rise for a second time that morning. At nine AM his parents arrived, closely followed by Siobhan and Kerry with William and Colleen. They all took ground cars into Washington DC where a huge carnival was already underway. There were military parades and police parades. Then came decorated floats and performance troupes. There were boy scouts, gospel choirs, cowboys on horseback, steel drums, brass bands, burlesque girls and every other form of entertainment imaginable. The audience stood at the side of the road and applauded them. It felt like the whole of America was out on the streets of their nation's capital to celebrate the end of the lifetrails.

At two PM, President Tavinor gave a speech from the West Front of the US Capitol. Apart from inaugurations this was a rare occurrence only ever done on very special occasions. President LaRey Tavinor was an elegant woman with a powerful voice. She was only four feet nine inches tall, but appeared to be a lot bigger. She always refused the footstools to boost her apparent height. It was only just over five weeks since her inauguration and she had got off to a roaring start. Already her fresh term of office was beginning to feel like the start of a new era, and the cessation of the lifetrail programme added to that. She was very different to her predecessor President William F Buckley whose eight year presidency had been controversial. A lot of people felt that his administration was something of an anachronism from the old order. His re-election in 1970 was mostly based on the standard American habit of "not changing horses in midstream". That was mixed with the fact that his rival was a rather insipid and sleazy old man called Lyndon B Johnson. The country had definitely returned to binary party politics; Buckley was henceforth an unashamed Republican, despite his four years as the Democrat President King's vice-president. As far as he was concerned, the interregnum of non-partisan executives was well and truly over. When the 1974 presidential election race began, the GOP's nomination for Buckley's replacement was Jim Rhodes, the Governor of Ohio. He was no match for the Democrat's selection. DuVille-LaRey Marceau Tavinor was the first successful female presidential candidate and she won. This both delighted and enraged the feminists. Delighted because she was the first ever woman to become President of the United States. She enraged them because she hardly ever referred to that fact in her campaign speeches and public interviews. At one point when a TV news pundit raised the matter, Tavinor replied with raised eyebrows: "Did you ask President Buckley how he felt about becoming the fortieth *man* to be President of the United States?" The reporter was struck dumb. Tavinor also disobeyed the advice of the Democratic Women's Welfare Organization to make sure that a full half of all her cabinet appointees and Federal agency directors were women. The final tally was fifteen percent. "I choose the best people for the jobs, men or women; it's that simple." she replied bluntly. President Tavinor was only forty-two on her inauguration day making her the second-youngest president in American history after Dr Martin Luther King Jr. She had been a US congresswoman for the first Congressional District of Maine, elected in 1967. She was a housewife and school dinner lady, and her three children were in high school. Her husband, jokingly referred to in the media as "the First Gentleman", was a public housing inspector for Kennebec County. She was intelligent and articulate, and she had a unique manner that was rarely seen in a politician; down to earth, sincere, modest, compassionate and friendly. She had a good sense of humour and a bubbly manner. Her voice was rich and warm. Whenever she was speaking she always sounded like she was about to burst into laughter. She also had a lot of moral courage. Most of the press had been against her yet she stood firm. She was not conventionally pretty and also slightly overweight, which was made more noticeable by her small stature; but she doggedly refused to go on a cosmetic diet. "Stop talking about my waistline and start talking about my party line!" she once bellowed, exasperated at a particularly tactless journalist. She won the nation's heart. Several foreign statesmen had also expressed an admiration for her just a few weeks into her administration. The economy was already booming and she had even somehow managed to resurrect the oil industry, using means still not understood by everybody. In the post-Disclosure world this had been denounced by all economists as impossible. Her nickname was "Daisy" which was the name of a heroine from a very popular 1960's children's fantasy book and film; a dwarf princess who was a very brave and kind character with a huge amount of spirit, strength and charisma within her tiny physical presence. At the end of her speech the crowds of over a million people slowly dispersed with dreamy smiles on their faces.

....

Two days after the March the first celebrations the world went back to its usual business under the new clear blue skies. Brendan and Clane headed for Derry in Clane's flyer. Very few people still called it "Londonderry" except a handful of the older conservative Protestants. It was a picturesque stone city with a row of conical church spires poking up to the clean heavens. It was framed by majestic hills, still browned for the winter, yet to react to the extra spring sunlight. "I don't want to do this." growled Clane.

"I know, dad; but it's just a one-off." Brendan looked down at their destination, a bland structure on the western outskirts of the city just inside the old border with Donegal. The flyer park was on the roof and the entrance sign was painted on the floor. It was partly covered by landed aerial vehicles, but was still legible: *LoWD&RO*- the League of the World Disclosure and Reconciliation Organization. They left the flyer and strode to the stairway down into the building. The receptionist gaped at Clane as he walked up to the desk. "Mr Quilley, isn't it?"

"Yes, I'm here for the O'Connor case." Clane replied impatiently.

The receptionist reached for his intercom with a trembling hand. "One moment, Mr Quilley. I'll just call the commissioner."

"There's no need. I'm only here to testify." He rolled his eyes. "Can't you just point me to the anteroom?"

The answer was of course no. Clane had been asked to attend various D and R hearings as a VIP observer, even before he retired and had been obliged to as part of his government duties. Now, as a private citizen, he was becoming increasingly less tolerant of his public prominence. However, it was unavoidable, especially when it came to the Disclosure issue. "There would never have *been* a Disclosure if it weren't for you, dad." Brendan had reminded him several times. Sure enough the LoW chief commissioner for the Derry hearings came striding down the corridor, tugged along by his diplomatic smile. He was accompanied by a pair of youthful and attractive female aides. "Mr Quilley! It's such an honour!" He held out his hand. Brendan and Clane were served tea and biscuits by the two aides in a sumptuous executive suite while they waited for Clane to be called. This happened after an hour and a half. An usher wearing a black gown came to the suite and knocked on the door. "Clane Quilley, you are required in Court Number Two now." As his father headed into court to give evidence, Brendan went to the public gallery. He had to hand in his roamphone at the door; another usher put it in a pigeonhole and gave him a chit to claim it back when he left. He disliked that because he'd just exchanged text messages with his wife and was concerned. Heather was still suffering from nausea and had not eaten at all that day. However he understood that a spectator with a roam might jeopardize the privacy and confidentiality of the hearing. The atmosphere changed considerably as Brendan entered the public gallery. He had never been in a courtroom before although he had seen many images of them in the media. The room resembled a theatre with the public gallery set in a tiered circle above the central pit where a cluster of people dressed in identical black gowns and strange white wigs sat around benches and tables. Everything was clean. The air was dry and set at a perfect temperature. The walls were covered in bright blue acoustic drapes to deaden echoes. Unlike American courtrooms, there was no flag or seal at the back behind the judge's bench. Instead the emblem of the League of the World loomed over them all.

The idea of a "truth commission" was absent from the history of most of the world's nations. There had been one or two minor legal investigations, mostly over matters relating to the two world wars, but after Disclosure the issue became paramount across the globe. It had begun after Disclosure Day in 1947 as soon as it became apparent that a large number of state actors had a lot of questions to answer. One of the last actions of President Truman before his assassination was to sign Federal pardons for a number of high-ranking figures at the War Office. Nobody knew why he had done this and hours later he was dead, so nobody ever would. The urgency for some new judicial device to untangle the unholy mess caused by Disclosure grew following Saucer Day and finally R-Day. With the three stages of Disclosure finally over, the cleanup operation could begin. During the months of the US Provisional Government, John F Kennedy had rounded up tens of thousands of suspects. Brendan remembered the street protests against it when he was a child, along with people weeping everywhere and the lynch mobs. Most of those apprehended were released without charge, but a few were put on trial. The issue eventually overlapped into other nations and became so vast that the backlog stretched to an estimate of several human lifetimes. For this reason the United States, along with most other countries outside the Red Bloc (sometimes dubbed the "Green Bloc"), signed the Tampico Accord in 1968 handing the entire process over to a specially established legal body within the League of the World. The domain of the League of the World Disclosure and Reconciliation Organization was not to prosecute criminal defendants under international law or the law of their own nations. It was simply to administer amnesty and commutations where appropriate. Obviously there were cases in which criminal prosecutions could not be overlooked; the most extreme example being with those behind the "underground children" and other real-life horror scandals. There were also a huge number of individuals charged with treason. All these were ruled as "returned"; the cases were referred back to the citizen's own country for a final trial and sentence. One of the most complex types of case was that of "indirect resultant harm" and it most often applied to those involved in the pre-Disclosure covert development of the new tech and the reverse engineering of extraterrestrial artefacts. The charge went along the lines of: the defendant was involved in a secret government and/or corporate project involving new tech. The fact that this new tech was kept secret caused a large amount of preventable human suffering, for example people dying of thirst in a drought when the new tech could have provided them with ample drinking water. Therefore even though the defendant did not actively cause damage, loss or injury to another, they did so passively by failing to make public their knowledge. It was a slippery issue and most of those in the dock trod a thin line. Those acting under security oaths were fairly safe; but, strangely enough, most of the senior figures in the projects did not. Some of them pleaded that they were simply obeying orders from senior members of their organizations, but that defence could be rejected under common law because it had been during the Nuremburg trials of 1946. Many of the accused would be refused amnesties and would end up being returned. The case Clane Quilley was involved in was exactly one of those.

Brendan took a seat. As his eye drifted across the scenario below him he stopped and gazed at the dock, immediately recognizing the person sitting there as Dr Melanie O'Connor. Everybody knew who she was and her media nickname was "the Banshee of Ballybay". She was a doctor who had begun her career in a conventional fashion, training at a medical school in England in the 1930's and then working in many different hospitals all over the UK and Ireland. She developed an excellent professional reputation and excelled at her work. Her intelligence quotient had once been tested at over a hundred and forty. In 1944 she had been recruited by a network of elite health clinics situated in southern Ulster that served the medical needs of the rich, famous and politically powerful of Ireland, Britain and other places across the world. These clinics offered interventions that were not available to the general public that had enormously beneficial effects. They were also deliberately omitted from all national drug schedules. The prosecution claimed that by collaborating with such a conspiracy Dr O'Connor had caused indirect resultant harm to the entire population of Ireland because many of them had lost their quality of life and suffered injuries, sickness and premature deaths as a result of being denied these interventions. They had also experienced the grief of loved ones being afflicted. Therefore the prosecution were pushing for a returnment.

Dr Melanie O'Connor looked very different to how she had when Brendan had arrested her at her hideout on Bentinck Island. She wore a smooth dark yellow velvet suit with black tights and shiny shoes, and her hair had been dyed brown and neatly pinned up. She was clutching a red leather handbag and a silver bracelet glinted at her wrist. She sat bolt upright in her chair with her head tilted confidently upwards over the assembled lawyers, clerks and stenographers. One of the barristers stood up. "Your honour, the defence calls Clane Quilley to testify." he declared.

"Call Clane Quilley." concurred the judge.

Brendan watched as his father entered from a door behind the witness box. He was wearing a brown corduroy suit and his tie flapped loosely from his chest. He looked flushed and nervous. He was made to hold a bible, raise his right hand and swear to tell the truth, the whole truth and nothing but the truth. He also had to confirm his name and other particulars to the court. After that he was allowed to sit down.

The defence barrister was an elderly black man with an educated English accent. His own grey frizzy hair peeked through the gap between his wig and nape. "Mr Quilley, please tell the court what happened to your wife in September of 1954."

Clane paused and coughed quietly. "She was diagnosed with cancer."

"Serious cancer?"

"Yes. Stage four metastatic breast cancer. It's a fatal condition; she was given a maximum of one year left to live."

The barrister sighed sympathetically. "That must have been terrible for you."

"It was. At the time my son Brendan was just short of his second birthday. My daughter was nineteen. My wife and I had remarried in early '52 after a divorce. We had moved to Ireland for a new start. I was beginning a career at the US Embassy."

"Could you please tell the court how you came into contact

with Dr Melanie O'Connor?"

"Gina, my wife, was referred to her clinic in County Louth. A friend of ours had the right connections. Dr O'Connor put her on a course of GMAT. It cleared up her cancer within a month."

"I'm very happy to hear that, Mr Quilley." smiled the defence counsel. "And how is your wife today?"

He smiled back. "Fit and well."

"How does this experience make you regard Dr O'Connor?"

Clane glanced across the room at the woman in the dock. "She saved Gina's life. I'm eternally grateful to her."

Brendan looked down at Dr O'Connor. Her expression was unmoved by Clane's sentiments and she kept her gaze dead ahead.

"'She saved Gina's life'!" quoted the barrister to the court. "Let that sink in, your honour. A doctor saved a life. A woman who did her job according to the universal ethics of her profession is sitting here before you being accused of not doing so. That doesn't make sense to me and I'm sure it doesn't make sense to you either... Thank you, Mr Quilley. No further questions."

"Your witness, Mr Conway." said the judge.

Another man sitting to the defence counsel's left stood up. He was a large fat man and he spoke with a treacly arrogant tone in a strange regional English accent Brendan couldn't recognize. "Mr Quilley, I would first like to echo Mr St Clare's delight that your good wife is no longer ill. I'm sure I join the whole court in expressing that."

Clane nodded. "Thank you."

"However, I must ask you, if Dr Melanie O'Connor is such a wonderful doctor then why is the Irish General Medical Council currently meeting with the intention of striking her off the register of practitioners?"

"Objection, your honour!" The defence counsel leapt to his feet. "The prosecution is asking the witness to comment on a matter he has no knowledge of."

The prosecutor looked over at his colleague. "Your honour, a patient or loved one of a patient is the perfect person to know whether or not a doctor is fit to practice medicine seeing as they experience the results first hand. Our fellows in the medical injuries litigation field know only too well how the scales of bias are weighted towards the negative when patients lodge complaints. A positive comment therefore deserves to be taken very seriously indeed."

"Overruled." said the judge woodenly. "You may answer the question, Mr Quilley."

Clane paused. "I was not aware of this matter and so don't know what kind of evidence is being used against Dr O'Connor in the complaint."

"Then allow me to enlighten you." said the prosecution counsel. "You told us that Dr O'Connor treated your wife's cancer with a course of GMAT, correct?"

"Yes."

"GMAT, glycoprotein macrophage activation therapy, is a very commonly prescribed treatment in modern oncology. I myself have taken it twice. When Dr O'Connor prescribed it to your wife, how many other people did you know who were also taking it?"

"None." replied Clane in a wary tone.

The prosecutor raised his eyebrows. "None?... But how can that be when GMAT is so powerful?"

Clane sighed. "GMAT was not available to the general public in Ireland at the time. It was only licensed in 1964 following R-Day."

"GMAT was developed in 1907. Why did it take almost sixty years for it to become generally available?"

"Because the pre-Disclosure authorities rationed it only to certain groups of private patients."

The prosecutor snorted contemptuously. "Do you know how many people used to die of cancer every year in the Republic of Ireland alone?"

"No, sir. I don't."

"Nine thousand... Thousands more were permanently maimed and sickened. This was because the government and major pharmaceutical corporations arranged a scheme to suppress the existence of GMAT. They ridiculed it in the media and persecuted its proponents as quacks."

Clane frowned. "You don't have to tell me that. I directed the post-Disclosure recovery programme in the United

States for eight years. The cancer cure cover-up was one of the biggest issues we had to deal with. Leaders in the health services, pharma and medical authorities were involved. Some were just interested in their profit. Chemotherapy, steroids, opioids, placebos. And the hardware too! Linacs, CAT scanners, panoramic radiographs. Do you know how much all that is worth? There was a psychological warfare element behind cancer too. It was one of the things people feared the most. Fear is the glue that held the pre-Disclosure world together."

"Then you should know..." He raised his voice and pointed at the dock. "Dr Melanie O'Connor colluded with that conspiracy! She did it willingly and in full knowledge of the consequences!... Your wife, Mr Quilley, was cured of cancer by Dr O'Connor, but you were extremely lucky. For every patient she cured she denied GMAT and other treatments to a thousand others who needed it! Whose lives she could have saved and chose not to! In doing so she broke the Hippocratic Oath! She contravened *primum nil nocere*, the principle of non-Malfeasance! She caused harm! Indirect resultant harm!... Why has the defence brought you in to testify? To make the point that Dr O'Connor is a good physician who cures people's cancer? No! She cured *your wife's* cancer, Mr Quilley! Your wife's and nobody else's!"

Clane shifted awkwardly and didn't speak.

"Do you wish to refute that?"

He paused. "I... I can't right now."

"You are an exception, Mr Quilley. A very tiny and very fortunate exception... And an exception does not disprove the rule... No further questions, your honour."

"You may step down, Mr Quilley." said the judge.

Brendan's father was shaking when he came out of the witness box and he went to the cafeteria for a cup of coffee with his son until he had recovered. After that, they both went back to the public gallery. Dr O'Connor was now testifying herself. She stood in the dock with her hands on the rail. "...It's difficult to explain to an outsider, somebody who has not been educated in the true complexities of modern medicine. You think it's a basic equation: sick person plus doctor equals well person. I'm afraid it's not that simple. Medical practitioners operate at the vanguard of an entire host of dedicated professionals and experts. I joined an elite group of geniuses because I wanted to see a world in control of such people. Yes, we were selective in who we treated. Yes, we chose to let most people remain sick or even die. I know doctors are not meant to think in those terms; we are supposed to be apolitical robots. Well that is why the world is in the mess that it is. Our organization did not enjoy seeing the people of the world suffer, but we understood that it was an unpleasant necessity. Our actions would eventually prevent far greater suffering in the future. We did not make decisions lightly. All factors, including moral ones, were taken into consideration. Nobody would benefit from the pharmaceutical industry collapsing. Without profit there would be no research, no production, no clinical trials, no hospitals... and no doctors for anybody! That is why I do not apologize for anything that I've done. I will not condemn myself or my organization in exchange for amnesty. The Illuminati reptilians were not our destroyers, they were our saviours! But you stupid people couldn't see it and you rejected them! A day will come soon when the whole of mankind will regret it!..."

Brendan looked at his father's face. It wore a very sad expression. They stood up and left the public gallery before the end of O'Connor's speech. When they got outside Brendan asked his father. "Do you think she'll get a returnment?"

He sighed and stared at the floor. "I hope she does."

Chapter 14

"I'll need the flyer today." said Heather. She and Brendan were making breakfast.

"What for?"

"I'm going to the docs again."

"I thought you said you didn't feel sick anymore."

"Hmm, kind of; but I still don't feel right. I puked a bit yesterday while you were at work."

"But you don't need the flyer to go to the base clinic."

"I'm not going to the base clinic. I've got an appointment with Dr Flynn in Rockville."

Brendan sighed. "Why him?"

"He's been our family doctor for my whole life. Yours too. Sorry, babe, but I trust him. He's the only one I want to see."

He chuckled. "Fair enough, honey. When's your appointment?"

"First thing eastern standard, so I'll be leaving at about midday."

"Okay, but could you drop me off in Dublin first? I'm going to see mom and dad. Seeing as I can't go by flyer I'll have to take the frightener."

"Sure." She spoke with an apologetic look.

It was Thursday, just three days after Clane's attendance at the Derry hearings. Dr Melanie O'Conner had been returned from the *LoWD&RO* court and was in custody at Dublin's Mountjoy Prison. Clane was back at home with Gina. Siobhan was at her Maryland apartment with Kerry and the twins. Brendan's submarine was settled in port and he had the rest of the week off work so he thought he would visit his parents. He kissed Heather goodbye and wandered into the Dublin frightener terminal wishing he had not sold his motorflyer the previous month. Luckily there was a speed-frightener about to leave for Accra. Once there he changed for a second frightener and arrived in Tamale only just over two hours after leaving Dublin. The searing heat and blazing sunshine struck him as he stepped out of the sliding doors at the regional airport. He went to a taxi rank and caught a cab to his parents' house. The vehicle was a flyer, but the driver insisted on travelling in ground-hugging mode. He explained in rapid English-native creole that a bylaw obliged him to during daylight hours. They drove slowly through the thick ground traffic down the straight busy market streets. The pavements were covered with shoulder-to-shoulder pedestrians all dressed in multicoloured traditional garments. Brendan had no local currency so when he arrived he had to ask his mother to lend him the fare. When they were both inside she tutted. "Honestly, Brendan. Didn't you think of switching your cash?"

He explained how Heather was using the flyer and that he had had to travel on public transport.

"They've got a bureau-de-change at the terminal don't they?"

"Jeez, mom! It's just a few dollars and I'll pay you back as soon as I've been to the goddamn bank." He was dismayed at his mother's attitude. She seemed to be in an irritable mood. He guessed she and her husband had been arguing again. "Where's dad?"

"Where he always is these days! Playing fucking golf!" She kicked the door of the washing machine shut with a crash.

Brendan eagerly escaped from the house and his mother's bleak manner. He wandered along the streets of the expatriate suburb towards the golf course. The white painted gates were wide open and just inside was the low bungalow of the clubhouse. Inside a number of men were drinking beer in the bar or on the patio. They were all old or in late middle age. "Good afternoon." said Brendan. "Anybody seen Clane?"

"I did a few minutes ago. He's on the back nine at the moment." The man was a Briton. Nearly everybody in the suburb was American, Irish or British; and, unlike the Pearson's hometown in Bawku, they were almost all white.

Brendan left the clubhouse smirking. In maritime slang "playing the back nine" meant something rude. He wandered onto the clean gravel paths between the fairways. Several golfers passed him, some wheeling their clubs on a portable trolley and others driving small electric cars. It was almost at the end of the dry season and the land was parched, but the golf course was always lush and green because of the watering pipes buried just under the surface. The players looked relaxed and cheerful, and they talked in quiet voices. The heat was intense. This was the hottest time of year in the Volta Union. Brendan deliberately tried to walk under trees to maximize his shade. Clane was about to tee off on the fifteenth hole. Three of his friends were playing with him. Brendan let him swing his driver against the ball before interrupting. "Hey, Bren." Clane's red sweaty face grinned beneath his white sunhat. "I've just had my second birdie! One more and I could break my course record."

Brendan waited patiently, following his father and his friends as they finished the round. Clane gulped down two pints of Guinness in the clubhouse and then father and son walked home together. They passed by the grocery shops on the way and Clane picked up a jar of coffee and some butter. There was some graffiti daubed on a blank white wall at the side of the shop, the crude black painted words: "*FORBAKO GO HOME.*" Clane looked uncomfortable as they passed it. "What's that all about, dad?" asked Brendan pointing.

"It means us. *Forbako* is a native word for expats."

"Do the VU folk not like us living here?"

"Not all of them. There's a new political party, set up last year. It's getting pretty popular in the polls. Its core policy is stopping immigration."

"If it gets into government does that mean you and mom will have to leave?"

He nodded. "Possibly. Even if we're allowed to stay we won't be treated as well. I've noticed that growing in the time we've been here. The natives aren't as friendly as they used to be... I guess I can see it from their point of view. When your mom and I came here there were only about a hundred thousand of us. Now there are more than five million, all living in these little enclaves, none of us speaking the local lingo. It must feel a bit like an invasion. The locals feel we're displacing their native culture... Also politics in the VU has got more radical in the last two or three years, probably because Nkrumah died."

"And will it get worse?"

"Yeah. With flyers and free energy, what's to stop everybody moving wherever they like and almost everybody who can afford it wants to come and live here where the weather's nice and the sea is warm. Not just in the VU, right across West and Central Africa or India, Vietnam, Thailand, Peru. It can't go on forever or these places will just turn into copies of America and Europe and the natives will have nowhere of their own. And of course the communists know this and are stirring up trouble as a result... We're petitioning the mayor-council's office to build a security fence around the area and make it a gated community."

Brendan paused. "That's a problem nobody predicted after Disclosure."

"One of many." Clane muttered grimly.

Brendan woke the next morning from a disturbing dream. It was about his childhood experience of being released from quarantine in Fort Detrick after he had come down with Morgellons disease. He was watching Farid, the Canadian boy he had been incarcerated with. He was crying and kicking out, desperately clinging on to every solid object he could find while the quarantine staff tried to drag him out of his confines. "*I'm not leaving! I can't leave!... Go away and let me stay here!*" Brendan checked his roam, but there was no message from Heather. He had not heard from her since the previous day. He frowned with worry. When Brendan went downstairs for breakfast his parents were talking in the tones that he recognized as a herald of an upcoming row, as sure as distant thunder foretold an imminent storm. "Can't you get off his case?" demanded Clane as Brendan walked in.

"No." Gina looked at Brendan in a way that made it clear they were talking about him.

Brendan shrugged in annoyance. "What!"

"Brendan, your father and I were just talking about that wife of yours."

"What about Heather?"

"You're too soft on her. She's taking advantage of you."

"No, she's not!" interjected his father.

Gina slapped his arm hard. "Shut up, Clane!... Brendan, you're doing all the giving and she's doing all the taking. You have to stand up to her."

Brendan was momentarily struck dumb with anger. "How dare you, mom! Who the hell do you think you are!?"

She snorted. Gina Quilley was sixty-two years old. Her hair was half grey but some streaks of the reddish brown locks that filled his childhood memory were still there. Her face was lined around the eyes and the sides of her lips, and she had a mole on her cheek that had grown over the years, but her beauty as a youth lingered like an echo on her face. It would for the rest of her life. Her figure was as muscular and upright as a younger woman's. She looked so much like Siobhan; that calm analysis poked up between the flanks of Brendan's outrage. She had suffered a nervous breakdown fourteen years earlier and had to be hospitalized, but she had completely recovered. In fact she had become by far the most conventional member of the family. "She stole your flyer!"

"Bullshit! It's *our* flyer and she hasn't stolen it; she's using it 'cos she needs it. I told her she could. She's got to go to the doctors!"

"Go ahead, make more excuses for her!"

"Holy shit, mom! Why are you making so much fuss about something so minor?"

Gina snorted and rolled her eyes again.

"You've always hated Heather, haven't you? That's why she won't come here!"

She softened slightly and bowed her head. "I don't hate Heather, Bren."

He guffawed. "In that case I dread to think how you'd treat somebody you *did* hate!"

"Please!... Stop this!" Clane raised his hands palms outwards. He seemed unusually upset at this exchange when normally he could be as aggressive as his wife.

There was a long silence, and then Gina shrugged and sighed. "Well, I'll leave you two to waste time by yourselves. Right now I have to go to Leeto's because we need a new bedside table seeing as your father leaned on it and broke it last week."

"Why do we need a new one?" asked Clane. "I'll glue the old one together."

"Like you were going to last week? Be honest, Clane! Never in a month of Sundays!" She strutted out of the kitchen. Clane and Brendan shared a pot of coffee. Five minutes later Gina came back with a summer dress on and pumps on her feet. She wore no tights and her tanned legs were spotted with reddened stubble where she had shaved them. "Right then, I'll see you later." she sneered. "Not sure how much later, mind you. I might decide to eat there in the cafeteria. They do splendid meatballs... Have a nice day." She yelled the last sentence sarcastically as she slammed the kitchen door. They heard her footsteps on the stairs. There was a buzzing sound from the roof and the windows flickered as the shadow of her flyer passed over them. The sound of the aircraft diminished and there was silence.

Brendan wandered through downtown Tamale. He window-shopped along the shiny atrium of the modern mall and the dusty smell-kaleidoscope of the traditional markets. He thought about his mother with sadness. She had worn a forced smile at his wedding to Heather in 1972. She had gone through the motions of course, but he could tell she was unhappy with his marriage. Since then she had offered his wife only very minimal and perfunctory courtesy. Clane on the other hand had wept with delight in the chapel at Fort Batten and he embraced Heather as if she were his daughter every time he saw her. This contrast made Gina's antipathy all the more obvious. Brendan and Heather had never talked about it, but he was sure Heather understood how poorly her mother-in-law regarded her.

Brendan sat down sadly on a bench. There was a flicker in the sunbeams and he looked up. A number of cruciform objects were circling overhead. At first Brendan thought they were fixed-wing aeroplanes, a rare sight those days, but then he identified them as vultures. These huge scavenging birds had become a pest in recent years. As sub-Saharan Africa became more urbanized, vultures had taken to the habit of raiding dustbins. It was easier than following dying antelopes across the savannah for hours on end. Their sharp powerful beaks could easily tear apart the side of a household wheelie-bin and pull out it contents to find something edible. Unfortunately they did not then put the non-edible rubbish back into the bin and it was left for humans to clean up after them.

The air temperature in Tamale rose through the morning. The natives continued their usual activity, smiling and cheerful as they tended to be, lugging bags of shopping and bunches of bananas, riding around quite happily on scooters and soaring over the corrugated metal rooftops on motorflyers.

However Brendan was sweating and his head ached. He went to a cafe and had a long chilled cola in the air-conditioned interior. After he finished the drink, he lay back and relaxed on a large sofa and sighed. At that moment his roamphone beeped in his pocket. He whipped the instrument out and saw a message from Heather. "Thank God!" he muttered as he opened it. It read: *"Brendan. Call me. H x."* He pressed the call button and waited as it rang.

Heather answered within two seconds. "Hi, Bren."

"Hi, Heather. Are you alright?"

"Yeah... Well, kind of." Her voice was breathy and tense.

"What do you mean 'kind of'?"

"Well... I'm pregnant."

Brendan heard the words; they reverberated a few times around his brain before registering. He felt the cafe tip and lurch around him. "What?"

"I'm pregnant, honey. We're having a baby."

Brendan struggled to form the words in his mouth. "So... you're going to be a mom and I'm going to be a dad."

She laughed. "I guess so."

"Are you sure?"

"Dr Flynn just called to confirm the test results."

"When will... will..."

"The baby be born? Early in October he reckons."

"Oh my God!" he gasped. "I'm going to be a dad!"

"Yes." She chuckled.

"Okay!... Okay!" he gasped. "I need to calm down."

"It's alright, babe." she laughed.

"Right, I'm coming home. I just have to tell mom and dad. I'll be with you soon... I love you, Heather."

"I love you too, Brendan."

Brendan ended to call and ran out into the street. He tried to call his father, but the phone was engaged. He flagged down a taxi and headed for his parent's house. He only needed his passport from his luggage and would not bother to pack. He kept repeatedly redialling his father's roam with his right hand as he rummaged through his rucksack with his left. As soon as he had his passport he heard the buzzing of a flyer outside. As he reached the hallway his father burst in holding his own roam to his ear, talking frantically. As he saw Brendan he lowered it. His face was ashen and taut. "Brendan!"

"What's the matter, dad?"

"It's your mom. She's had an accident."

....

Gina Quilley's face was surrounded by bandages, but it was easily recognisable. One of the most painful memories of Brendan's childhood was being eight years old and visiting his father in hospital just after he had had a stroke. Clane had been like a stranger, stripped naked and wrapped in dressings. When he was conscious he didn't know anybody and had no memory of his past. Gina was different. Her eyes were closed peacefully and her lips were slightly raised at the edges as if in a subtle smile. Despite the silvery pipe stuck between her lips like a teat to help her breathe, it was definitely her. A lock of brownish grey hair looped out from underneath the pressure dressing covering her scalp. It lay across her throat like a necklace. Beside the bed was a whirring, bubbling collection of electronic devices that monitored her heart, lungs and other vital organs. A ventilator hissed and clicked in a five second cycle and Gina's chest rose and fell in time with it as her lungs were inflated and deflated remotely by the mechanical diaphragm. Brendan's father stood beside him staring down at his wife. His mouth was trembling and his eyes blinked repeatedly. After a few minutes a group of nurses drew the curtains around the cubicle and they had to leave. They padded out of the neurological intensive care ward and went and sat in the visitor's lounge, a cheerless room covered in cheerful decorations in the ultimate portrait of futility. They sipped coffee and tea for half an hour and then the door burst open. It was Siobhan, Kerry and the twins. "Dad!" Siobhan exclaimed. Clane jumped up and hugged her desperately. "What happened, dad?"

"She was at the Leeto store in Port Sudan and a crate of flat pack dining tables collapsed on top of her... Incompetent Swedish motherfuckers!"

"Oh, dad." She rubbed the back of his neck.

"She was only buying a bloody cabinet for the bedroom!... How did this happen!? *Why* did it happen!?"

They all turned towards the door as a doctor in a white coat walked in. He was a thin dark-skinned man with thick-rimmed spectacles. "Mr Quilley, Ms Quilley." he said in a strong foreign accent.

"Yes!?" Clane barked expectantly.

"I am Dr Al-Azari and I'm looking after Mrs Quilley. We're about to take her to the theatres. I'll be operating on her."

"Will she be okay?"

He paused. "She has suffered severe head injuries. Fractured skull and multiple brain insults. We will know more once we start the surgery."

"Please, do what you can."

"We will, sir. I will give you news as soon as we have some."

In the oasis of calm that followed the drawn-out afternoon of panic, Brendan suddenly realized that Heather must be wondering where he was. He had completely forgotten about their conversation earlier. He even wondered if it had been a dream, but when he turned on his roam there was a whole list of messages for him. He thumbed a hasty lean-to explanation. He was standing on a terrace at the Al-Remila Hospital in Khartoum, renowned for its neurological trauma unit. The sun was setting over the city skyline and the muddy waters of the White Nile churned past beneath the parapet. A caravan of camels meandered back and forth on the far bank. He talked to Heather for a few minutes and then wandered back inside the hospital, following the Arabic and English signs back to the neurological department. There was a window in the door of the visitors' lounge and as Brendan approached he saw Dr Al-Azari standing with his back towards the entrance. He was wearing surgical scrubs darkened by patches of perspiration. Clane was sitting on the settee with his head in his hands. His shoulders were convulsing and Brendan could hear his howls of grief through the door. An icy wave of horror filled Brendan's stomach. Siobhan was sitting beside their father, her arms around him in a comforting cuddle, but her own expression was deadpan and composed.

....

By the mid-1970's virtually every person on earth had the ability to travel anywhere on the planet within three or four hours for almost no money at all. This led to the largest population shift in human history. The "global village" long predicted by science fiction was now a reality. However, the natural human tribal instincts were still there and they manifested in various ways. One of them was death rites. No matter where a person lived, nearly all of them were buried in their ancestors' native homeland. In the case of the Quilley family this was New York City, specifically the Most Holy Trinity Cemetery in Brooklyn. Georgina Lillian Quilley *née* O'Reilly was laid to rest just a few plots away from her father and grandparents. The antediluvian Bishop Seamus O'Shaughnessy came out of retirement specially to perform the funeral for the woman he had baptized as a baby and had married to Clane Quilley (the first time) when he was their parish priest. There was a full Requiem Mass at the church and then they moved to the graveside for the final act. The collection of black clad mourners arranged themselves respectfully into rows based on the immediacy of relation to the deceased. Clane, Siobhan and Brendan stood at the front. Kerry was there too. She was not a blood relative, but was as good as. William and Colleen were on each side of their mother. Nobody cried; those who had any tears had exhausted them days ago. After the coffin had been lowered to the bottom of the oblong pit, Gina's two brothers picked up spades and filled in the grave themselves, wet loam staining their spit-polished shoes. Gina's mother was smiling cheerfully, but she was eighty-eight years old and in the later stages of Alzheimer's disease. She sat in her wheelchair blissfully unaware of her own tragedy. After the burial there was a wake in a function room above a local pub. A large framed photograph of Gina was placed on the mantelpiece and the mood lightened as her loved ones reminisced affectionately about her life. John F Kennedy and a few other old friends raised glasses in a toast to the Quilleys and their lost member. After a few hours the mourners scattered to go home, some of them drunkenly. There were final hugs and kisses; a few comforting words as life went back to normal. Clane and Brendan flew in convoy with Siobhan; Kerry and the twins went in their own flyer. The sun plummeted towards the horizon like a time-lapse film as they headed eastwards across the Atlantic. "You know something, Brendan." began Clane. His voice made Brendan jump; he had been silent during the drive up till then.

"Your mom and I always knew one day you would be an engineer. You always wanted to know what was inside everything. We'd give you a toy and you would tear it to pieces to find out how it worked." He laughed. "Your mom called you her 'little mechanic'."

It was pitch dark when they got back to the house in Tamale. "It doesn't feel like home to me anymore." said Clane. He wandered around, picking things up, Gina's recipe books in the kitchen, her jewellery, ornaments she had chosen. At ten PM all six of them collapsed onto armchairs and the settee in the lounge to watch the first landing on the moon. There had been a faked event in 1952 shortly before Brendan's birth, but this was the real thing. What also didn't qualify was the secret space programme and the existing abandoned Illuminati bases on the moon and other planets. The spacecraft was powered by antigravity, like a modified flyer, and it took only twelve hours to fly from its launch pad in Mexico City to the surface of the moon. Appropriately, it looked like a huge black steel Mexican hat. It lifted off from a modified platform on a crossroads at the end of *Cinco de Mayo* Avenue with thousands of people cheering in the street. Their voices were drowned out by the humming of the spacecraft's engines, far louder and deeper in pitch than a flyer. The astronauts bounced around on the dusty lunar ground, not looking very different to those in the earth studio of the previous hoax. The principle difference was that the surface was dustier. Two of the eight astronauts were American and President Tavinor made a speech thanking them from the White House Press Briefing Room. The family shared a bottle of whiskey and for a while it was like nothing had happened. Gina was not there, but it was as if she had just popped down the road to the shops. As the family were watching the people in spacesuits plodding awkwardly across the grey moonscape, Brendan looked surreptitiously at the side of Siobhan's head. Her facial expression had not once changed since the moment of her mother's death. It was sedate, even sleepy. Her eyes blinked slowly. It was almost a dreamy look, as if she had had a busy energetic day and had just begun to relax. She had not cried in his presence yet. In fact she had not spoken much either. They went to bed at two AM. Brendan looked out of his bedroom door and watched his father walk slowly from the bathroom to his own bedroom alone. He had not yet told his family about Heather's pregnancy. He simply couldn't; it felt wrong at that time. Brendan lay on his back in bed with darkness surrounding him for a long time. He thought about his mother and images from his early childhood flicked across his mind. He sobbed quietly, tears flowing down his temples onto the pillow by his ears.

He awoke at dawn. He got up before the rest of the family and went out for a walk. His mother still dominated his thoughts. He had dreamed about her all night and now scenes he remembered of her life were replaying over and over on the cinema screen of his inner dialogue. He walked through the early morning bustle. Tamale was beautiful at the start of the day. The sun was low, peeking through the tree trunks of the woods; the sky was a patchwork of pink clouds and blue heavens. He still marvelled at the chemtrail-free firmament. He walked past a house with a pre-Disclosure classic car parked in its driveway. It was a British Riley, an early model from Morris Motors built in the late 1930's. The owner had clearly taken good care of it. It had spotless vanilla blue paintwork and chrome like a mirror. There was not one speck of rust anywhere on its body. Its number plate was an old British imperial Gold Coast one. The owner came out of the house with a bucket of soapy water and began washing the vehicle. He then filled the petrol tank from a can. IC fuels were expensive those days. Nearly all filling stations had closed and they had to be bought in cans from motorists' suppliers. He looked up and noticed Brendan admiring it. He smiled and waved.

"You got a great car there, sir." said Brendan.

The man was an elderly native, heavily built with skin smooth and dark as a chestnut. He had pure white hair and a sideboard moustache. He replied in a language Brendan couldn't understand; French pidgin, the local Niger-Congo vernacular or a mixture thereof.

Brendan nodded politely, not wanting to admit his lack of comprehension. As he watched the old man tenderly caring for his beautiful old car he felt tears well up in his eyes again. He walked hastily on down the road after he and the man waved goodbye to each other. He ducked into an alleyway between two other houses and pressed his hands to his face so that he could wail silently. After a few minutes he had recovered and continued down the street. He would not normally be so deeply moved by the experience he had just had. It was clear that he was very emotionally delicate. He ate breakfast at a diner in the city centre and felt stronger. He sent Dave Pearson a text and got a positive response so he went home and borrowed his father's flyer. Dave was enrolled on some indefinable humanities course at University of Dar Es Salaam in Tanganyika. It was a pleasant half-hour flight eastwards across the continent with just a three-hour time difference so it was only lunchtime when he arrived. Dave met him at the landing pad and they went to the students' union for food and drink. Brendan was delighted to be with his old friend and his emotions shot to the opposite extreme from the morning. He drank a few more beers than he normally would at lunchtime and became manic, laughing excessively at even the weakest joke. Dave tolerated him and so did his other friends. He must have told them about Brendan's maternal loss. They watched a movie at the cinema and then at five PM he said farewell to Dave and headed home. His father's flyer had a programmable autopilot so he didn't have to drive, which was just as well considering he was still mildly over the legal alcohol limit for aerial traffic.

The flyer touched down on the rooftop pad and Brendan locked it. He opened the door and descended the steep steps off the roof. He hung the flyer keys on the hook on the landing where they were always kept, and then he froze. Something was wrong, he could just feel it. "Dad?... Siobhan?..." There was no reply. Then he heard somebody sniffing in one of the bedrooms. He ran along the corridor in the direction of the noise and saw Colleen sitting on her bed. She was crying. "Coll, what's wrong?" he asked his niece.

"It's mom." Her hands were trembling. "She's had a fight with grandpa."

"Where is she?"

"She went out." said another voice from the doorway. William was standing there. He was tall and mature for a twelve-year-old. He was composed, but looked downcast.

"What was it about, Will?"

"She... she told grandpa she was happy grandma's dead."

"She what!?"

The boy shrank back awkwardly. "Uncle Brendan... we know mom never liked grandma."

Brendan stared at him. He felt a moment of shock, but it quickly passed. "You could hardly miss it could you?" He placed a comforting hand on his nephew's shoulder. "Do you know where your mom went?"

He shook his head.

Brendan sent Siobhan a quick text then ran downstairs. The lower floor of the house was as quiet as a tomb. "Dad?" Brendan blurted out in fear.

"I'm here." Clane Quilley's voice sounded like a stranger's. It was quiet, aspirate, almost inaudible.

Brendan looked in the direction of the voice. His father was sitting at the kitchen table. His back was turned towards the door and his shoulders were slumped. The bald patch on the top of his head was flushed and sweaty like a skinned watermelon. The frame of reddish-grey hair around it was ruffled. "Oh... dad..." Brendan began, but then he stopped. He instinctively knew not to approach his father or try to talk to him. "I'm going out." he continued and walked towards the door. He turned to the right outside the front door, in the direction of the main road into the city, but he was stumped as to how he would find Siobhan; then a text appeared on his roam: "*B. I'm in the park by the golf course. S.*" Brendan reversed direction and broke into a jog. Ten minutes later he arrived at the park out of breath. The evening shadows of the trees surrounding the park were long, almost covering the grass. A dozen or so people were walking their dogs or playing sports. Siobhan was sitting on a bench at the far end of the green space in the depth of the shade. She was alone, perched right in the middle of the seat with her legs pressed together and her hands on her lap. She turned her head and smiled thinly as she saw Brendan approach. "Hi, Bren."

"Siobhan." he puffed. "What's going on?"

She shrugged. The redness of her eyes revealed that she had been crying. For the first time ever she looked aged in Brendan's eyes. She was thirty-nine years old, but there were just a few grey hairs sprouting from the crown of her head. There were wrinkles on her face. She now looked more like her mother than ever before.

Brendan sat down beside her. "What's going on?" he repeated.

"I told dad the truth."

"Why?"

"Would it be better to lie to him?"

"Yes! At the moment. Mom is not even cold in the ground. You should have given him some more time."

She chuckled. "That's what *he* said."

"Who, dad?"

"No... Flying Buffalo."

He paused. "Who!?"

"I saw him. He came to me."

"The Indian?... When?"

"About half an hour ago."

Brendan gasped. "Oh my God!"

"I've not seen him for about ten years. I still don't know for sure if he is real. Half of me still thinks I just fantasize him."

"He's still here!... Why haven't I seen him?" Conflicted feelings poured through his system.

"He wasn't mad at me or anything. He was as nice as always. He just said... I shouldn't have said those things to dad... I don't want to tell you the rest."

"Was your fight with dad like your fight with mom about the school?"

"No. Dad and I were just sitting there and he asked me why I hadn't cried. He asked me if I had cried when I was alone. He said I needed to let it all out. 'It's not healthy to bottle up your feelings. Don't suffer in silence'. And that's when I told him."

"You told him you weren't sad?"

She nodded. "It wasn't like that day after school with mom. I wasn't angry. I'm not angry with dad still. I just told him the truth and he freaked out." She sighed sadly. "It was awful to see. At once I knew I thought I'd made a mistake, but it was too late."

"'Thought'?"

"Yeah. Now I'm not so sure. You see, he asked me in a

way that meant I'd have to lie and I didn't want to lie to him. Deep down I just wanted to say it. I really hate living this double life, Bren... At the same time, I know it's wrong. There is something very very wrong with anybody who feels glad when their mother dies... But I can't help it."

Brendan nodded. "Nobody can help their feelings, Siobhan."

"It was only after she was dead that I realized that it was something I had wanted for a long time, but I couldn't admit it to myself. It was too grotesque to see your mom alive and think to yourself: 'I wish you were dead!' and of course I could never have said that to her, or told anybody else... Or if I had, it would have been an evil thing to do... But if I died, mom would be just as happy. In fact she'd be overjoyed! She would dance on my grave and cheer. And unlike me, she would gloat about it in dad's face!"

"She wouldn't have done that!"

"Yes she would!"

Brendan didn't reply.

"Bren, now I'd like to be alone for a while." Siobhan spoke without looking at him. She stared at the ground in front of her.

"Sure. See you later."

When Brendan got home it was almost dark; night falls quickly in the tropics. His father was exactly how he had left him; sitting in the same chair in the same posture. William and Colleen were lurking in the lounge next door, either out of curiosity or concern for their grandfather's wellbeing. This time Brendan entered the kitchen and sat down beside him. "Hi, dad."

Clane nodded. His features were white. He looked stunned, as if his existing grief over his wife's death had just doubled. His eyes were those of a man who had just seen his wife die a second time. "Hi, Brendan."

"Want a coffee?"

He shook his head.

Brendan hesitated. "I saw Siobhan. She's really sorry about what happened."

Clane breathed in deeply through his nose and pulled his lips tight. "I keep thinking back to when your grandpa killed himself. How I felt then. I had my differences with him, very big differences, but he was still my dad... When Siobhan stood there and said she felt no sadness about your mom dying, just twenty-four hours after standing beside me as we committed her remains to the earth... it was like one of those weird nightmares when somebody you know and love starts acting completely different, acting in a violent and hostile manner."

"You know about Siobhan and mom... that they drove themselves apart from each other."

"Your mom is still the woman who gave her life." replied Clane slowly. "For Siobhan to... to be insensitive to that. To totally disregard that as if it was an irrelevant triviality. It's like she turned into another person. I felt I was looking at a total stranger who had suddenly invaded the body of my child."

"She saw Flying Buffalo."

Clane laughed sardonically. "And what riddles and double-talk did our old disappearing family friend have to say this time?"

"That she shouldn't have told you."

He snorted with painful irony. "Maybe it's better that she did. If my own daughter did not love her own mother it's something I'd rather be aware of, however heartbreaking it is."

There was a click as the front door opened. Siobhan walked in and stood still in the hallway outside the kitchen. She remained facing side on and turned her head. Her face was blank. Clane jerked round, startled by the sound. He looked at her for a second then swung back to face the table. His eyelids trembled and his corneas dampened. Siobhan sadly looked away and walked on. Brendan heard her in the lounge talking to her children. After about twenty more minutes the three of them padded upstairs.

....

Brendan slept better that night, mostly because he was drowsy from lying awake for much of the night before. He had unpleasant dreams again about his mother, but also Siobhan and his father. He saw them all fighting brutally, stabbing each other with knives and tearing each other's skin with their fingernails. When he woke up it was light outside and the clock said eight-twenty. He sighed with relief that his dreams were not real. He got up, put on a dressing gown and went out onto the landing. He could hear his father snoring gently in his own bedroom. Siobhan and the twins were all silent. He went downstairs into the kitchen. He had taken a coffee mug out of the cupboard and pressed the button to start the kettle before he noticed something unusual on the table. It was an oblong white object a few inches across propped up between two bottles of the cruet set. He picked it up and saw that it was an envelope. On the front were the words "*Dad and Brendan*" in Siobhan's handwriting. He ripped it open. Inside was a folded piece of blue notepaper:

"Dear Dad and Brendan. By the time you read this Will, Coll and I will have left the house. We don't know when we'll be back, maybe never. I am taking my children to be with their father. This time we will not give up until we have found him. I don't feel I have a place in this family anymore. I'm sorry about how I feel about mom, but I can't help it. I think if I was meant to be with this family I would be as sad as you both are. Don't try to follow me because you will not find me. I may be ready to come back to you someday, but it won't be for a very long time, a few years at least. We have taken mom's flyer, sorry about that. To stop you from following me I have stolen the keys to the other two flyers. Don't worry, I will mail them to you when we get clear of town and they will arrive back in a day or two. By then it will be too late. We have all left our roams and slates behind so you can't contact us. Goodbye. Siobhan."

Brendan's hands shook as he read and reread the letter. "DAD!" he yelled.

....

It was difficult to know where to start. Clane called the police, but they couldn't help. No crime had been committed. Siobhan could not be listed as a missing person because she had told them where she was going. She was also William and Colleen's mother so how could she kidnap them? Brendan and his father went along the street knocking on doors to ask if they could borrow any transport or be given a lift. The neighbours were rather alarmed by the request and in the end the best they could manage was a small hatchback ground car. Brendan thanked the lender and jumped into the driving seat. Clane leaned down to the window. "I'll stay at home in case she calls the landline or E-grams." he said.

"Right. I'm going to drive north to the TSSR. She will be somewhere in the Red Bloc and even if I'm not granted entry, maybe I can make enquiries or pass on a message at the border post."

"Text me and let me know how you're getting on." said Clane. He was holding back tears. "I want her back, Bren. I want my sweet little baby back home with me. Please bring her back to me!"

"I'll do my best, dad."

Brendan drove north in the Digby-powered vehicle. The main road to Bolgatanga ran through savannah, thin forests and lush cocoa farms. These were interspersed with small pastures speckled with goats. He arrived in the town at eleven AM and drove around the outskirts, not stopping. The weather was hot and humid as the rainy season announced its impending arrival. He had the car's windows shut and the air-conditioning on full power. The road he took ran northeast. The landscape became drier and hillier. Over the next two hours the road-signs changed from English to bilingual French-English and eventually to just French alone. The road moved from a dual to single carriageway and began to decrease in quality. He noticed more potholes and cracks, and the ride felt bumpier. West Africa had been through a brief hiatus of mass road building between the advent of the Digby Carrousel and the rise of antigravity. The results of that decade were large concrete and tarmac routes that were less than twenty years old, but had not been maintained for half that time. As transportation took to the air, the network was returning to its pre-Disclosure squalor. Brendan stopped to eat and drink at a roadside refectory and sent a long text to Heather explaining the problem. He had not seen her for almost a fortnight, since he had left to attend the Derry hearings before his mother's death. She had stayed away from the funeral and its aftermath and nobody had criticized her, knowing why she did it. She had been sending Brendan regular updates about her health and wellbeing. *"Oh no! Bren, I'm really sorry. She can't be serious about leaving for good, can she? Knowing Siobhan she'll change her mind and come home soon. H xx.*" Brendan sighed deeply and shuddered. "I hope so, babe." he mumbled to himself.

As Brendan continued through the north-eastern region of the Volta Union the land became more and more mountainous until the road ran in circuitous meanders along valleys between desiccated rubble-strewn peaks that reminded Brendan of the high desert of the United States. However the road was way below American standards. It was wider than it previously was, but it grew rougher and rougher until Brendan began to worry about damaging the car or puncturing the tyres. The ground car was a low power four-mill Digby rear-wheel-drive with normal street tyres. A four-by-four heavy-duty vehicle would be better and indeed all the cars that passed him were of this category. Then another type of vehicle began to dominate the roadscape; large articulated lorries. They were painted grey and covered with dust, powered by anachronistic diesels with vertical exhaust pipes belching clouds of blue-black smoke. They passed him every few minutes, their horns lowing like bulls, all of them heading in the opposite direction. There was something chilling about them and Brendan noticed that they all had yellow patches stencilled on their sides. When he got a closer look he saw that it was the radiation warning symbol. He frowned as he passed them, pressing down on the accelerator to be away from this unwholesome convoy as soon as possible.

He rounded a bend and finally saw the border of the Trans-Saharan Socialist Republic. It was heavily guarded by a group of soldiers who were busy inspecting another radioactive lorry that was parked waiting for permission to enter the VU. Because of the political situation, "Cold War II" as it was known, there was a lot of distrust between the TSSR and VU. Brendan had his passport with him, but no visa or other documentation. Would he be allowed through?

The border post was placed on the road where it ran between two mountain slopes. Beyond it ahead was flatter land, partly hidden by haze as the rain approached. It consisted of an inner Volta Union side and an outer TSSR side about a dozen yards apart. The VU border guards wore the uniform of the nation's army which Brendan was familiar with. They glimpsed at the hatchback as it passed, more out of curiosity then concern. They didn't really care who was leaving the country, only who was entering. Brendan coasted over the short no-man's-land into the Trans-Saharan Socialist Republic. A squad of half a dozen TSSR border guards stepped across the road in front of him and gestured at him to stop. Their uniforms were less elaborate, consisting of T-shirts with the TSSR flag on them and red berets with metallic badges whose meaning Brendan couldn't work out. Their trousers and footwear varied between individuals. Their outfit consisted of no unit flashes or insignia of rank. They were less orderly than the VU guards, rolling about on their feet casually and handling their service rifles in a lax manner. At one point Brendan almost ducked, not because the guard was about to shoot him, but because the guard accidentally let his weapon point at him. Brendan grinned inwardly as he thought what Training Sergeant Bayrooth would have done to the guard in that situation. One of the guards who was clearly in command pointed at Brendan and yelled something in heavily accented French. Brendan rolled down his side window and stuck his head out. "Come again?... I'm sorry, I don't understand."

The man switched to broken English. "Out from car! Out from car!"

Brendan opened the door and stepped out onto the searing dust of the road.

The guard leader continued to talk to him rapidly in French. Occasionally one of the others chimed in.

"Er... *Je m'appelle* Brendan Quilley." He faltered. It was one of the few phrases he recalled from his French classes at school. "I'm looking for... *ma sœur*. *Ma sœur, elle s'appelle* Siobhan. I think she has come here."

The chief guard poked him in the chest. "You *Anglais*?... 'Merican?"

"I'm American yes."

The guards turned to each other and began talking in their own language. After a few minutes of incomprehensible dialogue, they beckoned Brendan towards a wooden hut at the side of the road. "Come... come."

He followed, but looked over his shoulder. "What about

my car?"

"Come..." The man continued to goad him towards the hut.

"This is not my own car. It belongs to a friend. I can't leave in standing in the road."

"Come."

As he entered the hut he saw the other guards pushing the hatchback into a small carpark at the side of the road next to a few jeeps and a minibus. The hut had one small window and the heat inside was stifling. The guards offered him a cold drink from a refrigerator. They took his passport and examined it closely. There was a desk at the other side of the room with a rather dated telephone and the commander had a long conversation on it in babbling Afro-French. Brendan couldn't understand any of it, but twice the man read his name off the passport, pronouncing it wrongly: "*Bron-donn Kee-yay*". Brendan tried to send his father a text message, but the signal was very poor and it bounced. The border guards then led Brendan to the minibus. They tried and failed to explain what their plans were. Brendan looked at the parked hatchback and considered for a moment leaving and driving home, but then thought of Siobhan, and his nephew and niece. He stepped aboard. One of the guards got into the driving seat and started the engine. It rumbled into life with a noise that made Brendan jump. It was an IC, like the one he'd ridden in when he went to Australia. The vehicle moved jarringly out of its space onto the road and headed northeast into the TSSR. Brendan looked over his shoulder at the receding border post and gulped. There was no way he could go back now. Had he made a mistake?

The vehicle had no air conditioning and was very hot despite all the windows being open. It was old fashioned and in poor condition. Plastic foam stuffing was leaking out of the imitation leather seats. The driver never spoke during the entire journey, not that he and Brendan could have understood each other. He had laid his rifle casually on the front passenger seat so he could drive while Brendan sweated and glowed in the back. The countryside was less hilly now, but remained rocky with just a few succulent plants and small trees. After an hour the sun was mercifully dimmed by cloud and then deafening thunderclaps made the ground tremble like an earthquake. The most intense rain Brendan had ever seen then descended onto the landscape like an ocean wave. The road rippled with spattered water and the minibus' windscreen wipers could barely keep up with it. The air was still humid but considerably cooler. Water dripped onto his head from rusty holes in the roof. Visibility was reduced many-fold by the rain and the driver had to slow down and switch on the headlights. They passed other vehicles a few times, their own headlights shining out through the torrent like lighthouse beams. The road was now a river of brown mud and the minibus skidded a few times as it aquaplaned. After another hour the traffic grew heavier and they passed other cars every minute or so. Large buildings appeared at the side of the road as if they were entering a large town or city. Brendan leaned forward and tapped the driver's shoulder. "*Excusez-moi*... Where are we? What is this place? *Qu'est-ce que c'est, cette ville*? " He pointed at the structures on the roadside.

"Niamey."

Brendan nodded. He knew from his private studies that Niamey was a big city in the TSSR, formerly the capital of independent Niger it was now the second largest city in the socialist republic after Tripoli on the Mediterranean coast. He stared out of the window curiously. The buildings were all dark orangey-brown. The rain had reduced visibility to a few hundred feet. They drove over a wide bridge crossing a river that was swollen by a flash flood because of the deluge. It ran fast and high, almost to the top, threatening to submerge the bridge or wash it away. Brendan was relieved when they reached the far side safely. The driver eventually pulled up beside a cuboid house partly hidden behind a high wall topped by anti-climbing spikes. Several large satellite dishes sprouted from its flat roof. A metal sign by the gate announced that this was a US consulate. "*Ici*." The guard pointed at the building.

"*Merci beaucoup*." Brendan replied and slid open the back door. The vehicle drove off with a splash as Brendan ran towards the gate, raindrops hammering his scalp and trickling down the back of his neck. He rang the gate intercom and explained who he was. It opened immediately and the door to the building lay just inside. The entrance hall of the US consulate resembled that of a modern hospital. There was a glass desk beneath a flight of broad spiral stairs. The wall consisted mostly of tall windows and there was a mild background hiss of air-conditioning. The thin carpet squeaked under Brendan's wet feet. The receptionist was a dark-skinned woman in a traditional local dress and headscarf. Brendan walked up to her, rain dripping off his clothes, but before he had the chance to speak to her a booming voice yelled out from above: "Brendan, my boy!"

He looked up and an obese man in a suit was descending the spiral stairs. "Hello?"

The man chuckled. "Last time we met you were just starting school. You won't remember me, but I remember you well." He was a broad-faced man with a neatly trimmed white beard. He had a Southern accent. Altogether he looked and sounded like a Tennessee planter. "I'm Bart Tross the consul-general here in Niamey. I worked with your dad at the embassy in Dublin." He shook Brendan's hand warmly. "My goodness, how you've grown. How is your dad these days?"

"Pretty bad, sir. In fact, that's why I've come here." Brendan explained.

Tross' face fell with sympathy. "Oh, Brendan; I'm so sorry about your mother. Condolences to you all. May God comfort you at this difficult time. I'm sure I can help you find your sister. I recall that she was a charming young lady. But first, you must be hungry. Let me take you out for a meal."

Brendan was given accommodation in the consulate's comfortable guest flat. A change of clothes was left out for him. When he met Tross in reception it was almost dark outside and the rain had stopped. A taxi took them to an upmarket hotel, the grandest building he had seen so far in the TSSR. The other diners were all foreigners and a dozen of them were introduced to Brendan as staff from the consulate. The food consisted of spicy dishes based on millet, the staple crop of the region. As the evening wore on Brendan realized that Tross was using him to show off. As the son of the "man who gave us Disclosure" there was a pungent odour of celebrity worship among the people at their table. Tross spoke continuously about his friendship with Clane Quilley and his family in Ireland. Some of the younger women were ostentatiously flirting with Brendan. As they consumed their after-dinner brandies, Brendan's patience ran out. "Mr Tross... your Excellency." he began with a sarcastic grin. "I'm grateful for this exquisite meal and everything, but right now I am trying to find my missing sister and I need your help."

"Of course, my good fellow." Tross patted his shoulder. "I already have some of my team working on tracking her down. Until they do, by God Harry, there's no reason for us to have empty stomachs is there?" He patted his own stomach, which looked far from empty.

Back in his bedroom, Brendan once again tried to text his father, but there was no signal at all. He had not seen anybody in the TSSR using roamphones. They seemed to be unknown technology like flyers. He slept reasonably well and in the morning Tross allowed him access to the consulate's satellite telephone which could connect with the communications grid outside the Red Bloc, something which the Bloc's internal telecommunications system could not. First Brendan called his father to tell him what had been happening. He called Heather to check she was alright. In the afternoon, he dialled a number that he had to work hard to find. His father had to hack Siobhan's E-gram account from her slate by trying all of the passwords she had noted down in her diary. Brendan checked the time and realized that it would be early in the day for the people he was calling and hoped they would be awake. It rang and he heard a voice. "Good morning, the Spencer residence."

"Hello, is it possible to speak to Mr or Mrs Spencer please?"

"One moment, sir." There was a long silence for several minutes then a woman's voice with a grand English accent came onto the line. "Hello, Tanya Spencer speaking."

"Hello, Mrs Spencer. Apologies for disturbing you at this early hour. My name is Brendan Quilley and I'm the brother of Siobhan Quilley whom I think you have heard of."

There was a pause. "Oh yes. Of course." The voice was neutral, neither happy nor sad at the mention of her son's ex-lover. "I've not heard from Siobhan for a long time. How is she?"

"She's been alright, bringing up..." Brendan stopped himself abruptly with alarm. He was fairly sure that Tanya Spencer did not know about her two grandchildren. He didn't want to break the news to her at that moment. "Bringing up... herself to be a good writer, working on new articles for the press, a new book." He then told her about their mother's death and Siobhan's subsequent abscondment. "So I was wondering if you knew where Julian is living right now because that's probably where Siobhan is too, and where I will find her. Maybe then I can talk her into coming home."

There was a very long pause and he heard her sigh. "Brendan, I'm very sorry, but I can't help you. Neither Albert nor I have the faintest idea of Julian's whereabouts at the moment. In fact we haven't seen or spoken to him for fourteen years." There was a mixture of sadness and anger in her tone. "The last time we had any contact with him he told us in no uncertain terms that he wanted nothing more to do with us or anybody else in the family. He... he told us that he hated us. He called us the most awful names, accused us of the most heinous crimes, crimes of which we are completely innocent. Then he left us, telling us he intended never to see us again. It seems he has stood by his word."

"I see. I'm very sorry that happened, Mrs Spencer."

"Thank you, Brendan. I'm also very sorry about your mother's passing. Deepest sympathy to you all. Do give my very best wishes to Siobhan and your father when you next see them."

"I will. Good morning to you."

....

Bart Tross informed Brendan that a passage had been arranged for him on Monday, the day after the next; in the meantime Tross offered to take Brendan on a tour of Niamey and the surrounding country. Brendan reluctantly agreed; it was more appealing than hanging around the consulate building for the rest of the weekend. This was arranged for the following morning. As soon as they were out of the gates in the official car, it immediately became clear that this was to be an official diplomatic visit. As with the meal the evening before, the consul-general arranged this pomp and ceremony without telling his guest beforehand. He was escorted around several museums, sports grounds and government buildings. He nodded politely at the officials who spoke to him, but his nagging impatience needed effort to suppress. However, after they left the city things became more interesting. They drove northeast for several hours. The rainwashed countryside gave way to barren rocks and eventually sandy desert. They arrived at a town full of low square mud-brick buildings with camels roaming between them. On the far side of the settlement was a huge opencast mine. An artificial valley had been sunk into the Sahara landscape. Its sides consisted of tiered layers like a garden pond liner. This giant staircase led down onto a flat trench where bulldozers dug and huge dumper trucks the size of houses rolled across the exposed bedrock. Brendan stood at the edge of the quarry with a group of officers from the US embassy and the TSSR government. One of the latter was a white man called Janie Kevelaer whom he had met briefly at the restaurant the evening before. Kevelaer was so fat that his body was almost spherical. He had an inflated lower lip, giving him a permanent pout and huge earlobes that matched his lip in a triangle of globular flesh pulling his face downwards. He was introduced to Brendan as the "industrial organizer" of the TSSR's politburo. "What do you think of our mine, Mr Quilley?" he asked in a harsh South African accent.

"Very impressive." answered Brendan honestly. "I've never seen such an enormous quarry." His engineer's eye was passing an intrigued look at the machinery around the pit.

"It's the biggest in the world." said Kevelaer proudly. "We produce over five thousand tons of uranium a year from this site."

"Uranium?"

"Extracted from pitchblende ore. There is a processing plant at Arlit a few miles away where the ore is ground down and compounded to produce yellowcake. The yellowcake is the safest and most compact way to transport uranium. The pure metal itself can be extracted from the yellowcake by smelting."

"What are its applications?"

"Mostly energy, but also we export it to allied nations for weapons programmes."

Brendan nodded. He knew that two nations in the Red Bloc

had strategic nuclear weapons. The Green Bloc had then gone on to arm itself as a deterrent. This was the primary reason the current geopolitical dynamic had been christened "Cold War II". Then a thought came to him. He recalled the lorries he had seen two days earlier. He described them to the industrial organizer. "Mr Kevelaer, they had radiation warning symbols on them."

Kevelaer looked awkward. He shrugged his shoulders and looked away. "Yes... erm... those trucks were carrying our yellowcake."

"Into the Volta Union? Who are you exporting to there?"

"I'm afraid I'm not at liberty to say, Mr Quilley."

"Sorry, I don't mean to pry. It's just I'm American and I know that President Tavinor of United States initiated the TAPC Accord placing the entire Red Bloc under strict trade sanctions, especially for armaments. The VU has signed it. Almost the entire Green Bloc signed it... I think Martinique abstained..."

"I don't care!" snapped Kevelaer. He carried on in a defensive tone. "Maybe your President Tavinor and your other capitalist exploiters and masters have not been entirely honest with you... And I shall say no more." He waddled away angrily.

....

The following morning Brendan's journey to find his sister continued. A convoy of four TSSR government vehicles were waiting for him and he was surprised to see that Janie Kevelaer was in one of them. The globular government minister greeted Brendan genially and Bart Tross came out into the consulate courtyard to wish Brendan a pleasant journey. Brendan sat on the back seat of the third car next to Kevelaer. The vehicle was big and comfortable, much nicer than the minibus he had travelled to Niamey in. They set off northwards out of the city. The sky was cloudy, promising more rain. It would be a three-day drive to Tripoli and the international airport there. Brendan was acclimatizing himself to distances in a world without flyers. However, when the convoy had been on the move for just half an hour it slowed and took a sharp left. It headed down a much smaller and lower quality road. Despite not knowing the area, Brendan intuited that something was amiss. He had studied the route on the map the evening before and knew that it was a major highway right to the edge of the Sahara Desert from where they would cross open sand. He turned to his companion. "Mr Kevelaer, where are we going?"

"You'll see." He wore a partly crafty and partly embarrassed expression on his flabby face.

Brendan felt alarmed, but he didn't reply.

After another hour of bumping down the track they came to a series of buildings made from bricks and corrugated steel. There was no gate, but a crude signboard said *Ferme de Mamidou 2*. "Is this a farm?" asked Brendan.

"Yes." said Kevelaer gently with a thin smile. "You see, we need your help, Brendan. Get out."

All the occupants of the four cars opened the doors and alighted. Brendan hesitated and then copied them. His feet squelched onto the muddy verge of the track. In the background he heard goats bleating. "What's going on?" demanded Brendan fearfully.

Kevelaer sighed. "You see, Brendan; there is a catchphrase, one of the most classic socialist tenets. It was written by Marx himself: 'From each according to his abilities, to each according to his needs.' You have some abilities and there are people who need them."

"What the hell are you talking about?"

"We need you to work here for a while. Seeing as you've been a guest of the Trans-Saharan Socialist Republic and eaten some of our food in one of our finest restaurants with all your privileged white Yankee imperialist buddies, you are obliged to provide labour to cover its value."

"What the...!? I'm not obliged to do anything of the sort! I'm an American citizen..."

"Yes!" sneered Kevelaer. "You do things differently in the capitalist north don't you? You get other people to put in the labour and then you snatch its value from them. Well you are not in America now, *Boer*!"

Brendan looked around him. The men in the other cars were all crowding round the sides of their vehicles, preventing him from returning to them. "What's going to happen to me?" gasped Brendan.

Kevelaer pointed. "He will explain."

Brendan followed his finger and saw a thin elderly man in ragged dungarees and a desert headscarf walking towards them. He smiled and muttered to Brendan in French, holding out his hand. Brendan shook it without thinking.

"This is Comrade Alaqui, he is the organizer here." said Kevelaer cheerily. "He'll show you what to do... Right, we'll be off. Enjoy your stay, Brendan." The men all got into their cars.

"No wait! You can't do this! This is completely improper!" Brendan pounded on the roofs of the cars with his fists. He jerked his foot back to avoid it getting run over by a wheel. The cars trundled off down the lane, splashing through puddles. Brendan stared after them in disbelief. He looked round as farmer Alaqui tried to talk to him again. Even if Brendan had been able to speak French properly, this man would be hard to understand with his strong native accent and missing teeth. Brendan grabbed his arm making him recoil slightly. "Listen! Mr Alaqui, I need to use your phone... You understand? *Téléphone*." he made a mime of holding a telephone receiver to his ear.

"*A, oui*." the old man nodded cheerfully and beckoned him. He led Brendan into one of the metal buildings which contained an office with an old wooden desk covered with wads of paper and folders. In the middle was an old-fashioned rotary dial telephone. There was a directory in the drawer of the desk but it was all in French and only had a few dozen numbers. Eventually, with the help of the old farmer, Brendan managed to access a directory enquiries service and, again plundering his meagre French vocabulary, obtained the number for the US consulate in Niamey. As soon as Bart Tross was on the line Brendan babbled at him in fear and outrage.

"What?" replied the consul-general. "They dropped you where?

Brendan repeated his explanation more slowly, struggling to keep calm.

"Oh my goodness, I'm so sorry, Brendan. I'll call Mr Kevelaer's office at once. Give me your number so I can ring you back."

Brendan waited a tense twenty minutes by the phone.

When it rang, Alaqui picked it up. "*Allo*?... *Oui*." He handed it to Brendan.

"Brendan, my boy!" Tross' overly-exuberant tone was a portent. Brendan braced himself. "First of all, let me apologize for not warning you about this and letting you know in advance that it was going to happen. I must also tell you, I deplore Mr Kevelaer's conduct in this matter. He should have informed you as well. He should also have been more respectful when dropping you off."

"What's going on, Mr Tross?" demanded Brendan.

"I'm afraid Mr Kevelaer is right. Under TSSR law you are required to perform a period of service to the nation's agriculture. It's called *Nourriture*. All citizens and foreign visitors to the country have to do it. The only exceptions are those who stay less than twenty-four hours or have exemption visas. Hell, even I had to do it in '72 when I arrived here. I'm so sorry I never warned you, son."

Brendan bit his lip to keep his temper. "How long will I be stuck in this shithole?"

"It's sowing season... so probably about a month."

"A month!?"

"Yes... Look it's not so bad. You get free meals, a place to live. There are plenty of fun and games..."

"Mr Tross." Brendan was afraid he might cry. "I need to find my missing sister Siobhan."

"And you can when your service period is up... Look, I'll call your dad and tell him what's going on."

Brendan zoned out for the rest of the call. He hung up the receiver. He wandered outside. The farm was located in a shallow valley surrounded by low hills, dank and dark green with mud and new vegetation under the overcast. There were a few trees nearby where birds sang in strange tones different from the avians of North America. Brendan began walking towards the gate before he understood what he was doing. This was not a prison camp. There were no physical barriers preventing him from leaving. There was not even a fence of the kind normally seen around farms, one that is intended to keep animals in and is easy to climb over. He began walking down the lane the way the cars had gone. "I'll walk out of here." he mumbled to himself defiantly. "There's nothing to stop me leaving. Nothing to keep me here!" It was not an easy walk. The rain had turned the track into a mud pit. He walked in the wheel ruts of vehicles. His shoes quickly became saturated and filthy. He made and effort to be cheerful, whistling to himself and sloshing through the mire, ignoring the cold wetness soaking into his trousers. He worked out that it would take a few hours to reach the main road, but then there would be lot of traffic and he could hitchhike back to Niamey. The weather was cool so it wouldn't be too difficult. After about quarter of an hour of strolling he turned a corner and jerked to a halt with a yelp of alarm. A curtain of brown water flew into the air as his feet ground into the track's surface to stop his forward movement. Ahead of him was a lion. It was lying on its belly with its paws extended forward like the Sphinx. Its head was bowed down and its eyes were half-closed as if it were approaching sleep. It was on a patch of grass by the verge of the road, about twelve feet from the track. It was less than a hundred feet from where Brendan stood. Brendan took a deep breath and tried to remember everything he had learned about lions during his life, a life that might be about to end. He had seen them several times in zoos, but this was when there was a wall of steel bars separating them from him. There were none here. He was also unarmed. The lion had no mane which meant it was female and female lions did most of the hunting. He also knew that he must not turn his back on the beast or run, or that's what he had heard. Its behaviour would depend on how much it had eaten. A hungry lion is one of the most dangerous creatures in the animal kingdom, but a lion that has just had a decent meal is no more of a hazard than a domestic cat. He took a step backward; as he did so the lioness looked up. It turned its head and stared at him. Brendan whimpered in terror, but took another step backwards. "God, please help me!" he whispered. The lioness blinked and flicked its tail a few times, but did not stand up. It yawned widely and its ivory white teeth were all visible. He had never previously imagined that lions lived in that part of Africa, but then he remembered Dave Pearson telling him about various rewilding programmes that had been started across the continent by the LoWEHO. Eventually Brendan's backward tiptoe brought him around the corner he had come from. As soon as he was out of sight from the lioness he swung round and bolted. He sprinted faster than he had ever run before back towards the farm. He arrived gasping with exhaustion and relief, his lungs burning. Farmer Alaqui brought him some tea in a tin cup. When he had recovered, Brendan realized why there was no need for fences to keep people in the farm.

Farmer Alaqui escorted him to another larger building where a huge crowd of people were standing around. They were all dressed in similar dungarees to their boss. To his astonishment, they greeted Brendan warmly, as if he were an old and popular resident returning. There was about a hundred of them and they approached him one at a time to shake his hand. Some of them even embraced him. About twenty of them were children and they jumped up and down playfully in front of him. The people all spoke to him at great length and Brendan smiled back, shaking his head. He could barely understand a word they said to him, but their broad grins and open faces were unequivocal. Despite his predicament, he felt his spirits rise.

The job was fairly simple and despite the language barrier his new colleagues showed Brendan what he had to do successfully. He learned primarily by following their lead. They walked a few hundred yards to a field that had clearly been left fallow for quite a while. Half of it was weeded while the other half was in the process of being so. Most of the farmhands were busy at the latter, uprooting the weeds and emptying buckets of them onto a large pile of loamy vegetation at the corner of the field. It was on top of a darker base, presumably an older part of what was obviously a compost heap. Brendan joined a ploughing and sowing team on the half already weeded. A wooden plough was harnessed to a pony and directed by two men, one holding the plough handles and another guiding the pony's head. They headed off and left behind them a furrow in the soggy soil. Birds immediately landed to pick up the exposed worms and grubs. A handcart containing bags of millet seeds was parked at the side of the field and Brendan picked one up. It had a long strap that he slung over his shoulder. Another hand showed him how to measure out the right amount of seed to sprinkle into the furrow. The millet seeds were small dry white spheres less than a tenth of an inch across like tiny pearls. Brendan and his helper walked along behind the plough dropping the seed. It was quite pleasant work. The brown earth smelled nice and the air was cooled by the clouds. Behind them two other hands buried the seeds by pushed the displaced soil into the furrow with spades. The team doing the weeding struck up a chant in the local vernacular. It had a heavy beat and the people moved in time to their own singing. Brendan couldn't help doing the same. Suddenly there was a lavatorial noise. The pony raised its tail and released a clod of dung from its hindquarters. Brendan's helper spoke to him, pointing at the pile of excrement and then at the compost heap. "What?" said Brendan. "You mean you want me to move that over there?"

The man nodded. "*Oui, oui!*"

"Okay, can I borrow one of those?" He turned to the two men filling in the furrow. They looked at him blankly and clutched their spades close to their chests. Brendan sighed. "Come on, guys; you don't expect me to do it with my bare hands do you?" He was answered with silence. "You can't be serious!" He walked over the reeking pile of excrement and reached down. He dug his hands into the earth around the dung so he wouldn't be in contact with it directly and picked it up, cringing with disgust. He jogged over to the compost heap as quickly as he could and threw the muck on top of it, and then he walked back wiping his hands on his trousers, which were already getting as dirty as the others' dungarees. As he returned to the ploughing team he saw that they were all grinning. As he arrived they all burst into laughter. He realized that he'd just been the object of a practical joke. He looked over his shoulder and saw that the weeding team were laughing too. "You bastards!" he shouted, but in doing so felt himself half smile.

They carried on working. Then the sun came out and the temperature rose. Brendan felt the back of his neck become sore with sunburn. One of the others went back to the farm houses and brought him a cloth to cover his head and another let him drink from their own can of water. Everybody was drinking extra water and many of them had also covered their heads, but they were treating the newcomer with additional consideration. They stopped to eat lunch, which were some sweet dry fruits that Brendan didn't recognize, and then carried on within twenty minutes. Brendan's legs began to ache, but he looked over at the weeders on their hands and knees, tugging the weeds out by hand and throwing them onto bins strapped to their backs, and he realized he had been given the easiest job in the field. His new friends, and he was starting to think of them as such, were treating him with great kindness. As the sun dropped to the horizon the plough reached the end of the last furrow. The exhausted pony plunged its nose into a trough of water and drank desperately. The farmhands did the same from cans of water. Then they made their way back to the farmhouses carrying their tools.

Brendan was given the task of towing the handcart containing the seed bags by its long steel handle. It was a crude vehicle made from rotten planks and its four wheels were all odd. Brendan then noticed something about one of the wheels. It surprised him so much that he stopped pulling the cart and gawped. Two of the other wheels had clearly been cannibalized from a motorcycle and the third one was a carved wooden one, but the fourth wheel was solid and metallic. Brendan almost exclaimed aloud in surprise. It was a spinning disk from inside an antigravity generator. It was rusted and scratched, but it was still easily recognizable. Based on its size, about two feet in diameter, it was probably from a large flyer or small frightener, or from a domestic powerplant. He stood up and looked around himself in astonishment. He had spent the day farming using methods that dated back centuries; the horse-drawn plough, hand sowing, hand weeding. It was as if he had been working on a museum farm, as he had done once when he was at school. Yet this was a real working arable production outfit in 1975. Why was it so antiquated? He had heard stories about how when the Red Bloc first expanded into new areas, especially in Africa, it destroyed all new tech whenever it could. There were television images of communist party militias smashing flyers and Digby cars into pieces with sledgehammers. The prevailing view in the socialist world was that it didn't work. The new tech was just a bourgeois science fiction hoax to top up the opium of the people now that religion was less effective. This was of course flagrant nonsense, but the leftists of the world believed it; even those still living in the Green Bloc who saw the new tech every day. They rationalized it as conventional engineering in disguise as something esoteric. Somebody must have discovered this old antigravity disk on a scrap heap and decided that it would make a good wheel. They drilled a central hole to insert an axle and attached it to this rudimentary homemade cart. Brendan realized that the car he had borrowed from his father's neighbour to travel here, the Digby hatchback he'd left parked at the border, was probably in little pieces by now. He hoped this wouldn't cause too much aggravation for Clane.

When the team reached the farmhouse they all gathered in a large building where there was a kitchen with tables and chairs, and they drank mugs of steaming tea. The tea had no sugar, but Brendan chose the option of adding goat's milk. The farmers all praised the effort of their newest member. Brendan cheered with them. He still could only communicate using a few basic words, but he was already identifying names and personalities. The children were the most interested in him. A few of the younger ones were very keen to touch his skin. One girl of about five years old turned to her mother and said something in the local native tongue that Brendan guessed was something like: "Why is that man coloured white? Is he ill?" It was strange to think that these people, the younger ones at least, had never seen anybody of a different racial group to their own. They ate a meal of millet mixed with various vegetables and pieces of dried chicken and fish. It was not as tasty as the sumptuous dinner he had eaten in the Niamey hotel on Friday night, but Brendan enjoyed it a whole lot more. The company was far more pleasant. He quickly became drowsy as night fell. The long day in the field had given him a good level of sleep hygiene. The farmers all slept in a dormitory block that consisted of a row of bunk beds reminding Brendan a bit of the Seaguard training centre. There was an adjoining toilet that consisted of a pit latrine, whose contents would obviously contribute to the compost heap. The bathroom had a single small steel tub that was filled by water from a rain butt. A small wood brazier underneath it warmed the water. There was a separate room for the children, but the bedsteads in there were bare. The mattresses had all been laid on the floor in the main chamber next to the bunks each child's parents used. Some of the farm staff then laid decorated mats on the floor, knelt down and prayed; facing northeast in the direction of Mecca. Brendan drifted quickly off to sleep. His annoyance, concern and frustration had eased far more than he had expected.

Chapter 15

Everybody in the sowing team cheered. There was a ceremonial feeling among them as the plough ground to a halt and Yousef let the last handful of seeds fall into the furrow. Hosn and Jemel then pushed the earth over the furrow. Alaqui handed round everybody extra large cups of tea laced with mint, a special treat. "Brendan, in your country I suppose you would drink wine at a time like this." said Yousef.

"*Absolument, mon ami!*" replied Brendan. "A good bottle of champagne would be best."

"I bet Alaqui's tea is better." said Nyala.

Brendan raised his eyebrows at her. "I don't like to say yes or no." Everybody laughed.

Nyala patted his shoulder. It was the first time she had touched Brendan for a fortnight. There had been a rather embarrassing moment back then which had put their friendship on hold. He was glad that this hiatus was now over. Nyala was one of the first people he had bonded with on the farm. She was a lively and affectionate young woman, tall and elegant with Tuareg good looks. She was the mother of one of the children, a cute little six-year old boy who had become somewhat attached to Brendan. Her husband, the boy's father, had died five years previously. She and Brendan were constant companions. Then one night, completely uninvited, she had climbed into his bunk and put her arms around him. He knew such things went on of course. There were several married couples and common law partners on the farm. Sex did happen and in the dormitory there was no privacy so they did it as quietly as possible under the bedsheets or went off together alone into a nearby forest. Brendan had always assumed that this was a realm off-limits to him, and of course it was. He hated doing it, but he had to tell her to go away. They didn't speak for a few days, and then Brendan and she took a walk after dinner while the others were praying. He told her about Heather. As he did so he felt a prod of guilt. He had not thought much about his wife, nor her pregnancy since he had joined the farmers. Maybe it was a subconscious survival mechanism, seeing as he was so far away from her and could do nothing to help her or even contact her. He also felt a lot of shame over the fact that he was attracted to Nyala too and realized that a part of him had badly wanted her to stay in his bunk. Nyala nodded and replied that she understood. She added: "Your Heather is a very lucky woman." However she was somewhat distant from Brendan after that. Now finally, the moment the sowing was over, after more than three weeks of continuous work, they spoke to each other normally, as platonic friends. The tension between them had eased. They had had several normal conversations. Brendan could now speak fluent French. This still baffled him because it had been one of his worst subjects at school; yet a month after joining the farm he could speak it well enough to communicate almost perfectly. What he had learned in those boring classes in Rockville had never really gone away; it had lingered deep in his subconscious and burst out the moment he truly needed it. He had also picked up a handful words from the native vernaculars. The hundred or so people on the farm spoke three different native languages and would converse in them when alone with their own language group, but French was the agreed *lingua franca* of the entire community, as it was for the whole of former Niger. Apart from Brendan, nobody there spoke a word of English. The only time Brendan spoke his native language was when he was on the phone to Bart Tross. The United States consul-general called every few days and gave him updates on his father. He passed on messages between them. However, Brendan couldn't think of much to say. Clane Quilley and the world he lived in had faded into the past as if Brendan had left his homeland a far longer time ago than he had. He just told Tross to tell his father that he was thinking of him and wished him all the best. After the most recent call ended, Alaqui came back into the office. Brendan didn't mind the farm manager eavesdropping seeing as he couldn't understand what was being said. "Have you managed to talk to your father, Brendan?" asked the old man.

"No, *Monsieur* Alaqui" said Brendan. "It's not possible to connect him by a direct line."

"Where does he live?"

"The Volta Union... I miss him a lot and hope I get to see him again soon. My wife too. However, I must find my sister first. I promised my father that I would."

Alaqui smiled. "Naturally you have. My own dad died

about twenty years ago, but sometimes I still talk to him. In my home village none of us were religiously converted. We believed our ancestors stayed with us after death. They learned the wisdom of the spirits when they passed over and could communicate that knowledge to the land of the living if we were willing to listen. We had medicine men who knew the ancient traditions of spirit channelling. We used to speak openly about this and nobody minded; even the Muslims and Christians in our tribe... Only the revolution changed everything."

"Was the socialist revolution not a good thing?"

Alaqui merely snorted in reply. His private distain for the current political order manifested in other forms. In fact the most dramatic example took place at the end of the sowing operation. The team had wandered back to the farmhouses. Alaqui was walking ahead and the rest of them strolled along more slowly, sipping their tea. As they arrived they saw two cars parked inside the gateway. This was not in itself a major surprise because vehicles were always calling in on the farm, usually lorries or vans come to pick up produce or drop off supplies. In the early days of his stint Brendan had considered stowing away on a departing transport, but now the thought never occurred to him. These vehicles were different. They were off-road trucks with the TSSR flag stencilled on their doors. Everybody froze. "Oh no!" muttered Jemel.

"Come on, come on!" said Alaqui. The old organizer was walking back towards the farmers speaking in a jovial voice. However his face embodied panic. "Our comrades from the Inspectorate are here. How wonderful!" He spoke joyfully, but looked hard at Brendan with an expression that was far from joyful.

Brendan looked past Alaqui and saw a cluster of men wearing grey boiler suits with studded shoulder boards. Truncheons and pistol holsters hung obtrusively from their belts. They were officials from the TSSR's Agricultural Union. He immediately took Alaqui's hint and ducked out of sight while the officials' backs were turned. He dived into the accommodation block while the rest of the farming community kept the Inspectorate distracted. He dragged the children's mattresses as quickly as he could off the floor of the main dormitory and into the children's dormitory. He threw them onto the bedsteads there. Then he went round the bedside lockers hiding the Qurans, prayer books, ornaments and other religious artefacts from view. This was an activity everybody on the farm did as a habit on Saturday mornings because that was the day that the political commissar paid her weekly visits, however it was normally a more leisurely and routine activity. Today's visit was a snap inspection. The commissar was an old Arabian lady who wore a long shawl and had an affected geniality and exuberance about her. She reminded Brendan very much of Sister Margarita van de Kerk. She turned up at eleven AM on the dot every Saturday in a two-door open top car with her textbooks and film cans in an overstuffed satchel. Then all activity on the farm stopped and the entire community crowded into the dining hut to listen to the commissar's lecture on various aspects of Marxism. She read from books, showed them films on an old reel projector and asked her audience questions for which she expected good answers. The farmers nodded their heads and pretended to be interested. At exactly three PM she drove away. Sometimes she lent them books which nobody ever read. When she was gone everybody released suppressed yawns, laughed and made jokes about her. Nobody really disliked her, but she represented the difference between the lives they lived and the lives they were supposed to live. She was no major threat to them. This surprise visit from the Agricultural Union was though.

Brendan ran outside as soon as he had finished the cosmetic renovation of the living quarters and joined the crowd of farmers. They were not standing as formally as soldiers on parade, but they were clearly nestled together facing the gang of inspectors and were obliged to pay them full attention. The leader of the Inspectorate was a tall and wiry young man with abundant hair which formed a black puffball around his head. He had on thick plastic sunglasses and his mouth seemed to be stuck in a permanent sneer. "Right, comrades!" he barked. "This is an inspection. We have come from the Agricultural Union of the Trans-Saharan Socialist Republic to assess the quality, efficiency and revolutionary commitment of this agricultural project. We demand access to every part of this facility and we may wish to interview some of you personally." He had an assistant standing next to him who was making notes on a clipboard with a ballpoint pen whose end waggled as he wrote. "The Union expects the very highest standards of..." He stopped talking. He had noticed Brendan. Even behind his sunglasses Brendan could tell that the man was glaring at him. His sneer deepened. "Well, what have we here?" He walked over to Brendan, the crowd parted fearfully to let him through. "Looks like a..." he ended the sentence with a word Brendan didn't recognize, but he guessed that it was a derogatory term for a white person. The chief inspector turned his head slightly to address the farmers. "I hope you've been treating this colonialist the way he deserves, Comrade Alaqui."

"We've been making his life a living hell, Comrade Inspector!" growled Alaqui hatefully.

Brendan looked at the farm organizer sympathetically. He was not a very good actor. Then Brendan had no time to react as the inspector's fist impacted the bridge of his nose. He saw a flash of light and then the next thing he knew he was lying on the ground. The inspector leaned over him triumphantly. "How do you feel now, colonialist!? You're lying flat on your back in the dust of the country you stole from us! What does it feel like to know we've taken it back from you!?"

"I haven't stolen anybody's..."

"SHUT UP!" The inspector kicked him in the stomach, knocking the wind out of him.

Brendan rolled onto his side, gasping for air. His lungs heaved desperately. Stars wheeled in his vision. The other people in the community stood dead still, giving Brendan sorrowful but terrified sideways glances. The assistant continued scribbling on his clipboard.

"Alright, let's get on with this." said the inspector more quietly and the men in boiler suits all strutted towards the farmhouses fanning out as if they had rehearsed which building each one would examine. After a few minutes they came out. "Alright, comrades." said the chief inspector reluctantly. "I'm passing this facility as adequate pending above-adequate. Good day and long live the revolution!"

"Long live the revolution!" the farmers returned insincerely, lifting their fists in the air. The cars ground away through the dry dust. The moment they had passed around the bend the people rushed over to where Brendan was sitting and tended to him. His nose was painful. It was possibly slightly cracked. It had bled down his shirt. He had a bruise on his belly from the inspector's boot, but he was otherwise unharmed. The farmers cursed the inspector's name using French words Brendan had definitely not learned at school. They helped him walk over to the dining hut where Alaqui made him a mug of his mint tea. "I'm so sorry, Brendan." he said. "It's just the Agricultural Union has the power to arrest people. Some folk disappear forever."

"It's alright." said Brendan. He then made an effort to change the subject. "That inspection didn't last long."

"They never stay long." said Nyala. "They're not interested in the crops or the pasture or the yield statistics. All they care about is that our children are sleeping separately from their parents and that there is no other reactionary activity going on."

"That's why you did us a big favour today, Brendan." said Yousef. "If they had found our Qurans or knew that we let the children live as part of a family, we would be denounced as dissidents. If that happens in the TSSR you can be arrested and sent to a re-education camp in the desert for as long as five years. Most people die before the end of that period... You've just saved our lives." He laid a hand on Brendan's shoulder.

Brendan looked up at his farmer friends. A hundred faces were turned towards his with loving smiles. "I'll never leave you." he said.

....

There were no alarm clocks on the farm; people simply awoke when it was light outside. There was little seasonal variation in daylight hours at the latitude of the farm so there was no fixed time to arise. They all ate breakfast together and then went to work. Work ended when the sun was at an elevation of about twenty degrees, just above the tree line between two fields, as observed from the horse's water butt. There were clocks at the farm, but they were not really needed. The farm was primarily arable. The crops needed constant tending; watering weeding and pest control. There was also a small herb garden. There was a lot to do around the houses as well; cooking, cleaning, tidying and maintenance. A small schoolroom adjoined the children's dormitory where the children had lessons every evening taken by one of their mothers. There was also a small pasture where several dozen goats lived. Brendan was sometimes given the job of milking the goats. Nyala had showed him how to do it. He rather enjoyed it. The goats were happy and playful animals and he had quickly learned their names. One day just after breakfast had ended, he collected the tin milking pail and was walking from the dining hut to the goat pasture when there was the popping and rumbling of car tyres at the gate. All the farmers went to see who had arrived. They were not afraid of another inspection; it was just ten days since the last one. Brendan ran quickly just in case, ready to protect his friends again. Three cars had pulled up outside the farm; the cloud of dust kicked up by their tyres was blowing away on the breeze. They were government vehicles, but they were not from the Agricultural Union. The doors opened and several people got out. One of them was slower than the others; he had trouble squeezing his gelatinous frame out of the back seat. It was Janie Kevelaer. "Hello, hello, hello!" He greeted the assembled farmlands in English with a broad grin. "Comrade Alaqui, how are you? And all you friends and comrades, how are the crops growing?" He spotted Brendan. "Aha, here's the chap I've come for. Mr Quilley, how are you?"

Brendan stepped forward in astonishment. "Mr Kevelaer? What are you doing here?"

He tittered. "Did you just ask what I am doing here?... What do you think I'm doing here? I've come to take you to the bloody airport; in Tripoli where your flight is waiting."

"What?... Take me... *away*?" Brendan stammered.

Kevelaer frowned in confusion. "Don't you remember?... Come on, kid. I know you've been here nearly six weeks, but you must remember when I dropped you off. I know Bart Tross said it would only be a month... Six weeks toiling away on our own African land. I know you *blankes* aren't used to that."

"I do remember, but..." Brendan forced his memory back.

It seemed like years ago that he had arrived on the farm. Was it only six weeks?

"I thought you'd be really pissed off. I was bracing myself for an ear-bashing from you... Well come on then, Brendan. Get your gear. We've got a long drive ahead of us."

"I don't have any gear." It struck Brendan as strange for the first time that had come to the farm with no other possessions than the clothes he stood in. He had owned nothing the whole time he had been there and had not missed owning anything. There was a credit card and money in his wallet and it had not left his pocket once.

"Not to worry, we'll supply you with what you need. Get in the car then."

Brendan turned round and looked at the farm buildings, the fields, the dusty tracks, the lines of trees. These had been his whole world for such a long time. Then he saw the faces of his farming friends who had gathered round and his heart plummeted. He felt as if he were standing on the edge of a precipice. "I can't leave!" he hissed. "I *won't* leave!... Please don't take me away from here!"

Alaqui stepped forward and held both of Brendan's hands in his own. "It's been wonderful having you here at the farm, Brendan; but you must go. The sowing has been done and we need fewer people now. Remember, you have to find your sister. You have a wife in your own country and soon you will have a child. It's time for you to leave us. I'm sorry."

Brendan nodded, blinking back tears.

"What is this?" chuckled Kevelaer. "I thought you'd be gagging to get out of here. Bart Tross told me you faced down a man-eating lion trying to escape."

The farmers came past him one by one to shake his hand, as they had when he'd first arrived. Alaqui, Yousef, Jemel and so many others. Nyala kissed him hard on the lips and they looked at each other, each one knowing what the other was thinking. Brendan patted her son's head. "You be a good boy for your mother, Axmet." He could hardly speak; his nose was running. He kept his eyes on them all as he walked over to the car, not wanting to look away, knowing that it would be the last time he would ever see them. This was a moment he didn't want to end; he was afraid of it ending. Once inside the car, sitting on the back seat next to Kevelaer, he kept his gaze out of the rear window as the vehicle pulled away. His friends were all waving. He waved back, his hand trembling. The car rounded the bend and entered a cluster of trees and his line of sight to the farm gate was cut off. He had left the world he had lived in and was entering his old one. At that moment it felt like a new world; new, cold and hostile. It had taken less than ten minutes since the cars had arrived. Kevelaer looked at him, shook his head and sighed. "Goodness, Quilley. You *boere* really baffle me."

....

Brendan stood in front of a full-length mirror. He shook his head at his own appearance, a sight he barely recognized. His clothes were the same ones he had worn continuously for the last six weeks, taking them off only to wash and sleep. He had laundered them twice in the hot tub with everybody else's which had left them clean for about fifteen minutes. His skin had tanned deeply until he was almost as dark as the other farmers. His hair was overgrown and unkempt. He had a thin beard which was the same colour as his hair. The most unexpected change was that he had lost a lot of weight, about three or four stone. His body was tight and lean. He had not seen his own reflection for all that time; there were no mirrors on the farm. It was only now, in a hotel room in Tripoli, that he saw how much he had changed. He turned his thoughts away from the farm. Thinking of what he had left behind only caused him emotional pain. He had learned to direct his train of thoughts down the lines he wanted it during the drive from the farm. It had taken more than three days. They had crossed the biggest and driest desert on earth to reach this city on the coast of the Mediterranean Sea. The vehicles in his convoy were all off-road and for the second and third day there was no road and they had to cross bare sand. It was like a huge beach with no sea. The sand dunes stretched into the distance on either side to the horizon. The drivers needed to use a compass to keep themselves on course. It was a beautiful region, especially at sunset. They stopped both nights at Bedouin camps that were arranged around an oasis. The tent Brendan slept in was warm and snug. The sand under the groundsheet made an excellent mattress.

He was surprised how cold the desert was at night. He needed to wrap himself in several blankets. They had arrived at Tripoli, capital city of the Trans-Saharan Socialist Republic, just after midnight on the third day from the farm. Brendan had been given a plane ticket and installed at a hotel for the night. He had said goodbye to Janie Kevelaer, which he did without any regret. The industrial organizer lived in Tripoli and went straight home. Brendan had slept fitfully, expecting to feel his farm bunk under his back. In the morning he got up and bathed. The bath had proper hot water on tap. For the first time Brendan enjoyed an aspect of being out of the farm. He put on a new set of clothes that had been provided by the TSSR government and went to the dining room for breakfast. It felt so weird to be surrounded by strangers, people he didn't know and could not talk to without breaching social taboos.

Brendan took a taxi to the VI Lenin International Airport on the outskirts of the city. It was still early morning and traffic was light. The city consisted of square white buildings with small windows. He paid it very little attention. He was surprised at how little curiosity he had at being in a place he had never been to before and very few people from his part of the world ever visited. At the airport he was not treated as a VIP in the same way he had been in Niamey. He was a traveller from the Green Bloc, an extremely rare thing. He was asked a lot of searching questions about the reasons for his trip and he was honest: "I'm looking for my sister who has gone missing." The customs officer nodded and handed back his passport. At ten AM he boarded a fixed wing airliner for the flight. It was strange to be travelling in such an outmoded manner. The aeroplane was an aged Boeing 399. It's furniture and fittings were very 1950's in style. For the first time in years, Brendan heard jet engines spooling up. He fastened his seatbelt as it rolled onto the runway and wrenched itself up into the sky. The aircraft began its journey eastwards and soon passed out of TSSR airspace and into Egypt which was part of the Green Bloc. Brendan marvelled at how high they were flying. Flyer lanes were from two to seven thousand feet in altitude, depending on the cloud layer, while the remaining traditional jets flew at over thirty thousand feet. He had a window seat and could see flyers below him, zipping across the land like insects on a pond. They crossed the Arabian Peninsula and as the plane approached the Arabian Sea coast he saw that one of the flyers was ascending towards them. As it came close enough to recognize, he gasped. It was one made by Dr Jenny Bulstrode's company Spinning Disk Inc. It was a military model based on their standard heavy frame called the SDI Cormorant and, sure enough, on the side of it was the livery of Seaguard and its squadron crest. He was on a Red Bloc plane being shadowed by a Seaguard flyer, probably one deployed from one of the company's five aircraft carriers. Brendan felt an uncanny sense of reversal. There were many occasions that he'd been aboard one of his ships and even in a flyer like this one, and had tailed a Red Bloc aircraft or ship. It was like being in a looking glass world looking back into the outside universe.

The flight was the longest Brendan had ever taken; eighteen hours. That was the absolutely limit of the Boeing 399's range. That distance would have been two hours in a flyer. He sighed and lay back in his seat as the sun set artificially early because of their eastwards direction of travel. He thought of Siobhan and whether he would be able to find her. He contemplated his feelings for her and the difference between a man's love for his sister and sexual love, being *in* love; the feelings he had for Heather. He missed his wife as well; he hadn't seen her for over two months. She was pregnant, he reminded himself. "Oh God!" he groaned and hid his face in his hands. He reclined his seat and slept through the night, and woke up when the plane was descending into the airport at Perth on the western coast of Australia. The aircraft touched down and the passengers disembarked to a terminal building. It was an undecorated and uncomfortable place. Some did not pass customs but instead transferred to a smaller aircraft, a Boeing 397, for the final leg of the journey to Sydney. That took just over four hours.

Brendan's body was stiff from sitting in an airliner seat when he staggered down the jetway at Frederick Engels Airport in the south of the harbour city of Sydney. A young blonde woman in a badly fitted uniform glanced casually at his passport and handed it straight back. "Welcome to the SRA, mate." she said while chewing gum. He walked out of the arrivals lounge entrance and into Australia. It was a mild cloudy spring day. A row of minibuses were lined along the kerb driven by Arabs who accepted his US Dollars as fare, eager to obtain hard Green currency. He sat in the back next to other travellers with large suitcases and rucksacks. The vehicle drove for twenty minutes through the urban traffic and dropped its passengers off on a road near the harbour. The famous arch of the Sydney Harbour Bridge loomed over the vista. He leaned back to stare up at the steel riveted structure. "Right, where do I go from here?" he muttered to himself.

According to his research, Siobhan was likely to be somewhere in Sydney, but it was a city of three million people. He wandered along the streets, as if expecting to meet her just by chance. Sydney was similar to many American cities except that there were no public advertisements. Where elsewhere billboards would be placed marketing some product, on public telephones, on the sides of busses, on the doors to shops; there were instead political posters depicting strong men and women at work in factories and on farms. Words on them included slogans like: "*BUILD A NEW WORLD!*" and: "*LONG LIVE SOCIALIST AUSTRALIA!*" There were caricatures of rich people looking evil, sometimes depicted as anthropomorphic pigs, rats and slugs. There were images of Karl Marx, Frederick Engels, Vladimir Lenin and the current Australian Prime Minister John Pankhurst arranged in a row of profiles on a red background. There was a buzz of excitement among the public and some of the streets had been fenced off for a parade. This was May Day and, just as in the former Soviet Union, it was given over to celebration. The flag of the Socialist Republic of Australia flew everywhere it could be raised. A band marched along playing the *Internationale* and other communist anthems. Soldiers goose-stepped and tractors rolled. Crowds lined the streets cheering and singing to the music. Brendan scanned the faces of the spectators, looking for that familiar visage that he had known all his life. He decided to go to the US consulate which was in a basement beneath a square at a crossroads in the heart of the city. The main embassy was in Canberra, but that was a hundred and fifty miles away. He arrived at reception and explained who he was. He was allowed to use their telephone and for the first time in over six weeks managed to speak to his father. He had dialled his number without checking the time difference; it was three AM in the Volta Union. However Clane Quilley was overjoyed and became fully awake immediately as soon as he recognized his son's voice. Brendan also felt a deep shivering gladness as they conversed. Heather was staying with him, and she woke up and came on the line soon afterwards. Brendan blew her kisses into the receiver and promised to come home soon. "With my baby!" Clane added.

"Yes, dad." said Brendan. "I'll do everything I can to bring Siobhan home."

Brendan then had a meeting with the deputy to the assistant US consul-general in his windowless underground office. He was a small and mediocre individual with a monotone nasal voice, an Ivy League swagger and a bland manner. He appeared detached and almost autistic. He kept his eyes on his computer monitor the whole time and gave Brendan a political and historical précis while Brendan was asking for information about Siobhan. "'The Red Tiger', Mr Quilley. That's what Australia is being called. Not just within her borders, but all over the world. Unlike other socialist economies, the SRA's is currently booming. However they have done it, they've got it right. Financial pundits across the globe are wondering why."

"That's very interesting, Mr Mann." lied Brendan, "but how is this relevant to me finding my sister?"

He nodded and tapped his desktop console. "Well, according to SRA Customs and Immigration she arrived at Engels on March seventeenth on a flight from Manila."

"She must have dumped her flyer there... Did she have her children with her?"

"Yes, both the boy and the girl."

"Did anybody meet her at the airport?"

Mr Mann grimaced and straightened the grey tie of his grey suit. "The database does not record that information."

Brendan hesitated. "I believe she may be living with a man called Julian Spencer."

Mann looked up. "*The* Julian Spencer?

"Which one do you mean by 'the'?"

Mann took off his bifocal spectacles. "He's one of the most

famous and revered people in the country. He was one of the leaders of the revolution back in '66. In fact he led the military campaign against the provisional government. He was Sharkey's right hand man for a while. Then he broke with the CPA and disappeared."

"Where is he now?"

He shrugged. "I'm not sure. He has been back to Australia since then. I think he made his peace with the Pankhurst regime, to a certain extent. He did a couple of newspaper interviews about working with them."

"If he led the revolution then presumably he still has some kind of official capacity here in the parliament or military."

"Oh no. He has never taken up any political office, not in the SRA or anywhere else for that matter. His chosen role is as a guerrilla fighter. He goes wherever in the world he can do that."

"And then I suppose Siobhan will go with him."

"I doubt it. His life in the field would be very dangerous, no place for a mother with small children. My guess is that he has provided her with some form of lodgings here, if she has made contact with him."

"Well, where does Julian live?"

"He has no listed address in the SRA."

Brendan sighed and leaned back in his chair. "If Siobhan arrived here and Julian was not around, what would she do?... She'd probably wait for him. She told us she wouldn't give up until she found him... So where would she most likely wait?"

"In a family hostel probably, seeing as she has two kids with her."

"Are there any here in Sydney?"

Mann punched his keyboard. "Let's see... Yes, I've found quite a few." He clicked his mouse and a sheet of paper emerged from a printer behind him. He handed it to Brendan and it gave a list of addresses.

....

The hostel was in a seedy and dirty district of suburban Sydney. The ubiquitous political poster was pasted to the wall outside the door and it was an obscene caricature of the US President LaRey Tavinor. She was portrayed as an evil crone squatting down and urinating on a crowd of prostrate poor labourers. The caption said: "*S.R.A. WILL BOYCOTT ALL U.S. GOODS!*" Brendan walked through a set of revolving doors into the entrance. It was the third hostel he had visited. He had spent the night underground in a bedroom at the consulate and got up before breakfast to continue his search. The concierge was a dumpy woman with thick glasses who was sitting in a cubicle in the lobby reading a newspaper. When Brendan showed her the photograph of his sister he had printed out in Mann's office she looked up straight away. "Oh yeah. I know her; that's Siobhan."

Brendan felt his heart skip. "Great!" he puffed. "Is she here now?"

"Nah, she moved out last month. She was only here a couple of days. Nice gal though."

"Do you know where she went?"

"She told me she was leaving for Trotskygrad."

"Where's that?"

"West of the city, about five miles away."

Brendan had been offered the use of a hire car on the diplomatic budget, but he noticed that the urban light railway moved people a lot quicker than the roads. He went to the nearest station and studied a map. Trotskygrad was listed as a station on the network and it only took half an hour to reach it from where he was. When he arrived he was surprised to find that there was a cordon at the entrance to the station manned by very uncooperative security guards who refused to allow him through and provided no explanation. Brendan had no choice but to return to the consulate and seek advice. "Oh, I'm terribly sorry, Mr Quilley. If I had known you wanted to go there I'd have arranged the necessary permissions." Mr Mann's fingers danced on his keyboard as he spoke.

"So is that place a gated community?"

"Yes, of sorts. It's a demonstrational project set up as part of the SRA's truce with the Trotskyist and Spartacist camps. That's why I'm not surprised your sister has gone there; it's the most likely place Spencer will stop off whenever he visits Australia. The residents of the district are trying to live in accordance with what they believe is the perfect post-revolutionary lifestyle. You'll find it a bit weird in there."

Brendan returned to the station with a visitor's permit and this time the security guards let him through the gate. He had not been able to see past the cordon before because the path leading away from the station doglegged at a right angle and was lined by a brick wall and thick hedges. This was clearly designed to prevent people outside the area from seeing inside it, and as Brendan walked down the path from the station entrance he saw that the opaque barrier of foliage and cement carried on into the distance. He guessed that it completely encircled the settlement as if the interior was a holy sanctuary which unclean eyes must never view. Mr Mann had been right; Trotskygrad did indeed have an unusual atmosphere that was very different to the rest of Sydney. Brendan sensed it was somewhat like entering an urban monastery. There were a several large signboards set up along the side of the path which introduced the district and what its purpose was. These were long and detailed; they used a lot of terminology Brendan couldn't understand. There appeared to be no motor vehicles and the only means of transport was on foot; however somebody later passed him on a small motor scooter and he saw a few more people riding pushbikes. The community consisted of a set of blocks with straight paths running between them. Inside the blocks were long, low oblong concrete buildings two storeys high. Between the buildings were gardens growing all kinds of arable crops, fruit and root vegetables. People moved slowly around the gardens tending their produce. It reminded Brendan of his TSSR friends' farm that he had just left. However that one had a separate dwelling space. It was strange to see homes and farmland so close; it was as if a housing estate had been dropped into the middle of some allotments. Strangely, in a deviation to the rest of Sydney, nowhere was there flying the flag of the Socialist Republic of Australia. Brendan approached an elderly woman who was watering some flowers on a corner bed beside one of the buildings; it was the first example of purely decorative horticulture Brendan had seen so far in Trotskygrad. The path ran right past her. "Excuse me." he said.

The old lady looked up. Her clothes looked different and slightly old-fashioned. She wore a brown headscarf and wooden clogs. "Yes, comrade?"

"I'm looking for somebody called Siobhan Quilley. Do you know where she is?"

"No, comrade." the woman replied immediately and turned her back on him.

Brendan recoiled slightly in amazement, unsure of what to make of her abruptness. He stood for a moment looking at her. She continued sprinkling a patch of purple petunias, acting as if he wasn't there, forgetting the curt interaction they'd just had. Brendan paused and walked on.

All the people were dressed like the woman he had had his brief conversation with. The cloth of their garments was in pastel shades. Unlike every other city, town or village Brendan had been to or heard about, there didn't appear to be a centre to Trotskygrad. There were several buildings with a sign outside saying "Administration Centre" plus some letters and numbers of qualification. There were also theatres, libraries and sports arenas, both indoor and outdoor. However, there was nowhere Brendan walked where those kinds of facility were clustered or concentrated. They were dotted evenly and interspersed with the usual longhouses, that appeared to be mostly residential, and fields of wheat, barley and cabbages. The whole district was completely homogeneous. Brendan found it hard to judge where it began and ended, until he came to the wall at the far side about three miles from the railway station. He rotated in a circle with his hands on his hips, wondering where to go next. He turned eastwards and walked along the inside of the wall. Beyond it he could hear the normal traffic noises of Sydney. After a few hundred yards he came to another junction at the end of a block and turned right away from the wall. There was a sign on one of the buildings that said "*LFU 3*" and he heard the muffled sound of children chattering. The door clicked open and a child came out. It was a young boy. Brendan froze. He looked again carefully to be sure. It was William. Brendan began to run forward, a yell of greeting on his lips; but some instinct held him back. How would William react to his appearance? Had Siobhan told him to lure any visitors away? What had been going on in his nephew's life during the month and a half since he had last seen him? Brendan hid behind a row of plum trees and followed William covertly as the twelve-year old walked along the path, away from the wall and the direction Brendan came and into the heart of Trotskygrad. The boy stumbled slightly, as if tired or dizzy. He walked for ten minutes covering three blocks then turned into one of them and approached one of the house-cum-farm combinations. He vanished out of sight behind the building and Brendan heard him say "Mom..."

Brendan stopped and took a deep breath. He left the main path and walked along a smaller path that led diagonally across to the corner of the building. He rounded the corner. The space between that house and the next one was a pasture on which about a dozen sheep were grazing. A wire fence penned them in. In the field with the sheep stood William and in front of him stood Siobhan facing him. They were talking in low voices. She wore a pastel green archaic dress in accordance with the local fashion and her hair was covered by a headscarf of the same colour. She had a small handcart and held a small shovel in her hands that was stained brown with excrement. She had been gathering sheep droppings from the field. "Siobhan!" Brendan called.

She turned her head, straightened up in shock, gaped at him for a moment. She took a step away from him and then stopped, her facial expression going back to normal. She sighed sadly. "Hi, Brendan."

William's face lit up with joy. "Uncle Brendan!" He ran forward and almost knocked Brendan off his feet with a hug like a rugby player.

Siobhan scowled as her brother walked towards her, easing himself through the gate into the field. "Brendan, what are you doing here?"

"Don't you know?" For the first time since he had learned of her disappearance, Brendan felt angry with his sister.

"How did you find me?"

"How did you expect us *not* to find you?"

"Is dad with you?" she looked past him in alarm.

"No, he's at home."

She stared at him blankly. "Alright, you'd better come inside. Let me just clean up here."

Siobhan lived in an apartment on the upper floor of the two storey residential block. The block was home to several dozen people, she explained; mostly couples, a few of them homosexual. Her apartment consisted of a lounge, a bedroom, kitchen and bathroom; all of them were average in size. There were no doors sealing off any room from all the others, giving the home the atmosphere of a studio flat. Every home in Trotskygrad was the same, none bigger than any of the others. There was a double bed in the bedroom and a mattress propped against the wall of the lounge. "I insisted on Will and Coll living with us." said Siobhan as she lifted a kettle off the gas hob and poured it into three mugs. "Will sleeps on the settee and Coll is on the mattress that at night we lay out on the floor. Julian didn't like that, but I refused to back down."

"Where did he want them to live?"

"In the youth dormitories with all the other kids."

Brendan nodded, understanding immediately; and he told her of the official sleeping arrangements for children on the TSSR farm.

Siobhan groaned and shook her head. "It's not natural. I'm not surprised your farming friends broke the rules. Children belong with their moms and dads... Thing is, Julian says there's no such thing as natural."

"Do a lot of parents here keep their kids with them?"

"Yeah a few. Nobody forces them not to, unlike on your farm. It's not approved of though."

"Not approved of by whom?"

She tittered and shrugged. "People... generally. There'll never build any family apartments here."

"Why don't they do it?"

"It's not revolutionary." She rolled her eyes. "Ask Julian; he'll give you a two-hour lecture all about it. You know, the children technically aren't even supposed to call us 'mom' and 'dad'? They're supposed to call us 'comrade'."

"Seriously?"

She nodded. "I don't know any kids who obey that rule... But it's not shoved down our throats, as I said. That's not the methods of Trotskygrad. Julian reckons that change will come about automatically through the revolutionary process."

Brendan face-palmed. "No goddamn revolutionary whatnot would make me call dad 'comrade'... Where is Julian anyway?"

She shrugged and laughed ironically. "Where's the third seagull on the right?.. He's away again. He's away most of the time."

"When will he be back?"

"When he chooses to."

"Does he ever tell you why?"

"Nope." She sat down at the kitchen table and sipped her mug of tea. "He never tells me why, when or where. He leaves whenever he likes, without letting me know beforehand, and he just turns up again the same way. He doesn't even say hello or goodbye. Sometimes he's away for days."

Brendan hesitated, unsure of whether he should ask the question. "Are you and Julian... er..." He glanced at the bedroom.

She smiled. "A couple again?... No. We sleep together in the bed on the average one night in five that he comes home, but only in the literal sense. With the kids in the apartment there's nowhere else he can sleep... When he's here he spends almost every moment in his study area. He hardly ever talks to me." She showed Brendan Julian's study area. It consisted of a tiny desk about two feet square and an overfilled set of bookshelves in the corner of the bedroom. There was a folding seat for the desk to save space. The double bed filled most of the room. The drawers under the desk were stuffed with papers and writing pads; and there was a cracked teacup full of biros in the far corner. Photographs of Marx, Lenin and a few other people were secured to the wall with drawing pins. There were no electronic office devices at all, not even a telephone. Brendan peered closer at the books on the shelf: *The Wretched of the Earth* by Frantz Fanon, *Where Lenin meets Mao* by Saloth Sar, *Stalin* by Leon Trotsky and *Animal Farm* by George Orwell. There were some more books piled up below the shelves on the side of the desk, as if Julian had been reading them recently. Brendan read a title off one of the spines aloud: "'Embellished Armageddon- the Truth about the Nuclear Apocalypse by Jonas Lovelace'. Why's Julian reading that?" He pointed at the book.

"God knows." replied Siobhan without looking. "Oops! Sorry, I'm not meant to say 'God'. You may have noticed that there are no churches in Trotskygrad." She laughed bitterly and walked back out to the kitchen. "How are you feeling now, Will?" she asked her son.

William had been sent home from school early because he wasn't feeling well. "Better now, mom."

"Still feeling dopey?"

"A bit I guess."

"Okay, honey. Go and sleep on the settee."

"Siobhan." blurted out Brendan. "Why don't you come home?"

She looked up from her mug of tea; her face was pale. "No."

"But..."

"Brendan." she interrupted firmly. "I meant what I said when I left. I still mean it."

Brendan paused. "Dad misses you terribly. He's really sorry how things turned out."

"Dad also told me he would stop mom from doing what she used to do to me, but he never did. I only came home from Australia the first time because of his promise."

"Then why not come home and tell him that yourself?"

"It's too late... Mom is dead. It's a done deal now."

"You and dad are still alive!"

"So are my children and their father... Jesus, Bren! You know in a couple of weeks I'll be turning forty. Forty years old! I'm middle aged. What kind of mother have I been? What kind of family life have I provided for my children?"

"Well what kind of family life is Julian providing? What have you just told me about his fatherly commitment?... Whatever the differences you have with dad, you can do a way better job back home on your own with dad, Kerry and me; away from this lunatic asylum and away from the nuttiest guy in it!"

Siobhan lowered her head to the table; her hair flopped over her teacup. "There's more, Bren. Stuff I've never told you."

Something in her tone chilled him. "Like what?"

"Like what mom did when dad was in Japan after the war. It was years before you were born... She ran off with this guy called Norman, a millionaire from Long Island. She kept it secret from dad and told me to help her... I was only eleven years old. I... I couldn't bear it." Siobhan blinked back tears.

The memory still hurt her. "I told dad. He was gutted. He almost ended up in jail when he went to Norman's house. For a couple of hours I thought dad had killed him..."

Brendan sat back. He realized that he knew there was some deep and dark secret between his mother and father; he always had done, but he never realized what it was.

Siobhan continued, speaking slowly for emphasis. "Mom was a very very destructive woman. Dad knew this. He let her off far too lightly for Norman. Why was he so shocked at me celebrating her death?... Mom did everything she could to make my life a misery. Was I supposed to love her anyway just cos she was my mom?... Who am I!? Fucking Job!?"

There was a long silence. "Siobhan, why not just come to the consulate and talk to dad on the phone? He really wants to hear from you."

She shook her head. "I can't... I can't because I think that if I heard his voice on the phone I would cave in and go home, and I know that right now that's the wrong thing to do."

There was a fumbling at the door to the flat and Colleen walked in. She gaped at Brendan in the same way her brother had and ran over to him, leaping onto his lap and squealing with delight. Siobhan and Brendan's eyes met over Colleen's shoulder. Their expressions were sad, but affectionate.

....

Brendan returned to the consulate at five PM and had a long and emotional telephone conversation with his father. A lot of this consisted of Brendan persuading him not to jump into his flyer immediately and drive to her. "No, dad! Don't come here now. It would do no good. Trust me; I've been talking to her all day. Leave her be for now... I'm going to stay away myself for the weekend."

"But she needs to come home to me!"

"She will, dad. She will, but not right now. We have to handle her carefully." After he came off the phone he felt rueful and dismal. He wanted so badly the same thing that his father did; he felt awful dissuading him when he knew he had also to dissuade himself. He felt a longing for things to go back in time to before Siobhan's exodus, to play things differently with hindsight.

The entrance to the Sydney US consulate rose out of the

pavement like that of an underground railway station. Brendan climbed the stairs to street level and took a walk through Sydney, but could not shake off his depression. He couldn't be bothered to try the city's restaurants and pubs and decided to eat in the consulate's dining room. He felt even worse when he reached the docks and noticed that one of the ships berthed there was definitely a whaler. The SRA was still hunting whales against the ruling of the LoWEHO. He spat on the ground. "What are Seaguard doing about that?" he muttered to himself aloud, wishing he were back on board ship. He had been granted special leave due to his family problems, but now, for the first time, would have been happy returning to work. He went straight back to the consulate, not wanting to see any more of Sydney. When he arrived in his guest room there was an envelope waiting for him on his dressing table. Inside was a covering note from Mr Mann and a second envelope that contained a gilt compliments card: "*Dear Mr Quilley. Prime Minister Pankhurst requests the pleasure of your company tomorrow at an official luncheon...*" The card read on for a few more sentences, giving him instructions. "How did he know I was here?" Brendan asked himself aloud. Then he reread the note from Mr Mann and snorted. "You told him didn't you?" Brendan didn't feel he was in the mood to socialize formally with Australian bigwigs and decided to decline the invitation, but later reconsidered. He was due to return to Trotskygrad on Monday to visit Siobhan again and was preparing himself for a boring weekend of reading books and playing solo card games. He shrugged. "Might as well go. Got nothing better to do."

He ate dinner and went to bed. As soon as he lay down he felt his eyes watering. He blinked a few times, wondering if he might be allergic to something in the bedroom. He wiped his eyes a few times with his hands and eventually gave up and switched on the bedside light to locate a box of tissues that he had seen there earlier. His heart thudded. His hands were covered in black fluid. This had flowed onto the pillow and bed sheets staining them. He leaped out of bed, yelping in panic. He looked at himself in the mirror and saw that the source of the black liquid was his own eyes. At first he thought it was oil, but it was odourless. Then he remembered what had happened the previous year when he had been part of the crew of Seaguard *Heather* in its invasion of Southern Thule. "Black goo!" he hissed aloud. He ran to the bathroom and washed his face frantically. The flux from his eyes had now lessened. He returned to the bedroom and saw that the stains were evaporating like acetone, the same thing that had happened after the breakout in the wardroom. He went back to the mirror and was relieved to see that his spontaneous alien tears had now stopped. He stood back and scratched his head. He had worried for the first few days after the foreign substance had been absorbed into his body, but had forgotten about it when he suffered no ill effects. However, it had been inside his system the whole time and had just emerged. Why? Had it somehow come to life? What would this mean for his health? He fell into an uneasy sleep, but did not experience any more black goo discharge for the rest of the night.

....

The car that was sent for him was a vintage ZiL limousine from the former Soviet Union. It picked him up from the US consulate's entrance at eleven AM. Brendan had managed to hire a decent suit and felt dapper as the chauffeur held the door open for him. He thanked the man warmly. Servants like these felt incongruous in a state ruled by socialism, but the practicalities of political power had always been a good amnesiac for sentiments. Brendan expected to be driven to a grand hotel or government building somewhere, but instead he was taken to an airfield in the suburbs where a business jet was idling. The plane flew north for several hours across dry bush. The landscape turned greener as they crossed over into Queensland and forested mountains scrolled below. Eventually the sea appeared ahead, the deepest blue ocean Brendan had ever seen. It was marred by grey spots that a member of the crew told him was the Great Barrier Reef. The plane began descending and Brendan fastened his seatbelt to land. As soon as the plane's door was open, a blast of heat flooded into the cabin making Brendan break out in a sweat. He stepped down from the aircraft into a hot tropical day that reminded him on the Volta Union. A number of stewards in uniforms led him to a car which drove a mile or so to the coast. He then walked down a jetty and boarded a small boat.

The boat bounced across the sapphire waves to a small flat island covered with trees. It dropped him off at another jetty on the island and ahead he saw a plush beach villa. "Perhaps you'd like to change your clothes, sir." suggested one of the stewards.

Brendan had long since loosened his collar and removed his jacket, but he still felt out of place in his suit. "Yes. It would be nice to slip into something more comfortable." However when the man showed him to a changing room, the only garment hung up as an alternative was a pair of swimming trunks. He had not expected that, remembering the very decorous invitation card he had received. He stripped and stepped into them before exiting the changing room by the far door. He emerged onto a lido. A kidney shaped swimming pool ended just a few yards from a beach of clean golden sand at the foot of which the sea massaged the shore in calm lazy strokes of surf. Palm trees rose above the scene like giant flowers. At the near end of the pool underneath a row of parasols sat about ten people on deckchairs, men in swimming trunks and attractive women in bikinis. There was a barbecue steaming away to one side and a crate of ice cubes from which the tops of beer cans sprouted. A television set was in front of the row of deckchairs showing coverage of a sporting event. One of the men was John Pankhurst. He turned round and smiled as Brendan approached. "G'day, Brendan! Thanks for coming, mate. Grab yourself a snag and a tube."

"This is the formal luncheon is it?" Brendan gestured at their surroundings with one raised eyebrow.

Pankhurst shrugged. "You know what they say: When in Rome... do what the Aussies do 'cos it's much more fucken fun!" His companions laughed.

A servant set up another deckchair for Brendan and made him a sausage bap from the barbecue. Brendan cracked open a can of lager and sipped from it. He expected Pankhurst to come to the point and focus on whatever business he had the wherewithal to discuss, including why he had asked Brendan to join him; but instead he and the others stared at the TV screen talking animatedly about the unfolding game. At first Brendan thought the sport they were watching was rugby, but then he saw that the shape of the pitch was oval.

The rules were obviously different too. On the other hand, perhaps there were no rules. Indeed every few minutes the players stopped to shout at each other and even trade blows. Pankhurst's posse cheered that on too as if it were merely part of the object of the game and this was a blend of a team sport and boxing. Finally it was over and Pankhurst groaned. "Fuck it! St Kilda arseholes!"

"Did your side lose?" asked Brendan, his patience wearing thin.

He nodded.

"Then perhaps you could explain what I'm doing here."

He paused and then chuckled. "Leverage."

"What do you mean?"

"I need you as a witness, because you're a Yank. I've been involved in a business deal and I want to raise the stakes." He winked.

"A business deal with whom?"

"Somebody who's due to arrive any minute now." He looked away, indicating that he would reveal no more at this juncture.

Twenty minutes later a large black flyer appeared in the sky. Brendan was amazed because he knew that new tech was shunned within the Red Bloc, however the people in the deckchairs were unperturbed by the appearance of this futuristic behemoth entering their midst. Brendan stood up and stared. The vehicle buzzed down in a steep dive from a high altitude as if afraid of being spotted from the shore and landed on the beach. The driver and front seat passenger got out. They were both men in dark suits open at the front and the armbands they wore looked familiar. One of them opened the rear passenger door and a small feminine figure emerged. "The president!" Brendan gasped.

President LaRey Tavinor strutted up the beach, her smart office slippers sinking into the sand, leaving a sprinkling of grains stuck to her black tights. The two Secret Service bodyguards flanked her on either side. Apart from Brendan, nobody in the lido stood up. "Mr Pankhurst." She greeted him in a brisk tone.

"LaRey! Great to see you again. How's it going?" The Australian Prime Minister cast a critical eye over her smooth linen suit. "Where's your cozzie?"

"I beg your pardon."

He imitated an upper-class English accent: "Bathing costume."

She rolled her eyes. "I'm not here for a beach party, Mr Pankhurst. You know why I've come. Shall we get this over with?"

"Sure, but first of all I'd like to make you aware that one of your countrymen is here as a potential witness." He pointed to Brendan.

Tavinor looked at Brendan and did a double take. She glared at the Australians. "What the hell do you think you're doing!? You assured me that this would remain strictly sub rosa!"

"Yes, but my comrades and I decided to take out a unilateral insurance policy."

She sighed and glanced briefly at Brendan again. "As you wish, Pankhurst. Do you have the shipments prepared?"

"Yes, two thousand five hundred tons, as we agreed; and you?"

"Ten point seven million barrels. Adjusted according to last week's oil pices, as we agreed." She removed a sheet of paper from her jacket and handed it to Pankhurst.

"Thanks." He handed her a similar document. The two national leaders examined the papers. "Well that all seems in order." he said. "It's a pleasure doing business with you, LaRey, as always." He held out his hand.

She ignored it. Instead she turned to Brendan. "May I speak with you in private a moment?" She beckoned him over to the far side of the pool beside a row of surfboards stacked up in a pile. "Forgive me, but aren't you Clane Quilley's son?"

"Yes, ma'am."

She smiled nervously. "How is your dad?"

Brendan was about to respond in kind. Everything that had happened during the last few minutes was churning round his mind. Instead he said: "Madam President... what are you doing here?"

She faltered. "Erm... Barclay is it?..."

"Brendan."

"Brendan... can I ask you to forget you saw me here?"

"Why? What's going on? It sounded like you were doing... doing some kind of trade over there."

She blushed. "I was."

"But... the SRA is under TAPC sanctions."

"I know."

"Madam President, that was your policy. You organized the summit..."

"I know, Brendan." she repeated more slowly and firmly.

"So what's going on?"

She closed her eyes and breathed deeply. Then she chuckled. "You're just like your dad. I know you're not going to be fobbed off... I have a covert deal running with the SRA. I'm bartering oil for uranium."

"Uranium!?... What for?"

"Weapons. I'm importing uranium from mines in the TSSR in exchange for American sweet light crude. This is because America needs a nuclear deterrent and there's nowhere else we can get the uranium of the grade and in the quantities we need."

"But that's illegal!"

"I know."

"That's why you're doing it here, on your own, miles from anywhere. You want to keep it secret. If you're caught..."

"I'll be impeached and sent to jail." she finished his sentence.

He looked at her with resentment. "How could you!?"

She frowned back. "Jesus Christ, Brendan! Have you any idea what the affairs of state involve? This isn't a goddamn church camp! Every day I have moral dilemmas coming out of my fucking ears!... And guess what? That makes me the same as every other president America has ever had! No better, no worse... It's the same in most other nations as well. My country needs to be protected by force and sometimes that involves means that won't win me the best Girl Guide award!... That's the dark side of democracy nobody wants to face, until they *have* to! Welcome to real life in government, Brendan!"

He paused sadly. "Everybody thinks you're honest. Everybody thinks you're different to the others."

"I *am* honest!" she said with exasperation. "Look,

compare me to that filthy bum Pankhurst." She glanced over her shoulder at the Australian leader as he fiddled with the remote control of the TV set. "Why do you think he's in on this? Does he care about his country? No! He's doing this because he gets a commission from the industry. He's out to make money... Or did you think he was different from other communists." She gave him a sarcastic half smile.

Brendan opened his mouth to speak, but no words came out.

She moved in on his reticence. "Brendan, if you don't want to weaken your country, work with me. Say nothing to anybody." She patted his shoulder and summoned her USSS escorts.

"Hey, LaRey!" called Pankhurst from the row of deckchairs. "You leaving already? Why not stay and have a beer?"

She turned her back on Pankhurst, strutted over to her flyer and got into the back seat. The two bodyguards climbed into the front and the machine started humming with that familiar bees nest sound that was so taboo in the Red Bloc. It rose into the air, spun round and sped away until it was just a small dot in the sky. Then it was gone.

....

On Monday morning Brendan returned to Trotskygrad. It took him a while to find Siobhan's residence because of the uniformity of the district's architecture and urban layout. When he arrived there, a group of children were playing in the field amongst the sheep, but none of them were William or Colleen. A baby was crying through an open window on the ground floor. He climbed the stairs to the upper floor and went to the door he was pretty sure was the entrance to Siobhan's flat. He knocked; nobody answered. He tried the handle almost out of habit, expecting the door to be locked; but it was not. As he pulled the door open and looked at the latch, he saw that there was no way to lock the door, as if this was an internal door instead of a front door to a private home. There was nobody in the apartment. Brendan decided to wait for a while. He looked into the bedroom out of curiosity. The lights were off and it was dark inside the windowless chamber; the only light was sifting in from the open plan doorway. A wave of curiosity came over him, as well as expectant boredom-to-come if he had to wait too long. He stepped through the entrance and found a light switch. He glanced over his shoulder once more to verify that he was alone and walked over to the desk on the left hand side of the bed. There was a second light there, a small desk lamp. Brendan switched it on. In the middle of the desk was a large ring bound writing book with a sticky label on the cover which read: *An Introduction to Marxism-Spencerism by Julian Spencer*. He opened it up. It was about half filled in with neat, but rushed handwriting on every line. There were numerous crossings out, footnotes and insertions in the margin. He read a few lines, but it was very jargon heavy and made no sense to him.

"Looking for some political education?"

Brendan jumped in shock, letting out and involuntary yelp. A man was standing in the doorway. With the desk lamp on, Brendan had not noticed his shadow appear.

"Sorry, I didn't mean to startle you." The man was tall and thin. He wore a crumpled and dirty short-sleeved shirt of military grey cotton with half the buttons undone. He had long dark hair and a thick beard. Steel-framed sunglasses hid his eyes.

"The door was open and..." Brendan stammered.

"It's alright." The man took off his sunglasses and his chestnut eyes peered from beneath strong furrowed brows. "I'm Julian. Aren't you Brendan?"

"Yes."

"Siobhan mentioned that you had come to visit... You've grown up of course, but I recognize you. When was it we last met?"

"Erm... about 1960 I think." Brendan rustled up the memories he had of his sister's boyfriend. He recognized Julian Spencer at once from the media images he had been studying at the embassy. He also recalled the years he and Siobhan were lovers; when Brendan himself had been a small boy. His memory was of a young man with shorter hair and no beard, but with the same intense and fresh features.

"Take a seat. I'll get some beers." Julian strode into the kitchen and pulled two bottles out of the refrigerator. "Fosters alright?"

"Yeah sure." Brendan sat down at the kitchen table.

"I bought these yesterday. I can drink this brand now because the brewery had just been nationalized." He opened the bottles with an opener hanging from the ceiling by a coiled cord and slammed one of them down in front of Brendan. "Get it down you. There's plenty more after that... Cheers."

"Cheers." Brendan took a sip from the bottle. He noticed that Julian handled the bottle awkwardly with his right hand as if it were partly disabled. There was a long lateral scar across his right inner forearm. "I must apologize for entering your apartment while you were out. It's just..."

"It's not *my* apartment." Julian interrupted. "It's not Siobhan's, it's not Will's or Colleen's. It belongs to nobody and everybody. We have no private property in Trotskygrad. That's why there is no lock on the door. There are no locks anywhere here... Property is theft." He drained the bottle in three swigs and got up to get a second one.

"Where are Siobhan and the twins?"

"Colleen is at the learning facilitation unit... Like a school." He added the explanation with a half smile when he saw Brendan's bemused face. "Siobhan has taken Will to the doctor." He growled in disgust. "There are perfectly good doctors at the medical centre here in Trotskygrad, but she insisted on going to this stupid old petty-bourgeois fool in the clinic at Rushcutters Bay. Why for fuck's sake!?" He swore in his English accent.

"How has Will been?"

"Sick all weekend. He's been lying around on the couch whinging, taking up space where I normally sit, throwing up on the floor."

Brendan was dismayed and irritated by Julian's lack of compassion for his son. "How did it feel when you found out you had children?"

He guffawed. "I don't *have* any children, nor does Siobhan. Having children is another form of private property. Children are born as free citizens of the proletarian state. A day will come soon when even possessive pronouns are removed from all human languages!... Anyway, I already knew. Siobhan had sent me about a dozen letters telling me."

Brendan gasped. "So those letters got through!?"

"Yup." He finished his second beer and grabbed a third

from the fridge.

"Why didn't you reply?"

Julian raised his eyebrows and glared as if finding the question foolish. "I had more important things to do. I was fighting for the revolution in seven countries!"

Brendan paused, collecting his thoughts. "I'm going to become a father myself in a few months. My wife and unborn child are the most important things in my life right now."

Julian looked at him in genuine sympathy, as if Brendan were a mentally ill teenager suffering from a naive delusion. "Brendan, I know it seems like that to you, but your perspectives are warped because you have lived your whole life under the jackboot of Green Bloc fascism. Your view of the world is shallow and totally distorted. Mine is deep and perfectly clear. I have learned the truth about how society really works. History is purposive! It is leading up to an appointed end! But society needs skilled guidance as it enters the final period of capitalism if it is not to falter and collapse."

Brendan wasn't sure what that all meant, but he replied as best as he could: "But, Julian. You've had your revolution now. The communist party is in complete power."

He tittered. "In case you hadn't noticed, Brendan; the Red Bloc only covers a quarter of the earth's landmass. Besides, what we have in Australia is not..." He broke off and paused. "Well, it needs replacing."

"In what way?"

"I don't know if you managed to read any of my manuscript before I came in, but I'm formulating a new idea that I think will drive the revolution forward. It's complicated, but I'll give you the basics. You see, in *Anti-Dühring*, Engels explains what he believes is the process of transition from socialism to communism. I think he was wrong. I am certain that there has to be two stages of transformation. I call them 'Phase One Socialism' and 'Phase Two Socialism'. What we have in the SRA today, as in the rest of the Red Bloc, is Phase One Socialism. And because the international vanguard is too arrogant, corrupt and stupid to understand their error, we are stuck there. Phase One Socialism plays an important role. It creates the economic and financial foundation for the future transformation of society; and, unlike Trotsky, I believe it can be introduced in one country or several countries before the revolution has spread globally. The transition to communism cannot begin until both stages of socialism have been fully achieved across the earth. However, the world revolution is currently floundering because it is run by people who don't know how to transition to Phase Two Socialism, the political element. If we don't break this impasse soon then the entire Red Bloc will logjam and regress. I estimate we have three to four years left at the most. I mean... I think Orwell saw it, at least partly. This was what *Animal Farm* really revealed, even if he only had a subconscious inkling."

"Is that the book about pigs acting like humans?" Brendan was interested despite himself.

Julian's face brightened. "You've read it?... Yes."

Brendan recalled the island meeting he'd had on Saturday. There was something very decadent and obtuse about the behaviour of Australia's leaders that reminded him of the final scene in George Orwell's classic barnyard fable. He described his experience to Julian.

His sister's ex-lover listened attentively, but then sat up and raised his head with a scowl. "What!?"

Brendan bit his tongue. He had just let slip about President Tavinor's visit. He momentarily cursed himself, but then stopped. He had not sworn himself to secrecy in front of her; LaRey Tavinor had merely requested his collusion. He was under no obligation to honour that. He wasn't even sure he agreed with her that it was the right thing to do so. He told Julian the whole story.

Julian stared at the table with a furious expression on his face, deep in thought. "Stalinist bastards!" he hissed. After that he relaxed slightly. "I shouldn't be surprised. Pankhurst is nothing but a greedy careerist reactionary bureaucrat; everybody knows that. It stands to reason that he would do something like this. I mean... selling the Americans uranium for nuclear weapons!? Arming the biggest counterrevolutionary force on earth!" He laughed out loud. "Of course Pankhurst would do that! The odious little shit-bag!" Julian stood up. "Thanks for letting me know, Brendan. I'll make sure I bring that up at tonight's meeting."

"Meeting? Of what?"

Julian paused. "I can't tell you." He then reached into a broom cupboard and removed a large object that he threw onto the table with a crash, knocking over an empty beer bottle.

Brendan recoiled in shock. It was an assault rifle, an AK47 from the former Soviet Union. There was a magazine inserted and Brendan was relieved to notice that the safety catch was selected. "Is that loaded?"

"Yup."

"What have you got it for?"

"I can't tell you." he repeated, then added with a sly grin: "You'll find out soon enough." He picked up the weapon and headed for the door. "I've got to go now, Brendan. Feel free to wait for Siobhan; she'll be back soon. Help yourself to another beer."

After he had gone, Brendan sat at the table for a while in pensive stillness; then he got up and returned to Julian's study area. The manuscript for his book was still lying on the desktop. Julian seemed undaunted at the possibility of it being stolen or lost, or of any passer-by reading it. Brendan sat down on the folding chair, opened the pad and flicked through. The pages which had already been written in were rough and crinkled from the pen lines. He froze when he caught the words "*nuclear weapons*" out of the corner of his eye. He stopped flickering and turned back, scanning each page until he found the passage with those words. He also glanced to his right and saw that the book *Embellished Armageddon* was still on the study pile. He began reading Julian's tight and spidery handwriting: "*...For many years now, since the start of the first Cold War, the media has been focused on the possibility of full global nuclear warfare. Along with this focus have come the visions of the 'post-apocalyptic' world, the remnants of nature and human life surviving on a planet shattered and comatose, possibly terminally, by multiple nuclear explosions. In these scenarios, the heat and blast of nuclear ordnance combined with radioactive fallout renders the earth uninhabitable. Sometimes rudimentary human life endures, sometimes life has to begin again from very basic forms; and in others the earth is killed stone dead* *and becomes another Mars or Venus. The best known of these dystopian fantasies is probably Nevil Shute's* On The Beach. *I believe that this nightmarish projection is based on the cultural archetype of the apocalypse, also found in myths of Judgement Day and the Kali Yuga etc, and has very little scientific foundation. Following the publications by Laktov, Lovelace, De Franco* et al *in various journals (1969 to 73) it is clear that the devastation of a nuclear holocaust would be far more attenuated and confined than the bleak cataclysmic scribblings we're all familiar with. Yes, it would annihilate the world's major cities and the death toll would be gargantuan, but the effect on the earth's biosphere would be negligible and temporary. Radioactive fallout disperses quickly, a mile-per-REM-per-megaton, within days of the detonation, and blends with natural background radioactivity within a mere few miles from ground zero, in less than four weeks. This is especially true of the most advanced nuclear bombs which are of lower yield than their 1940's predecessors and also are designed for air bursts, so-called, and correctly called, 'clean nukes'. You'd have to be living very close to the individual blasts, and stay there afterwards, to suffer radiation poisoning. Even the dreaded 'nuclear winter' would not last longer than those caused by major volcanic eruptions such as Krakatoa in 1883."* The next few sentences were scribbled out. *"The true post-apocalyptic world after a nuclear war would be one of a fully-functioning natural planet with a vastly reduced human population and destroyed infrastructure. Recovery from that situation would be difficult; but, given time, civilization could be restored. For the Marxist-Spencerist this poses an obvious question: Why restore society according to a model based on the previous capitalist democratic regime, or the deformed workers' state of Stalinism? Why not take that precious opportunity and make it a shortcut to building an international socialist order?"* A sentence was obliterated here. *"According to the preparedness plans of many nations for maintaining continuity of government in the event of nuclear war, including all the big developed bourgeois democratic capitalist ones, the world after nuclear war is astonishingly similar to pure socialism; a resource-based planned economy, personal allowances for all necessities, state control of the essential public service industries bestowed under capitalism to the corporate monopolies. In fact the radical and remarkable progression from this fact is that a nuclear holocaust ought to be something a Marxist should not fear, but hope for and welcome; if, and when, it occurs. It is, after all, the most revolutionary societal backdrop imaginable. However, I wonder how many comrades would have the audacity to take this theory one step even further. What I am about to say is extreme and it will shock many readers, but please entertain it as a thought experiment: the ultimate revolutionary act would be* actively to initiate *a nuclear holocaust, not merely wait with fingers crossed in case one might happen. Would you consider that immoral? In which case, think it over some more. There is only one moral scale for a Marxist; revolutionary is good, counterrevolutionary is bad. Full stop. You may balk at the mega-deaths resulting. Even Lovelace admits that in all likelihood the majority of mankind will be culled; between fifty and eighty percent. The only quandary therefore is whether the deaths of two to three billion people are a price worth paying for the success of the revolution. My answer is simple and given without hesitation or qualification: Yes...*"

Brendan shut the book with a snap and leaned back. His hands were trembling. "Jesus!... He's a fuckin' madman!"

At that moment he heard the front door open and Siobhan's and William's voices. Brendan switched off the desk lamp, folded the chair and left the bedroom to greet his family. "Hi, Siobhan. Hi, William." He patted his nephew's shoulder. "How did it go?"

"He's got to go back for more tests." answered Siobhan.

William looked pale and bleary-eyed.

Chapter 16

It was a lazy Sunday afternoon in the Kilmacsimon barracks. Heather and Brendan were on sun loungers in the garden of their married quarters with their eyes half closed. It was a warm day and woodpigeons cooed in the nearby trees. Bees orbited the flowers and a gentle breeze ruffled their hair. Heather's belly had expanded over the last two months and she rested her hands on top of it. Brendan was enjoying not having to work. Seaguard *Foyle* was coming to the conclusion of a minor refit but was still not deploying for the foreseeable future. Her engines were being picked over by a specialized team from the company's head office in Dublin. Brendan had been needed for the first stage of the overhaul, but this week he had been asked to stand aside. At first this irritated him, but now he was glad of the time off. Apart from a touch of paperwork he had been able to relax for the last seven days. He had a book by his side that he read in snatches between dozing and daydreaming. The phone rang. Brendan raised his head and saw the handset lying on the footstool nearest to him. He groaned and reached down to grab it, failed the first time and reached again. This time he seized it. He lay back with an annoyed sigh and put it to his ear. "Hello?"

"Is that Mr Quilley? It's John Mann from the US consulate here in Sydney."

Brendan sat up. "Mr Mann? Of course, we met a few weeks ago. What can I do for you?"

"Your sister has asked me to pass on a message to you. Could you please come and visit her, as soon as possible?"

"Why? What's the problem?"

"I don't know I'm afraid. She left me a voicemail earlier this evening and didn't specify. Her tone sounded insistent though."

Brendan paused. "Alright. How can I get there? Do I have to go via the TSSR again?"

"No no, not at all. The ambassador has arranged permission for you to travel by flyer, but not to Sydney. You're authorized to land at an airbase near Canberra."

When he had come off the phone, Brendan met Heather's inquisitive gaze. "Shall I call your dad?" she asked.

Brendan was about to say "yes", but stopped himself. "No.

Let me find out first what's up with Siobhan. If necessary, I'll let dad know."

Brendan's route took him over Scandinavia and Asia. On the three-hour flight he worried about what might have happened to Siobhan for her to demand his immediate presence on the other side of the world. She couldn't even come to the consulate and call herself. Just a few days ago she had spoken on the phone from Mann's office to him and their father so they could wish her a happy fortieth birthday. Night fell as he headed across Siberia, China and Indonesia. He was contacted by radio and told to land on the same helicopter pad that he had landed on when Siobhan first took him to Australia in 1968. The US embassy provided a ground car so that he could drive immediately to Sydney. It was three AM when he set off and the roads were devoid of all but a token level of traffic. Because of the time difference he was wide awake. The car was an IC and so he had to keep a close eye on the fuel gauge. He also had to remember to drive on the left. At one point he had to stop to buy IC fuel with Australian money provided by the embassy. It was almost six AM and the sky was starting to brighten. It was fairly easy; there were filling stations every few dozen miles on the main road and the car's fuel tank was accessed through a hole in the rear fender. A hook like probe attached to a rubber pipe was inserted into the hole via a machine called a "petrol pump" and he squeezed a trigger to make the fuel flow through it. After that he paid at a counter inside a small adjoining shop. When he reached Sydney it was Monday morning local time and the rush-hour was underway. A light rain fell from the grey sky. It took him a long time to reach Trotskygrad and when he did he had to leave the car in a large carpark at the edge of the experimental live project. Inside it was still strictly a pedestrian zone. His heart was pounding as he entered the residential block and opened the door to Siobhan's flat. It was empty. A woman from the apartment next door heard him and came out. "She's not in, comrade. She's at the hospital."

"Which one?"

Siobhan had gone to the Jock Garden Memorial Hospital near the city centre. The car's tyres screeched as Brendan skidded to halt in the short stay carpark and he ran into reception. His subconscious sense of urgency had increased. He told the receptionist who he was and she made some calls. He waited on a row of settees, wringing his hands in worry. He jumped up as his sister marched down the corridor towards him. Her face was taut with anxiety. "It's William." she gasped. "He's got leukaemia."

Brendan paused and then burst out laughing with relief. "Is that all? Is that what you summoned me from the other side of the world for? I thought he had been run over by a bus or something!... Damnit, you made me scared for nothing!"

Siobhan gave him a scowl of confusion. "Brendan... what's wrong with you? This is not nothing! This is leukaemia! It's cancer! It's serious."

"Serious? Of course it's not. He can just take GMAT or something..." He broke off as he noticed the sad realization morph across her face. "Oh no! You can't get it here, can you?"

"The doc's going to put him on a course of chemotherapy."

"What!?"

"His chances of survival are less than sixty percent over three years."

There was a long silence. Then a new comprehension materialized in Brendan's jetlagged brain. It was followed by a burst of triumph, a nasty feeling for his sister that resembled momentary hatred. "Right, Siobhan. Decision made! You'll have to come home." He couldn't resist a vainglorious snigger.

"Home?"

"Hasn't it dawned on you, Siobhan?... Holy shit, why haven't *you* thought of this yourself!? How long have you been living over here! That Julian has got inside your head!... Will needs treatment to save his life that he can only get back home. It's either that or he stays here and takes his meagre chances with commie chemo. You know that's the wrong thing to do."

Siobhan looked out of a window at ambulances rolling past. She slowly nodded. "Yes. That's true... Okay, we'll take Will home, but only till he's better. I'm still not ready to see dad. Talking to him on the phone last week was bad enough."

"Sure, Siobhan." Brendan grinned inwardly, thinking she might change her mind during her stay in the Green Bloc.

William was staying on an oncology ward on the third floor of the hospital. He was lying in bed, his skin grey like parchment. Brendan went upstairs to see him, but the twelve year old remained asleep. Siobhan stayed with him, sitting in the chair by his bedside while Brendan went back to the car and drove to the US consulate. He explained the situation to Mr Mann. The official wiped his glasses on a clean handkerchief. "I see. Well that explains Miss Quilley's phone-call... Of course you can take him home, but you must be careful how you go about it. It would be best not to tell the hospital staff what your plans are. They mustn't suspect you're leaving the SRA. From their point of view it would be like removing a child from all suitable care. They could then demand a retraining order. How long do they plan to keep him as an inpatient?"

"Until Wednesday." said Brendan. "He's due for his first chemo treatment tomorrow."

"Right, well you can see if you can get that appointment delayed, but that's unlikely. You might have to let him have a single treatment and then go home when he's discharged afterwards."

"We'd rather he had no chemo at all."

"One session shouldn't hurt him."

"Nevertheless, if we can spare him that we'd like to."

"Then you'll need to find some way to get him discharged before tomorrow."

"How?"

Mann hesitated. "Tell the staff you want to take him out this evening for a couple of hours. Tell them he's got to visit his dying aunt or something. Then, as soon as you're clear of the hospital, drive to Canberra, get in your flyer and head for home."

"Alright." Brendan nodded with a relieved smile.

When Brendan returned from the hospital William was still asleep and Siobhan had gone. A nurse told Brendan that she had left because Colleen was about to finish school. When Brendan arrived at Trotskygrad something strange was going on. The paths between the buildings were full of people, mostly men, all armed. They were scruffy in appearance and not uniformed. Some had red bandanas or red star badges on their shirts and hats. They strutted around in no particular order, their rifles pointing at the sky, not talking to each other or the Trotskygrad residents. The local people went about their business, pretending to ignore these intimidating newcomers. The armed men did not harass them. When he reached Siobhan's home she and Colleen were sitting in the kitchen. "What's going on with all these heavies?" asked Brendan.

"It's something to do with Julian." she answered. "He was here this morning."

Brendan remembered the AK47 Julian had been hiding in the broom cupboard. Siobhan had found out about it herself earlier. "What's he been up to? He's been storing weapons here and keeps talking about having 'meetings'."

She shrugged. "He split a few hours ago while you were at the consulate. Before he left, he told me to switch on the TV at four PM."

Colleen interjected. "Uncle Brendan, are we going home to the States?"

"Yes, Coll, but don't tell anybody about that. We're leaving tonight. We've got to pick up Will from the hospital first of course."

Siobhan looked at the clock. "It's five-to-four now. Let's see what all this is about." The television set in the apartment was primitive, like everything else in the Red Bloc. It was a cathode ray tube in a boxy wooden cabinet with a small screen. Brendan had not watched much television while he had been in the SRA. There were just two terrestrial channels and they both only ran in the afternoons and evenings. The quality of programming was poor; it reminded him of old Soviet propaganda films. As Siobhan flicked the set on there was a public information film playing, warning people not to waste electricity by leaving lights on or appliances running unnecessarily. When it ended, the screen went blank and there was a pause. A voiceover began: "*We interrupt our normal schedule for a special announcement by the Prime Minister of the Socialist Republic of Australia.*" The screen went dark again for a few seconds and then it lit up. The picture showed a familiar sight, the office of the Australian Prime Minister, the location from where he delivered inspiring live speeches to the nation, a regular occurrence since the revolution in 1966. However, the man sitting behind the desk was not John Pankhurst; it was Julian Spencer.

"What the fuck!?" Siobhan leapt to her feet.

Julian faced the camera with a hard expression and began speaking. "*People of Australia. Free people of the socialist world. Friends, comrades, brothers and sisters. My name is Julian Spencer. I speak to you this afternoon for the first time as your new Prime Minister, the third Prime Minister of the Socialist Republic of Australia. I have relieved Prime Minister Pankhurst of his office in accordance with the constitution of the Communist Party of Australia for contravening Articles Two, Three and Seven. He has been charged with high treason and counterrevolutionary interests. We are also investigating allegations that he has conspired to break the 1972 Wollongong Act by engaging in a secret economic relationship with an enemy nation, specifically the United States of America...*"

"Oh God!" Brendan bowed his head.

"*Therefore, with the assistance of loyal members of the politburo and the Australian Red Army, I have invested myself as Prime Minister of the SRA. It is my intention to redirect the revolutionary efforts of the nation towards a more robust and expansionist programme. I believe the SRA, as the leading nation within the Red Bloc, has a duty to the people of the world, to spread socialism to the fullest extent of our abilities.*" He paused and leaned back slightly in his high-backed leather swivel chair. He continued in a more personal tone. "*Many comrades watching will not know my name. Today I am almost forgotten in a nation I helped to liberate. In 1966 I was the closest friend and comrade of our first Prime Minister and leader of the glorious revolution, Lance Sharkey. Having fought and struggled to build the Socialist Republic of Australia I left it for foreign shores to continue the revolution there. I knew that the country was safe and would do well in Sharkey's hands. However it was not to be. Our beloved leader died suddenly the year after the revolution and this office passed into the hands of one John Pankhurst. Under*

Pankhurst's regime the nation slid into lassitude. The forces of reaction, both internal and external, took hold of Australian hearts and minds. Today, the SRA, and as a consequence the entire Red Bloc, teeters of the edge of destruction. All we have fought for, all so many of our comrades gave their lives for, will be thoughtlessly squandered and the revolution defeated. Global capitalism will continue for the foreseeable future, possibly until the entire earth is destroyed. I will not allow that to happen. I will now consult with the new politburo and in a few hours I will provide a public update about my proposal on this channel. The normal television schedule is suspended until further notice and this emergency broadcast will continue. Please keep your set switched on so as not to miss any news. Thank you very much for your support and long live the revolution!" He raised his right fist in the air and the screen went blank.

Brendan, Siobhan and Colleen sat back. Siobhan sighed tremulously. "I think we'd better get a move on."

"Yes." said Brendan. "We need to go now. Colleen, go and pack your stuff. Hurry!"

....

The armed militia that had been hanging out in Trotskygrad had vanished. Brendan and Siobhan walked speedily along the ruler straight lanes of the demonstrational settlement with Colleen between them. The only belongings they carried were in handheld cases. When they reached the carpark they jumped aboard the embassy hire car and headed to the hospital. The disappearance of the militia was explained. They had left Trotskygrad to patrol the streets of Sydney in a rough paramilitary style like vigilantes. They paid Brendan and his family no attention as they weaved their car through the evening rush hour traffic. At the hospital they made their way to the oncology ward, whispering to each other to make sure they had their cover story straight. The doctor treating William met them at the door to his room. He shook his head as they told him of their intentions. "I'm terribly sorry, comrades. I've just put William on a course of intravenous antibiotics to treat his bronchitis. He can't leave until the course is complete."

"How long will that take?"

"Four or five days."

Siobhan groaned. "Comrade doctor, is this strictly necessary? Will a bottle of pills not do the same job?"

He shook his head. "This is Amoxicillin and at this high dose it can only be given intravenously. William could come down with pneumonia if we don't treat the infection this way. The leukaemia is compromising his immune system..."

"Comrade doctor." interrupted Siobhan. "I don't think you realize the emotional trauma William might face if he did not get one last chance to speak to his aunt Agnes. She was like a mother to him when I was in hospital for six months after my hysterectomy. She has been at every one of his birthday parties, every Christmas Day. He adores her! Please! Allow him just a few hours this evening to go and visit her, to say goodbye properly."

The doctor gave a guilty sigh. "I'm so sorry, comrade. I really cannot allow that. I have a duty to William's proper care. It would be highly detrimental for me to permit him to leave hospital at this point in his treatment."

Brendan suddenly had an idea. He reached into his pocket and pulled out his wallet. He removed all the cash that the embassy had given him for expenses and held it out in front of the doctor's nose. He did not understand the Australian currency and had no idea how much he was holding.

The doctors eyes bulged and his jaw dropped. He glanced over his shoulder and then snatched the money from Brendan's hand. He smiled and cleared his throat. "Keep warm clothes on him and make sure he drinks plenty of water. Have him back here by nine this evening."

Brendan chuckled as Siobhan roused William from his sleep. "That used to work in the USSR so I'm told."

William took a long time to wake up and he complained as Siobhan ordered him to dress. He could walk and talk normally, but he was feeling very much under the weather and was vocal about it. He dragged his heels as they walked along the hospital corridors. "Keep up, Will!" Siobhan snapped at him, shoving him in the small of his back. As soon as he was in the car he fell asleep on the back seat. Colleen objected when he laid his head on her lap. Eventually he dozed with his head propped against the rear door pillar. Brendan drove carefully and correctly through Sydney, praying fervently that this was the last time he would have to see these streets again. He joined the same main road he had driven up that morning and headed in the opposite direction. He checked the fuel gauge every so often to see how fast the liquid was draining into the engine. He would then know whether he needed to stop for more before they reached their destination. He had given all his money to the doctor, but Siobhan had some in her handbag. The sun set as the overcast broke and stars appeared. Brendan switched on the headlights. He felt drowsy, having missed a night's sleep by the time zone he was attuned to. They stopped for a meal at a roadside service station. William had no appetite so Colleen ate his share. They arrived in Canberra and headed straight for the airbase where the flyer was parked. To Brendan's consternation, they were refused entry at the gate. The regular military guards had been replaced by militiamen like those wandering around Sydney. "Sorry, guys." he said insincerely. "Your aircraft has been impounded. New regulations direct from the PM. All foreign materiel is to be acquisitioned."

"How do we get it back?" Brendan demanded.

The man huffed. "Get it back?... You can't, mate. We've already broken it up for scrap."

"What!?... That's my flyer! You can't do that!"

"We just did, mate. It's a piece of fake fascist junk anyhow... Look, we're just obeying orders. Take it up with the PM's office if you want to lodge a complaint."

"We damn well will!" The family were subdued as they roared out of the airbase and straight through the city of Canberra towards Parliament House. "We've got nothing to lose." said Siobhan. "Either we ask Julian direct or we're stuck here anyway." A trio of militiamen were standing on the entrance driveway. They were even more heavily armed than usual. One was holding a machinegun which was probably more for show than anything else. It was manifestly weighing him down and there was no way he could fire the weapon in that position. "Who are you?" he asked aggressively.

Siobhan leaned out of the window. "We want to see Prime Minister Spencer."

"Bugger off! He's not taking visitors."

"He will take me! I'm his wife! These are his children."

The three men stared at them skeptically. Then one walked a few feet away and had a conversation on a shortwave radio. He came back and nodded to his companions. "Alright, you can go through." The three of them stood aside.

As soon as they arrived at the entrance to the parliament of the SRA they saw that the atmosphere of the place was very different to how it had been when they had first been there seven years earlier. The crates of beer, overflowing boxes and barbecues were nowhere to be seen. Many of the people wandering the corridors were wearing smart military uniforms as well as those in the casual rags of the militia. One of the latter escorted them to a large room with French windows and a terrace. It was clearly not the Prime Minister's office from which Julian had spoken from a few hours ago. The place was brightly lit and full of people, many of them part of a television crew and the place was being set up as a TV studio. Several large cameras were being positioned and cables snaked across the floor. A microphone boom swung around under the ceiling like a crane. The world outside the windows was shrouded by night and the panes reflected the interior like a mirror. The Prime Minister himself was standing in a corner in conversation with two of the crew, one of whom was wearing earphones.

"Julian!" Siobhan yelled as soon as she saw him.

He turned round and gave her a blank glare as she strode over. "Will this take long, Siobhan? I'm due to address the nation again in twenty minutes."

"Why have you destroyed Brendan's flyer?"

"Why do you need it?"

"It was *mine*, Julian!" chimed in Brendan.

Julian jabbed a finger at him. "Never use that word in my country again!"

"Goddammit, Julian!" yelled Siobhan. "I need to take Will to a hospital! He needs treatment!"

"What's wrong with the hospitals in the SRA?"

"They can't give him the medication he needs!"

"Of course they can! SRA hospitals are the best in the world! William can stay here and have chemotherapy. It's what every other SRA citizen is offered, therefore it's good enough for him."

"He needs GMAT!"

"GMAT is fascist pseudoscientific Green Bloc quackery!"

Siobhan paused. She sniffed as tears rose in her. "Please, Jules. Just let us leave the country. I know you don't care about our son, but... can you do it for me? Do it for what we had? I... I know you don't love me anymore. I no longer love you either, but we *used* to! We loved each other! We have happy memories..."

"Speak for yourself!" he sneered.

Siobhan stepped back with a sob. "Julian, please let us leave. *Please!*"

He gazed at her contemptuously. "Go and get yourselves a coffee. We'll talk about it later... And don't forget to keep the TV on."

Siobhan, Brendan and the twins sat in another room similar to the one they'd just left. A CRT television set the size of a grand piano had been placed in one corner showing a screen with the words on it: "*STANDBY FOR AN ADDRESS BY THE PRIME MINISTER*". They were all sipping from cups of coffee except William who was slouched in one of the armchairs. His forehead was covered in sweat and he shivered under the blanket that one of the staff had given him. A few other people sat in the room too on various chairs and others were perched on tables. The TV screen flickered and then the picture formed. It showed Julian Spencer again. This time he was standing upright in the room his family had just left. He lifted his hand to look at his wristwatch. "*People of Australia. Free people of the socialist world. Friends, comrades, brothers and sisters.*" the Prime Minister began. "*The words I speak to you tonight are the most important ever spoken by anybody in history. This moment will be remembered for the rest of the life of humanity and planet earth as its greatest turning point. We have struggled, comrades. We have struggled long and hard! I have watched men and women die. I have watched them die in agony and terror. Comrades I loved and admired. I have watched them die by violence and by exhaustion. I have watched them die by their own hand. I have watched them die with the hope sucked dry from their very bones! I have known that at their last moment, they were certain that the revolution was over. Socialism was a dead dream."* His voice rose to a passionate roar. *"Never again will that happen!... It ends NOW!... Tonight the revolution will be realized and everybody on earth will know it!"* He wiped tears away from his eyes. He looked at his watch again and then continued in a calmer tone. *"It's something that I've never spoken openly about before, but I now know the truth behind all Marxist theory. I have finally completed the work started by Marx over a century ago. I have placed the last piece of the jigsaw puzzle into its space. I have worked out the one and only way we can win the last fight... I've been writing about it in a new book, one not yet published, but one day it will be rediscovered and will become the greatest historical document ever written..."*

A pang of horror passed through Brendan's body as he stared at the TV screen. "Oh my God!"

Siobhan looked at him in alarm. "What is it?"

"Surely not! Surely he's not really *that* insane!"

"What are you talking about?"

"...with commitment never before seen in the world." Julian looked at his watch again. *"Those heroes of the proletarian movement deserve better than failure! For their sake, not just ours! Not just future generations! Let us enter into this new and ultimate challenge boldly!... Do not be afraid. We have merely done what we have to do. There is no other way than this!"* He looked at his watch again. *"Comrades, people of the world, brothers and sisters whom I love with all my being... It is almost time!"* He turned his back on the camera for a moment and opened a pair of the French windows. He threw them wide dramatically. A night-time breeze ruffled his silky black hair.

There was a flash of light and a rumble of thunder outside the windows of the spectators' room that was echoed a split second later on the television signal. Brendan turned his head and looked at the windows. He had not seen any signs before arriving at Parliament House that a thunderstorm was brewing. The lightning flickered again.

In Julian's makeshift studio, the camera moved towards the window. Julian stepped out onto the terrace and was partly dimmed by the gloom. His body was glowing at the edges by reflection coming out from the interior. Ahead was bright flickering light, but it was not lightning. Five huge columns of fire towered into the sky above the northern skyline of Canberra. The outlines of the hills at the edge of the capital were plainly silhouetted. The noise was a rumbling rolling bass roar, but it was continuous; it didn't dissipate like thunder.

Brendan jumped up and ran to the window. He saw with his own eyes what he'd just seen on television. Other people in the room were doing the same. The glow from the towers of flame lit up the roofs and streets of the city. "What are those?" he asked.

"Redsear ballistic missiles." said a man standing beside him, staring upwards with the same wide-eyed disbelief. "They're on their way to America... and other places."

Brendan looked back at the TV screen. The camera angle had changed and the operator skilfully, or luckily, captured the iconic image of the light from the missiles' tail fire reflected in Julian Spencer's eyes as he gazed upwards at the departing weapons. He had raised his arms in the air at forty-five degree angles, his palms turned outwards as if trying to embrace the globe. He was laughing joyously at the top of his voice. *"Observe, comrades!"* he yelled. *"Behold the instruments of revolution!... As the great Lenin said: We shall now proceed to construct the socialist order!"*

Brendan was out of the spectators' room before he knew what he was doing. He ran down the corridor and into the studio. Nobody tried to stop him. The militiamen and soldiers were like statues, gazing into thin air with shock. They clearly had not been expecting this. Brendan burst in and ran over to the French windows. He didn't look to see or care whether the camera was still rolling. The cool night air surrounded his body. The noise of the missiles' rocket engines had faded to a low sound like a dog growling. Their exhaust was just a series of white specks in the sky like a shower of shooting stars. In the distance more missiles were launching. Their sound was just a distant growl, their light just rising specks like fireflies. Julian was still giggling as if drunk. He turned and looked at Brendan.

"We're dead." Brendan panted. "You've just killed us all."

"No, Brendan!" answered Julian emphatically. "I have just

given birth to us all!"

"How many missiles did you just launch?"

"All of them!"

"The Green Bloc has its own deterrent. They're going to shoot back! We're all dead!"

Siobhan and Colleen ran up to Brendan's shoulder. All three of them took in Julian.

The Prime Minister was standing like a Greek hero on the terrace, his hair rustling in the wind. His face became tender. "If you want to leave now, you can. I won't stop you."

"You'll let us use the airport, take a plane?"

"In an hour's time there won't be any airport or planes... Take a car. Get out of Canberra, drive as fast as you can. You may be able to get far enough away to survive... at least at first."

"Jules." Siobhan spoke so quietly she was almost inaudible. "Come with us."

He shook his head. "No."

"Why not?"

"I've done what I have had to do. My whole life has led up to this point. There's no need for any more of it. I shall die happy."

Siobhan and Colleen stepped forward. Siobhan kissed his lips and Colleen grabbed his hand. Julian looked down at his daughter and stroked her hair.

Chapter 17

The streets of Canberra were devoid of traffic. The pavements were crammed with people, but nobody tried to flee. They were like the staff at Parliament House; they just stood there like waxworks staring at the sky. A few families clutched each other and lovers held hands. Brendan rocketed down the streets with ease. He had taken a large military pursuit vehicle after finding one with the keys in the ignition. William and Colleen crouched in the back seat while Siobhan sat beside him. She turned to him. "Brendan."

"Yes?"

"Maybe we should stop too."

"Why?"

"I'm not sure I want to live through this."

He paused. Similar thoughts had been going through his head. "We have to try."

They reached the main road to Sydney. Brendan pressed his foot to the floor and the powerful IC engine dug into the tarmac. After half an hour's driving there was sudden flash of light from behind them as if the sun had risen in a split second. Brendan slammed on the brakes. "Cover your eyes! Don't look!" He could still see the deadly illumination through the gaps between his fingers, through his eyelids. The radiated heat on the back of his neck was like an open oven door. After a few seconds it eased. They all got out of the car and looked back. A ball of writhing plasma hung in the sky above the Australian capital, its base connected to the ground by a stalk of burning red vapour. After a few minutes it faded back into the black of night. The family got back into the car and drove on.

....

It was three AM when they reached the coast. They had stolen a road atlas from a deserted service station to find their way. There were no people anywhere in the villages and towns they drove through. It was as if the bombs had made them vaporize into thin air even if they hadn't been close enough to the explosions to do so physically. Siobhan had navigated their way to Bateman's Bay on the shores of New South Wales. A large marina lay before them. The electric lights had failed but there was a torch in the vehicle's cab. They walked slowly along the jetties looking at the inert craft that were tied up there. "We can only escape by sea." said Brendan. "Australia is an island continent. We've lost the flyer and there are no aircraft; a boat is the only way... We'll need a big one if we're going to cross the open ocean."

"How about that one?" Colleen was pointing at a large motor yacht.

Brendan patted her on the shoulder. "It's big enough, Coll. A hundred and twenty-footer I reckon. Ideally we should get one with sails in case the engine fails... Like that one!"

The perfect boat was a ninety-foot hybrid sailing yacht with a five hundred horsepower auxiliary diesel engine. Brendan had had to break into the cockpit. Luckily he found some tools in the car that allowed him to hotwire the engine ignition. They helped William up the gangplank and let him lie down in one of the cabins. Then Siobhan and Colleen cast off the lines while Brendan hit the throttle. The boat backed down out of her berth and between the two lifeless beacons that marked the sides of the entrance to the marina. Brendan put the wheel over and reversed the throttle. The diesel reacted politely and the vessel moved forward. He turned the wheel until the craft was heading out to sea. "I'm glad you're a sailor, Uncle Brendan." smiled Colleen at him when they were all in the cockpit.

"I'm glad you're an engineer" added Siobhan.

Colleen sighed. "It's a shame we had to steal the boat. Not very nice for the owners."

"We can return it to them afterwards." said Brendan. "I'll even pay them for the broken window." He added silently to himself: *If by a miracle they're still alive.*

"Where do we go now?" asked Siobhan.

"The closest place in the Green Bloc is New Zealand, but that's still a long way. Go check if there are any charts on the boat." Luckily there was a good set of charts in a drawer and a full-sized navigation table. Brendan plotted a course. The diesel bunkers were full and he reckoned there was just enough fuel for the journey. "It's a long voyage." he said. "Over a thousand miles. Pray to God for fine weather. We should be alright though. We can do it in about three days. We'll steer straight there, one hundred and twenty degrees true. We'll probably hit New Zealand somewhere on the South Island."

"Will New Zealand still be there though?" Siobhan asked grimly.

He looked at her sadly. "Do you have any better idea than we just go find out?"

She shook her head.

By the time the sun rose they were out of sight of land. The Tasman Sea was purple-blue with a slight chop of whitecaps. The wind was from the northwest. Brendan had been at the wheel for four hours and was close to unconsciousness from lack of sleep so Siobhan took over from him after brief instructions. "Leave the throttle where it is. Just concentrate on the compass binnacle. This line is the ship's head; keep our course as close as possible to a hundred and twenty degrees. If we drift off it, turn the rudder port or starboard until we're back on it."

"Aye aye, captain." Siobhan answered with a chuckle.

As Brendan was falling asleep in a cabin he marvelled at her cheeriness. Was it a psychological defence mechanism?

Colleen did a stint in the cockpit for the afternoon while Siobhan tended to William. When Brendan once again was back at the helm for the nightshift the weather had worsened. The gale was only a force eight, nothing major. A large ship would hardly have noticed it, but it made this sailing yacht pitch up and down like a seesaw. The windscreen was regularly dashed with spray. William's illness grew worse during the night. He coughed ceaselessly. His fever increased and he talked in his sleep during his delirious dreams. Siobhan and Colleen both sat in the cabin with him, bathing his head with a wet flannel and trying to keep him hydrated by encouraging him to drink as much as possible. "I think he's got pneumonia." said Siobhan in a fearful voice. The sun rose behind a sky of tar. Rain fell but the wind eased. William remained sick, but his condition was stable. Brendan slept again and woke up. There were some victuals on board the boat, but not enough for full meals for the whole voyage. He ate a can of custard before taking his place at the helm. Along with the worry was the boredom. Brendan worked hard at daydreaming and avoided watching the clock. He had not used his imagination much throughout his life, but now, with nothing else to stimulate his mind, it became a cinema, WorldMesh and library all rolled into one. He enjoyed extraordinary mental trips as he stared at raindrops on the window and the horizons reeling over the prow.

When he fell asleep at the end of the second night he dreamed of Farid again, the Canadian boy who he had met at Fort Detrick. *"I'm not leaving! I can't leave! Go away and let me stay here!"* He kicked and yelled as the staff tried to remove him from his prison. Brendan had had this dream many times during his life. Perhaps he was now beginning to understand why. "Farid is all of us." he muttered aloud. "The prison is the pre-Disclosure world and everything outside it is the post-Disclosure world." Wasn't Julian, in his own way, just like Farid? Freedom sounds so wonderful to those who do not have it that they never stop to think how frightening it might be if they ever obtain it. It can so frightening that people will run from it like the plague.

Brendan enjoyed his third night in the cockpit more because he knew it would be their last one. He had no navigation aids; no sextant, no sat-director, no radar, no inertial gyroscope. He had been running by dead reckoning alone, but he had stayed on course and at a steady speed which meant they had to hit the coast of New Zealand sometime within the next twenty-four hours. The only electronic communicator was a shortwave analogue radio. Brendan switched it on, but it was silent right along the dial. Sure enough they sighted land just after ten AM. It was a row of woody hills ahead to the southwest. There were large rocks in the shallows, but no cliffs. They stayed about two miles out to sea and turned north. They came across a harbour just before midday. The fuel bunkers were down to their last gallon, making Brendan breathe a sigh of relief as he entered the river estuary that made up the port. He was also very happy to see that things looked normal. There was no damage and no sign of war. Vehicles drove along the roads and people wandered the seafront. A flyer zipped overhead. The houses were all detached and most were single storey. A man in oilskins on the quayside helped them tie the boat up. "Thanks." yelled Brendan. "How are you coping with the war?"

"We're not sure." he shouted back. "New Zealand has not been hit, but the grid is totally down; we're in a media blackout."

The family went ashore into the town and found out that it was called Greymouth. The first priority was to find treatment for William. They took him to the local emergency clinic where he was put onto antibiotics to treat his pneumonia. However the medics there refused to prescribe GMAT or any other anticancer drug for his leukaemia. "But he'll die if you don't give him some!" shrilled Siobhan in the waiting room.

"Not immediately." pacified the doctor in an accent that sounded similar to the Australian one, but had several differences. "We're under martial law at the moment and drugs are rationed. Your son does not count as an urgent case."

Siobhan stormed out of the surgery and fumed on the street for a few minutes before going back to William's bed on the ward. "It's not so bad, Siobhan." said Brendan. "Will is out of immediate danger now they've got his pneumonia under control. When martial law is lifted they'll give him GMAT."

"And how long will that be?"

Brendan sighed. "If New Zealand has survived then other parts of the world will have too."

"How can we find out?... And how can we get Will GMAT?"

The local people filled Brendan in on what had been happening. The news that Canberra had been bombed on Monday evening was the last they heard before the communications grid had been silenced. Everything had gone, international television, international telephones, radio and WorldMesh. "For all we know we're the only people left alive on the planet!" A sales assistant in the local grocery shop had told him. Brendan had an idea. He called the US embassy in Wellington on the North Island and the ambassador made an appointment for a meeting with him. It turned out he was another old friend of Clane Quilley's and remembered Brendan as a child. He promised to send a flyer to pick up Brendan from Greymouth. The aircraft was a typical big government saloon with tinted windows. As soon as it was airborne, Brendan leaned forward and spoke to the driver. "Here, buddy. Could we take a little detour?"

"Where?" The chauffeur was a large man with swarthy features typical of the *Māori*, the indigenous New Zealanders. He had their traditional tattoos on his cheeks.

"The United States."

"What? No way! The government has banned international travel during this state of emergency. What's more it's two hours away. My boss would get suspicious if it took that long to drop you off."

"I shall accept full responsibility... Please." Brendan wished he had not given quite all his cash to the doctor in Sydney. "I'll make sure you get a good tip as soon as I have the money."

"Why do you want to go there?"

"My nephew is very sick and I need to get him medicine... Have you got kids?"

The man nodded. "Yeah, a boy and a girl."

"Then surely you'll understand."

The driver hesitated. "Alright... but I can only go as far as the west coast, California. Then you get the medicine and we turn straight back. No sightseeing. Okay?"

"Agreed."

The sky cleared as the embassy flyer headed across the South Seas. Brendan noticed something about the blue post-lifetrail sky above. There were multiple brightly lit objects scattered across it. They were yellow in colour and arranged in groups of three. He leaned close to the window and squinted. They were not just points of light, they were structured. They were circular, or they could have been discs seen from below. "Are those flyers?" he asked.

"Are what?" said the driver.

"Those." Brendan pointed.

The driver leaned forward so that he could see upwards through the windscreen. He gasped. "*Rangi!*"

"Pardon?"

"It's *Rangi!*" The man looked delighted.

"What's that?"

"Sorry, mate. *Rangi* is kind of what my people call God."

Brendan was about to chuckle dismissively, but then stopped and looked up at the objects again. More were appearing on the forward horizon. Judging by their apparent change of position relative to the sea below, they were clearly at a very high altitude. The fact that he could make out their shape meant that they must be of some considerable size. "They're MFO's." he said. "They're extraterrestrial."

"They're *Rangi*." insisted the driver.

Brendan shrugged. He knew that he couldn't rule it out. Even the most serious and level-headed MFOlogists admitted that there was a spiritual element to the phenomenon. Maybe MFO's were something to do with God.

The first sign that they were approaching the coast of California was a huge swathe of grey haze ahead. It looked like a cloud of ash from a volcano. Brendan gulped down bile and braced himself. The land appeared on the horizon and it was a line of blackness. He recognized the outline of Catalina Island below them and knew they were approaching Metropolitan Los Angeles, or what should have been that. In place of the city was a plain of broken black masonry, like cinders from a giant's fire pit. Palls of smoke rose from patches of it and the glowing of fires still alight dotted the infernal landscape as if it were cooling lava. There was not a single living thing to be seen. Brendan had been expecting this and preparing himself for it. He recalled his father's descriptions of Hiroshima from his time in Japan after World War II. The driver started weeping and chanting quietly in his own language.

"Can we go on a bit further?" Brendan asked him tremulously. "Please... This is my country and I want to see how much of it is left."

"Of course." replied the driver.

Away from Los Angeles the devastation was less complete. In San Bernardino County a few buildings were still standing and people could be seen walking along the pavements. Brendan's hopes rose when they reached Phoenix, Arizona and saw no sign of any bombing.

The driver exclaimed as two flyers suddenly appeared on both sides. "Shit!"

Brendan looked out and saw that they were US Army Air Force interceptors. "Do you have a radio?"

"Sure." He switched it on.

A voice came through from one of the interceptors. "USFS vehicle, state your business! This is restricted airspace."

The driver handed Brendan the microphone. "This is Brendan Quilley. I'm seeking urgent medical treatment for my family who are US citizens stranded in New Zealand."

There was a long pause. "Very well. Lay to out quarters and follow us." The two escorts flew northwest across the United States. Brendan's spirits were restored as he failed to see any more signs of nuclear attack. They flew over bustling cities, sweet towns, green forests and blue clean rivers. "I don't believe it." said Brendan. "They're safe. There was no further bombing... But I saw the missiles launch! Julian fired every single one of them."

"*Rangi* saved us." said the driver brightly.

Brendan looked up. The MFO's were still there, hanging over the land like golden lace.

They landed in a carpark on the side of a wooded hill in Pennsylvania. A cluster of important looking military officers were waiting for them. "Mr Quilley, follow us please."

Brendan waved goodbye to the driver and walked off in the wake of the officers. He wondered where they were taking him, seeing as he had landed in the middle of nowhere. However he soon understood when they walked down a stairway in a tunnel leading downwards into the ground. Below the carpark was a sizeable underground military base. He had been in a few such facilities before when his father was in government service. He had also seen the ones declassified and converted into museums like Area 51 and Montauk. This one was clearly active though, and he had never heard of it before. The officers took him down in a lift. He walked along a quiet corridor to an office with a large conference table in it. He was left alone sitting in one of the chairs around the table and dozed heavily; he had not slept well on the boat and was still suffering from sleep deprivation. He woke up with a jolt when two of the officers came back in. They sat down in chairs opposite him and asked him an array of questions about his experiences in Australia and what happened during the nuclear attack. He answered as best as he could, but wished the men would offer him as bed to sleep in. Then they asked him a question that made him alert: "Have you at any time experienced symptoms such as having black liquid exude from your body, from they eyes, mouth or nose?"

He nodded.

The two men looked at each other.

"May I ask why?"

"It's something a lot of people are experiencing at the moment." After a few more questions they left him in the room. The lights on the ceiling were bright and his head began to ache. The door opened again and this time another group of suited and uniformed men entered and in the middle of them was the compact figure of President LaRey Tavinor. Brendan instinctively got to his feet. "Madam President."

She smiled at him as she sat down on a chair at the head of the table. "It's good to see you again, Brendan." she said. "After what's happened since we last met..." She stopped.

"I know."

"You tell me you have family abroad who survived."

"Yes, my sister and her two children. They're safe at the moment. They're in New Zealand, but my nephew has leukaemia and needs treatment which the health service there will not provide."

"We'll do our best to make sure he has the care he needs... Sit down, gentlemen." Her entourage took their seats at the table; there were just enough chairs for them all.

"Madam President." said Brendan. "What has been happening?... Why are we all still alive?"

She paused. "We're not sure. We all ought to be dead. This is something we've been mulling over and over in theory since the start of Cold War One. We have computer models and impact assessment studies..."

"I saw LA." he interrupted.

"Los Angeles is gone, as is most of Houston. Warheads also impacted Brasilia, Johannesburg and an English town called Milton Keynes. However of the hundred and ninety units launched by the Red Bloc, all but seven of them malfunctioned. All but three of our two hundred and eleven did. One of the successful ones was the bomb that landed on Canberra."

"You fired back didn't you?" he asked rhetorically.

"Of course." she answered deadpan. "As soon as we

detected the incoming strike we immediately launched a full retaliatory spread. That has always been our policy... Along with Canberra we also took out part of Brisbane and Tripoli."

There was a long silence, then Brendan said: "So the Volta Union was not bombed?"

"No."

He sighed deeply. "Then my dad is safe."

She nodded awkwardly. "Quite likely. Although there have been reports of conventional fighting in the north of the country between the VU army and TSSR forces."

"How do you know, seeing as the global communications network is down?"

"We're using emergency encrypted VHF relays via our embassies and regional commands."

"Ah!" Brendan ran a hand across his face. "So Ireland wasn't hit either. Heather is okay too. Thank God!... What happened to those missiles? Why did they all malfunction?"

LaRey Tavinor responded with a half smile. She slowly raised her head to look up at the ceiling.

"The MFO's!"

One of the officers raised his hand.

The president was clearly chairing the meeting. "General Leyton?"

"As head of Strategic Strike Command I witnessed it happen, Mr Quilley." he said. "At first the missiles all ran normally. They completed their boost phase and entered their ballistic trajectory. By then they were above the earth's atmosphere. Then... these things appeared; brightly lit saucer-shaped objects, just like the Roswell craft. They just plucked them out of space. It was like watching somebody pick up sticks from a river. Then they disappeared back out into deep space. Our observer corps telescopes filmed the whole thing." General Leyton was trying to keep his professional composure, but his shock, relief and numbness were all painted on his face like a road sign.

"We obviously have a lot to thank the MFO's for." Tavinor said fervently.

Brendan suddenly remembered something he had seen many years ago when he was sitting in a parked flyer with

Siobhan monitoring Dave Pearson's house in case he was abducted by aliens. He had watched a video which featured a Capt. Robert Salas talking about how visiting MFO's disabled the nuclear missiles at his launch facility. As his mind drifted, Brendan yawned again.

"Are you tired, Brendan?" asked Tavinor.

"Yes, exhausted." He was grateful she had asked. He felt embarrassed to raise the subject himself. "If fact I was wondering if you had a cot handy I could use for the night."

Her expression changed instantly to a frown. "Absolutely not, Lt. Quilley! You are still an active operative with Seaguard. You will report to your ship for duty with all dispatch."

"Why? What for? The war's over!"

"No it's not. We're invading the Red Bloc."

There was a long silence. The military officers around the table didn't flinch.

"Whether or not their missiles malfunctioned, the union of nations we call the Red Bloc has proven itself to be a threat to the United States... and everywhere else for that matter, and it is willing to take hostile action. That threat must be removed!"

"Make this a clean war." Brendan did not speak those words intentionally. They were out of his mouth before he understood what they meant.

"What do you mean?"

"We fight in accordance with the code of the warrior, not the Illuminati puppet. We engage combatants only, not civilians. Let's make history, Madam President. Let's make the United States the pioneer of a new code of military ethics."

She guffawed sarcastically. "I had no idea you'd been trained as a strategist, Lt. Quilley... We'll do whatever we have to do to keep America safe. That means whatever it takes to win; and you will obey all orders in accordance with your company's contract. Understood?"

He jumped to his feet and saluted her. "Yes, Ma'am."

Chapter 18

Brendan had another black goo attack on the US Navy flyer. The substance dripped down his cheeks and onto his flight suit. None of the crew members spotted it. He blinked and wiped his eyes with the back of his hands. As before, in the guest room at the Sydney US consulate, the flow stopped after a few minutes and the sentient oil dissolved into nothing. He was on his way out to sea to be picked up by Seaguard *Foyle*. When war broke out, the refit had just finished and so the submarine put to sea. Luckily the work being done was minor and the boat had not been cut open in a dry-dock. The flyer began to descend and out of his window Brendan could see a tiny speck on the surface of the ocean, too small to recognise, but as they came closer he could see that it was a submarine. The flyer manoeuvred carefully as it slowed to match the submarine's speed and course. Then it eased itself down onto the rear casing. It kept its engines running and its lift active as Brendan stepped from the open door of the craft onto the rubber acoustic coating of the submarine's deck. He looked up at the bridge and saw Capt. Vine's white hair and beard whipping in the breeze. He laughed and saluted his captain. Vine returned the salute with a smile that was visible even from that distance.

....

"Conn, sonar. Master seventeen now bears three-oh-two." came Ears Keen's voice in Brendan's voicelink earphones.

"Conn, aye." he replied. He was standing on the conn by the periscope, which was lowered at their current depth. He had been directing the underwater vessel for the last three hours. "Helm, all ahead two-thirds. Keep periscope depth." he ordered. The submarine responded and the hull creaked to accompany the water pressure being released as they came shallow. Capt. Vine walked in through the control room door. He did not interfere with Brendan's actions, but he watched carefully. Brendan ordered the periscope raised and quickly gained a visual contact. There were four ships in the surface action group, all from the Socialist Republic of Australia. The air was so clear that their shapes were distinct, even at the range of eight nautical miles. The previous day they had bombarded a convoy of LoW troop carriers emerging from the Straits of Gibraltar and were now heading toward the Canary Islands, possibly to destroy the LoW naval base on Lanzarote. That base would shortly come into range of their SS-N-22 land attack cruise missiles. Brendan looked round at the captain; Vine nodded. "Battle stations!" Brendan called. A warbling alarm echoed through the steel pressure hull and it was mixed with the pattering of feet as the crew rushed though the boat. The footwear of all personnel was "still-shoes", specially designed with a soft sole to prevent the noise of footfalls being picked up by enemy hydrophones. As soon as Lt. Gary Marsden arrived, Brendan handed the conn over to him and made his way towards his own battle station at the front of the control room, the target motion analyzer. Gary was at the periscope and he fed details of the targets and Brendan used the electronic system to generate a firing solution. The accuracy gauge began to stack up and the arrows and lines on the display became more solid. He had to work out not where the targets were now, but where they would be when the torpedoes met them. "Attackie, I have a firing solution on Targets seven, eight and nine."

"Very well. Make the weapons in tubes one to six ready in all respects."

"Flooding tubes and opening bow caps." said a weapons technician.

"Fire tubes ones and two!"

"Shoot and vent!" The torpedoes were launched in three pairs. They rasped through the Atlantic Ocean towards the SRA ships. These warships were not such soft targets as the whalers. They detected the incoming torpedoes with their own hydrophones, turned tail and bolted at over thirty knots. This speed was no match for the torpedoes sixty knots in a flat race, but the ships had a good head start. There was a risk the weapons would run out of fuel before catching them up or that the opening range would make the submarine lose sonar contact on the ships. Then the ships could carry out evasive manoeuvres and dodge the torpedoes. The ships were also dropping noisemakers and bubble generators into the sea to confuse *Foyle*'s sonar and neutralize the torpedoes' homing sounders. Ears worked hard to keep the ships in contact. Brendan and the firecon tech guided the torpedoes via the trailing wires. Just when they had seriously begun the think that they had missed, that the attack had failed and that the vessels would then be free to fire their missiles at Lanzarote, there came the audible crump of a marine explosion followed by two more. Everybody in the control room cheered. Ears then reported the sound of the ships breaking apart as they sank to the bottom of the sea. Since the war had begun two months earlier their current score was three attacks made and all were successful.

....

Conn, radio. Receiving flash ELF." called the sailor in the communications room. Seaguard *Foyle* had picked up its call sign on the extremely low frequency band, the only radio waves that could penetrate the ocean to any extent. This was an order to come to periscope depth and receive a more detailed message via a satellite link. Brendan was officer-of-the-deck again and he ordered the vessel upwards from its cruising depth of six hundred feet. When they were shallow enough, he raised the radio antenna and downloaded the message. Captain Vine emerged from his stateroom where he had been enjoying a rare nap and read the printed out transmission. He reached for the ship wide public address. "Attention all hands, this is the captain." Everybody aboard stopped what they were doing to listen. "We have been ordered to carry out a missile attack against a target on land. Battle stations in five minutes."

Brendan was once again working in the fire control section of the control room. His job was different from when they were pursuing a seaborne target. The torpedo tubes were loaded with cruise missiles, similar to those the SRA ships were planning to fire onto Lanzarote a few days earlier. He programmed the navigation computers inside the missiles with the coordinates of the land target that was to be eliminated. There was a pause as the missiles' engines were activated. During those three minutes, just for curiosity's sake, Brendan looked up the location of the target on the map. It was in the Trans-Saharan Socialist Republic just a few miles north of Niamey... He stopped as still as a statue. He couldn't be absolutely certain; but, according to the map, the grid reference was close to the farm he had lived on back in

March. Even if it wasn't, it still made him wonder what was in the area of military value. He had been in that location and seen nothing, but sand, scrub and earth. He tried to dismiss such thoughts. This was one of the problems of serving in a submarine. Because of the isolation from the outside world, none of the men knew how the war was progressing outside their own small role in it. They operated purely on orders received from operations command. It was quite possible that the TSSR authorities had found a nuclear missile they'd forgotten they had and built a launch silo where *Foyle* had been ordered to fire its missiles...

"Mr Quilley!" yelled the captain.

"Yes, sir?"

"Are you paying attention? I repeat: status of land attack missile in tube one."

"Sorry, sir. Compressor is at fifty percent and rising correctly." A cold bath of guilt and insecurity came over him. He checked the map again and this time blended the display with a civilian satellite image. "Oh no!" he muttered. Even from above he recognized the school hut, the millet fields, Alaqui's office, the parked handcart. There was no doubt about it. He saw human figures in the image, made visible by their shadows. They could have been Nyala, Yousef, Hosn or Jemel... One of the smaller shadows might be little Axmet.

"Flood and equalize tube one." ordered Capt. Vine.

Brendan's hand moved to the switch and stopped, frozen, unable to move as if embedded in stone. He felt a terrifying precariousness come over him, as if he were crossing a rope bridge over a chasm.

The captain frowned. "Mr Quilley, I said flood and equalize tube one!... What's wrong with you today?"

"Captain, I think there's been a mistake. There is no valid target at the coordinated point in the attack order."

"What are you talking about, man!?"

"I'm familiar with the place, sir. I spent six weeks there a few months ago. It's just a farm, sir; a simple farm."

Capt. Vine's face flushed red between his white hair and beard. "I don't give a damn about what's in your holiday diary, Quilley! We have orders to attack and destroy that location and we are going to do it!... Now obey your orders and flood that tube!"

"I can't do that, sir." Brendan's own voice sounded unrecognizable in his ears; it was a completely different tone.

There was a catatonic silence in the control room as all eyes turned to stare. The captain broke it: "Lt. Quilley, stand relieved! Coxswain! Place Lt. Quilley under arrest for gross insubordination and mutiny, and escort him to the brig."

Brendan got up from his seat as two burley sailors walked over to him. "Come quietly now, sir." said the coxswain. The men forced Brendan's arms behind his back and secured his wrists with handcuffs.

"Chief Meigs!" snapped the captain. "Take Mr Quilley's place in firecon. Flood tube one."

Another crewmember sat down in the seat Brendan had been sitting in and pulled the switch calmly and easily. His face was blank like a robot. There was a burbling sound as the torpedo tube filled with water. "Tube one flooded and equalized, sir." he recited. The missile was almost ready to fire.

Brendan was quivering with terror. He remembered his last conversation with President Tavinor: "*Make this a clean war.*"

"Open bow caps!" commanded Vine.

"Opening bow caps aye, sir!" responded Meigs.

"Prepare ignition, stand by to shoot!"

"Ignition prepared and firecon is standing by, sir!"

Suddenly the radioman's voice broke in over the emergency tannoy: "Conn, radio. Receiving flash traffic, status immediate! Repeat: status immediate! Recommend alert one!"

"Hold fire!" said Vine.

"Hold fire aye, sir." said Meigs quietly, looking over his shoulder at the skipper.

Vine ran forward to the radio room. He returned carrying a printout. His face changed from red to pale as he scanned the lines; his cheeks were now almost as white as his beard. "Shut bow caps, drain tube, secure missile." he almost whispered.

In the silence of the control room, everybody heard him.

He walked over to the conn and picked up to public address microphone. "Attention all hands. This is the captain. The land attack has been cancelled. Secure battle stations at the end of this pipe... We have just received this immediate message from ops command, and I quote: 'Coordinated unconditional surrender of all Red Bloc forces has been made. TSSR and SRA governments have agreed to resign and hand over all sovereignty to the League of the World. Cease all offensive operations with immediate effect.'... The war is over."

The submarine resounded and vibrated to a cheering and whooping that it had never experienced before. Crewmembers embraced each other, jumped for joy and prayed.

Capt. Vine replaced the microphone on its holder and slowly walked over to where Brendan was standing, handcuffed with two men-at-arms by his side, ready to be dragged off to the brig. He gazed hard into Brendan's eyes. "Release Mr Quilley." he ordered. The coxswain obediently unlocked the handcuffs and Brendan's arms swung free. "Lt. Quilley, under the circumstances..." began Vine. "I am willing to forget what happened here a few minutes ago. Your actions will be struck from the log."

Brendan nodded. He couldn't think of anything to say. He felt no gratitude or relief. His mind and heart were numb.

Chapter 19

"Pah!" scoffed Gary Marsden. "He probably just wants to avoid the paperwork."

Brendan took a sip of English beer. "The old man was right though. What I did was mutiny. If I had got a court for that I'd have been guilty as hell... But it's been a whole month and he still hasn't done anything. He must mean what he said; he's overlooked the whole thing... Christ that was lucky! What unbelievable timing. A few seconds later and that missile would have been away."

"Luck of the Irish!" Marsden took a drag on his cigarette and mixed the smoke in his mouth with a gulp of bitter. "Seaguard has a reputation for being a very lucky company and you, my friend, have procured about half of it." The two officers were sitting in a quaint country pub in a village called Peene just outside Folkestone in Kent. The place was just like the pubs Brendan had seen in tourist brochures, a flagstone floor, old wooden beams, thatched roof, a low ceiling and a jar of pickled eggs on the bar. The other patrons were mostly locals and they gave the strangers disapproving sideways glances. Brendan heard the epithets "yank" and "paddy" rise above the clamour occasionally. Brendan looked out of the window. The hostelry had a beautiful view of the coastline. There were numerous warships at anchor a mile or so out. Too many had put into Dover and Folkestone for the harbour to accommodate them all. A service of small boats connected the craft to the port and it was in one of these that the men of Seaguard *Foyle* had landed for a well-earned run ashore. Most of the crew had hit the urban centres, but Brendan and his friend preferred somewhere quieter where they could talk. Directly below the hill on which the pub stood, between Peene and Folkestone, was what looked like a huge building site full of chaotic arrangements of machinery and buildings. In the middle of it were three gigantic cylindrical objects hundreds of feet long and about forty feet in diameter. "Is that a tunnel boring machine?" Brendan pointed. "I thought there already was a tunnel here. Didn't they dig a tunnel under the English Channel back in the sixties?"

"They did." said Gary. "And now they're filling it in. That's not a tunnel boring machine; it's a tunnel filling machine.

If I've heard about it, how come a grease-monkey like you hasn't?"

"I guess I'm too blinkered by my speciality of nautical engineering... Tunnel *filling* machine?"

"Yes. See the flat face at the back? That's where they feed hot semi-fluid crushed rock and press it until it's solid. The grinders at the front break up the tunnel walls and the opening at the front is where the rubble is passed out and transported back along the tunnel to the other end. It'll take a few years, but eventually the machine will reach the other end and the tunnel will be gone."

"Hmm, I remember seeing something like that when I was a kid and they demolished the Hoover Dam. Why fill in a tunnel? I mean, I know it's been disused for a long time, but it seems a waste of effort to fill it in. Why not just leave it?"

"It's LoWEHO policy. The earth has to be returned to its natural state as much as possible, and that includes removing tunnels. When they've finished here it will be like that tunnel was never built in the first place."

Brendan laughed. "Why not just leave it be? Who will be the injured party if a disused tunnel is running under the English Channel? Will some rare seagull be threatened with extinction or something?... How much is this white elephant costing?"

Marsden laughed too. "Gawd knows! But it's an interesting story; I've been following it... You know they're also filling in cuts and gaps, land grading alterations on roads and railways and the like. They're using a similar system. They've got these huge machines called 'naaiers' that wander back and forth along the excavated space dropping red hot rock and patting it down. Eventually they plan to fill in everything that was dug out and the landscape will be natural again."

There was a long silence and then Gary said: "Isn't it about time we went home?"

Brendan nodded. "The war's been over a month. All we do is patrol empty seas."

"There's talk of guerrilla resistance in the former Red Bloc."

"But those guerrillas don't have ships. Let Landguard cope with it."

"Any news on the family?"

"None. The grid is still down. When's it going to be fixed?"

"Somebody's working on it, according to the news."

"Then this 'somebody' is having a rather long tea break. They must be English."

"Shh!" warned Gary as a few eyes turned their way.

Brendan lowered his voice. "I've tried to get a message through via the embassy and through ops command, but they couldn't do it... or wouldn't! Last time I saw the family it was in New Zealand back in May... I'm worried about William the most. He's very ill and needs treatment."

It was late when Brendan and Gary left the pub. Gary took a taxi, but Brendan chose to walk. It was a warm August evening and the sunset was still glowing slightly on the western horizon. The countryside was quiet as it always was in England at night. No crickets could be heard and the occasional hoot of an owl was the only sign of nature. He strolled down the narrow lane leading back into Folkestone and thought about Siobhan and the twins. They were surely thinking about him too. The sky was a dark blue hemisphere peppered with stars. The MFO's had gone now. They had dissipated the previous month over a period of a few days. The town of Folkestone was clean and well spread out. Apart from the occasional drunk coming out of a nightclub, including some he recognized from the Seaguard fleet, the place was peaceful. The St George's Cross, the flag of the Republic of England, flew from windows, lampposts and trees. His father had visited Britain in 1955 and Brendan always wanted to go too and see what the place was like. Twenty years later it had transformed as much as the rest of the world, although it had to do so quicker.

Most of the crew had to make their way back to the submarine after their night out, with all the danger that riding in a small boat while intoxicated with alcohol entailed. Brendan had booked himself into a small hotel ashore. The crew had three days liberty so the following morning he hired a motorflyer and took off to explore the country. He passed over London. He was not too bothered about seeing it and had indeed visited it for a few hours for his tenth birthday trip.

He still had unpleasant memories of how he'd felt after the show in the London Planetarium. He decided to visit another famous place and so headed northwest following a disused motorway that was in the process of being broken up. He saw some grey smoke ahead on a ridge of hills coming from a patch of red combustion. For a moment he thought that it was a forest fire, but when he got closer he saw that it was the LoWEHO doing their stuff again. He stitched to autopilot and used the motorflyer's built-in slate to look up what he was seeing online. He was above the Stokenchurch Gap, a huge cutting created by the Mosley regime the 1950's for the F-Forty motorway to cross the Chiltern Hills. It was now being filled in so that the countryside could be returned to its original natural condition. Brendan recalled talking about this with Gary in the pub the previous evening. Below him, the land filling operation was underway and the fire that he had seen was in fact the heated chalk gravel being deposited in layers by a naaier. The naaier was shaped like a starfish and was about a hundred feet across. It moved at less than a walking pace. In its wake the new surface cooled and turned black. More pure while chalk was piled up in a field to one side of the naaier waiting to be inserted into the remains of the Stokenchurch Gap. Some agitator-cum-artist on the cut-filling team had arranged some of the fill into giant letters, so big that they must have been invisible from the ground. They spelled the maxim of the LoWEHO across the green Oxfordshire meadow: "IT'S NOT TOO LATE".

Five minutes later he came to Oxford, home of the famous university. This was a place nobody in his family had ever been to and he felt quite proud to be the first Quilley to go there. He orbited the tall spires sprouting from grey slate roofs and looked down into quads of precise square lawns. He parked the motorflyer in a slot near the railway station and wandered through the streets lined by ancient yellow-brown stone. Students walked past him in knots of three or four. There were people on bicycles everywhere. Grotesque gargoyles peered down at pedestrians. He entered a college pronounced "maudlin", but for some reason was spelled *Magdalen*. Inside the college he saw a quad from ground level. The buttresses around the outside were topped by strange statues. Some were recognizable and others were more abstract. Brendan purchased a guidebook that explained that these images were created almost five hundred years age by an unknown sculptor. Some represented biblical scenes, others were heraldic, but two in particular were of interest in lieu of recent revelations. They appeared to be statues of reptilian humanoids. Did the sixteenth century artist who carved them know about the Illuminati and their true nature? How long had the reptilians been in control of planet earth? The guidebook had only questions in this regard and no answers, which was fairly common at that time. He left the college and wandered up a narrow winding road between the university's walls called Queen's Lane. It ran underneath a covered arched bridge that joined one building to another and right next to that was the internationally acclaimed Museum of Geoengineering. It was a structure in the so-called "heart of Oxford" from which experts had been recruited into the chemtrail programme. Today it was a memorial and a warning for the future. Brendan didn't enter it, but went instead to the tourist information office. After Disclosure, it had turned out that Oxford had been a major centre of global Illuminati power, especially in the field of education. There were numerous hidden chambers below the streets and colleges. There were secret scientific enclaves where unspeakable experiments had been carried out on animals and humans that matched the horrors of Montauk. There were archives of information accessible only to the initiated elite, especially inside the Bodleian Library, which had a secret vault containing millions of occult books. It was said to be one of the biggest depositories of secret knowledge in the world, along with the Vatican library. Both institutions were still being analyzed and the full results were yet to be published, but some historians were commenting that the information included lost texts from the Library of Alexandria which had been burnt down by the Illuminati in the fourth century. If this was a fact then the full worth of the covert knowledge buried beneath Oxford was beyond calculation.

Brendan was downhearted by all the tales of evil and clandestine enlightenment so he took himself out of the city centre and flew around the suburban districts of Oxford for a while. The most prominent structure outside of the university was a large ivory coloured oblong building that stood on the summit of a hill to the northeast. The carpark sign said: "*John Radcliffe Hospital*". As he cruised over its flat roof a warning alarm sounded from the dashboard that he was violating restricted airspace. He understood why when an ambulance flyer shot past him at high speed, its blue lights flickering, and speedily landed outside the accident and emergency entrance. He swung his aircraft onto a reciprocal course and descended to a parking area just outside the hospital. He walked up a long straight road and came out on a busy street than ran sharply uphill. Across the road was a pub with a signboard announcing its name as *The Britannia*. It was lunchtime and he was hungry and thirsty so Brendan entered the pub and saw that the majority of customers were staff from the hospital. Nurses with their own jackets thrown over their white dresses, doctors who had forgotten to remove the stethoscopes from around their necks and many others. He ordered a pint of bitter and sat down at a table. He watched with amusement as a benign but heated argument broke out between two men at the bar. One of them was a small thin individual with shoulder length brown hair and a crooked nose. He was sitting on a barstool with an overflowing ashtray beside him. "You're nothing, Ben!" He spat in a strong Glaswegian accent. "Honestly, you're nothing at all!"

"Well we'll have to differ on that, Jack." said his companion who was standing beside him. He was a much younger and taller man; but he was equally thin, so his stature gave him an emaciated appearance. He was wearing a uniform which included a pale blue polo shirt. He had a cherubic face and his head was surrounded by a huge afro of thick brown hair. He addressed Jack in a much calmer voice.

"You're absolutely fuck all!" Jack jabbed a finger at Ben.

"A few minutes ago you said that we were the heartbeat of the hospital."

"Don't fuck around with my head!"

"But you said it! How can we be the heartbeat and nothing at the same time?"

Jack stubbed out his cigarette with irritated movements. "Why don't you do your training, for fucks sake!?"

"I have done my training. I'm a qualified manual handling trainer..."

"No, I mean something better than fuckin' portering!... you could become a nurse! You could become a paramedic! You could become an ODP!"

Ben sighed. "Jack haven't we had this conversation before? I'm a grown man and I've made a decision about what I want to do with my own life."

"Yeah, but you've made the wrong decision!"

"I must respectfully disagree."

Jack gasped. "Are you seriously telling me you want to be a porter your entire life!?"

"You say 'porter' as if it's a dirty word."

"It *is* a dirty word for most people!"

"Well then you go and kiss the arses of these 'most people'. You go put them on a pedestal. I refuse to model my life on their stupidity... I mean seriously, why does this bug you so much? Have you ever stopped to wonder to yourself why you are so obsessed with another man's professional life?"

"I don't like watching you waste your life, Ben."

"To be a hospital porter is not a waste of anybody life." retorted Ben. "To be a hospital porter is to be an essential member of a lifesaving team doing one of the most important jobs in the world."

"How many people actually think that apart from *you*!?"

"How many people can explain logically why I am incorrect?"

Jack paused and lit another cigarette. "What you've got to understand is that you are on your own here! The people who agree with me are the overwhelming majority."

Ben shrugged emphatically. "Life is not an election."

He glared angrily and stuttered. "But... I used to be a porter too! I went up the ladder! I improved myself. That's all I want for you."

"Have you ever asked me if I actually want to be a Jack Mark 2?"

He paused. "For the last time, Ben... *Please*! Train! Get into nursing, get into tech, get into anything other than being a fuckin' porter till the day you die."

Ben took a step back and drew himself up to his full height.

He punched the air and shouted: "Never!... I say it clear and I say it loud! I'm a porter and I'm proud!"

Brendan had been enjoying being a spectator to this unique wrangle on an issue he had never considered before, and so had not been paying attention to the news programme that was playing on the television screen hanging on the far wall. "Hey!" somebody called. "Did you hear that? She said the grid is back up! Can that be true?"

"Anybody got their roam with them?" asked a man at a table.

"No, I stopped carrying mine around ages ago. There was no point." said another.

Brendan's hand automatically went to his pocket. His roamphone was there. He had had it in his pocket back in May when he drove to Australia following Siobhan's message. He had forgotten all about it because the instrument was useless in the Red Bloc and had been equally so outside it since the war began. He pressed the start-up button and the device came to life. The screen lit up and, sure enough, the signal indicator was fully barred. It immediately bleeped to alert him to incoming messages. "Wow!" he exclaimed.

The other pub patrons looked at him. "Hey! Have you got a signal, mate?... This bloke's got a signal!... I'm going home to get my roam!" People crowded round him in wonder as if seeing a roamphone for the first time.

Brendan took no notice; he just read the names of the torrents of text messages and E-grams that were pouring in. Four months of backlogged data: *Dad... Dad... Siobhan... Heather... Heather... Dad... Siobhan... Heather...* "I gotta go!" He jumped up and ran out of the pub leaving his pint half-finished.

....

It took Brendan hours to sift through the thousands of messages. They dated back to early May when he had first crossed the former SRA border, but some were time stamped to the present day. He sat on the pillion of his motorflyer in the carpark as he went through the most recent ones; those were the most important. He panted with emotion as he read the first communications he'd received from his family since the beginning of the war in May. He started the motorflyer and zoomed back to Folkestone as fast as he could. He arrived there within thirty minutes. The flyer hire firm then leased him a larger flyer that he could use for a longer journey. He drove westwards across the Atlantic Ocean and North America until the morning sun set in his windscreen. He knew his liberty pass expired the following morning and so, if he was not back at his ship he would be listed as absent-without-leave; but he didn't care. During the journey he activated the autopilot and spent the three-hour flight reading more of the epic of past E-grams.

The sun was about to rise again as he landed in Hawaii. There was a huge crowd of people outside the Pearl Harbour naval complex. They were all relatives of the people about to arrive on a dozen LoW frighteners that had been hastily deployed to bring home the hundred and fifty thousand US citizens who had been stranded abroad since the first missiles launched. The local police department and other authorities did their best to cope with the sudden influx of visitors. Flyers swooped down like a swarm of wasps. People crowded onto a patch of parkland near the Pearl Harbour visitors' centre. Brendan stayed with his flyer, sitting in the driving seat and waiting. As the sun rose, the first frightener appeared as a dot eclipsing it. The giant antigravity airship floated down, the League of the World emblem embossed on its side. Its open deck was crowded with passengers waving, far too distant for recognition. The frightener flew over the dark shape in the water, the wreck of battleship USS *Arizona* that had been sunk in its berth thirty-four years earlier. It settled above the water, covering the space between the visitors' centre and Ford Island. Gangways were lowered on both sides to allow the passengers to disembark.

It took all day to corral the refugees off the aerial vessel. The police had to seal off the gangways several times to prevent overcrowding and the risk of human crushes. Buses, both aerial and ground, were brought in to ferry the people away. It was not until three PM that Brendan saw them. Siobhan came out of the visitors' centre gate clutching Colleen by the hand. William was on a separate hospital flyer because of his illness, as Siobhan had explained in her texts. They spotted each other and yelled each others names, rushing forward, pushing past shoulders, kicking over suitcases. They embraced in a group hug of three that became four a few minutes later. Clane Quilley had also been waiting although Clane had not been able to find him in the throng. Father, son, daughter and granddaughter linked arms around each other's bodies and felt their love flow freely around them, smoothly and uninterrupted.

....

"Good morning, William." Dr Flynn grinned in a paternal way as William entered the GP's surgery. Brendan and Siobhan were helping him walk.

William was gaunt and thin. He had started coughing again a few days earlier. "Hi, Dr Flynn." he breathed.

"I've not seen you for a few years. Good to know what a healthy young man you are. What's the problem today?"

"I've got leukaemia." he replied.

The doctor looked up at his mother. Siobhan nodded. "I'm sorry, we have no records, but he was diagnosed by an oncologist back in May. We were living in the Red Bloc at the time."

"No problem. Let me have a look at you, Brendan."

"Will he have to have tests all over again?" asked Siobhan.

Dr Flynn felt William's throat. "No. I'm happy to accept the verdict. This certainly looks like leukaemia to me."

"So he can have GMAT?"

"No. That only works against tumour cancers, but we can give him laetrile. That should soon clear up his leukaemia."

Siobhan gave a huge sigh of relief. "Thank you, doc!... Thank God! At last."

Dr Flynn scribbled on a prescription pad and tore off a sheet. "Right, William. I'm giving you some pills to take. You must take one of these every day and there's a month's supply in here. If you're not better by the time these have run out, your mom will bring you back and we'll give you some more, okay?"

The three of them thanked their trusted family doctor and headed out of the surgery to the nearest chemists' shop. There Siobhan exchanged the small piece of paper for the bottle of little green pills that would save her son's life.

Chapter 20

Brendan wanted to continue watching a television programme about the LoWEHO operation to release captive dolphins and orcas into the wild while his father wanted to watch a baseball game on another channel. "Oh alright, dad." surrendered Brendan and tossed him the TV remote control. Siobhan, Heather, Kerry, Colleen and William laughed at Clane and Brendan's spat. Like all disputes in the family these days, they were token and good-natured. They were sitting in the lounge of Clane's house in Tamale. It was ten AM and outside birds were cawing. It was the middle of the dry season and the lawn was an ochre slab. "I don't know why you don't just spray it." said Brendan to his father. "It's not like you have the excuse of saving water anymore."

Clane shrugged. "I can't be bothered."

"Do the neighbours complain?"

"Constantly, but do I give a shit?"

The broadcast from the baseball game began. "Who are playing?" asked Brendan.

"Don't you follow our great American sport, Bren? The Dodgers of course!"

"I'm American and I've never got into baseball." put in Heather. She was reclined on the settee opposite Clane's armchair. Her belly was like a huge bowling ball beneath her maternity dress.

"Yeah, but you're a girl."

"A *woman*, Clane." corrected Heather. "I'll soon be a mom; I can't be a girl then."

He chuckled. "When you're as younger than me as you are, I can call you nothing else but a girl."

Heather laughed. "Oh, Clane! You make me laugh and that makes the baby kick."

Brendan stood up.

"The game's about to pitch off, Brendan. If you're going to the kitchen could you get me a beer from the fridge?"

Brendan was about to affirm, but then Siobhan cut in: "Dad, it's only ten in the morning."

"Yes, but it's three PM in the Apple and my body clock is permanently locked on New York time... I can't watch a game without a beer now, can I?"

Clane laughed at his father's humour as he reached into the refrigerator and took out one of the stack of chilled bottles lying on one of the shelves like pipes waiting to be laid. He broke off the top with the opener attached to the edge of the fridge door and dropped the buckled steel cap into the recycling bin. Then he walked back into the lounge. His father's armchair was turned with its back to the kitchen door. Clane's crop of grey hair surrounding the bald patch on his crown was visible above the top of the headrest. The sides of his hands could easily be seen resting on the arm. One of them rested on the TV remote like a spider upon its web. In front of him the TV screen flashed and bubbled. The sound of the commentator mixed with the cheering crowd fuzzed into the room from the speakers. Brendan reached the rear of the chair and held out the bottle expecting his father to reach up and take it, but he didn't. "Here you are, dad." he said.

There was no reply.

"Dad?" Brendan walked round to the front of the armchair.

Clane turned his head to look at his son. One of his eyes was closed. "Brendan?" His speech as distorted because only the right half of his mouth moved. A trickle of salvia ran down his chin from the opposite corner. His voice was completely calm and matter-of-fact. "Could you please call an ambulance? I'm having another stroke."

....

"My fellow Americans. Today is the eighth of July 1977. Thirty years ago this very day, at this very time, my predecessor Harry S Truman sat in this same office and addressed the American people to tell them the most important news in the history of the world. We are not alone... We don't know how many intelligent extraterrestrial species there are, we don't know where they come from, but we know they exist. We have decisive forensic evidence in the form of wreckage and corpses that have been salvaged, covertly at first, but now overtly. We know that many of these creatures also know that we exist. They have been visiting this planet and interacting with us since time immemorial. We regularly see their craft in our skies and seas; and many people have contact and abduction experiences. There is a taxonomy of

several hundred positively identified species. What few people knew at the time was that the world was ruled secretly by an organization called the Illuminati, many of whom themselves were a type of extraterrestrial, or extra-dimensional. They had been covering up the truth about this alien presence engaging the human race. This was a secret they were not willing to reveal without a fight and they went to enormous lengths to try and force the genie of Disclosure back into the bottle. Thanks to one of our greatest national heroes, Clane Quilley, they failed. On Saucer Day, all was revealed. However they made another attempt through the usurper Henry A Dealey who later was exposed by Siobhan Quilley and John F Kennedy. Thanks to Dr Jennifer Bulstrode and many others, the interdimensional reptilians were all unmasked on R-Day. Since then we have learned in a very dramatic context that the MFO's are willing to intervene in our affairs, or they were on this one occasion. It's no exaggeration to say that they saved the world from total destruction during the full-scale nuclear exchange that triggered the Red Bloc War. I'd like to say: Thank you, whoever you are... So goes the first thirty years of the post-Disclosure world. How will the next thirty go and the thirty after that, or the hundred after that? Nobody knows. However..."

"She's not really telling us anything we don't already know." said Alaqui. He was reading the French subtitles that were appearing at the bottom of the television screen. "Believe me; I've had to learn it all very quickly."

"*...I am going to endorse formally the League of the World resolution to change the zero date of the Gregorian calendar from the estimated year of the birth of Jesus Christ to the year currently designated as 1947...*"

"Can they do that?" asked Alaqui.

"If everybody else agrees." answered Brendan. "It would mean all dates would then become either after or before Disclosure. I was born in 1952 so I guess that would change to... erm... 5 AD, if it is 'AD'... I guess we could use the same letters to mean 'After Disclosure' instead of *Anno Domini*. Before that would be 'BD- Before Disclosure'. We could use the BC letters perhaps for... er... 'Before Confirmation'. Although that's English; we'd have to change it for other languages, unless we choose to use Latin again. I've no idea what that would be."

Alaqui put a finger to his head. "I was born in 1906, so that would become... 41 BD... I'll never get used to that!"

"It's just an LoW resolution; it's not the word of law yet... Okay I've seen enough. I watched it live last night."

Alaqui switched off the TV showing the recording of the speech made the evening before by President Tavinor.

Brendan said goodbye to his friends on the farm and flew back to Niamey. *Ferme de Mamidou 2*, recently renamed *Ferme d'Alaqui*, had just taken delivery of an antigravity tractor and Brendan wanted to go along when it was delivered. The farmhouses already had had a free energy generator installed a few months earlier. It was what powered the new television set which Alaqui had bought. The old man was very proud of his little millet farm, and it really was his now. He had been allowed to buy it off the League of the World Provisional Government at a discount price. The LoW were selling off all the former TSSR state assets to the citizenry as quickly as they could in order to liberate the former Red Bloc from its state bureaucracy. As his flyer took off, Brendan looked down and saw Jemel and Yousef gleefully sitting in the cab of their new tractor which was hovering two feet above the field. The instructor from the manufacturer was sitting behind them. It moved forward and they ploughed a test furrow. The old pony, named Doudou, was grazing happily in the pasture with the goats as he would for the rest of his life. He would never again have to pull a plough.

In the centre of Niamey, people were putting up decorations to prepare for the upcoming celebration the following Saturday when the Republic of Niger was formally re-established after more than a decade of being a vassal state of the TSSR. The League of the World was eager to end its occupation as soon as possible. This celebration had upstaged Disclosure Thirty, but that was understandable. Brendan drank a cup of tea at a cafe in Niamey and then set off for London. He had an appointment at St Bartholomew's Hospital. The International Sentient Oil Clinic was a new building on the ancient site in London. The doctor who saw Brendan was called Prof. Jeremy Oldfield and he was the world's leading authority in this new medical speciality. "Only three attacks since we last saw you, Mr Quilley. That's good."

"The last one was only a few drops." said Brendan. "Mostly out of my nose."

"There is a general decline in the prevalence. Although there are still over a million people in the world who experience BGS, it seems to be easing."

"Is anybody closer to an answer to what Black Goo Syndrome actually is?"

"No. The substance itself is so unstable that we can't get it to stay in one place long enough to be examined. The fact that it's emerged now indicates that it has in some way been... activated."

"Activated by whom?"

"Nobody knows, but it might be related to Disclosure and the MFO's."

After leaving the doctors, Brendan walked through the streets of London to St Paul's Cathedral. The giant seventeenth century edifice was about to be moved. It had been purchased by a billionaire in Scotland after the Greater London Council threatened to demolish it. Documents from the secret vault in the Bodleian Library in Oxford showed that its architect, Sir Christopher Wren, was a high initiate Freemason and had built the cathedral as a secret Illuminati Satanic temple. Human sacrifices had been carried out inside it. The new owner couldn't bear to see it destroyed, along with a WorldMesh social media group with over ten million members. For over two years workmen had been digging tunnels under St Paul's and installing antigravity lifters. They were creating a giant flying platform to levitate the entire cathedral into the air. A hole of just the right size and shape had been dug on the philanthropist's estate in Midlothian. In a few weeks' time St Paul's Cathedral would be floated through the air to its new home. It would be a delicate operation. Any failure of the platform would cause the load to fall to the ground and break apart. It also had to avoid flying over built-up areas for the sake of safety. It would be flown down the Thames and up the North Sea coast. The weather conditions had to be perfect. Brendan worried over the excessive haste some people were moving in to change everything. There was a movement to change some of the city's names, such anything with "Victoria" in them, and there were other places that were in jeopardy. As Brendan got off the underground train at Victoria Station and looked up at it, he wondered what else people might call it.

The weather was warm and fresh with an affectionate breeze as Brendan crossed the street and left the station forecourt. He walked up Buckingham Palace Road until he got to the square and straight-sided stone edifice. The home of the Illuminati's House of Windsor was completely open to the public now, including the secret basements where the reptilians had carried out their unspeakable Satanic rituals. It had the atmosphere of the preserved World War I trenches. Some of the reproductions were a bit kitsch and excessive, thought Brendan. For instance there were mannequins outside the palace doors dressed as old Household guards and the golden coronation carriage stood in the forecourt. He stopped by the open gates and looked in, watching a group of young children excitedly playing around the coach, unaware of the macabre historical shadow it represented. The children's parents were gathered in a group a few yards away staring up at the palace facade, clustered together for comfort. A handful of people appeared on the balcony where the bloodlines had once stood to greet their minions and looked around curiously, taking a few photos. Brendan left the palace and walked up to Mall towards Trafalgar Square, a location that had been altered. The phallic monolith of Nelson's Column was gone. It had been felled by the communists during their brief ascendancy post R-Day and the square now felt very open and airy, more so than it should have after the loss of the column. The energy and ambiance of the whole area had been altered by the destruction of Nelson's Column. Here Brendan came across one of the few working buildings in the area, the National Gallery. It remained virtually as it had always been and he poked his head inside to examine one or two paintings before heading out to Whitehall. He strolled along the wide, straight imposing road with Big Ben looming over its end. He passed the fibreglass rider and horse that stood outside the Horseguards Entrance and let his eyes wander over the disused old ministry buildings. After R-Day the LoW transitional government had considered moving into these buildings, but had wisely chosen not too. It would have been an insult to themselves and the people of the past, present and future. Then Brendan came to Downing Street and walked up towards Number Ten. The famous black door was shut, preserved in its original form; visitors to the home of the old UK Prime Ministers had to pass in and out of a side entrance. A pair of happy looking young women sat on the steps outside the front door laughing at something, perhaps a joke about the old regime. Brendan turned back to Whitehall and made his way to the houses of Parliament. He had now entered the former operational heartland of the country, where the Illuminati-occupied government had dominated and abused the entire nation and empire. He crossed over the now pedestrianized roads and sat on a bench in Parliament Square in front of the pavement where protesters had once had their tents. The afternoon sun warmed his back. Visitors were coming in and out of the building, blinking in the sunlight like freed miners, all wearing dazed expressions on their faces from their experience of wandering the dark, echoing chambers. Some couldn't face it. Some people hated those buildings with a passion. There was another social media group with over ten million members calling for the place to be immediately demolished, along with all the other putrid oblong piles of the Illuminati's *Ancien Regime*. Brendan felt no repulsion from these buildings; in fact they looked and felt to him like innocuous facsimiles of their former selves. The gloom and menace that they had once radiated was dulled. He actually felt a sense of gloating as he looked at them; they were like the enemies' heads impaled on poles, the broken spear of the invading general. Where men in dark suits had once sat together over brandy and cigars and plotted the enslavement of the British people, tourists and school parties now wandered. Couples from Japan now sat at the Commons Dispatch Box and students from Scotland reclined in the Speaker's Chair laughing as their friends took photos of them.

Flyers zoomed past Big Ben. The air he was breathing in was clean; in fact Brendan had recently seen a news story stating that there was now little difference between urban and rural air quality. As for the people who walked the pavement, they were a contrast beyond striking. People didn't walk so much these days as glide. It was now three PM and the after work rush-hour was beginning. Brendan found that few people in England wore suits. The cipher of the Illuminati gopher was now something of a taboo wear, revived only by the most stalwart conservative. Nowadays the London pedestrians usually wore casual clothes or multicoloured smart shirts and trousers, the new office dress. Pastel-hued open-collars and short sleeves without buttons and slack ankle length trousers seemed to be the form. Many blouses and shirts sported eye-catching patterns, emblems and pictures. A number of women wore skirts which were long and thin. Many of their hems were ragged and decorated with beads and embroidery. Brooches punctuated busts and bright buckled and tie-died sashes divided costumes at the waist. Brendan raised his eyebrows to himself as this thought went through his mind. He left the bench and strolled through the subway to the Embankment. The River Thames was a shimmering crystalline plate of china blue with a hint of grey from the silt that it carried from its watershed. The musty smell of life, soil, fish and plants wafted over from it on the light easterly breeze. The refreshing vapour from its surface moistened his airways. Riverboats were cruising back and forth, mostly pleasure craft full of sightseers and people relaxing with a drink or meal. The Schauberger ducts of the vessels produced a much less visible wake than screws. Happy voices echoed off the facades of the disused government buildings as crowds of people poured down the streets from their workplaces to the pubs and cafes. There was a large food market on the corner from which columns of people filed in and out. Brendan approached and entered, breathing deeply as delicious aromas met his nose. The door was propped open on a warm afternoon like this. A plaque above the lintel stated: *Glasson's Lush-Mart- Operated in partnership by the Glasson and London Retail Force Workers Cooperatives*. He smiled and looked around for the shop's staff. One walked towards him carrying a box of pineapples. She was a young woman with black hair tied back. She was wholesome and rosy-cheeked. She hummed to herself and her steps were light and energetic. She had on a dark green tabard with the Glasson's Lush-Mart motif on the breast, but underneath she wore casual clothes. She lowered the box into a stall rim and puffed to herself. "Phew, them pinies are heavy!" Then she raised her head and called out in a thick cockney accent: "Carrie! What price are we putting on the pinies today?"

Another older woman turned towards her and yelled back: "Four magows or two bob and six."

"Blimey! That's cheap; can we afford it?"

"Yeah, they've only got one day left on 'em. We're getting in a new shipment tomorrow and I want space for 'em."

The woman picked up one of the pineapples and examined it with a proud smile on her face. "These South African ones are my favourite. Ain't they gorgeous!? Maybe now the war has ended for good, the price'll go down and stay down." She carefully put it back on the shelf then walked off to find something else to do. Brendan looked at the shelf she'd just been attending to and picked up one of the pineapples she'd just replaced. He hefted it in his hand and felt its weight. Its rough skin pushed against the palm of his hand, its barbs spiking uncomfortably. He lifted it to his nose and breathed in. The scent of the fruit triggered exotic images in his mind: hot sun, miles of beaches, blue sea. He licked his lips as his mouth watered.

"Want one of our pinies, mate?"

Brendan swung around with a start; the woman he'd first seen when he entered the shop was grinning at him from his shoulder.

"Top quality, direct from South Africa's finest plantation."

"Erm... sure. How much?"

"Four Magows or two bob and six."

He prospected in his pocket. "OK."

"The till's over there. Hope you enjoy it!" The woman gave him a green plastic basket to put his purchase in. He took the basket and continued along the stalls, examining the fruit which was laid out on display like artwork. He picked up an immaculate apple from Somerset and sniffed it, feeling like Eve. Its sweetness seemed to seep through the pores of his skin as he held it. The tomatoes were, like most fruits and vegetables, much bigger than those he recalled from his childhood. Their skin was firm and unblemished and their texture strong. He noticed that the woman was still watching him.

"Try one if you like, governor." She said as she arranged price tags on the opposite shelf.

"What, are you giving them away?" he chuckled.

"One or two. It's a fair investment 'cos we know one taste and you'll be back for more."

Brendan placed the tomato's rump between his teeth and took a bite. The skin cracked under the pressure of his incisors and cold juice flooded over his tongue. Its perfume and taste of Earth, sun and sky sent shivers through his body. Slippery, wet seeds followed and then tougher flesh. He closed his teeth and extracted the mouthful, wiping juice away with the back of his hand. "Mmm! Yes lovely." he said indistinctly as he chewed. "Are they totally organic?"

She shrugged. "What ain't these days?... Well, these are from ex-Rothamstead land so they're about 99.8% plus. The farmer has to wait another season for his certificate."

"Well he obviously cares about what he grows so I hope he gets it soon."

"He'd have had to wait another twenty years without the lifetrails." She lowered her voice and for the first time didn't meet his eyes and she spoke, aware that she was raising a very controversial subject.

He lightened the conversation, aware of her discomfort. "Have you got any grapes?"

She turned back to him and smiled more broadly than ever. "Of course. They're five and seven a pound... or four-point-six-five if you're a magow man." She winked cheekily, perhaps acknowledging his lack of a local accent. He bought a bunch of grapes, some pears and a Cypriot orange; he took them to the till and fished in his pocket for his wallet to pay. He had twelve Oxford Hours which were not legal tender in London, but fortunately he had withdrawn fifty magows from the bank before going into the hospital. Nowadays there was no Bank of England. Like so many other artefacts of the Illuminati-occupied regime the building in the City which had housed the Bank was just a museum with roped off reproductions of offices and waxwork mannequins in suits. Today every city and county, and many small towns too, had their own currency and independent banking system. Of course this presented problems when travelling outside the jurisdiction of these small monetary zones, like the need to change money while travelling abroad in the old days, but far worse. So to avoid the necessity for a Bureau de Change on the outskirts of every tiny hamlet a duel currency system had emerged. Local means of exchange now operated in tandem with the magow; a global currency, but not in the same way as the one originally intended by the Illuminati. After the Illuminati banking system collapsed, the gold reserves of all the nations, including the US Federal Reserves at Fort Knox, were released to the public and were available for all citizens to buy, although some were incorporated into the US dollar to make it a gold standard currency. Far from deflating the price of gold, as the conservative economists had warned, the price had almost doubled since then as more and more people bought up the gold stocks that had been off limits to them for so many centuries. These stocks were sold in smaller and smaller portions until they were eventually made available in minute amounts; and as a result had to be put in a larger container for the purposes of basic dexterity. The easiest way to do this was to embed individual milligrams of pure twenty-four carat gold in plastic cards that resembled old-fashioned credit cards. These became known as Mg-Au, or "magow" cards. Even tinier portions of bullion were released in hundred and fifty microgram cards. It wasn't long before magows naturally evolved into a universal unit of tender that solved the mini-currency exchange problem. The teller was short of magows and so gave him change in London Shillings, directing him to the local branch of the Bank of London where he could change it back into magows or US dollars.

Brendan returned to his flyer in the hospital carpark and headed for another hospital, the Neurological Center in New York. It stood on the north extremity of Manhattan in Hudson Heights. Clane Quilley had been there for the last few days undergoing a brand new treatment to repair his brain following his stroke in 1975. He was lying on a couch in a hermetically sealed room while doctors operated on him from a control gallery. It was called "endosurgery" and it had been developed from new tech retrieved from one of the secret laboratories in Oxford. Tiny machines flowed through Clane's bloodstream to his brain where they reconstructed the injured segments neuron by neuron. "I'm glad some good has come out of Oxford's secrets." said Brendan to one of the doctors. After the treatment a porter took Clane back to his ward in a wheelchair. Brendan walked beside him. "Hi, dad. It's Brendan." He had to introduce himself every time he met his father because Clane could no longer recognize faces.

"Hey, Brendan. Thanks for coming to see me. How's Heather? Has she had the baby yet?"

Brendan paused. "Lil is almost two, dad."

He nodded and blushed. At least it wasn't one of the days when he only spoke Irish Gaelic. Brendan prayed that the treatment would work.

Brendan then flew home to the Seaguard base in Belfast where he was currently posted. Heather was giving Lillian her evening meal. "Daaaa!" The little girl beamed up at him from her highchair making his heart dance. He walked over and kissed the soft hair on the top of her head. Then he kissed his wife. He was glad he had a shore assignment now, teaching at the Power School. He hated going away to sea and leaving his family. Since he had heard his daughter laugh and seen her smile, and conversed with her as she attempted to speak, he had discovered a landscape of joy that he never could have previously imagined.

....

Clane responded well to the treatment and when Brendan went to visit him his father the following month, he waved and called out: "Morning, Brendan. All set to go?"

Brendan smiled. "Dad, you know it's me!"

"Yes." he grinned back. "I feel like a new man." They left Clane's flat and walked down the corridor towards the entrance of the sheltered accommodation block where he lived. His home was a aboard a residential frightener. More and more people were moving into such communities in the last few years. These frighteners were similar to the ones designed for transport except they were much bigger. The one Clane lived on was two miles across and cruised around the environs of Lake Placid, New York. It couldn't stay in one place for too long otherwise the residents on the ground below would complain about being in its continuous shadow, so it looped back and forth at a very low speed. The concierge in the sheltered accommodation block was a beaky woman with thick glasses who wore a white dress like a chemist. "Now, you be careful, Clane. Don't go doing anything too strenuous or wander off on your own or anything. And wear that jumper I knitted for you!"

"Alright, Maggie. Stop fussing will ya!" He rolled his eyes at Brendan. "This winter I intend to go skiing... I'm kidding!" he added as Maggie opened her mouth to respond.

They flew westwards to the Rocky Mountains and then turned north into Canada. Eventually they came to a beauty spot in British Columbia that Brendan had located on WorldMesh. They landed in a small carpark and wandered up a pathway overlooking a majestic granite gorge. A waterfall tumbled down from a gap in the mountainside above them. There was a wooden bench underneath a shady tree set up at the perfect location to enjoy the scenery. To their right, away from the waterfall the landscape descended into green plains fading into the distance. It was a sunny but cool day with a light film of cloud, almost like an old chemtrail haze. Drops of water from the stream glittered like glass beads in the air. "The doc says this will do you good." said Brendan.

Clane opened up the picnic hamper and removed a can of Guinness. "This won't." He chuckled and cracked it open.

Brendan laughed too and pulled out a can of lager.

"You're driving." warned Clane.

"I'll put her on autopilot."

They discussed old times and absent friends, Gina, Brendan's grandparents, places they'd lived. They talked about the difference between the US Navy in World War II and service in modern Seaguard. "We've seen a lot of changes in our lives." said Brendan. "I've often wondered if we would survive the changes. I used to think we could never be free because we humans are hardwired not to be."

"Well, the fact is we let the Illuminati in." said Clane, opening his third can of Guinness. "It's like what Siobhan says about it being like the Parable of the Sower. It's what

Jesus says when he talks about the seed falling on good soil and sometimes it falls on stony ground or amongst the thorns. The reptilians are like the seeds, only they're intelligent seeds. They fly across hyperspace looking for suitable universes to land in. When they find one, they close in on it like leeches. They are true parasites. They came here because we were good hosts for them to suck off. Maybe that was what is meant by the fall of man. It's not literally eating a forbidden apple; it's just symbolic of something. It's the same with the story of Atlantis. We fell from grace and we've had to climb back up again... That's been the hardest pill to swallow. We can't play victim; it's really all our fault. You can get angry with a leech for biting you so maybe we can't get angry with the Illuminati either."

Brendan grinned at him. "You're in a philosophical mood today, dad."

"*Slainte*!" He took a pull of his can. "I don't know how long this will last though. Grace is difficult to get up to and even harder to stay. The president called this a 'golden age' on TV back at Disclosure Thirty..."

"Well, I think she likes the idea that she's in the White House to take the credit for it."

"No doubt. Does this mean utopia? I know Siobhan and I had a fight about that a few years ago, but... well, maybe she was right. It's not healthy to hope for a world of perfection and can be dangerous if you try to create one. It's that which led Julian to the idea that it would be a good idea to launch those missiles."

Brendan nodded and told him about the thoughtless drive for change he had witnessed in London.

"Do you know, Bren; there are people who want gladiatorial combat legalized?"

"Like in the old days, when people really killed each other for sport?"

"Yup. I was watching a TV show about it the other day... although there are many variants now involving modern warfare. There are people who want to play war games; but not just with blanks, with live munitions."

"That's crazy!"

"If it's between consenting adults would it be right

to stop them?"

Brendan opened his mouth to answer and then stopped.

"It's a conundrum, isn't it?... You see, I don't think human beings are hardwired to reject freedom, but we do have a natural aggression inside us, especially men. Sport is a good outlet for that aggression, but is it enough? You know, there used to be totally peaceful Indian tribes where they never fought any wars, but those tribes invented some of the most violent sports the world has ever seen. Lacrosse used to be one of them."

"Lacrosse is violent? Nah, girls play it."

"These days yes, but the way it was played in the traditional way by the Indians, you used to lose a couple of players every match!"

There was a long silence. They listened to the sound of the waterfall. "If that's the way we are naturally, then so be it." said Brendan. "We have to play our best with the hand nature has dealt us."

Clane looked up at the crags on the far side of the gorge. "I sometimes regret the fact that I'm too old to see the future. By the time the post-Disclosure world has settled down I'll be long gone... Maybe you will too, Bren. Depends how long it takes. It might be something only Lil can enjoy."

"But it's like what you said earlier about human nature. We don't choose when we're born any more than we choose our innate nature."

"Come to think of it, maybe we are the lucky ones. We've been here to witness Disclosure and the changes that it brings. This means we will appreciate it in a way future generations born into the post-Disclosure world will not. They'll just take it for granted like a man with water in his faucet every day will never enjoy a glass of water as much as a man dying of thirst... Yeah, this a great time to be alive." He reached down into the hamper. "Darn it! We've run out of beer."

"Have we? Damn, I could do with another... Tell you what, dad; I'll go and buy some in a nearby town. Are you okay to wait here for half an hour by yourself?"

"Sure, here's a great spot to wait."

"Right you are. Back soon." As Brendan wandered down the path, he looked back over his shoulder at his father sitting on the bench under the tree. Clane waved. Brendan smiled and waved back. Clane yelled something, but his son was too far away to hear it.

Because he had been drinking he had to programme the flyer's autopilot. He flew to a town about twenty miles away called Prince George and found a supermarket. There he purchased a six-pack of lager and one of Guinness. He paid with magows and then flew back to the waterfall. He landed the flyer and picked the beer cans off the back seat where he had thrown them; then he walked back up the path whistling cheerily.

The weather had changed; a chilly wind now blew down the gully from the waterfall. His father came into view. Clane was still on the bench, but he was slumped over. "Dad!" Brendan called, thinking he had fallen asleep. As he got closer he saw the pallor of Clane's skin. His chest was not moving. Brendan stopped, frightened to approach any closer in the same way as he would be frightened to jump off the cliff. "Dad?" He felt his mouth quiver as he spoke. He walked forward until he was right by the bench. He touched his father's forehead. Clane Quilley was dead. His body was cold. He must have expired soon after Brendan left him half an hour ago. Brendan fell to his knees and laid his face on his father's shoulder. His tears soaked into the sweater Maggie the carer had knitted for him.

"I'm very sorry, Brendan."

Brendan looked up at the sound of the voice. "You!" He sneered. "Where have you been, you bastard!?"

Flying Buffalo was dressed in a white suit with an open shirt collar. His shoes were black with pure white spats. He looked as if he had just been to watch a polo match. "Brendan, please try to understand, death is not the end. Your father has not ceased to exist. He will continue to live in another form, in another world; as will you when your time of transition comes. This is a cycle that every unit of consciousness experiences for eternity... There's a good chance that you and he will meet again in the future."

"I don't want to meet him again in the future. I want him here now... Bring him back!"

"I can't do that; and if I could I would refuse to."

Brendan glared into his eyes. The peace in them was as immovable as the mountain they were on. "Get out of my sight!"

Flying Buffalo bowed his head sorrowfully.

Brendan looked down at his father's lifeless face and when he looked up again, Flying Buffalo had vanished.

Chapter 21
"This is the best time of year to visit." said Brendan. "In summer it's too hot, in winter it's too cold." He wandered down the gangway from the frightener and stepped onto the hard, dry concrete of what used to be a flight line. Siobhan and Kerry followed with Siobhan's husband Graham. Lillian was clutching onto her father's hand as she always did. Little Clane was sleeping in his pushchair as Heather wheeled him out of the frightener's hatch. Brendan looked back at his wife with his one-year-old son and smiled with love and pride. William and Colleen came out last. The sixteen-year-old twins were lagging behind as usual. The hangars, workshops and office blocks of what used to be Roswell Army Air Field, today called the Roswell Business Park, were still standing, but they had been adapted for numerous other functions. One of them was the terminal for the frightener service. Hangar Eighty-Four though was untouched; it was part of the Roswell museum circuit. Graham pointed at it. "So that's where they took the bodies?"

"Yes." said Siobhan. "And the wreckage too. They kept it there for a few days before transferring it to Wright Field. In 1955 it was moved to Area 51." A decorated sign, made to look like a flying saucer, loomed above the frightener pad with the words *Welcome to Roswell* being held up by a novelty alien. "They really ought to take these things more seriously." tutted Siobhan.

Graham shaded his eyes as he looked up at the sign. He was a sociable and modest man who Brendan had grown to like in the two years he had known him. As the newest member of the Quilley family he had been shy at first, but today he fitted in as well as the others. He looked at his younger brother-in-law. "I appreciate you paying for us all to come with you to Roswell, Brendan."

Brendan shrugged modestly. "I wanted the whole family to see this place... And besides, what else am I going to spend this year's cap-div on? Myself?" He laughed.

"Come on, Abbott and Costello!" chuckled Graham and put his arms around the shoulders of William and Colleen. They picked up their pace, holding onto their stepfather's elbows.

Brendan stopped to watch. He felt so happy at how the

twins had warmed to Graham. They had fallen in love with him almost as quickly as Siobhan had.

The family took a ground bus into the city of Roswell. It was exactly as Brendan had imagined it to be, based on his father's descriptions and photographs. Roswell was a place of straight wide square roads and the buildings were all low and oblong. Few were more than two storeys in height. The city centre was the crossroads where Main Street and West 2nd Street met. On one corner of the crossroads was the world famous Museum of Disclosure. "Shall we go in?" asked Colleen.

"Maybe later." answered Siobhan. "We've got more important things to show you first."

"I hope nobody recognizes us." said Brendan. "I don't want to be treated as a VIP."

"We should come back for Disclosure Day." said William. "But I bet we'd be recognized then."

"We wouldn't be able to move either." said Brendan. "The place gets jammed packed on the eighth of July. In that museum you can see lots of pictures of dad, some of the wreckage from the crash and photos of the bodies."

"Where are the actual bodies kept?" asked William.

"At the Battelle Memorial Institute in Ohio. They have them on ice there. Every so often they put them on public display."

"Look over there." Siobhan pointed to a metal sign above a doorway leading to a flight of stairs. "That used to be the office of the *Roswell Daily Record*. That's where dad worked. He wrote the famous July 8th 1947 news story in the offices up there: *RAAF Captures Flying Disk*."

"Used to be?" said Heather.

"Yes, they've moved to new premises now on the edge of town. I don't know what this place is now; maybe somebody lives there. I'm surprised it's not been made into a museum too... But it's nice of them to leave the old sign up."

The family took the bus to the north of town to visit a row of motel rooms. They weren't sure if they would still be standing, but they were. They were still open too. One of them had a blue plaque on its wall that said: *Clane Quilley MFOlogist and Disclosure activist lived here 1946-1947*.

Brendan sighed. "Somebody's going to recognize us sooner or later." They were indeed recognized when they took the tour bus out to the crash site in Lincoln County. The driver talked non-stop about his own MFO sightings and his sisters' abductions. The crash site was marked by a cairn and a stone slab with a message carved on it. There was not much else to see except a slight depression in the ground. The expanse of New Mexico scrubland stretched into the distance on all sides, as flat as a calm sea. Crickets clicked invisibly in the coarse grass. After that they went to the debris field a few miles away which was fairly similar. Then they went back to Roswell and checked into their hotel. Heather had to care for Little Clane and so she stayed in the hotel. Siobhan and Graham stayed to keep her company so Clane took Lillian and the twins back to see the Museum of Disclosure. The exhibitions were laid out neatly and included official documents talking truthfully about the MFO reality and the manila envelopes containing information packages that were about to be given out to the press before President Truman was assassinated and the Illuminati initiated their cover-up. There was an advance notice for a lecture in the adjoining auditorium by Jesse Marcel, an old friend of Clane Quilley's who had handled to original RAAF investigation. After Brendan and the others had been round the museum Lillian became tired so they all went back to the hotel for dinner. After they had eaten, Brendan went out for a walk alone. He crossed some of the empty spaces where buildings used to be, or had yet to be built, in the vast open space that Roswell seemed to consist of. The sun was setting between two houses and a well could be seen between them with a bucket and chain hanging from a stand above it. He didn't speak at first when he noticed Flying Buffalo walking beside him. "In just two months." began the old Indian. "It will be the year 1980. The twentieth century is aging fast."

Brendan stopped walking and looked at him. The old man was wearing a Stetson hat and poncho, the same clothes he had worn the first day he appeared in front of Clane in 1947. "I'm sorry I got angry at you, when dad died."

Flying Buffalo shook his head. "What else were you supposed to do in response to what I said? It was the right thing to say, but that doesn't make it less hurtful."

"It's just, I never believed he would die like that, so suddenly. He was getting better. The doctors had been fixing his brain... How is he?"

"Very well. He misses you."

"I miss him." There was a long pause. "When 1980 comes, it sounds like it's almost 2000, a new century and even a new millennium. What does the future hold for the world?"

"Nobody knows. That is for you to decide."

"The new tech has done a lot of good, but it could be made into a weapon. Look at what Dr Bulstrode constructed. That could be used against the people by somebody evil."

"Indeed it could."

"Suppose another Julian Spencer pops up."

"Suppose he does."

"What can we do?"

"Everything. There are people like Julian all over the world. None of them threaten to destroy the earth. Julian's power came from his ability to convince other people to follow him. If they had not been convinced, he would have been helpless."

"We must teach ourselves not to be easily convinced."

"Correct." Flying Buffalo grinned. "I think you will do well."

Brendan blinked and his eyes filled with black goo. "Oh no, not another attack. Damn it." He pulled out a handkerchief and wiped his eyes. When he could see again Flying Buffalo was gone. "Of course." Brendan snorted sarcastically. "Don't bother to say goodbye or anything!"

He walked back to the main road and saw the staff at the Museum of Disclosure locking the doors for the night. They walked off down the street chatting to each other. "So that's it." said Brendan. "One story ends and another begins."

High above Roswell, an MFO hovered, a yellow luminescent disk. It was like a hawk looking for prey, or an angel keeping watch. Brendan watched it for many minutes. People walked past him on the pavement, but he didn't bother to alert them. Some of them saw it for themselves and also stopped to watch it. The extraterrestrial craft departed so quickly that

Brendan's eyes only just caught it. It rose into the air with the abruptness of a fish caught on an angler's line. Within a second it had faded from visibility near the starry zenith.

<u>The End</u>

Also by Ben Emlyn-Jones.

The Roswell Trilogy

Book One:
Roswell Rising- A Novel of Disclosure

Book Two:
Roswell Revealed- A World After Disclosure

Book Three:
Roswell Redeemed- Humanity After Disclosure

Ben Emlyn-Jones' second novel Rockall is available free to read online at:
http://hpanwo-bb.blogspot.co.uk/2009/02/rockall-chapter-1.html

Ben Emlyn-Jones' first novel Evan's Land is available via private sale in limited numbers. Please email the publisher at:
bennyjay74@gmx.co.uk

All published by

The Aldyth Press

www.ingramcontent.com/pod-product-compliance
Lightning Source LLC
Chambersburg PA
CBHW050610300426
44112CB00012B/1448